Smart
TOEFL® iBT
Pre-Intermediate
2

Smart TOEFL® iBT Pre-Intermediate Book 2

Publisher Chung Kyudo
Editors Cho Sangik, Hong Inpyo
Author Darakwon TOEFL Research Team
Proofreader Michael A. Putlack
Designers Zo Hwayon, Park Sunyoung

First published in August 2012
By Darakwon, Inc.
Darakwon Bldg., 211, Munbal-ro, Paju-si, Gyeonggi-do 10881
Republic of Korea
Tel: 82-2-736-2031 (Ext. 250)
Fax: 82-2-732-2037

ISBN 978-89-277-0655-7 18740
978-89-277-0648-9 18740 (set)

www.darakwon.co.kr

Components Main Book / Answer Book / Free MP3 Downloads
10 9 8 7 6 5 4   25 26 27 28 29

Smart TOEFL® iBT

iBT

Pre-Intermediate 2

DARAKWON

Table of Contents

Introduction

Chapter 1
Reading

Chapter 2
Listening

Chapter 3

Speaking

Chapter 4 Writing

Chapter 5 Actual Test

Introduction

One of the most important standardized tests students of the English language may ever take is the TOEFL® iBT. Because getting a high score on the test is so crucial, it is important to prepare for the test as much as possible prior to taking it.

That is the purpose of *Smart TOEFL® iBT Pre-Intermediate*. This book focuses on all four sections on the TOEFL® iBT: Reading, Listening, Speaking, and Writing. In the Reading and Listening sections, all of the question types are explained. There are also hints as well as sample passages and questions. Finally, each unit contains two passages along with questions for test takers to answer. As for the Speaking and Writing sections, they contain sample questions and answers for all of the tasks found in those sections. The Reading passages and Listening lectures and conversations in *Smart TOEFL® iBT Pre-Intermediate* cover many of the topics that have recently appeared on the TOEFL® iBT. The questions and topics found in the Speaking and Writing units are also those that have recently appeared. This should help students when they sit for the actual test.

Smart TOEFL® iBT Pre-Intermediate is intended for students with a low-intermediate knowledge of English. Therefore the passages are shorter, and the questions are easier than those found on the TOEFL® iBT. Nevertheless, the passages and questions are written in the TOEFL® iBT style, so students will be able to prepare themselves for the test when they actually take it. *Smart TOEFL® iBT Pre-Intermediate* will also provide students with a basic introduction to many different academic topics. Thus students will learn important information and specialized vocabulary in a number of topics.

This book, however, is merely a tool. Both students and teachers must make use of this tool in the best possible manner so that students may do as well as possible when they take the TOEFL® iBT.

About This Book

Smart TOEFL® iBT Pre-Intermediate consists of thirty units. There are ten Reading units, ten Listening units, five Speaking units, and five Writing units. Each unit contains passages, questions, and, in the Speaking and Writing units, sample answers. The passages and questions are similar to those found on the TOEFL® iBT.

The subjects of the passages in both the Reading and the Listening units have occurred on recent TOEFL® iBT tests. Since many topics on the TOEFL® iBT Reading section are repeated, this can benefit students. By becoming familiar with the topics, subject matter, and vocabulary used in the passages in the Reading and Listening units, students can be more confident when they take the Reading and Listening sections of the TOEFL® iBT.

The same is true of the sample questions and passages in the Speaking and Writing units. The questions are those that have recently appeared on the TOEFL® iBT tests, and so are the passages, which include lectures, reading passages, and conversations. By becoming familiar with the topics, situations, and vocabulary used in the Speaking and Writing units, students can be more confident when they take the Speaking and Writing sections of the TOEFL® iBT. The sample answers can also show students how to speak or write answers that can result in high scores on the TOEFL® iBT.

READING

Each Reading unit contains an explanation of a type of question that appears after a Reading passage. Then, there are hints for answering that type of question and a short passage with a sample question. Finally, there are two Reading passages of around 300-350 words. They are each followed by four or five questions.

LISTENING

Each Listening unit contains an explanation of a type of question that appears after a Listening lecture or conversation. Then, there are also hints for answering that type of question and a short lecture or conversation with a sample questions. Finally, there are a conversation of around 250-300 words and a lecture of around 450-500 words. They are each followed by three or four questions.

SPEAKING

Each Speaking unit is made of five parts. Each part covers one of the five tasks that appear on the Speaking section of the TOEFL® iBT. In addition to the question, lecture, reading passage, and/or conversation, each task contains a brainstorming section, an organizing section, and a sample answer.

WRITING

Each Writing unit is made of two parts. The first part covers the integrated task while the second part covers the independent task. For each integrated task, in addition to the reading passage and lecture, there are a section for note-taking and a sample answer. For each independent task, there are a planning section and a sample answer to the question.

Chapter 1

Reading

Unit 01

Question Type 1 **Factual Information**

Factual Information questions focus on the facts that are found in the passage. These types of questions ask the test taker about various details, definitions, explanation, events, and other data in the passage. The test taker must examine the answer choices and determine which one has factual information from the passage. There are 3-6 Factual Information questions for each passage.

Recognizing Factual Information questions:

- According to the paragraph, which of the following is true of X?
- The author's description of X mentions which of the following?
- According to the paragraph, X occurred because . . .

Helpful hints for answering the questions correctly:

- Many answer choices have information that is partially correct. However, the information in the answer choice must be 100% correct. Do not select answer choices that have information that is only partially correct.

- Many times, the question mentions a paragraph. In order to answer the question properly, focus only on the information in that paragraph.

- Some answer choices contain information that is correct but which does not appear in the passage. Do not select these answer choices. Only select answer choices that have information from the passage.

- These questions ask for facts, not opinions. Do not select any answer choices that are opinions.

Sample Factual Information Question

2 → For centuries, people have found uses for the various plants that grow in the oceans. Kelp, a type of seaweed, is one of these. There are many species of kelp. Most have some value either as food or medicine. For instance, in several cultures, people have long consumed it. This is particularly true of people in Asian countries. They mostly dry the kelp and then eat it alongside other foods, such as fish. More recently, kelp is sometimes included as an ingredient in ice cream, and it is also used as a thickener for certain foods. Kelp has value as a medicine, too. People with thyroid problems commonly consume it because kelp produces a hormone that can improve the body's metabolism. Finally, kelp is valued by many elderly individuals since it is able to ease pain in their joints. For sufferers of arthritis, it is quite beneficial.

According to paragraph 2, some old people like kelp because

(A) it can be used to make ice cream
(B) they like how it thickens some foods
(C) it makes their joints feel better
(D) they prefer eating it with their meals

Answer Explanation

Choice C is the correct answer. The passage notes, "Finally, kelp is valued by many elderly individuals since it is able to ease pain in their joints. For sufferers of arthritis, it is quite beneficial." Thus, when elderly people consume it, it can make their joints feel better by easing their pain. Choices A and B are mentioned in the passage, but they are not named as reasons the elderly like kelp. So they are incorrect. Choice D is not mentioned in the passage, so it is incorrect, too.

Totem Poles

Native American tribes are often noted for their artwork. In some cases, they produce beautiful works of jewelry. A few tribes make rock art while others have created art on cave walls. Yet arguably the most impressive works of Native American art come from the Pacific Northwest region of North America. This includes the American states of Washington and Alaska as well as British Columbia in Canada. The members of the tribes in these areas have been creating totem poles for hundreds of years.

Totem poles are large monuments made from the trunks of trees. They differ in size. Some are a meter or so in height, and others soar to heights of twelve meters or greater. Totem poles have various features carved into them. There are regularly both human and animal faces cut into the wood. Some totem poles have extensions that are shaped like bird wings. No two totem poles are alike as they all vary in their design and the objects that are carved in them.

3 → Most totem poles are made from the trunks of red cedar trees. First, the tree is cut to the required length, and its <u>bark</u> is stripped. The master carver then draws the basic outline for the totem pole. The bottom of the totem pole is shaped first as the master carver works upward. After the carving is complete, the totem pole is then painted. The entire process can take from two to eight months. Once the paint dries, the totem pole is raised upright in its final location while a special ceremony, called a potlatch, is held.

4 → When Captain James Cook first saw some totem poles in the 1700s, he thought that they were "monstrous figures." But he erred in his description. Totem poles are beautiful and serve important purposes. They often tell stories. They may <u>recount</u> tribal legends or the history of an individual family. They can indicate the cultural beliefs of a tribe. And they may be used to honor individuals of note. They are not, however, religious icons and thus are not involved in any religious ceremonies.

Glossary
bark: the hard external covering of a plant's trunk and branches
recount: to tell, as in a story

1   Which of the sentences below best expresses the essential information in the highlighted sentence in the passage? Incorrect answer choices change the meaning in important ways or leave out essential information.

Ⓐ Some totem poles have unique designs and shapes.
Ⓑ Totem poles all look different from one another.
Ⓒ A wide variety of objects may be carved into totem poles.
Ⓓ It takes time to cut an object into a totem pole.

2   In paragraph 3, the author's description of how totem poles are made mentions which of the following?

Ⓐ The person making them starts at the bottom.
Ⓑ It can take up to a year to make one of them.
Ⓒ They can be made from different types of trees.
Ⓓ After a figure is carved, it is immediately painted.

3   In paragraph 4, the author implies that totem poles

Ⓐ have written stories carved onto them
Ⓑ cost thousands of dollars to make
Ⓒ were first seen by Captain James Cook
Ⓓ are never worshipped by people

4   **Directions:** An introductory sentence for a brief summary of the passage is provided below. Complete the summary by selecting the THREE answer choices that express the most important ideas of the passage. Some sentences do not belong because they express ideas that are not presented in the passage or are minor ideas in the passage. **This question is worth 2 points.**

Some Native American tribes create totem poles as monuments that have several different purposes.

-
-
-

Answer Choices

1. Totem poles are one type of art made by Native Americans.
2. Captain James Cook was not impressed upon seeing totem poles.
3. Tribes in the northwest part of North America create totem poles.
4. Red cedar trees and commonly used to make totem poles.
5. The figures and designs on totem poles are all of importance.
6. Some totem poles may tell stories or legends from the past.

Swamps

There are a variety of bodies of water, including oceans, seas, lakes, rivers, and streams. Swamps are another. Swamps are wetlands but are unique from other bodies of water in one way: They are forested.

2 → While swamps exist in many places, they are inclined to be located near large bodies of water, especially lakes and rivers. They frequently form when a river slows down as it flows through low-lying land. The Mississippi, Amazon, and Nile rivers all have swamps near them. ■ There are also swamps that form near oceans and seas. ■ These swamps are found in low-lying coastal regions and contain either salt water or brackish water. ■ And a few swamps are not found near any other large bodies of water. ■ These swamps are usually seasonal, forming during rainy seasons and drying up at other times of the year.

The fact that swamps are found in so many places results in there being a <u>myriad</u> of different types of them. The two most common kinds are forest swamps and shrub swamps. Forest swamps are common in places where the land is not that wet. There are two kinds of forest swamps: conifer swamps and hardwood swamps. Conifer swamps are dominated by pine, spruce, and cedar trees while hardwood swamps mostly contain maple, elm, birch, and oak trees. As for shrub swamps, they proliferate in areas where the land is covered with water for most of the year. They also have smaller trees, such as alders and willows. Of the other types of swamps, saltwater swamps are the most common. Mangrove trees, one of the rare trees that can survive in salt water, dominate them.

4 → Swamps are crucial parts of ecosystems. They typically have an abundant supply of life. Fish and reptiles in particular <u>thrive</u> in them, but mammals as well as numerous species of birds reside in swamps as well. They are also home to many species of plants, some of which are rare or endangered. Finally, they can help prevent flooding as they can absorb large amounts of water from nearby overflowing rivers.

Glossary
myriad: a large number; many; a multitude
thrive: to do well; to succeed; to increase

1 In paragraph 2, the author uses The Mississippi, Amazon, and Nile rivers as examples of
    (A) rivers that have swamps alongside them
    (B) some of the world's longest rivers
    (C) places that flow close to large lakes
    (D) rivers that contain brackish or salty water

2 Which of the following can be inferred from paragraph 2 about swamps?
    (A) They can be as long as some rivers at times.
    (B) A lot of them have swiftly flowing water.
    (C) Most of them are found near lakes and rivers.
    (D) Those with salt water have the greatest amount of life.

3 The word proliferate in the passage is closest in meaning to
    (A) recede
    (B) flourish
    (C) formulate
    (D) exceed

4 According to paragraph 4, swamps are important to ecosystems because
    (A) they instigate flooding in some areas
    (B) some people make their homes in them
    (C) a variety of animal species dwell in them
    (D) humans cannot use them for other purposes

5 Look at the four squares [■] that indicate where the following sentence could be added to the passage.

Kenya has a number of these types of swamps beside the Indian Ocean.

Where would the sentence best fit?
Click on a square [■] to add the sentence to the passage.

Question Type 2 · Vocabulary

Vocabulary questions focus on both words and phrases that appear in the passage. These types of questions ask the test taker to determine the meanings of these words and phrases. Most of the time, the words and phrases have multiple meanings. The test taker must determine the context of the word or phrase in order to select the correct meaning. There are 3-5 Vocabulary questions for each passage.

Recognizing Vocabulary questions:

- The word X in the passage is closest in meaning to

- In stating X, the author means that

Helpful hints for answering the questions correctly:

- Many words have several meanings in English. Do not simply choose the most common meaning of the word since it is often not the correct answer.

- Pay attention to the context of the word or phrase. Do this by reading the sentences both before and after the highlighted word or phrase. By doing that, you can find the correct answer.

- Replace the highlighted word or phrase with all of the answer choices. See how each answer choice reads in the sentence. The correct answer choice can always be substituted into the passage without any grammatical problems.

Sample Vocabulary Question

> Nowadays, it is common for people to purchase goods and services with credit cards. This provides them with several benefits. For instance, they do not have to carry large amounts of cash with them. This helps protect them from thieves. In addition, using a credit card enables a person to receive goods and services instantly while paying for them at a later time. While these cards are frequently used today, they are relatively new. The concept of credit has been around for centuries. But credit cards were first introduced during the 1900s. These cards were different from those of contemporary times in several ways. The most obvious is where they could be used. The first credit cards could only be used at the stores or businesses that issued them. However, modern-day credit cards are accepted at a wide number of places of business all around the world.

The word contemporary in the passage is closest in meaning to

(A) current
(B) advanced
(C) regular
(D) traditional

🔷 Answer Explanation

> Choice A is the correct answer. Contemporary times are modern or current times. Thus "current" is the correct answer. There is a context clue in the passage. The last sentence reads, "However, modern-day credit cards are accepted at a wide number of places of business all around the world." The word "modern-day" is a synonym of "contemporary." The passage is comparing credit cards in the past with modern-day cards. Thus, by reading carefully, you can find the context clue and then determine the answer. Choices B, C, and D are all incorrect answers.

The Manhattan Project

During World War I (1914-1918), millions of soldiers were killed on the battlefields of Europe. Yet despite already having many weapons capable of killing large numbers of people, people continually tried to create even more destructive weapons. Some scientists realized that it would be possible to make an incredibly powerful bomb by <u>splitting</u> the atom. This, they realized, would let them make an atomic bomb. It would be the most powerful weapon in the world.

2 → In the 1930s, scientists working for Adolf Hitler's Nazi Germany began to research how to make an atomic bomb. This fact came to be known to scientists in the United States. In 1939, Albert Einstein and some other well-known physicists wrote a letter to American President Franklin D. Roosevelt. They warned the president about what the Nazis were doing. Furthermore, they urged him to initiate the country's own atomic bomb project. This prompted Roosevelt to start the Manhattan Project in 1942. This happened in the middle of World War II. The goal of the Manhattan Project was the building of an atomic bomb. The Americans were joined by both Canada and Great Britain.

The Manhattan Project had facilities at more than thirty sites in three countries. It was centered on Los Alamos, New Mexico, though. Army General Leslie Groves was in charge of the military aspect of the project. Robert Oppenheimer was the chief scientist. He led the civilian scientists working on the project. Some of the most <u>brilliant</u> scientists in the world were involved in the Manhattan Project. They included Enrico Fermi, Niels Bohr, and Richard Feynman.

For three years, the team moved toward its goal. They had to solve various complex scientific and engineering problems. The main difficulty was making the nuclear material needed for the weapon. Ultimately, the scientists built two types of bombs. One used plutonium. The other used uranium. On July 16, 1945, an atomic bomb was successfully detonated in New Mexico. By then, Germany had been defeated. But, in early August, two atomic bombs were dropped on Japan. This forced the Japanese to surrender and ended World War II.

Glossary
split: to divide into two; to halve
brilliant: intelligent; very smart

1. Which of the sentences below best expresses the essential information in the highlighted sentence in the passage? Incorrect answer choices change the meaning in important ways or leave out essential information.

   Ⓐ Armies around the world suddenly possessed weapons that made them more powerful than ever before.

   Ⓑ There were already a large number of powerful weapons that could kill many people at the same time.

   Ⓒ Some people began to conduct research on weapons that were capable of mass destruction.

   Ⓓ Individuals attempted to make very deadly weapons even though many of them already existed.

2. According to paragraph 2, Albert Einstein and others sent a letter to the American president because

   Ⓐ they wanted the United States to win World War II

   Ⓑ they hoped to get extra funding from the government

   Ⓒ they believed that it was possible to split the atom

   Ⓓ they were concerned about activities in Nazi Germany

3. The word detonated in the passage is closest in meaning to

   Ⓐ experimented with

   Ⓑ exploded

   Ⓒ constructed

   Ⓓ developed

4. **Directions:** An introductory sentence for a brief summary of the passage is provided below. Complete the summary by selecting the THREE answer choices that express the most important ideas of the passage. Some sentences do not belong because they express ideas that are not presented in the passage or are minor ideas in the passage. **This question is worth 2 points.**

   The Manhattan Project was an enormous effort to build an atomic bomb before scientists in Nazi Germany could do so.

   -
   -
   -

Answer Choices

1. Robert Oppenheimer and many other famous men worked in Los Alamos.
2. The entire project involved intelligent people working in many places.
3. The American president at the time of the project was Franklin D. Roosevelt.
4. The first atomic bomb was tested successfully in the summer of 1945.
5. It cost more than two billion dollars to do all of the research on the project.
6. Einstein and others were concerned about German research on atomic weapons.

Henri Matisse

Henri Matisse is widely considered one of the most influential artists of the twentieth century. While his art career began in the 1800s, he did the bulk of his work during the 1900s. During his lifetime, he created more than 200 paintings. He also made a large number of drawings, sculptures, and collages. His works are noted for their <u>vivid</u> use of colors, and he is often associated with the art movement called Fauvism.

Matisse originally intended to become a lawyer. But he had a change of heart and decided to become an artist instead. So he moved to Paris to study at an art school in 1891. Matisse's early works were mostly dark and gloomy. Then, he met John Peter Russell, an impressionist painter. Russell introduced the work of Vincent van Gogh and other impressionists to Matisse. The result was that Matisse's style underwent a radical change. He began to paint in brighter colors from then.

3 → The first work of Matisse's to be considered a masterpiece was *The Dinner Table*, which he completed in 1897. He held his initial solo exposition in 1904. It was around that time that he became involved with Fauvism. By 1905, he was considered one of the most important people in that movement. Matisse's work in Fauvism lasted only from 1904 to 1908, but it was a crucial period in his life. His Fauvist works emphasized the use of vibrant colors over realism. The colors often appeared as solid <u>slabs</u> in one tone. Matisse was rather prolific during this period as well. At first, many Fauvist works were ridiculed. Over time, however, people came to appreciate them.

■ During the 1920s and until his death in 1954, Matisse mostly engaged in traditional styles of artwork.■ However, as he aged, he painted less often. ■ Instead, he turned to making paper collages since he was often confined to a wheelchair and could no longer paint. ■ When he died, he was widely hailed as one of the giants of twentieth century art.

Glossary
vivid: bright; glowing; colorful
slab: a block; a chunk

1 In stating that he had a change of heart, the author means that he
   Ⓐ thought of something else
   Ⓑ considered his emotions
   Ⓒ changed his mind
   Ⓓ became emotional

2 The word radical in the passage is closest in meaning to
   Ⓐ simplistic
   Ⓑ fundamental
   Ⓒ periodic
   Ⓓ noteworthy

3 According to paragraph 3, which of the following is true of Fauvism?
   Ⓐ It emphasized dark, solid colors.
   Ⓑ Fauvist works were always praised.
   Ⓒ It was founded by Matisse in 1905.
   Ⓓ Matisse was a leader in that movement.

4 In paragraph 3, the author implies that Matisse
   Ⓐ made many paintings during his Fauvist years
   Ⓑ sold his first painting when he was a Fauvist
   Ⓒ became famous thanks to his Fauvist paintings
   Ⓓ came to reject the works he made as a Fauvist

5 Look at the four squares [■] that indicate where the following sentence could be added to the
   passage.

   Perhaps the most famous of those works is _Blue Nude II_.

   Where would the sentence best fit?
   Click on a square [■] to add the sentence to the passage.

Question Type 3 — Inference

Inference questions focus on arguments and information that are not stated in the passage. These types of questions ask the test taker to determine information that is implied or must be inferred. So the test taker must be able to read between the lines to answer these questions. There are 0-2 Inference questions for each passage.

Recognizing Inference questions:

- Which of the following can be inferred about X?

- The author of the passage implies that X . . .

- Which of the following can be inferred from paragraph 1 about X?

Helpful hints for answering the questions correctly:

- Words and phrases such as *many*, *most of the time*, *the majority*, *on occasion*, and other similar expressions are often important for inference questions. Pay close attention whenever these words are used in a passage.

- Learn to recognize any cause-effect relationships that are in a passage. Think about what the results of various actions could be.

Sample Inference Question

[3] → It is often stated that Elisha Otis invented the elevator. Yet that is not actually true. In fact, the first elevator was invented more than 2,000 years ago. However, it was not until the 1800s that people began making better elevators. One reason for this was that, prior to the 1800s, most buildings were only a few stories high. Thus elevators were not needed. But, in the 1800s, people started to use new building materials. These enabled people to make buildings ten stories or higher. Without a mechanical device to take people up and down the floors, erecting high buildings was impractical though. Thus inventors worked on a variety of elevators. As for Elisha Otis, he did not invent an elevator. Instead, he made a safety brake for it in 1852. The next year, he founded a company that sold elevators. Since then, millions of people around the world have ridden in—and continue to use—Otis elevators.

In paragraph 3, the author of the passage implies that Elisha Otis

(A) became a rich man thanks to his invention
(B) founded a company that still exists today
(C) experimented with some new building materials
(D) encouraged the building of skyscrapers

🎲 Answer Explanation

> Choice B is the correct answer. The important sentences are "The next year, he founded a company that sold elevators. Since then, millions of people around the world have ridden in—and continue to use—Otis elevators." First, the passage notes that Elisha Otis founded a company. Then, it mentions that people "continue to use" Otis elevators. Thus the passage implies that his company still exists today. The statements made in choices A, C, and D are not implied in the passage.

Windmills

Prior to the Industrial Revolution in the 1700s, there were few sources of power that people used. They mostly relied upon animals or themselves. However, some people used water power, and others utilized the wind to provide power. They did this by constructing windmills.

2 → A windmill is a structure that employs the power of the wind to operate machinery. There are many types of windmills, but the most common is the vertical windmill. It has a set of four long blades that have the appearance of an airplane propeller. These blades catch the wind as it blows and revolve around a central axis. As they move, the blades rotate a driveshaft that is connected to machinery inside the windmill itself. In many cases, the top of the windmill— the part with the blades—can rotate. This enables the blades to be moved to face the wind.

3 → Various kinds of windmills have been used since ancient times. They are known to have been built in the Middle East, China, and India many centuries ago. It is believed that windmills were introduced to Europe during the 1100s. Most early windmills were employed to grind grain such as wheat and corn. The process of turning grain into flour is backbreaking work when done by hand. Windmills, however, allowed people to let machines do the work.

4 → Another use that people found for windmills was to pump water. This led to thousands of windmills being constructed in Holland. Holland is a low-lying country located beside the North Sea. ■ A large amount of land there has been reclaimed from the sea. ■ To do that, the Dutch people constructed dikes to keep the sea water out of an area of land. ■ Then, they utilized windmills to pump the water out of these enclosed spaces. ■ Once the land was dry, the Dutch could plant crops or erect buildings on it.

When the Industrial Revolution began, the usage of windmills declined. Steam engines promptly replaced wind-powered machinery. Today, windmills are sometimes used to create electricity. But they are not nearly as prevalent as they once were.

Glossary

driveshaft: a device that rotates and sends power from an engine to an area that receives the power

grind: to crush; to mill; to turn into powder

1. In paragraph 2, why does the author mention an airplane propeller?
   - (A) To make a comparison
   - (B) To imply a solution
   - (C) To discuss a problem
   - (D) To describe an effect

2. In paragraph 3, which of the following can be inferred about grinding grain?
   - (A) Few people know how to do it.
   - (B) People use windmills to do it today.
   - (C) It is difficult to do without machinery.
   - (D) It improves the taste of the grain.

3. According to paragraph 4, people in Holland build windmills in order to
   - (A) assist them with growing their crops
   - (B) remove water from some areas of land
   - (C) build dikes to hold back floodwaters
   - (D) construct buildings throughout the country

4. The word prevalent in the passage is closest in meaning to
   - (A) utilized
   - (B) widespread
   - (C) powerful
   - (D) impressive

5. Look at the four squares [■] that indicate where the following sentence could be added to the passage.

   In fact, so much land has been reclaimed that around a quarter of the country presently lies beneath sea level.

   Where would the sentence best fit?
   Click on a square [■] to add the sentence to the passage.

The Medieval Origins of the University

[1] → In the year 800, Charlemagne was crowned the Holy Roman Emperor. The land he ruled became known as the Holy Roman Empire. His empire covered a great amount of Central and Western Europe. Charlemagne was a forward-looking ruler. So he attempted to implement reforms in many aspects of society. One of these was education. He desired an educated clergy. Therefore he ordered the cathedrals and monasteries in his empire to open schools to train boys to become priests. Charlemagne died in 814, so his plans were not fully carried out. However, some places opened schools. These were the roots of what later became universities.

[2] → There were famous cathedral schools as places such as Chartres, Cluny, and Reims during the Middle Ages. The curriculum was mostly religious. Students learned Latin, grammar, rhetoric, logic, and theology. Over time, other subjects were added to the course of study. These included arithmetic, geometry, astronomy, and music. The instructors were priests and monks. They taught their lessons in Latin since it was the language of the Church and the educated. Most of the students were from the upper class. These schools only taught boys since girls were not permitted to enter the priesthood.

[3] → Over time, these schools started to evolve. It is from them that the first universities emerged. The first university was established at Bologna, Italy, in 1088. The University of Paris was recognized as a university in 1150. During the next century, there were universities established in many places in Western Europe. Most of them were founded in Italy, France, Spain, and England. During the medieval period, these schools rid themselves of outside interference, including from the Church. This gave them a certain amount of freedom. They expanded the courses they taught. These new classes included medicine, law, and music. Large numbers of young men were trained in the scholastic arts. Thus these universities helped spark the Renaissance in the 1400s.

Glossary

clergy: a group of priests; a group of people approved by the church to be religious leaders

curriculum: a set of classes; the classes that are taught at a school or institute

1 In paragraph 1, the author's description of Charlemagne mentions which of the following?
  Ⓐ the year in which he was born
  Ⓑ the changes he made in his empire
  Ⓒ the name of the land that he ruled
  Ⓓ the reason he wanted to join the clergy

2 According to paragraph 2, which of the following is NOT true of cathedral schools?
  Ⓐ Only the children of nobles were allowed to attend them.
  Ⓑ They forbade girls from taking their classes.
  Ⓒ They focused on teaching religious studies to students.
  Ⓓ The instructors used Latin to teach their classes.

3 In paragraph 3, the author implies that the Church
  Ⓐ wanted its clergy to attend universities
  Ⓑ attempted to influence some universities
  Ⓒ donated large amounts of money to some schools
  Ⓓ considered universities a threat to cathedral schools

4 **Directions:** An introductory sentence for a brief summary of the passage is provided below. Complete the summary by selecting the THREE answer choices that express the most important ideas of the passage. Some sentences do not belong because they express ideas that are not presented in the passage or are minor ideas in the passage. **This question is worth 2 points.**

The cathedral schools started by Charlemagne later transformed into the first universities during medieval times.
  -
  -
  -

Answer Choices

1. The first universities were founded during the 1100s and 1200s.
2. Charlemagne ruled the Holy Roman Empire from 800 to 814.
3. Most students were from the upper class, but some were from poor families.

4. Thanks to universities, the Renaissance was able to take place.
5. Charlemagne ordered cathedrals to open schools that would teach boys.
6. Early cathedral schools taught a wide variety of subjects to their students.

Question Type 4 Negative Factual Information

Negative Factual Information questions focus on the facts that are found in the passage. These types of questions ask the test taker about various details, definitions, explanation, events, and other data in the passage. However, three of the answer choices contain correct information while one answer choice has incorrect information. The test taker must examine the answer choices and determine which answer choice has incorrect information. There are 0-2 Negative Factual Information questions for each passage.

Recognizing Negative Factual Information questions:

- According to the passage, which of the following is NOT true of X?

- The author's description of X mentions all of the following EXCEPT:

Helpful hints for answering the questions correctly:

- Look for facts, not opinions, in the passage in order to answer these questions.

- Many times, the question mentions a paragraph. In order to answer the question properly, focus only on the information in that paragraph.

- Sometimes an answer choice has correct information, but that information is not mentioned in the passage. That is the answer that must be chosen.

Sample Negative Factual Information Question

According to paragraph 2, which of the following is NOT true of projection?

(A) It happens when people think others feel the same way they do.
(B) It is the act of transferring one's feelings to other people.
(C) People often employ it as a defense mechanism.
(D) It mostly involves positive feelings rather than negative ones.

📖 Answer Explanation

Choice D is the correct answer. The author notes, "For the most part, people project negative feelings or opinions onto others." This is the opposite of Choice D. Choice D claims that people project positive feelings more than negative ones. This is incorrect. Since Choice D is a false statement, it is the correct answer. Choices A, B, and C are correct statements. So they are all incorrect answer choices.

Animal Nurturing

All animals have an instinct that drives them to breed and to produce offspring. Once mating is done though, animals react differently. In some instances, the male goes away and has nothing to do with his offspring. This is common behavior among fish and reptiles. Often, the male remains with the female until the offspring are born or hatched. Once the babies are alive, one or both parents may depart. However, most bird and mammal species stay with their young and nurture them to adulthood.

One of the two most important aspects of animal nurturing involves the providing of food. When mammals are born, the female provides milk for her young. Later, as they grow older, they stop drinking milk and consume solid food. Then, the mammals—typically both the mother and father—provide food for their babies. They do this by killing animals and bringing the <u>carcasses</u> back to the den. Or, in the case of herbivores, they bring fruits or vegetables to their young or take them to places where they can find food for themselves. As for birds, they carry food back to their nests and feed it to their young.

³ →As the animals age, their parents teach them how to feed themselves. Animals have various ways of doing this. For instance, cheetahs bring dead animals to their young. The baby cheetahs then learn to hunt by attacking the bodies. Other animals, especially <u>felines</u>, bring back live prey and let their babies kill it. Many times, young animals follow their parents as they search for food. By observing, they can figure out how to hunt or acquire food for themselves.

The second major aspect of animal nurturing involves parents protecting their young. Animals build nests, dens, and other shelters to protect their babies. They stand guard to protect eggs and newborns from predators. Many young animals stay with their parents for several months or years. For example, male lion cubs remain with their mothers for around two years. Once the young animals are capable of living away from their parents, they set out on their own.

Glossary
carcass: a dead body
feline: a cat; a member of the cat family

1   The word depart in the passage is closest in meaning to

(A) approve

(B) endure

(C) observe

(D) leave

2   Which of the sentences below best expresses the essential information in the highlighted sentence in the passage? Incorrect answer choices change the meaning in important ways or leave out essential information.

(A) In many cases, certain animals show their babies where they can find food.

(B) Parents that are herbivores do very little to provide food for their offspring.

(C) Certain animals simply bring back some vegetation for their young to eat.

(D) Plant-eating parents provide food for their young or show them how to get it.

3   In paragraph 3, the author's description of how parents teach their young to feed themselves mentions all of the following EXCEPT:

(A) which animals bring live prey to their young

(B) how quickly some animals learn to hunt others

(C) how young cheetahs learn to hunt animals

(D) why some animals accompany their parents on hunts

4   **Directions:** Select the appropriate statements from the answer choices and match them to the aspect of animal nurturing to which they relate. TWO of the answer choices will NOT be used. **This question is worth 3 points.**

<table>
<tr><td align="center">**Answer Choices**</td><td align="center">**ANIMAL NURTURING**</td></tr>
<tr><td>1. Reptiles often have nothing to do with raising their offspring.</td><td>**Providing Food** (Select 2)
•
•</td></tr>
<tr><td>2. Parents may watch over eggs that have not hatched.</td><td>**Protecting Young** (Select 3)</td></tr>
<tr><td>3. Female mammals provide milk for their newborn babies.</td><td>•</td></tr>
<tr><td>4. Some animals build nests for their young to live in.</td><td>•</td></tr>
<tr><td>5. Young animals remain with their parents for months or years.</td><td>•</td></tr>
<tr><td>6. The father often abandons the mother after mating.</td><td></td></tr>
<tr><td>7. Animals take carcasses back to their nests or dens.</td><td></td></tr>
</table>

The Holy Roman Empire

[1] → On Christmas Day in the year 800, Pope Leo III crowned Charlemagne the Holy Roman Emperor. The pope had a number of enemies. So he was seeking protection from the strongest ruler in Europe at the time. Charlemagne was one of the greatest men of his time. Yet he only lived until 814. The Holy Roman Empire, as his realm was called, transferred to his descendants. But they split his once-vast empire. So the Holy Roman Empire slowly disappeared in both power and name.

[2] → Nearly 150 years after the death of Charlemagne, another pope found himself threatened. Much like Leo III did before, the pope turned to the Germanic people to be protected from his enemies. In 962, Pope John XII crowned Otto I of Saxony the Holy Roman Empire. Otto had unified most of the Germanic tribes under his rule. He also ruled parts of northern Italy. He was thus seen as an ideal ally for the pope. With Otto's crowning, the Holy Roman Empire was once again renewed.

[3] → Otto and later emperors proceeded to involve themselves in the affairs of the Church. They often fought with the popes. They dismissed those popes with whom they disagreed. Then, they had their allies elected to the office instead. The Church resented this interference by the emperors. It fought back, and the Holy Roman Empire later ended its involvement in church affairs.

[4] → The empire itself changed over time. The emperor slowly lost power as local nobles in the land began to accrue more power. The empire then changed. It became a collection of powerful states, small principalities, and free city-states. The position of Holy Roman Emperor stopped being hereditary. Instead, it became an elected one. Over the centuries, the individual states in the empire came to control most of their own affairs. By the 1700s, Prussia and Austria dominated the empire. When Napoleon defeated Francis II of Austria in 1805, the Holy Roman Empire was a weak entity. It was abolished the next year in 1806.

Glossary

descendant: a person who descends from another; an offspring; a younger direct relation of another

principality: a state that is ruled by a prince

1. According to paragraph 1, the Holy Roman Empire became less powerful after the death of Charlemagne because
   (A) Charlemagne failed to prepare his children to rule
   (B) it fought a number of wars with neighboring countries
   (C) the rulers who came after him divided the empire
   (D) the pope was interested in seeing it become weak

2. The author discusses Otto I of Saxony in paragraph 2 in order to
   (A) compare his accomplishments with Charlemagne's
   (B) explain why the pope crowned him Holy Roman Emperor
   (C) describe some of his accomplishments as emperor
   (D) explain how he helped the pope fight his enemies

3. In paragraph 3, the author implies that the Church
   (A) always had a major role in choosing the Holy Roman Emperor
   (B) asked the Holy Roman Emperor to approve the popes it chose
   (C) had an unsteady relationship with the Holy Roman Empire
   (D) went to war with the Holy Roman Empire on occasion

4. The word accrue in the passage is closest in meaning to
   (A) cede
   (B) observe
   (C) desire
   (D) amass

5. According to paragraph 4, which of the following is NOT true of the Holy Roman Empire?
   (A) Napoleon ruled it as the last Holy Roman Emperor.
   (B) The nature of the empire changed over time.
   (C) It came to an end in the nineteenth century.
   (D) Many of its member states retained their own power.

Reference questions focus on how certain words in the passage relate to other words or phrases. These types of questions ask the test taker to look at a highlighted word and then to decide which word or phrase in the passage the highlighted word refers to. Most of the time, the highlighted word is a pronoun such as *he, she, it, they, this,* or *that*. There are 0-2 Reference questions for each passage.

Recognizing Reference questions:

- The word X in the passage refers to

Helpful hints for answering the questions correctly:

- When a singular pronoun is highlighted, the correct answer is always a singular word or phrase. When a plural pronoun is highlighted, the correct answer is always a plural word or phrase.

- Replace the highlighted word or phrase with all of the answer choices. See how each answer choice reads in the sentence. The correct answer choice can always be substituted into the passage without any grammatical problems.

- The answer choices always appear in the same order that they appear in the passage.

- Most of the answer choices come before the highlighted word. Occasionally, an answer choice may appear after the highlighted word.

Sample Reference Question

A person observing the night sky is likely to see an occasional streak of light. This light typically moves across a portion of the sky before disappearing. This is a meteor. A meteor may be a speck of dust or a rock. The reason it creates the light is that it is burning up in Earth's atmosphere. Due to their small size, few meteors ever reach the planet's surface intact. Most are consumed completely in the atmosphere. At some times during the year, Earth passes through clouds of interstellar dust during its orbit around the sun. The result of this is a meteor shower. In ideal viewing conditions, people can see more than fifty meteors per hour during a meteor shower. The Perseid meteor shower is one of the most famous. It usually starts in late July and lasts until late August. Another is the Leonid meteor shower, which takes place annually in November.

The word its in the passage refers to

(A) the atmosphere

(B) the year

(C) Earth

(D) interstellar dust

🔷 Answer Explanation

Choice C is the correct answer. The "its" that is in orbit around the sun is Earth. Simply substitute all of the answer choices with "its." Only one of the four answer choices orbits the sun: Earth. By substituting the answer choices, you can quickly find the correct answer. Choices A, B, and D are all incorrect.

High-Speed Trains

[1] → Trains have been transporting both people and cargo since the middle of the nineteenth century. At that time, they were the fastest means of transportation on land. However, during the twentieth century, automobiles and airplanes began to replace trains as the primary means of transportation. To counter this, engineers worked to increase the speed that trains could travel. The result was the development of high-speed trains.

The purpose of a high-speed rail system is to deliver people and goods from one place to another very quickly. Today, most high-speed trains operate at speeds ranging from 100 to 300 kilometers per hour. However, some are capable of attaining speeds as high as 580 kilometers per hour. Engineers believe they can get them to move even faster in the future. There are several types of high-speed trains. Most operate on electricity, but maglev trains are an exception. They employ magnetic <u>levitation</u> techniques to move at great speeds.

[3] → The majority of high-speed trains run on tracks that have been specifically designed for their usage. These tracks have continuously welded rails, so there are no gaps in their rails. They are mostly straight with only a few curves. This allows the trains to run at constant high speeds since they have to decelerate when going through a curve. There are also no road crossings for high-speed trains like there are for regular trains. This too prevents the trains from having to slow down or stop because of road traffic. The trains themselves have <u>aerodynamic</u> designs to reduce drag, which increases their speed. Because of their shape and speed, they are often called bullet trains.

The primary advantage of a high-speed rail system is its speed. Large distances can be crossed in a short amount of time. This has made high-speed rail systems popular in regions with large urban populations that are relatively close to one another. Japan, for instance, has an extensive network of high-speed trains. So does Europe. At present, China has the largest high-speed rail network in the world, with more than 6,000 kilometers of tracks throughout the country.

Glossary
levitation: the act of raising something in the air
aerodynamic: designed to reduce the amount of drag on an object

1 According to paragraph 1, engineers developed high-speed trains because
- Ⓐ trains were losing business to cars and airplanes
- Ⓑ passengers demanded a faster means of transportation
- Ⓒ it would let railway companies earn more money
- Ⓓ they were needed to transport goods cross country

2 The word their in the passage refers to
- Ⓐ high-speed trains
- Ⓑ these tracks
- Ⓒ continuously welded rails
- Ⓓ gaps

3 In paragraph 3, the author uses bullet trains as an example of
- Ⓐ a competitor of high-speed trains
- Ⓑ a unique form of maglev trains
- Ⓒ the most aerodynamic of all trains
- Ⓓ a nickname for high-speed trains

4 **Directions:** An introductory sentence for a brief summary of the passage is provided below. Complete the summary by selecting the THREE answer choices that express the most important ideas of the passage. Some sentences do not belong because they express ideas that are not presented in the passage or are minor ideas in the passage. **This question is worth 2 points.**

High-speed trains are used to transport both goods and people at extremely high rates of speed.
-
-
-

Answer Choices

1. Some high-speed trains can move almost 600 kilometers per hour.
2. The first high-speed train appeared in Japan in the 1960s.
3. High-speed trains are popular in urban centers in Japan and Europe.
4. The design of the trains and their tracks let the trains move swiftly.
5. The most extensive high-speed railway system is in China.
6. Maglev trains rely upon magnetic levitation rather than electricity.

Maple Trees

Every fall, forests in parts of Asia, Europe, and North America transform from green into brilliant red, orange, and yellow. Many of the trees responsible for these bright colors are maples. The maple tree is a deciduous tree common in temperate climates. There are around 125 species of maple tree that grow all over the world. The leaves of maple trees have a distinctive shape that makes them easily recognizable: They have a long stem and three large extensions, which have many points.

2 → Maple trees vary in height. The vine maple typically reaches a height of only around six meters and is therefore considered a shrub. Sugar maples may grow to be around twenty-five meters tall. And silver maples and other species can grow higher than forty meters. Maple trees have small flowers that mostly bloom early in spring. Depending on the species, these flowers are orange, yellow, red, or green. The leaves of the maple start as <u>crimson</u> in spring, change to green in summer, and then transform into resplendent colors of red, orange, and yellow in fall. Maple tree seeds have distinctive shapes that resemble wings. ■ The seed is encased at one end of the wing. ■ The shape of the seed makes it twirl in a circle as it falls to the ground. ■ This twirling motion can carry a seed far from its tree, especially in windy conditions. ■

3 → While maple trees are beautiful to look at, particularly in fall, many have a commercial value as well. Some species are planted in parks and people's yards to beautify them, so there are plant nurseries that specialize in maple trees. Some maple trees are valued for their timber. Their wood is used on construction projects, and it is also employed to make musical instruments since it has good <u>acoustic</u> properties. The sugar maple is prized for its sap. The sap is drained from the tree by using taps. It is then boiled and processed to make maple syrup, a type of sweetener.

Glossary
crimson: a deep red color
acoustic: related to hearing; auditory

1 The word which in the passage refers to
  Ⓐ maple trees
  Ⓑ a distinctive shape
  Ⓒ a long stem
  Ⓓ three large extensions

2 In paragraph 2, the author's description of the height of maple trees mentions all of the following EXCEPT:
  Ⓐ how long it takes maple trees to reach their full height
  Ⓑ how high the sugar maple may grow to be
  Ⓒ why people call the vine maple tree a shrub
  Ⓓ which maple tree can be more than forty meters high

3 The word resplendent in the passage is closest in meaning to
  Ⓐ magnificent
  Ⓑ excessive
  Ⓒ apparent
  Ⓓ considerable

4 According to paragraph 3, some maple trees are used to make musical instruments because
  Ⓐ the trees are easy to cut and shape
  Ⓑ musicians like the way that they look
  Ⓒ their wood has good sound qualities
  Ⓓ the high sap content increases the wood's value

5 Look at the four squares [■] that indicate where the following sentence could be added to the passage.

This enables maple trees rather easily to expand the area in which they grow.

Where would the sentence best fit?
Click on a square [■] to add the sentence to the passage.

Unit 06

Question Type 6 — Rhetorical Purpose

Rhetorical Purpose questions focus on the reasons that certain information appears in the passage. These types of questions ask the test taker to determine the function of specific information included in the passage. The test taker should be able to recognize why the author of the passage mentions the information that is being asked about. There are 0-2 Rhetorical Purpose questions for each passage.

Recognizing Rhetorical Purpose questions:

- The author discusses X in paragraph 2 in order to . . .

- Why does the author mention X?

- The author uses X as an example of . . .

Helpful hints for answering the questions correctly:

- The information that is asked about is often highlighted. It can be a single word, or it can be a longer phrase. Read the sentences around the highlighted information in order to determine its relationship with the passage.

- There are often context clues that can help you determine the function of the information. These context clues include the words *definition*, *example*, *explain*, *illustrate*, *note*, *contrast*, *refute*, and *criticize*. Use these words to help find the correct answer.

Sample Rhetorical Purpose Question

4 → Many people are aware of John D. Rockefeller's success as a businessman. In the late 1800s and early 1900s, he was one of the richest men in the world. His company, Standard Oil, was a leader in the oil industry. But what many people do not realize about him is that he was a great philanthropist. People often know of the work that Andrew Carnegie, one of his contemporaries, did to found libraries. Yet they do not know about Rockefeller's donations. It is estimated that he gave more than half a billion dollars to charity during his life. He did not wait to make his donations until he was wealthy either. He donated ten percent of his earnings to charity as a young man. Rockefeller gave funds to many causes. He was very interested in education. He donated more than eighty million dollars to the University of Chicago. He gave large sums to medical research as well.

In paragraph 4, why does the author mention the University of Chicago?

(A) To state that Rockefeller went to school there
(B) To note how it benefitted from Rockefeller's charity
(C) To claim that Rockefeller founded the school
(D) To stress the medical research that was done there

Answer Explanation

Choice B is the correct answer. The author mentions that Rockefeller gave a lot of money to charity. Then, the author writes, "He donated more than eighty million dollars to the University of Chicago." In writing that sentence, the author notes how the university benefitted from Rockefeller's charity. Choices A and D are untrue statements, so they are both incorrect. Choice C is true but is not mentioned in the passage, so it is incorrect as well.

Blaise Pascal

Blaise Pascal was a French scientist and philosopher who lived from 1623 to 1662. During his time, it was common for scientists to work in many fields. For that reason, Pascal became accomplished in several areas. He mainly focused on mathematics, especially geometry. Yet he also invented a mechanical calculator, worked in hydrodynamics, and did research on vacuums.

2 → When Pascal was a child, he showed a great deal of intelligence. He was considered a child prodigy, especially in the field of mathematics. Unfortunately, his father lost the family fortune. So he had to take a job as a tax collector. Interested in helping his father, Pascal invented a calculating machine when he was only nineteen years of age. This was the forerunner of all modern calculators. Known as the Pascaline, it was a fairly intricate machine. Yet it was difficult to build and expensive, too. Pascal built a total of twenty machines, some of which are in museums today.

3 → Pascal made a number of contributions to the field of mathematics. His most famous is called Pascal's triangle. This is a triangle in which the numbers placed at the top of the triangle add together to form the numbers beneath them. Pascal devised the triangle while trying to think of all of the probability outcomes in a card game. Pascal's triangle had been known to the ancient Chinese. But he was the first person to recognize how important it was. His work with the triangle laid the foundation for the theory of probabilities.

4 → In the field of hydrodynamics, Pascal contributed what is today called Pascal's Law. It states that the pressure exerted on a fluid in a combined space is transmitted equally in all directions. He also proved the existence of vacuums. As far back as Aristotle, people had theorized that vacuums did not exist. Pascal, however, proved them all wrong. Sadly, Pascal died at a young age. Had he not done so, his contributions to the world of science might have been even greater.

Glossary
forerunner: something that comes before another; a predecessor; a prototype
outcome: a result

1 The word prodigy in the passage is closest in meaning to
   (A) genius
   (B) laborer
   (C) assistant
   (D) student

2 The word he in the passage refers to
   (A) Pascal
   (B) a child
   (C) a child prodigy
   (D) his father

3 According to paragraph 2, which of the following is true of the Pascaline?
   (A) The machine only had a few moving parts.
   (B) Pascal earned a lot of money from selling it.
   (C) The idea for it came from Pascal's father.
   (D) It was invented when Pascal was a teenager.

4 In paragraph 3, the author's description of Pascal's triangle mentions all of the following EXCEPT:
   (A) The Chinese were the first to invent it.
   (B) Pascal used it while playing card games.
   (C) It was useful for probability theory.
   (D) Pascal realized how important it was.

5 In paragraph 4, the author uses Pascal's Law as an example of
   (A) an instance in which Pascal proved Aristotle wrong
   (B) some work that Pascal did in hydrodynamics
   (C) a law based on research done by Aristotle
   (D) a discovery as important as Pascal's Triangle

Planetary Rings

In 1610, Galileo Galilei pointed his telescope at Saturn. He was surprised by what he saw. Saturn appeared to have a bump on each side. Decades later, in 1659, astronomer Christian Huygens observed that there was a flat disk which appeared to surround the entire planet. What both men had seen were the rings of Saturn.

2 → The eight planets in the solar system are divided into two groups: terrestrial planets and Jovian planets. Mercury, Venus, Earth, and Mars are the terrestrial planets. The larger Jovians are Jupiter, Saturn, Uranus, and Neptune. The Jovian planets share several characteristics. One is that they all have rings around them. Saturn's are the most evident. But Jupiter, Uranus, and Neptune have ring systems as well. The rings themselves are comprised of ice crystals, dust, and rocks. Most of the material that makes them up is quite small. However, there are some rocks in Saturn's rings that are hundreds of meters in diameter. In addition, some moons even orbit their planets from within ring systems.

Astronomers believe these rings were created in one of three ways. First, they may be made of material that remained in orbit around the planet after it originally formed. Second, some rings may be made from material from a moon that orbited too close to its planet. Due to the strength of the planet's gravity, the moon was ripped apart, and the debris that resulted from its gravity formed a ring. Third, some rings may have formed from debris ejected from nearby moons that were struck by meteoroids, comets, or asteroids.

Saturn has the most extensive ring system, with fourteen major groups. Within each of these groups are thousands of individual rings. In comparison, Uranus has thirteen distinct ring groups, Neptune has five, and Jupiter has four. Jupiter's ring system is the least dense and is mainly composed of dust. This makes astronomers believe that its rings mostly formed due to various impacts on its moon. Neptune's rings are not very dense. As for Uranus, its ring systems are mostly made of ice crystals.

Glossary
eject: to expel; to throw out
distinct: separate; individual

1 In paragraph 2, why does the author mention terrestrial planets and Jovian planets?
   - Ⓐ To describe the characteristics of each type of planet
   - Ⓑ To name the two groups of planets in the solar system
   - Ⓒ To compare the compositions of both types of planets
   - Ⓓ To point out which planets have rings and which do not

2 The word evident in the passage is closest in meaning to
   - Ⓐ comprehensive
   - Ⓑ stunning
   - Ⓒ expansive
   - Ⓓ visible

3 Which of the sentences below best expresses the essential information in the highlighted sentence in the passage? Incorrect answer choices change the meaning in important ways or leave out essential information.
   - Ⓐ The planet's powerful gravity destroyed the moon and turned it into a ring.
   - Ⓑ The ring formed when a moon crashed into the planet and destroyed itself.
   - Ⓒ Some planets have gravity that is powerful enough to help them create moons.
   - Ⓓ The force of gravity caused one of the planet's moons to break apart.

4 **Directions:** Select the appropriate statements from the answer choices and match them to the planet to which they relate. TWO of the answer choices will NOT be used. **This question is worth 3 points.**

Answer Choices	PLANET
1. Has rings that were likely created by moon impacts	**Jupiter** (Select 2)
2. Contains rings that are mostly made of ice	•
3. Has a total of thirteen unique ring systems	•
4. Has more rings than any other planet	**Saturn** (Select 3)
5. Contains thousands of rings in each ring system	•
6. Has some large rocks in its ring systems	•
7. Has the least number of ring systems	•

07

Question Type 7 — Insert Text

Insert Text questions focus on where a new sentence would best fit in the passage. These types of questions present a new sentence that is related to the passage in some way. The test taker needs to find the best place in the passage where the sentence could be inserted without interrupting the flow of the passage. There are 0-1 Insert Text questions for each passage.

Recognizing Insert Text questions:

- Look at the four squares [■] that indicate where the following sentence could be added to the passage.

  [You will see a sentence in bold.]

  Where would the sentence best fit?
  [Click on a square [■] to add the sentence to the passage.]

Helpful hints for answering the questions correctly:

- There will be four black squares in the passage. These squares always appear in four consecutive sentences. The new sentence should go in one of those squares.

- Try reading the new sentence in each of the four squares. This will help you determine the best place for the sentence to be inserted.

- The new sentences often contain important connecting words. These include *for example, for instance, consequently, as a result, on the other hand, meanwhile, however, thus,* and *therefore*. Take note of these connecting words and pay attention to how they relate to the rest of the passage.

Sample Insert Text Question

It is often clear when and why some cultures disappear. ■ A civilization may be defeated by another in a war. ■ Or perhaps a disease or natural disaster kills another group of people. ■ However, there are numerous instances in history in which a civilization vanishes but leaves no records concerning its disappearance. ■ This is the case of the Anasazi. They were a Native American tribe. They once lived in the land that is in the Four Corners area of the United States today. They lived there from around the years 200 to 1300. Archaeologists have done extensive work on many Anasazi settlements. They have learned a great deal about their culture. They know about the types of crafts that the Anasazi once made. And they are aware of which crops the Anasazi grew. What they do not know is why the Anasazi suddenly vanished. They do, however, have a number of theories about this matter.

Look at the four squares [■] that indicate where the following sentence could be added to the passage.

Many Native American tribes, for instance, were wiped out by smallpox epidemics in the 1500s.

Where would the sentence best fit?
Click on a square [■] to add the sentence to the passage.

🎲 Answer Explanation

The sentence best fits after the third square. The sentence before the third square reads, "Or perhaps a disease or natural disaster kills another group of people." The sentence to be added notes that many tribes "were wiped out by smallpox epidemics." In this case, the key words are "disease" and "smallpox epidemics." Notice the connection between the words. So the sentence to be added provides an example of some civilizations being wiped out by a disease.

Dinosaur Fossils in Antarctica

[1] → Antarctica has one of the most inhospitable climates in the world. Most of it is covered in ice and snow. The temperature there can get as low as minus eighty-nine degrees Celsius. As a result, it was the last place that scientists ever expected to find dinosaur fossils. Nevertheless, in the 1980s, the fossilized remains of some dinosaurs were found. Since then, the bones of at least eleven species of dinosaurs have been discovered there. These include both plant- and meat-eating dinosaurs. All of the dinosaurs lived in either the Jurassic or Cretaceous Period. These two periods took place from 200 to sixty-five million years ago.

[2] → At first glance, it may appear strange that dinosaurs once lived in Antarctica. After all, dinosaurs were suited for warm and hot climates. In addition, hardly any plants grow in the land's frigid climate. So the presence of herbivores seems mysterious to some. Yet these facts are easily explained. Antarctica was not always cold. In fact, it was once much warmer than it currently is. Millions of years ago, Antarctica was not in its present location; it was located much farther north. There, it joined with all of the other continents to form a gigantic landmass near the equator. ■ Later, this supercontinent split into two smaller landmasses. ■ One was in the north. ■ The other was in the south. ■ The southern landmass was comprised of what would become South America, India, Australia, Africa, and Antarctica.

When Antarctica was a part of these two landmasses, its climate was quite different. It was warmer, and plants grew there. Thus it had an ideal habitat for many species of dinosaurs. Even when it moved to its present location, some scientists believe that it stayed fairly warm for a while. This was during the Cretaceous Period. It happened between 144 and sixty-five million years ago. So it is likely that dinosaurs and other animals lived in Antarctica for millions of years. Only after its climate became harsher did most life there die out.

Glossary
herbivore: an animal that only eats vegetation
supercontinent: an extremely large continent

1   The word inhospitable in the passage is closest in meaning to
    Ⓐ inhumane
    Ⓑ varied
    Ⓒ intense
    Ⓓ hostile

2   In paragraph 1, the author's description of Antarctica mentions all of the following EXCEPT:
    Ⓐ what kinds of dinosaur fossils were found there
    Ⓑ why the climate there can be so harsh
    Ⓒ when the dinosaurs found there lived
    Ⓓ how cold the temperature can get there

3   According to paragraph 2, Antarctica was once warmer than it currently is because
    Ⓐ the sun made the planet warmer in the past
    Ⓑ it was located elsewhere near the equator
    Ⓒ there was more volcanic activity back then
    Ⓓ the Earth as a whole was warmer in the past

4   The word It in the passage refers to
    Ⓐ Antarctica
    Ⓑ An ideal habitat for many species of dinosaurs
    Ⓒ Its present location
    Ⓓ The Cretaceous Period

5   Look at the four squares [■] that indicate where the following sentence could be added to the passage.

    Today, it is known to scientists as Pangaea, which means "all of the Earth."

    Where would the sentence best fit?
    Click on a square [■] to add the sentence to the passage.

The Development of Rock and Roll Music

Several genres of music have their origins in the United States. One of these is rock and roll. There is some debate about the genesis of rock music. Yet most musicologists agree that there were two major factors involved in its development. The first was the combining of various musical genres. The second was the creating of electric musical instruments and tools.

In the 1940s, the American South was a land rich in different types of music. During that period, many musicians experimented with music. They combined elements of various genres. These genres included blues, country, jazz, and gospel music. With them, some musicians created an <u>innovative</u> sound. This new music was further influenced by black musicians. They introduced elements of jazz and rhythm and blues into the music. They played dance rhythms in two new forms of music, called jump blues and boogie-woogie. These were highly popular with both black and white Americans.

3 → Around the same time, better electric guitars, basses, <u>amplifiers</u>, and microphones were invented. They accelerated the development of rock and roll. Musicians used these electric instruments to play the new sound that they had created. Soon, the basic rock and roll combo began to emerge. It was a group that had one or two electric guitarists, an electric bassist, a drummer, and sometimes a keyboardist. Some bands used horns and acoustic instruments. But they were less popular.

By the early 1950s, these two elements had formed the beginnings of rock and roll. In 1951, radio disc jockey Alan Freed in Cleveland started regularly playing recordings of this new music. ■ He also coined the term "rock and roll" to refer to the music itself. ■ In 1955, Bill Haley and the Comets recorded *Rock around the Clock*. ■ It became the first big rock and roll hit. ■ Around the same time, Elvis Presley made his initial recordings. He caused a worldwide sensation with his music and stage performances. Rock and roll soon became a mainstream form of music. Today, it ranks among the most popular of all musical genres.

Glossary
innovative: new; original
amplifier: an electronic device that increases the strength of a signal that is sent to it

1   The word These in the passage refers to
   (A) Black musicians
   (B) Elements of jazz and rhythm and blues
   (C) Dance rhythms
   (D) Jump blues and boogie-woogie

2   According to paragraph 3, which of the following is true of the basic rock and roll combo?
   (A) It emphasized the use of acoustic guitars.
   (B) It did not always have a keyboardist.
   (C) It focused more on singing than on playing instruments.
   (D) It rejected the use of electric instruments.

3   Look at the four squares [■] that indicate where the following sentence could be added to the passage.

   The name that he came up with for the new music was an instant hit with people.

   Where would the sentence best fit?
   Click on a square [■] to add the sentence to the passage.

4   **Directions:** An introductory sentence for a brief summary of the passage is provided below. Complete the summary by selecting the THREE answer choices that express the most important ideas of the passage. Some sentences do not belong because they express ideas that are not presented in the passage or are minor ideas in the passage. **This question is worth 2 points.**

   There were two major factors that involved the creation of rock and roll music in the mid-1900s.

   -
   -
   -

Answer Choices

1. Some musicians combined aspects of several types of music to make a new sound.
2. Elvis Presley became one of the greatest performers in history.
3. Country and jazz music were integral to the development of rock music.
4. Rock and roll musicians mostly focused on using electric instruments.
5. Alan Freed was a disc jockey who created the name "rock and roll" for the music.
6. No one is exactly sure when the first rock and roll music was played.

Question Type 8 — Sentence Simplification

Sentence Simplification questions focus on a single sentence in the passage. This sentence is usually both long and complex and has two or more clauses. These types of questions ask the test taker to choose the sentence that best simplifies the sentence that has been highlighted. This correct answer must convey all of the important information in the highlighted sentence. There are 0-1 Sentence Simplification questions for each passage.

Recognizing Sentence Simplification questions:

- Which of the sentences below best expresses the essential information in the highlighted sentence in the passage? Incorrect answer choices change the meaning in important ways or leave out essential information.

Helpful hints for answering the questions correctly:

- Read the highlighted sentence carefully to determine the important information in it. Be sure that this information is contained in the answer choice that you select.

- Find the main point of the highlighted sentence. This is always included in the correct answer choice.

- The highlighted sentence typically contains multiple clauses. Break down the sentence by looking at the clauses individually. Doing this will help you better understand the sentence.

Sample Sentence Simplification Question

In the 1800s, much of the United States was still unsettled. Few humans had ever visited many of its regions. This provided landscape artists with a great opportunity. They were able to draw and paint pictures of areas of untamed wilderness. The American public was often stunned by the pictures the artists created since most people were unaware that such beauty existed in their country. As a result, many artists gained great fame. One such artist was Thomas Moran. While he was born in England in 1837, his family soon moved to the United States. It was there that Moran became interested in art. Moran spent some time drawing and painting around the Great Lakes. However, it was not there that he gained fame. It was at Yellowstone where he accomplished that. In 1871, Moran was hired as an artist on an expedition to the Yellowstone area. That job changed his life.

Which of the sentences below best expresses the essential information in the highlighted sentence in the passage? Incorrect answer choices change the meaning in important ways or leave out essential information.

(A) The majority of Americans became interested in art for the first time because of the stunning work made by the artists.

(B) Most Americans were shocked by the art because they had never seen any pictures painted so well before.

(C) It was the first time that many Americans were introduced to art, so they were amazed by the pictures they saw.

(D) The art that they made surprised a lot of Americans, who did not know how beautiful parts of their country were.

Answer Explanation

Choice D is the correct answer. The highlighted sentence notes that Americans were surprised by the art since they did not know that certain regions in their country were so beautiful. This idea is best expressed by Choice D. Choices A, B, and C are all incorrect statements.

Clipper Ships

People have been trading for thousands of years. To engage in trade with others, they have transported goods over land and by sea. Merchants have always been able to move more products by ship. So, for centuries, people attempted to build faster sailing ships that would allow merchants to move their goods more quickly from one place to another. In the 1800s, the fastest ship ever to sail the oceans was built: the clipper ship.

The first real clipper ships were built in the United States in the early 1830s. The design was soon imitated in Britain and elsewhere. By the 1840s, clipper ships were common sights on the world's oceans. Clipper ships were designed to be fast. Most had three masts equipped with many sails. These sails were square shaped, which allowed them to catch a lot of wind. The ships also had narrow <u>hulls</u>, which further increased their speed but prevented them from carrying large amounts of cargo.

3 → At the time clipper ships were first built, most sailors considered it a good day when they covered around 240 kilometers. Clipper ships, however, averaged about 400 kilometers a day. The fastest clipper ships could sail more than 600 kilometers in a single day. This great speed made them invaluable when it was necessary to transport goods quickly. For instance, clipper ships often brought tea from China and India to Europe and the United States. They were utilized to transport tropical fruit to northern lands while other merchants shipped ice from northern places to warmer lands. And, during the California Gold Rush, which began in 1849, thousands of <u>prospectors</u> sailed on clipper ships. They made the extensive voyage past the southern tip of South America much faster than those who took the land route across the United States.

The age of the clipper ship came to a sudden end though. Steamships started being used during the mid-1800s. They traveled faster than clipper ships and did not rely upon the wind to move. By the 1870s, there were only a handful of clipper ships still transporting goods across the oceans.

Glossary
hull: the hollow low part of a ship
prospector: a miner, often one who is searching for gold

1 Which of the sentences below best expresses the essential information in the highlighted sentence in the passage? Incorrect answer choices change the meaning in important ways or leave out essential information.

Ⓐ Merchants have tried for centuries to get their goods to markets as quickly as they can.
Ⓑ The fastest ships were always preferred by merchants since they could make more money with them.
Ⓒ People tried to make swift ships for the purpose of transporting goods for hundreds of years.
Ⓓ There have been several different types of fast sailing ships that people have used for centuries.

2 The word extensive in the passage is closest in meaning to

Ⓐ lengthy
Ⓑ expensive
Ⓒ roundabout
Ⓓ perilous

3 According to paragraph 3, which of the following is NOT true of clipper ships?

Ⓐ They were utilized to transport both goods and people.
Ⓑ Most of them averaged 600 kilometers a day when sailing.
Ⓒ Merchants used them to move various goods great distances.
Ⓓ They carried products as varied as ice, tea, and fruit.

4 **Directions:** An introductory sentence for a brief summary of the passage is provided below. Complete the summary by selecting the THREE answer choices that express the most important ideas of the passage. Some sentences do not belong because they express ideas that are not presented in the passage or are minor ideas in the passage. **This question is worth 2 points.**

For a few decades, clipper ships were used as swift forms of transport of goods all around the world.

●

●

●

Answer Choices

1. A typical clipper ship had three masts with square-shaped sails on them.
2. Merchants use clipper ships to transport all manner of goods that needed to be moved fast.
3. When the steamship was invented, the popularity of clipper ships decreased.
4. The average clipper ship could sail much faster than other ships of its time.
5. Clipper ships had many sails, which let them capture a great amount of wind.
6. Clipper ships first appeared in the 1830s and mostly disappeared by the 1870s.

The Valley of the Kings

In ancient Egypt, the burial sites of the pharaohs were of great importance. Many pharaohs built pyramids to serve as their final resting places. Others had underground tombs constructed. On the west bank of the Nile River near the modern-day city of Luxor is an area known as the Valley of the Kings. For centuries, Egyptian pharaohs belonging to the Eighteenth, Nineteenth, and Twentieth dynasties had their tombs constructed there. Since then, both archaeologists and grave robbers have combed the area in search of the hidden tombs.

Most archaeologists agree that members of royal families were buried in the valley from the sixteenth to eleventh centuries B.C. The ancient city of Thebes—Luxor today—sits at the entrance to the valley. The tombs of the pharaohs and their family members were either cut into the limestone in the valley or were dug into the ground there. Efforts were made to hide the tombs to keep them safe from intruders. But many of them have been found.

3 → Thus far, archaeologists have discovered sixty-three tombs. Some are simple rooms while others have numerous chambers. A typical tomb has a long <u>corridor</u> that leads to the main burial chamber. Side rooms often branch off from the corridor. The Egyptians placed treasures as well as whatever other items they believed the deceased would need in the afterlife in these rooms. Among the pharaohs buried in the Valley of the Kings were Seti I, Ramses II, and Tutankhamen.

4 → King Tutankhamen's tomb was discovered by Howard Carter in 1922. He was a minor pharaoh and died as a teenager. But the discovery of his tomb sparked interest all over the globe. The reason was that King Tut's tomb was found intact. It was full of all kinds of treasures. This was a rare event because, ever since ancient times, looters have <u>plundered</u> the treasures from the tombs in the Valley of the Kings. After Carter's discovery, only three more tombs have been unearthed there. It is likely that more tombs exist. They are merely waiting to be found by someone in the desert.

Glossary

corridor: a long hallway; a passageway
plunder: to steal; to rob

1   In stating that archaeologists and grave robbers have combed the area, the author means that archaeologists and grave robbers have
Ⓐ looked very hard
Ⓑ conducted research
Ⓒ gone on some digs
Ⓓ asked questions

2   Which of the sentences below best expresses the essential information in the highlighted sentence in the passage? Incorrect answer choices change the meaning in important ways or leave out essential information.
Ⓐ Some pharaohs shared limestone tombs with their family members.
Ⓑ Most of the pharaohs and their families were buried in tombs.
Ⓒ People have found tombs made of limestone and dug in the earth.
Ⓓ The royal tombs were made in rock or were dug underground.

3   The word them in the passage refers to
Ⓐ the pharaohs and their family members
Ⓑ efforts
Ⓒ the tombs
Ⓓ intruders

4   In paragraph 3, the author uses Seti I, Ramses II, and Tutankhamen as examples of
Ⓐ the pharaohs with the most famous tombs in the Valley of the Kings
Ⓑ the pharaohs with the most recently discovered Egyptian tombs
Ⓒ three pharaohs who were buried in the Valley of the Kings
Ⓓ the three pharaohs who had the largest tombs in the Valley of the Kings

5   In paragraph 4, the author's description of King Tutankhamen's tomb mentions which of the following?
Ⓐ It is the largest of all the tombs of the pharaohs.
Ⓑ It had not been robbed of any of its treasures.
Ⓒ It is the last tomb discovered in the Valley of the Kings.
Ⓓ It changed how archaeologists studied ancient Egypt.

Unit 09

Question Type 9 ## Fill in a Table

Fill in a Table question focus on the information that is contained in the entire passage. These types of questions are about the theme, main idea, or main topic of the passage. There are either two or three categories along with seven to nine answer choices. The test taker must match the answer choices with the correct categories. There are 0-1 Fill in a Table questions for each passage.

Recognizing Fill in a Table questions:

- **Directions:** Select the appropriate phrases from the answer choices and match them to the type of X to which they relate. TWO of the answer choices will NOT be used. **This question is worth 3 [4] points.**

Helpful hints for answering the questions correctly:

- Recognize the main theme, idea, or topic of the passage.

- These questions often ask about causes and effects or problems and solutions. In other cases, they require you to compare and contrast two or three topics from the passage.

- There are always two incorrect answer choices. So these answer choices should not be selected.

Sample Fill in a Table Question

One of the most exciting fields in archaeology does not take place on land. It happens under the water. It is underwater archaeology. In recent years, many shipwrecks have been found and explored. Yet this type of archaeology is hard to do. There are several reasons for this. For one, finding shipwrecks buried under layers of silt and mud is difficult. Many times, archaeologists must use scuba gear when examining a find. This poses dangers as well. Preserving artifacts that have been underwater for centuries can also be problematic. And, finally, the cost of doing maritime excavations is high.

Fortunately, archaeologists have come up with some solutions to these issues. They use modern technology such as sonar to detect shipwrecks. This way, they do not have to dive until they know exactly where a wreck is. Practicing safety methods ensures that divers can be safe while in the water. And laboratories can keep artifacts from being damaged after they are brought to the surface.

Directions: Select the appropriate statements from the answer choices and match them to the problem and solution of underwater archaeology to which they relate. TWO of the answer choices will NOT be used. **This question is worth 3 points.**

Answer Choices

1. People are exploring a lot of ships underwater.
2. Doing underwater archaeology is expensive.
3. Archaeologists can employ sonar to find buried ships.
4. Many individuals are conducting underwater archaeology.
5. Using scuba gear is not always safe.
6. Shipwrecks are often buried in the mud.
7. Laboratories preserve the artifacts that people find.

UNDERWATER ARCHAEOLOGY

Problem (Select 3)
-
-
-

Solution (Select 2)
-
-

🔷 Answer Explanation

Choices 2, 5, and 6 refer to problems. Concerning the problems involved in underwater archaeology, the passage reads, "The cost of doing maritime excavations is high." The author also mentions, "Many times, archaeologists must use scuba gear when examining a find. This poses dangers as well," and, "Finding shipwrecks buried under layers of silt and mud is difficult." Choices 3 and 7 refer to solutions for the problems in underwater archaeology. The passage notes, "They use modern technology such as sonar to detect shipwrecks," and, "And laboratories can keep artifacts from being damaged after they are brought to the surface." Choices 1 and 4 are statements that are mentioned in the passage but are neither problems nor solutions. So they are incorrect.

Joseph Conrad

Joseph Conrad was one of the greatest writers of the late nineteenth and early twentieth centuries. Although he was born in Poland, he moved to Great Britain in his twenties. There, he learned to speak and write English. For many years, Conrad was a seaman. His journeys took him to the <u>Far East</u>, South America, and other parts of the world. His personal experiences frequently served as the basis for his adventure stories.

2 → During Conrad's time, many people were traveling to unique places around the world. This was especially true of writers. Herman Melville, for instance, based *Moby Dick* and *Omoo* on his experiences as a sailor. Jack London, author of *The Call of the Wild*, traveled to Alaska and Northern Canada. Rudyard Kipling wrote numerous stories about the time that he spent in India. His works included *The Jungle Book* and *Kim*. Conrad was similar to his contemporaries in that matter. He used his travels in exotic lands as the basis for many of his stories.

Conrad published his first book in 1895. It was entitled *Almayer's Folly*. It was set in the Dutch East Indies, a place he had visited previously. Much of Conrad's works were seagoing adventure stories that were full of exotic characters. He sometimes created fictional lands, but they were mostly based on places he had visited. For instance, *Nostromo*, one of his greatest works, is set in a fictional South American country.

4 → Conrad's works were usually complex and contained many characters and themes. His stories tended to be <u>pessimistic</u> in tone. The main character was often an anti-hero. These features are all evident in what is perhaps his most famous work, *The Heart of Darkness*. Set in the Congo in Africa, the theme of the book is the colonization of Africa by white Europeans. It tells the tale of a white European who goes mad in the jungle and sets himself up as a kinglike leader.

Altogether, Conrad wrote eighteen novels before his death in 1924. Today, many of his novels are still hailed as works of great literature.

Glossary

Far East: the countries that are located in East Asia, including China, Korea, and Japan

pessimistic: negative in attitude or outlook

1   The word His in the passage refers to
   (A) Herman Melville
   (B) Jack London
   (C) Rudyard Kipling
   (D) Conrad

2   The author's description of Jack London in paragraph 2 mentions which of the following?
   (A) He spent some time employed as a sailor.
   (B) He visited both Alaska and Canada.
   (C) He was a famous nineteenth-century writer.
   (D) He was the author of *The Jungle Book*.

3   The word exotic in the passage is closest in meaning to
   (A) fictional
   (B) creative
   (C) villainous
   (D) unusual

4   Which of the sentences below best expresses the essential information in the highlighted
   sentence in the passage? Incorrect answer choices change the meaning in important ways or
   leave out essential information.
   (A) It is about an insane European who becomes a king in the jungle.
   (B) A European becomes king and then goes mad while trekking in the jungle.
   (C) The story is about a madman who visits the jungles of Africa.
   (D) There is a king in the jungle that becomes mad at the Europeans.

5   According to paragraph 4, which of the following is NOT true of Joseph Conrad's writing?
   (A) His stories were upbeat tales of adventure.
   (B) He included a number of themes in his writing.
   (C) He often wrote novels that were complicated.
   (D) His main characters were not typical heroes.

Types of Galaxies

[1] → A galaxy is a large collection of stars in outer space. Earth's galaxy is the Milky Way. Astronomers are not sure, but they believe between 200 and 400 billion stars are in the Milky Way. The Milky Way is merely one of billions of galaxies in the universe. These galaxies do not all look alike. They have various shapes. In the 1920s, American astronomer Edwin Hubble created a system to classify galaxies based upon their shapes. He determined that there are two basic shapes: elliptical and spiral. He also identified a third group, called irregular galaxies.

Elliptical galaxies have spherical shapes. Some are more elongated than others. These galaxies have classifications that range from E0 to E7. An E0 galaxy is almost a perfect circle. As for an E7 galaxy, it has a highly elongated oval shape that gives it a rather flat appearance. Elliptical galaxies have extremely bright centers and become dim at their edges. For the most part, they consist of stars that have already formed. So they contain little of the interstellar matter needed to make new stars. Elliptical galaxies are the largest in the universe. Some contain trillions of stars. Astronomers believe that many of them formed when two or more galaxies collided.

[3] → Spiral galaxies have a bright central bulge and arms that extend from the bulge. They also have a halo, which contains very old stars. The central bulge has two shapes: spherical and barred. The bulge has old stars while the arms, which are brighter, contain newer stars. Earth's sun rests in one of the arms of the Milky Way. These galaxies are classified as S or SB galaxies. S galaxies have spherical central bulges while SB galaxies have barred central bulges. There are other subgroups of spiral galaxies that depend upon the shape and appearance of the arms.

[4] → Irregular galaxies have no particular shape or structure. Astronomers have divided them into Irr I and Irr II galaxies. The former has many young stars that are very hot. The latter contain so much dust that it is impossible to see the stars in them.

Glossary
interstellar: between the stars
trillion: 1,000,000,000,000

1 According to paragraph 1, which of the following is true of the Milky Way?
   - (A) Astronomers believe it is an irregular galaxy.
   - (B) It is the largest galaxy in the universe.
   - (C) Edwin Hubble was the first man to see it.
   - (D) There are a few hundred billion stars in it.

2 In paragraph 3, the author implies that Earth's sun
   - (A) is in the Milky Way's central bulge
   - (B) is a relatively new star
   - (C) will continue to burn for billions of years
   - (D) is not as bright as other stars

3 The author discusses Irregular galaxies in paragraph 4 in order to
   - (A) explain how often they appear in the universe
   - (B) focus on the hotness and youth of their stars
   - (C) provide some of their notable features
   - (D) mention why some of them have so much dust

4 **Directions:** Select the appropriate statements from the answer choices and match them to the type of galaxy to which they relate. TWO of the answer choices will NOT be used. **This question is worth 3 points.**

Answer Choices	TYPE OF GALAXY
1. Is the type of galaxy that Earth is found in	**Elliptical** (Select 2)
2. Contains so much dust that its stars cannot be seen	•
3. May have more than a trillion stars in it	•
4. Has arms that extend from its center	**Spiral** (Select 3)
5. Lacks a particular shape or structure	•
6. Has a bright center with edges that are less bright	•
7. May be listed as an S or SB galaxy	•

Question Type 10 — Prose Summary

Prose Summary questions focus on the main idea of the entire passage. These types of questions contain one sentence that provides a summary of the passage. The test taker must then read six sentences and determine which three contain information that is related to the summary statement. There are 0-1 Prose Summary questions for each passage.

Recognizing Prose Summary questions:

- **Directions:** An introductory sentence for a brief summary of the passage is provided below. Complete the summary by selecting the THREE answer choices that express the most important ideas of the passage. Some sentences do not belong because they express ideas that are not presented in the passage or are minor ideas in the passage. **This question is worth 2 points.**

Helpful hints for answering the questions correctly:

- The summary statement always includes information about the main ideas or themes of the passage.

- Think about the main points of the passage when selecting answer choices. Ignore all of the minor points.

- Some answer choices contain information that is correct but which was not mentioned in the passage. Do not select these answer choices.

Sample Prose Summary Question

Some places around the world endure periods of time when they receive heavy rainfall. Melting snow and ice in spring can also cause water levels to rise. In both cases, flooding may occur. There are some positive benefits of flooding. Yet there are more negative effects. The most obvious result is the damage that flooding causes to manmade structures. Floods can destroy buildings and roads and wash away bridges and other structures. Floods—especially flashfloods—may kill people as well when river and stream levels suddenly rise. Floods cause damage to the natural environment, too. They can wash away valuable topsoil, which makes the land less fertile. They can cause erosion in some areas, which changes how the land itself looks. The excess of water can kill numerous plants and animals. Finally, flooding may lead to outbreaks of diseases. In the aftermath of a flood, it is common for both people and animals to fall ill with various sicknesses.

Directions: An introductory sentence for a brief summary of the passage is provided below. Complete the summary by selecting the THREE answer choices that express the most important ideas of the passage. Some sentences do not belong because they express ideas that are not presented in the passage or are minor ideas in the passage. **This question is worth 2 points.**

There are many negative effects of flooding.

-
-
-

Answer Choices

1. Some floods in the past killed thousands of people.
2. Humans and animals may become ill due to floods.
3. Floodwaters can destroy buildings, roads, and bridges.
4. Floods occur when river or stream levels rise.
5. There is sometimes great loss of life because of floods.
6. Flooding happens during the rainy season in some places.

Answer Explanation

Choices 2, 3, and 5 are all correct. The passage reads, "In the aftermath of a flood, it is common for both people and animals to fall ill with various sicknesses." It also notes, "Floods can destroy buildings and roads and wash away bridges and other structures," and, "Floods—especially flashfloods—may kill people." Choice 1 is not mentioned in the passage. So it is an incorrect answer choice. Choices 4 and 6 are minor points. So they should not be chosen.

Bird Nests

Virtually all bird species make nests of some sort. The main reason that birds build nests is so that they can have a place to lay their eggs and then to <u>incubate</u> them. In addition, birds often sleep in their nests and utilize them as places of refuge from predators. Yet all bird nests are not alike; birds build their nests in different places and construct them out of differing materials.

2 → The location of a bird's nest is typically of great importance. Although many birds simply make their nests in the branches of trees, others are more creative. Seabirds, for instance, frequently build nests in natural holes found in cliffs near the shore. Many species of woodpecker carve holes in trees and build their nests inside the trees themselves. ■ Eagles, hawks, and other high-flying birds make their nests high in the mountains or at the tops of the tallest trees. ■ Birds that cannot fly, such as penguins, make their nests on the ground. ■ Many birds have adapted to the presence of humans by building their nests in manmade structures. ■ Swallows sometimes build nests in the eaves of houses or inside barns while falcons and hawks make them on the ledges of skyscrapers in large metropolitan areas.

3 → Birds can be creative in the materials that they utilize to build their nests as well. Most birds take advantage of whatever natural materials they can find. For the most part, they construct their nests out of twigs, leaves, and grass. The harder twigs serve as the <u>backbone</u> of the nest and thereby provide both strength and support. Then, the birds add leaves and grass to soften the nest and to fill in the gaps. Some birds also make their nests with stones, moss, mud, and feathers. It is not uncommon to see various manmade items in bird nests as well. Essentially, birds use anything they can to construct nests that are capable of holding their eggs and then keeping their hatchlings in the nest once they are born.

Glossary
incubate: to keep warm
backbone: a spine; the strongest part of something

1   According to paragraph 2, which of the following is true of some birds?

    Ⓐ They build their nests on the lowest branches of trees.
    Ⓑ They find nesting places in manmade buildings.
    Ⓒ They prefer making nests on the ground instead of in trees.
    Ⓓ They look for holes in the ground to lay their eggs in.

2   In paragraph 3, why does the author mention twigs, leaves, and grass?

    Ⓐ To name the most common materials nests are made of
    Ⓑ To say that they are easy materials for birds to find
    Ⓒ To claim that some birds avoid making nests out of them
    Ⓓ To compare their value with stones, moss, mud, and feathers

3   Look at the four squares [■] that indicate where the following sentence could be added to the passage.

The ostrich, another flightless bird, does the same thing.

Where would the sentence best fit?
Click on a square [■] to add the sentence to the passage.

4   **Directions:** An introductory sentence for a brief summary of the passage is provided below. Complete the summary by selecting the THREE answer choices that express the most important ideas of the passage. Some sentences do not belong because they express ideas that are not presented in the passage or are minor ideas in the passage. **This question is worth 2 points.**

Almost all birds build nests, but they are located in different areas and are not made with the same materials.

-
-
-

Answer Choices

1. Predators have a harder time hunting birds when they are in their nests.
2. There are some bird nests that are found in high mountains, trees, and buildings.
3. Birds usually stay in their nests for weeks at a time to incubate their eggs.
4. Most birds use natural materials to make nests while others use manmade items.
5. Birds often employ twigs to strengthen their nests and then add other materials.
6. Penguins, falcons, and swallows all build their nests in different locations.

Alloys

For thousands of years, prehistoric humans lived in the Stone Age. They made primitive tools from stone. Then, around 3300 B.C., humans learned to make bronze and entered the Bronze Age. Bronze is not a basic metal; it is a combination of tin and copper. Thanks to bronze, people could make tools that were stronger and sharper. This enabled civilization to develop much faster.

Bronze is an alloy. An alloy is a combination of two or more elements that makes a new metal. There is always one base metal in an alloy. The additional elements that are added may be either metals or nonmetals. Bronze was the first alloy that humans invented. But there are many others. Brass is a combination of copper and zinc. Electrum is a combination of silver and copper. Steel is another alloy. It is made of iron and carbon. They are three well-known alloys.

3 → The main metal in an alloy is called the base metal. Any others are the solutes. Alloys are typically created by melting the elements and then combining them. This can require very high heat since all elements have different melting points. The newly formed alloy often retains the melting points of its individual metals. Thus part of the alloy may begin to melt at one temperature while a higher one is required to melt it entirely. However, if the elements are combined in certain proportions, the alloy usually gains a new melting point.

4 → The appeal of alloys is that their physical properties are different than those of their original elements. An alloy may be harder, lighter, or stronger than its component metals. Its ability to resist heat and to conduct electricity may change, too. Steel is an example of an alloy that is both stronger and harder than its individual components. Nowadays, many alloys are created for special purposes. For example, airplanes, rockets, and spacecraft require special alloys. They must be light yet strong and able to resist both heat and pressure. Titanium— a combination of aluminum, iron, and other elements—is a common alloy in the aerospace industry.

Glossary
retain: to keep; to maintain
proportion: a ratio; an amount

1   The word primitive in the passage is closest in meaning to

    Ⓐ ancient

    Ⓑ efficient

    Ⓒ simple

    Ⓓ passable

2   The word It in the passage refers to

    Ⓐ Bronze

    Ⓑ Brass

    Ⓒ Electrum

    Ⓓ Steel

3   In paragraph 3, the author's description of the melting points of metals mentions which of the following?

    Ⓐ what temperatures they typically melt at

    Ⓑ how they may change when they become alloys

    Ⓒ how long they must be heated in order to melt

    Ⓓ what the lowest melting point of any metal is

4   According to paragraph 4, people like alloys because

    Ⓐ they are relatively simple to make

    Ⓑ it does not cost much to purchase them

    Ⓒ they are stronger than base elements

    Ⓓ many of them contain precious metals

5   In paragraph 4, the author implies that titanium

    Ⓐ is used to build some spacecraft

    Ⓑ is more valuable than gold

    Ⓒ is the hardest substance known to man

    Ⓓ is almost as light as aluminum

Chapter 2

Listening

Question Type 1 **Gist-Content**

Gist-Content questions focus on the main topic or main idea of the passage. These questions appear after both lectures and conversations. However, they are more common after lectures. These types of questions require the test taker to think about the entire conversation or lecture and then to determine what it is about.

Recognizing Gist-Content questions:

- What are the speakers mainly discussing?

- What is the main topic of the lecture?

- What aspect of X does the professor mainly discuss?

Helpful hints for answering the questions correctly:

- Focus on the entire passage and consider what it is mostly about. Think about the main topic or idea of the lecture or conversation.

- Choose the answer choice that covers the greatest amount of material that was mentioned in the passage. Avoid answer choices that are only about minor topics.

- The speakers in conversations often state the main topic at the beginning of the talk. Listen carefully to be able to identify it.

Sample Gist-Content Question

Listen to part of a lecture in an economics class.  1-01

M Professor: People have been trading with each other for thousands of years. The first trades were carried out by people who swapped, uh, you know, bartered with their neighbors. Perhaps one person traded some grain for some meat that another person had. Or maybe someone traded a weapon for an animal skin. Who knows really? I'm sure there were all kinds of trades that people made.

Over time, people began to trade with others further away from them. Merchants started traveling, um, to new areas to sell or trade their products. As these merchants traveled, they established trade routes. Trade routes are, hmm . . . I guess I should say that they're paths that merchants take when they're transporting goods from one place to another. Trade routes can be on land or water. Many of the first trade routes were actually over water. The reason is that it's easier to transport large amounts of goods by ship than by horse or wagon.

All throughout history, there have been water trade routes. Some were simple. They merely involved putting goods on rafts and floating the rafts downriver. Others involved transoceanic voyages. For instance, uh, the Europeans discovered a trade route to India by sailing south around Africa. They also established trade routes to North and South America. Of course, there are land trade routes as well. The Silk Road is probably the most famous of these. It started in China, passed through India, and ended in Rome.

You're probably wondering why people established trade routes. There are a number of reasons for this. And that's what I'd like to discuss with you now. Do any of you have any ideas? What do you think? Why did people establish trade routes . . . ?

What is the lecture mainly about?

Ⓐ Bartering
Ⓑ Trade routes
Ⓒ The Silk Road
Ⓓ European trade with the Americas

🔷 Answer Explanation

The correct answer is Choice B. The professor focuses on trade routes during his entire talk. He gives a definition of trade routes. He notes that people traded over land and by water. And he describes some trade routes from the past. The professor mentions all of the information in choices A, C, and D. However, he does not focus on them. They are merely minor details. So these choices are all incorrect.

Listen to part of a conversation between a student and a professor. 🎧 1-02

> *Notes*

1 What are the speakers mainly discussing?
- Ⓐ The most recent lecture
- Ⓑ A paper the student must write
- Ⓒ The student's grade in the class
- Ⓓ The upcoming final exam

2 What does the professor ask the student to do?
- Ⓐ Come to class on time
- Ⓑ Pay more attention in class
- Ⓒ Consider dropping his class
- Ⓓ Turn in her paper early

3 What is the student's opinion of the professor's suggestion?
- Ⓐ She is offended by it.
- Ⓑ She supports it.
- Ⓒ She disagrees with it.
- Ⓓ She will consider it.

4 What can be inferred about the professor?
- Ⓐ He is eager to assist the student.
- Ⓑ He gives most students low grades.
- Ⓒ He thinks that the student has average ability.
- Ⓓ He has little concern for the student's welfare.

Mini Test 2 : Lecture

Listen to part of a lecture in a meteorology class. 1-03

> *Notes*

1. What is the lecture mainly about?
   - (A) The changing of the seasons
   - (B) Some abnormal climates
   - (C) The Earth's climate zones
   - (D) Standard types of weather

2. Based on the information in the lecture, indicate which climate zone the statements refer to.
   Click in the correct box for each statement.

	Temperate Zone	Tropical Zone
1 Is located between the other two zones		
2 Has a high level of humidity		
3 Has four seasons that are distinct		
4 Receives a variety of weather		

3. Why does the professor mention the Sahara Desert?
   - (A) To state the degree of latitude that it is found at
   - (B) To note its heat despite being in the temperate zone
   - (C) To compare its weather with a region in Uganda
   - (D) To emphasize the complete lack of seasons there

4. According to the professor, what is the importance of the tilt of the Earth's axis?
   - (A) It causes individual seasons to occur.
   - (B) It makes some places hotter than normal.
   - (C) It reduces the rainfall in some regions.
   - (D) It produces some ocean currents.

Unit 02

Question Type 2 **Gist-Purpose**

Gist-Purpose questions focus on the overall theme of the passage. These questions appear after both lectures and conversations. However, they are more common after conversations. These types of questions require the test taker to understand the purpose of the conversation or the theme of the lecture.

Recognizing Gist-Purpose questions:

- Why does the student visit the Registrar's Office?

- Why did the professor ask to see the student?

- Why does the professor explain X?

Helpful hints for answering the questions correctly:

- These questions always start by asking "why."

- In conversations, the student usually gives the reason for speaking with the other person at the beginning of the conversation. In other situations, the professor or other person will explain why he or she wants to speak with the student at the beginning of the conversation.

- In lectures, the professor usually states the importance or relevance of the information that he or she is telling the class. This information can appear at any time in the lecture.

Sample Gist-Purpose Question

Listen to part of a conversation between a student and a student housing office employee.  1-04

> **W1 Student Housing Office Employee:** Yes? Is there something I can help you with?
>
> **W2 Student:** I hope so. Is it too late to change dorm rooms?
>
> **W1:** No, it's not too late. The deadline for changing is the day after tomorrow. However, you need to have a good reason for doing that. Why do you want to move elsewhere?
>
> **W2:** My dorm is way too noisy. I mean, uh, students are constantly playing music, running around the halls, and . . . well, they're making too much noise.
>
> **W1:** I see. And where would you like to move?
>
> **W2:** I heard there's a quiet dormitory on campus. Is that true?
>
> **W1:** Yes, it is. Deacon Hall is the quiet dormitory. Students are not allowed to play music or make any loud noises there at any time.
>
> **W2:** Oh, it sounds perfect. I really need to move there before my grades start to suffer. Please tell me there's at least one empty room in Deacon Hall.
>
> **W1:** Let me check . . . You're in luck. There happen to be three available spots in that dorm. Do you have a preference for a floor?
>
> **W2:** Hmm . . . I'd like to be on the highest floor possible. I don't enjoy being down near the ground. What floor can you get me on?

Why does the student visit the student housing office?

- Ⓐ To ask about changing dormitories
- Ⓑ To complain about her roommate
- Ⓒ To mention a problem with her room
- Ⓓ To say that she dislikes Deacon Hall

🔲 Answer Explanation

The correct answer is Choice A. The student starts the conversation by asking, "Is it too late to change dorm rooms?" She says that her current dormitory is very noisy. And she states that she wants to move to a quiet dormitory. So she goes to the student housing office to ask about changing dormitories. Choices B, C, and D are all incorrect.

Listen to part of a conversation between a student and a Bursar's office employee. 1-05

> *Notes*

1 Why does the student visit the Bursar's office?
- (A) To solve a financial problem
- (B) To submit an application
- (C) To apply for a scholarship
- (D) To receive a refund

2 What did the Bursar's office send to the student?
- (A) An email
- (B) A letter
- (C) An application form
- (D) A facsimile

3 Why does the student tell the woman about the charity?
- (A) To tell the woman to contact it for some answers
- (B) To explain why his tuition has not yet been paid
- (C) To state that it might give him a scholarship soon
- (D) To blame it for not paying all of his school fees

4 What will the woman probably do next?
- (A) Help the student complete the application
- (B) Look at the student's financial records
- (C) Give the student a consultation
- (D) Read the letter the student gave her

Listen to part of a lecture in a biology class. 1-06

> *Notes*

1 What is the lecture mainly about?

- (A) Why animals live in a certain area
- (B) How animals defend their territory
- (C) Which animals mark the land they live on
- (D) When animals become territorial

2 Why does the professor explain the ways that animals mark their territory?

- (A) To introduce her talk about wolves
- (B) To point out what lions usually do
- (C) To respond to a student's question
- (D) To prove a theory she mentioned

3 According to the professor, how do birds let other animals know that they have claimed an area as their own?

- (A) By making sounds
- (B) By secreting certain liquids
- (C) By acting aggressively
- (D) By flapping their wings loudly

4 What does the professor imply about animals that defend their territory?

- (A) They might attack animals of the same species.
- (B) A large majority of them are predators.
- (C) They prefer to defend their area in large groups.
- (D) They tend to be mammals instead of birds.

Question Type 3 ## Detail

Detail questions focus on the factual information contained in the passage. These questions appear after both lectures and conversations. These types of questions require the test taker to listen for and recognize the details that are provided in the passage. These questions are about the main topic of the passage instead of the minor topics.

Recognizing Detail questions:

- According to the professor, what is one way that X can affect Y?
- What are X?
- What resulted from the invention of the X?

Helpful hints for answering the questions correctly:

- ◉ The questions will be about the main topic or the most important information in the passage.
- ◉ Ignore the minor facts and details in the passage since the questions will not ask about them.
- ◉ Correct answer choices are often restatements of the words and phrases that are used in the passage. Think about how the information can be restated. Be careful about words and phrases in the answer choices that are used exactly as they were in the passage. These are often incorrect answer choices.

Sample Detail Question

Listen to part of a lecture in an education class.  1-07

M Professor: Okay, um, I think that's enough about the Montessori Method. Let's move on to another kind of alternative schooling method. It's becoming more and more popular every year. And that should come as no surprise. After all, it was the preferred method of learning for centuries. I'm referring to homeschooling.

Remember that the schools we have today are relatively new creations. We've only had mass education since the 1800s. Prior to that, people mostly learned in two ways: They attended small schools at churches or other religious centers. Or they were taught in their homes.

In the 1800s and 1900s, most parents sent their children to public or private schools. Yet, for the past, oh, the past couple of decades, many American parents have started homeschooling their children. They do this for a number of reasons. First, they aren't satisfied with the educations their children are getting at school. A lot of parents feel that they can teach their children better at home. Other parents homeschool their children for religious reasons. Some do it to prevent bullying. Whatever the reason may be, homeschooled children stay home and learn there.

Now, you may think that these children are getting poor educations. Um, that's definitely not the case. As a matter of fact, many homeschooled children get outstanding educations. Parents these days have access to various resources that help them educate their children. For example, there are teaching packets they can use. They can download lectures from the Internet. They can purchase homeschooling software programs. They can hire special tutors for some subjects. In many cases, homeschooled children get advanced educations while also studying for fewer hours. That's pretty impressive, isn't it? Let me show you some homeschooling curricula. I think you'll find it quite fascinating.

According to the professor, how do some homeschooled children learn?
Click on 2 answers.

1.   By reading public school textbooks
2.   By using Internet-based lectures
3.   By attending classes with other homeschoolers
4.   By studying with private teachers

Answer Explanation

> The correct answers are choices 2 and 4. The professor tells the students, "They can download lectures from the Internet." He also states, "They can hire special tutors for some subjects." He does not mention the methods in choices 1 and 3. These are actually both ways that some homeschooled students study, but they are not mentioned in the lecture. So both choices are incorrect.

Listen to part of a conversation between a student and a student housing office employee. 🎧 1-08

<table><tr><td>Notes</td></tr></table>

1   What problem does the student have?
    Ⓐ He does not get along with his roommate.
    Ⓑ His dormitory room is too small.
    Ⓒ There is a mistake on his bill.
    Ⓓ Robinson Hall is too noisy for him.

2   Where was the student before he went to the student housing office?
    Ⓐ The library
    Ⓑ The Bursar's office
    Ⓒ Robinson Hall
    Ⓓ His advisor's office

3   What can be inferred about the student's university?
    Ⓐ It is currently renovating some student dormitories.
    Ⓑ It charges different rates for dormitory rooms.
    Ⓒ It has frequent problems with its computer system.
    Ⓓ It is raising the price of tuition next semester.

4   What does the woman say she will do for the student?
Click on 2 answers.
    1 Call the Bursar's office
    2 Print a copy of a form
    3 Remove a charge from his bill
    4 Change his room status

Listen to part of a lecture in a musicology class. 

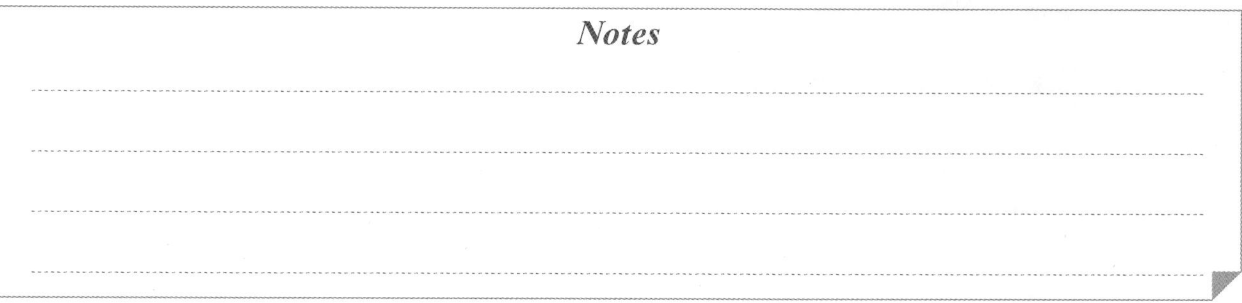

1   What can be inferred about the *Brandenburg Concertos*?
   Ⓐ They became the most famous works of the Baroque Period.
   Ⓑ They were written as pieces of secular music.
   Ⓒ They were composed during the Renaissance.
   Ⓓ They had both choral and instrumental parts.

2   Why does the professor discuss patrons in the Baroque Period?
   Ⓐ To note that most of them were in the Church
   Ⓑ To claim they had too much influence
   Ⓒ To explain their influence on music then
   Ⓓ To name some pieces of music they sponsored

3   According to the professor, how did music in the Baroque Period change?
   Ⓐ Several new instruments were invented at that time.
   Ⓑ Operas became the most prevalent type of music.
   Ⓒ Instrumental sounds were stressed more than singing.
   Ⓓ Individual notes became more important than chords.

4   Listen again to part of the lecture. Then answer the question.
   What does the professor mean when she says this:
   Ⓐ The Renaissance greatly influenced the Baroque Period.
   Ⓑ The Baroque Period lasted longer than the Renaissance.
   Ⓒ There were many differences between Baroque and Renaissance music.
   Ⓓ Baroque music was greater than Renaissance music.

Question Type 4 — Detail (Chart)

Detail questions may appear as charts. These questions can appear after both lectures and conversations. These types of questions require the test taker to determine if some statements about the passage are facts or not. These questions focus on major topics in the passage, not minor ones.

Recognizing Detail questions:

- In the lecture, the professor describes a number of facts about reptiles. Indicate whether each of the following is a fact or not. [Click in the correct box for each sentence.]

Helpful hints for answering the questions correctly:

- These questions are about the main topics of the conversations and lectures. So listen carefully to determine what the main topics are.

- Ignore minor facts and details. These questions do not ask about them.

- A single word in the answer choice can make it wrong. This is especially true of adverbs such as *always*, *usually*, and *never* as well as the use of singular and plural words.

Sample Detail Question

Listen to part of a lecture in a history class. 

W Professor: One towering figure in history is Julius Caesar. He's one of the most important individuals we're going to study this semester. He was alive—and involved in—the destruction of the Roman Republic. He also had a connection to the creation of the Roman Empire. Of course, he wasn't alive for that. He was assassinated in the Roman Senate years prior to the formation of the Roman Empire. Anyway, um, you simply cannot understate how important Julius Caesar was to the history of Rome.

Caesar was born sometime between 102 and 100 B.C. He was born into a noble family. They weren't rich, but they were in the upper class. Caesar therefore had a fairly privileged upbringing. That meant he got to serve as an officer in the Roman legions. That was where Caesar became widely known. During his time in the legions, Caesar was responsible for conquering Gaul. Uh, that's the area that France is in today.

We know a lot about what happened in Gaul thanks to Caesar himself. You see, uh, most people just know Caesar as a dictator or general. But he was much more than that. He was a brilliant public speaker. He was also a great writer. His work *The Gallic Wars* described the military campaigns that enabled him to conquer Gaul. His prose in that book is simple and straightforward. Actually, all throughout his life, he wrote numerous memorable lines. For instance, after one crushing victory . . . uh, not in Gaul but somewhere else . . . he sent word back to Rome. He wrote "*Veni vidi vici*." That Latin phrase translates as "I came. I saw. I conquered." Simple and straight to the point, isn't it? Anyway, let me get back to Caesar's life rather than his words.

In the lecture, the professor describes a number of facts about Julius Caesar. Indicate whether each of the following is a fact or not.
Click in the correct box for each statement.

	Fact	Not a Fact
1 **Was the son of a wealthy Roman family**		
2 **Was considered a great speaker and writer**		
3 **Was the author of *The Gallic Wars***		
4 **Was the first ruler of the Roman Empire**		

Answer Explanation

The facts are choices 2 and 3. About Julius Caesar, the professor claims, "He was a brilliant public speaker. He was also a great writer." She also mentions, "His work *The Gallic Wars* described the military campaigns that enabled him to conquer Gaul." Choices 1 and 4 are not facts. The professor states, "He was born into a noble family. They weren't rich, but they were in the upper class." Thus Caesar's family was not wealthy. Also, she notes, "He also had a connection to the creation of the Roman Empire. Of course, he wasn't alive for that." So Caesar was not a ruler during the Roman Empire.

Listen to part of a conversation between a student and a professor. 🎧 1-11

Notes

---

1 What problem does the student have?

   Ⓐ He cannot decide which subject to major in.
   Ⓑ He has to choose between two different options.
   Ⓒ He thinks he is enrolled in too many classes.
   Ⓓ He does not have enough time to get a job.

2 Why does the student tell the professor when the psychology class meets?

   Ⓐ To say that it interferes with his part-time job
   Ⓑ To explain why he cannot take her class
   Ⓒ To note that he has a scheduling problem
   Ⓓ To complain about how early in the morning it starts

3 What is the student's opinion of the professor?

   Ⓐ He trusts her enough to take her advice.
   Ⓑ He thinks she is the best teacher at the school.
   Ⓒ He values her opinions in her field of study.
   Ⓓ He respects the way she handles other students.

4 In the conversation, the student describes a number of facts about the internship. Indicate whether each of the following is a fact or not.
Click in the correct box for each statement.

	Fact	Not a Fact
1 It is a paid position.		
2 It requires the student to work twice a week.		
3 It is a position at a consulting company.		
4 It is in the field of psychology.		

Listen to part of a lecture in an architecture class. 1-12

> *Notes*

1   What is the main topic of the lecture?
     Ⓐ Some uses of arabesque in Islamic architecture
     Ⓑ The most famous mosques in the world
     Ⓒ Some notable features in Islamic architecture
     Ⓓ The manner in which most mosques are built

2   In the lecture, the professor describes a number of facts about mosques. Indicate whether each of the following is a fact or not.
Click in the correct box for each statement.

	Fact	Not a Fact
1 May have either a dome or a flat roof		
2 Have tall towers known as minarets		
3 Often have pictures of humans and animals in them		
4 Do not have any central courtyards		

3   What is the professor's opinion of Islamic architecture?
     Ⓐ He finds much of it to be original.
     Ⓑ He thinks that it can be impressive.
     Ⓒ He dislikes its lack of human images.
     Ⓓ He believes arabesque should be used more.

4   How does the professor organize the information about Islamic architecture that he presents to the class?
     Ⓐ By covering its development chronologically
     Ⓑ By lecturing to the students as he shows them slides
     Ⓒ By listing some major features and explaining them
     Ⓓ By showing them pictures from the textbook as he talks

Question Type 5 — Understanding the Function of What Is Said

Understanding the Function of What Is Said questions focus on statements in the passage that the speakers make. These questions appear after both lectures and conversations. These types of questions require the test taker to infer the meaning or purpose of a speaker's comment. Sometimes these are replay questions. So a short part of the lecture or conversation is played again.

Recognizing Understanding the Function of What Is Said questions:

- What does the professor imply when he says this: (replay)
- Why does the student say this: (replay)
- Why does the professor ask the student about his grades?

Helpful hints for answering the questions correctly:

- Think about the hidden meanings of what people are saying. Learn how to read between the lines to determine what people are implying in their comments.
- Listen closely to the speaker's tone of voice. This can help you determine what the speaker actually means.
- When there is a replay question, listen closely to the entire part that is replayed. Do not only focus on the sentence that is played a second time. The entire section is important in determining the correct answer.

Sample Understanding the Function of What Is Said Question

Listen to part of a conversation between a student and a professor. 

W1 Student: Professor McDaniel, are you leaving your office now?

W2 Professor: Er, yes, Patricia. I've finished my classes for the day. So I am getting ready to go home. Do you need to speak with me about something?

W1: Yes, please. Could you spare one or two minutes of your time for me?

W2: Of course I can. What's going on?

W1: I need a really big favor from you. I, uh, I need you to write a letter of recommendation for me. I've got a job interview coming up, and the person at the company asked me to bring a couple of letters of recommendation with me.

W2: This interview wouldn't happen to be tomorrow, would it?

W1: Oh, no, ma'am. It's next Tuesday.

W2: That's a relief. I thought I might have to write it tonight. But Tuesday's fine. I can do that.

W1: Thank you so much. I was worried you might say no to me.

W2: Ah, there's no chance of that happening. But you can do me a big favor. It will help me out when I write your letter. Why don't you send me an email? In the email, list everything you want me to mention in the letter. Then, I will try to include those things.

Listen again to part of the conversation. Then answer the question.

W2: I can do that.

W1: Thank you so much. I was worried you might say no to me.

W2: Ah, there's no chance of that happening.

Why does the professor say this:

W2: Ah, there's no chance of that happening.

- Ⓐ To warn the student not to be late with the email
- Ⓑ To ask the student to do a small favor for her
- Ⓒ To indicate that the student should not be worried
- Ⓓ To let the student know she can write the letter

Answer Explanation

The correct answer is Choice C. The student asks the professor to write a letter of recommendation. The professor agrees to do that. Then, the student says, "I was worried you might say no to me." When the professor responds by saying, "Ah, there's no chance of that happening," she is telling the student that she would not reject her request. Therefore, the student should not be worried. Choices A, B, and D are all incorrect.

Listen to part of a conversation between a student and a Registrar's office employee. 🎧 1-14

Notes

1   Why does the student visit the Registrar's office?
- Ⓐ To submit a change-of-grade form
- Ⓑ To get some copies of her transcript
- Ⓒ To pay the rest of her tuition bill
- Ⓓ To find out about some graduate schools

2   What does the woman ask the student to give her?
Click on 2 answers.
- 1   A credit card
- 2   Her student transcript
- 3   Her ID card
- 4   A form

3   What will the student probably do next?
- Ⓐ Give some money to the woman
- Ⓑ Leave the Registrar's office
- Ⓒ Finish filling out a form
- Ⓓ Take a look at her transcript

4   Listen again to part of the conversation. Then answer the question.
What can be inferred from the woman's response to the student: 🎧
- Ⓐ She cannot fulfill the student's request.
- Ⓑ She wants the student to repeat herself.
- Ⓒ She is surprised by the student's answer.
- Ⓓ She thinks the student is making a mistake.

Listen to part of a lecture in a zoology class. 1-15

> ### Notes

---

1   What aspect of megafauna does the professor mainly discuss?
   - Ⓐ Which ones lived in North America
   - Ⓑ How they differed from modern-day animals
   - Ⓒ Why many of them went extinct
   - Ⓓ Which characteristics they had

2   According to the professor, how did most megafauna in North America die out?
   Click on 2 answers.
   - ☐1 They lost territory because of humans.
   - ☐2 They were killed during the last ice age.
   - ☐3 Humans hunted and killed many of them.
   - ☐4 Droughts and natural disasters made them extinct.

3   What will the professor probably do next?
   - Ⓐ Lecture about North American megafauna
   - Ⓑ Discuss the most recent ice age
   - Ⓒ Explain the characteristics of megafauna
   - Ⓓ Tell the students about the moa

4   Listen again to part of the lecture. Then answer the question.
   What does the professor imply when he says this:
   - Ⓐ Hearing examples will help the students understand.
   - Ⓑ He wants the students to think of some megafauna.
   - Ⓒ Students should know just how large the animals were.
   - Ⓓ It is possible that some megafauna still exist today.

Question Type 6 **Understanding the Speaker's Attitude**

Understanding the Speaker's Attitude questions focus on the attitude or the opinion of one of the speakers in the passage. These questions appear after both lectures and conversations. These types of questions require the test taker to determine either what the speaker means or to understand how the speaker feels about someone or something. Sometimes these are replay questions. So a short part of the lecture or conversation is played again.

Recognizing Understanding the Speaker's Attitude questions:

- What is the professor's opinion of X?

- What does the woman mean when she says this: (replay)

- What does the professor imply about the student's paper?

Helpful hints for answering the questions correctly:

- Listen closely to the speaker's tone of voice. This can help you determine what the speaker actually means.

- Pay attention when the speaker gives his or her opinion about something. When giving an opinion, the speaker might say phrases such as "I believe," "I feel," or "in my opinion."

- When there is a replay question, listen closely to the entire part that is replayed. Do not only focus on the sentence that is played a second time. The entire section is important in determining the correct answer.

Sample Understanding the Speaker's Attitude Question

Listen to part of a conversation between a student and a professor. 

W Professor: Jeff, have you made up your mind about next semester's classes yet?

M Student: Pretty much. I'm going to take the four classes we talked about before. Just to remind you . . . They're classes in biology, economics, math and English literature.

W: Ah, right. I remember. I believe those are good choices. And I'm sure you'll do well in them.

M: I hope so.

W: So do I. Now, uh, what about your last class? Remind me again . . . Which two classes are you trying to decide between?

M: I'm thinking about taking a class in the Astronomy Department. It's Astronomy 102. It's a basic introductory class. The other class I'm considering is History 115. It's a course in early American history.

W: And why can't you make up your mind?

M: Well, uh, basically . . . I like both subjects. And, as an economics major, both classes will fulfill requirements. So I won't benefit more by taking one class instead of the other. I simply don't know what to do.

W: Hmm . . . As far as I know, the astronomy class is offered every semester. However, the history class won't be offered for three more years. And you're a sophomore . . .

M: Oh, I see. Okay. I think I'll pass on the astronomy class then.

Listen again to part of the conversation. Then answer the question.

M: I simply don't know what to do.

W: Hmm . . . As far as I know, the astronomy class is offered every semester. However, the history class won't be offered for three more years. And you're a sophomore . . .

What can be inferred about the professor when she says this:

W: However, the history class won't be offered for three more years. And you're a sophomore . . .

- Ⓐ She thinks the astronomy class is the better choice.
- Ⓑ She believes that the student can take the history class later.
- Ⓒ She supposes that the history class is too hard for a sophomore.
- Ⓓ She feels that the student ought to sign up for the history class.

Answer Explanation

The correct answer is Choice D. The student says that he does not know which class to take. The professor answers, "As far as I know, the astronomy class is offered every semester. However, the history class won't be offered for three more years. And you're a sophomore." The student is a sophomore. He will be finished with school the next time the history class is offered. So the professor implies that he should take the history class instead. Choices A, B, and C are all incorrect answer choices.

"

Listen to part of a conversation between a student and a professor.　1-17

Notes

1　Why did the professor ask to see the student?

(A) To discuss the student's test grade

(B) To give the student information on a scholarship

(C) To encourage the student to try harder

(D) To tell the student to talk more in class

2　What does the student imply about the professor's class?

(A) It is in the History Department.

(B) It is an upper-level class.

(C) It has four tests during the semester.

(D) It requires each student to give a presentation.

3　Why does the student have two jobs?

(A) She is planning to study abroad next semester.

(B) The school recently increased tuition.

(C) She wants to take a trip during the summer.

(D) Her parents cannot pay for her tuition.

4　Listen again to part of the conversation. Then answer the question.
What does the professor mean when he says this:

(A) The student has not turned in any assignments yet.

(B) The student should consider dropping the class.

(C) The student has not been doing well lately.

(D) The student needs to work harder than before.

Listen to part of a lecture in an astronomy class. 1-18

Notes

1 According to the professor, how do hyperspace drives operate?

Ⓐ They rely on advanced mathematics.
Ⓑ They utilize special fuel.
Ⓒ They create warp bubbles.
Ⓓ They change the way time flows.

2 What is the professor's opinion of generation ships?

Ⓐ They are the most likely way humans will reach the stars.
Ⓑ He does not find them personally appealing.
Ⓒ They will be the fastest way to travel.
Ⓓ He thinks they will cost too much money to build.

3 Based on the information in the lecture, indicate which type of interstellar travel the statements refer to.
Click in the correct box for each statement.

	Generation Ship	Wormhole
1 Might involve centuries of traveling		
2 Has been mathematically proven to exist		
3 Could enable people to travel hundreds of light years instantaneously		
4 Involves travel that is slower than light speed		

4 How does the professor organize the information about interstellar travel that he presents to the class?

Ⓐ He focuses on the methods most likely to work.
Ⓑ He names some methods and gets the students to discuss them.
Ⓒ He describes several methods in detail.
Ⓓ He only talks about the methods he prefers.

Unit 07

Question Type 7 Understanding Organization

Understanding Organization questions focus on the organization of the passage. They almost always appear after lectures. These types of questions require the test taker to understand how the information in the lecture is organized and presented. They also require the test taker to know why certain information is included in the lecture.

Recognizing Understanding Organization questions:

- How does the professor organize the information about X that he presents to the class?
- Why does the professor discuss X?
- Why does the professor mention X?

Helpful hints for answering the questions correctly:

- Think about the manner in which the lecture is organized. Lectures are typically organized by chronology, by describing a problem and a solution, by classifying, by providing examples, by making comparisons or contrasts, by categorizing, and by describing a cause and an effect.
- The professor sometimes tells the class at the beginning of the lecture how the information will be presented. Listen carefully to be able to identify the method.

Sample Understanding Organization Question

Listen to part of a lecture in an astronomy class.  1-19

W Professor: Some of the more unique bodies in the solar system are comets. Comets are much smaller than planets and moons. They're typically around the size of asteroids. Uh, not the bigger ones like Ceres and Vesta though. Most comets are about one to ten kilometers in diameter. A few, um, super comets that are up to eighty kilometers in diameter have been found. But they're extremely rare.

Comets are basically giant balls of ice and dust. The ice is a mixture of both frozen water and other gases that have been frozen. Many of the ones in the solar system are periodic comets. This means that they orbit the sun in fewer than 200 years. However, other comets have extremely long orbits. They often wander deep into the outer solar system. These comets may complete a single orbit of the sun in hundreds or even thousands of years.

The most famous comet is Halley's Comet. It's a periodic comet that completes a single orbit every seventy-six years. The last time it made an appearance was 1986. It was, sadly, a rather unimpressive appearance. It was much brighter in both 1910 and 1835. Actually, Halley's Comet has been known for more than 2,000 years. The Chinese noticed it back in 240 B.C. The comet got its name from the astronomer Edmund Halley. He calculated the comet's orbit and predicted when it would return to the solar system. Halley, unfortunately, died before the comet returned. So he never knew if his prediction was right or not.

Anyway, let's get back to comets in general. All comets have several distinct parts. The three most important parts are the nucleus, coma, and tail. The tail is the most spectacular of the three. But the nucleus forms the body of the comet itself. So let's examine the nucleus first.

Why does the professor discuss Halley's Comet?

(A) To provide a brief history of it

(B) To explain how it was discovered

(C) To talk about its large size

(D) To state when it will return near Earth

Answer Explanation

The correct answer is Choice A. The professor talks briefly about the years that Halley's Comet appeared, who discovered it, and how it got its name. Thus the professor provides a brief history of the comet. The professor does not explain how Halley's Comet was discovered. She does not mention the comet's size. And she does not give the year when it will return near Earth. So choices B, C, and D are all incorrect.

Listen to part of a conversation between a student and a computer laboratory employee. 🎧 1-20

Notes

____

____

____

1 Why does the student visit the computer laboratory?

   Ⓐ To introduce herself to the person she will work for
   Ⓑ To find out what her work schedule will be
   Ⓒ To ask the man working there for a job
   Ⓓ To learn when the next lab class is going to be held

2 What does the man say he will do for the student?
   Click on 2 answers.

   1 Talk to Professor Jackson about her
   2 Tell her how to teach a laboratory class
   3 Let her know what her job duties will be
   4 Show her where some chemicals are

3 What is the student's attitude toward her job?

   Ⓐ She is afraid she will make a mistake.
   Ⓑ She is nervous about teaching a class.
   Ⓒ She is looking forward to doing it.
   Ⓓ She is positive that she will do well.

4 Listen again to part of the conversation. Then answer the question.
   What does the man imply when he says this: 🎧

   Ⓐ The student will not work tomorrow.
   Ⓑ He is enrolled in graduate school.
   Ⓒ He is teaching for the first time.
   Ⓓ The student should leave the laboratory.

Listen to part of a lecture in a history of cinema class. 1-21

Notes

---

1 What is the lecture mainly about?
   Ⓐ Animated movies that used sound
   Ⓑ The usage of cels in animation
   Ⓒ Walt Disney and his creations
   Ⓓ The early history of animation

2 According to the professor, why were most of the first animated films short?
   Ⓐ All of the pictures were drawn by hand.
   Ⓑ Cels could not be used to make long movies.
   Ⓒ All films at that time were fairly short.
   Ⓓ People were not interested in long animated films.

3 Why does the professor mention *Steamboat Willie*?
   Ⓐ To note that it was a popular animated film
   Ⓑ To say that it was a film made by Walt Disney
   Ⓒ To claim that it became a commercial success
   Ⓓ To name it as an animated movie with sound

4 Listen again to part of the lecture. Then answer the question.
   What can be inferred about the professor when he says this:
   Ⓐ He expects the students to understand the point he makes.
   Ⓑ He believes students commonly misspell that word.
   Ⓒ He dislikes being interrupted during his lecture.
   Ⓓ He wants the students to know the material for their test.

 Connecting Content

Connecting Content questions focus on how the different pieces of information in the passage are connected to one another. They almost always appear after lectures. These types of questions require the test taker to think about the major relationships in the passage. These relationships typically involve the themes, ideas, objects, or individuals discussed in the lecture.

Recognizing Connecting Content questions:

- What is the likely outcome of doing procedure X before procedure Y?
- What comparison does the professor make between X and Y?

Helpful hints for answering the questions correctly:

- Think about the relationships between the facts, concepts, and ideas that are mentioned in the lecture. Consider their similarities as well as their differences.
- Think about what the results of certain actions or events that are described in the lecture may be.

Sample Connecting Content Question

Listen to part of a lecture in a meteorology class. 

> **W Professor:** So, uh, let me recap really quickly because I named several different instruments. There are three instruments you really need to remember. The first, of course, is the thermometer. We use it to measure the temperature. Next is the barometer. It measures air pressure. Third is the anemometer. That tool measures the speed of the air. The other instruments are important, so you should remember them, too. But I want to talk about something else now.
>
> Here's what I'd like to examine: the tools meteorologists use to help them predict the weather. You see, uh, thermometers and anemometers don't predict the weather. All they can do is tell you about the present conditions. Well, uh, I suppose barometers can predict the weather. After all, you can use a barometer to figure out whether or not it's going to rain soon.
>
> But what about the high-tech tools meteorologists have these days? We're extremely fortunate to have advanced technology on our side. It helps us forecast the weather. Of course, we still don't get it right all the time. Weather is just, uh . . . It's just too unpredictable. Anyway, what are these tools I'm referring to . . . ? First are satellites. There are numerous weather satellites in orbit. They provide images of virtually the entire planet. They do things like show us where storms are forming and which direction they're heading. Doppler radar is another important tool. It tells us about the intensity of storms and which places are getting rain. Additionally, balloons are sent into the air with numerous instruments. These measure the temperature and air pressure. So they note changes in the atmosphere that indicate the weather is changing. Let me see. What else is there . . . ?

What comparison does the professor make between the barometer and Doppler radar?

- (A) The manner in which each of them works
- (B) How they are used in weather forecasting
- (C) The process through which they were developed
- (D) What kind of technology they utilize

🔷 Answer Explanation

The correct answer is Choice B. About the barometer, the professor states, "I suppose barometers can predict the weather. After all, you can use a barometer to figure out whether or not it's going to rain soon." Then, about Doppler radar, she says, "Doppler radar is another important tool. It tells us about the intensity of storms and which places are getting rain." So she is comparing how both of these instruments are used in weather forecasting. Choices A, C, and D are all incorrect.

Listen to part of a conversation between a student and a librarian. 🎧 1-23

> *Notes*
>
> ---
> ---
> ---
> ---

1   What is the student looking for?

   (A) Some journal articles
   (B) Some books
   (C) Some microfilm
   (D) Some newspaper articles

2   What can be inferred about the student?

   (A) He frequently checks out books from the library.
   (B) He has never done an interlibrary loan.
   (C) He must submit his paper by the end of the week.
   (D) He is majoring in English literature.

3   What is the likely outcome of the student asking for a book through interlibrary loan?

   (A) The book will arrive within a week.
   (B) The student must pay to get the book.
   (C) His request will be denied.
   (D) He will receive photocopied pages of the book.

4   What is the man's attitude toward the student?

   (A) He ignores the student until he is asked for help.
   (B) He provides some unwanted advice.
   (C) He makes an effort to be helpful.
   (D) He is slightly insulting to the student.

Listen to part of a lecture in a history class. 1-24

> *Notes*

1   What aspect of food preservation does the professor mainly discuss?
    - Ⓐ Common ways to preserve meat and fish
    - Ⓑ The early methods that people used
    - Ⓒ How long preserved food was good for
    - Ⓓ The importance of grain silos

2   What does the professor imply about hunter-gatherers?
    - Ⓐ Preserving food was of little importance to them.
    - Ⓑ They lived in places located all around the world.
    - Ⓒ All humans were like them for thousands of years.
    - Ⓓ They sometimes dried the food they acquired.

3   What comparison does the professor make between caves and silos?
    - Ⓐ The civilizations that utilized them
    - Ⓑ The types of food that were kept in them
    - Ⓒ The manner in which they preserved food
    - Ⓓ How effective they were at food preservation

4   According to the professor, what was the most effective way that people preserved meat?
    - Ⓐ Pickling
    - Ⓑ Salting
    - Ⓒ Smoking
    - Ⓓ Drying

Unit 09

 Connecting Content (Chart)

Connecting Content questions may appear as charts or tables. They almost always appear after lectures. These types of questions require the test taker to match four sentences or phrases with two or three themes, ideas, causes and effects, problems and solutions, objects, or individuals.

Recognizing Connecting Content questions:

- Based on the information in the lecture, do the following sentences refer to X or Y? [Click in the correct box for each statement.]

	X	Y
1 [a statement]		
2 [a statement]		
3 [a statement]		
4 [a statement]		

Helpful hints for answering the questions correctly:

- Listen carefully when the professor makes comparisons, talks about causes and effects, mentions problems and solutions, covers a sequence of events, or describes two or more ideas, people, or themes.

- The professor may sometimes describe how to do some type of procedure. Listen carefully to determine the order of the steps involved in doing the procedure.

Sample Connecting Content Question

Listen to part of a lecture in a geology class. 

> **M Professor:** Before people can mine for valuable minerals, they have to find them first. In the past, people didn't have access to advanced tools. So they mostly discovered minerals by luck. Fortunately for us, we don't have to rely on luck nowadays. Geologists instead utilize lots of special equipment.
>
> What's some of the special equipment we use . . . ? Let me see . . . There are Geiger counters, gravimeters, magnetometers, and, uh, explosive devices, among others. Let me tell you about each. Take a look at page eighty-two in your books. Check out the picture in the top left-hand corner. That's a Geiger counter. Geiger counters are effective at finding radioactive substances such as uranium. Uranium, um, I'm sure you know, is a valuable element that's used for both nuclear power and nuclear weapons.
>
> The picture next to the Geiger counter shows a gravimeter. These machines show the differences in the density of different layers of rock. Why is that important . . . ? Well, geologists can look at the density of the rocks underground and then figure out what they're made of. That saves them from actually having to dig and look at the rocks up close. Take a look at the third picture in your books . . . uh, the one below the Geiger counter. That's a magnetometer. As you can figure out from its name, it works with magnetism. Basically, it, uh, it produces magnetic fields that help find iron ore. Finally, what about explosive devices? Those are actually quite fun to work with. Anyway, explosives produce shock waves that go deep underground and then bounce back. The speed they travel indicates the type of rocks in the ground. Explosives are useful for finding coal, oil, and gas.

Based on the information in the lecture, indicate which type of special equipment the statements refer to.
Click in the correct box for each statement.

	Geiger Counter	Magnetometer	Explosive Device
1 Results in shock waves that go underground			
2 Can find radioactive material			
3 May be utilized to detect coal and oil			
4 Is used to locate iron ore			

🔷 Answer Explanation

Geiger counter is Choice 2. The professor states, "Geiger counters are effective at finding radioactive substances such as uranium." Magnetometer is Choice 4. About the magnetometer, the professor tells the students, "Basically, it, uh, it produces magnetic fields that help find iron ore." And explosive device is choices 1 and 3. The professor notes, "Anyway, explosives produce shock waves that go deep underground and then bounce back." He further says, "Explosives are useful for finding coal, oil, and gas."

Listen to part of a conversation between a student and a professor. 1-26

> *Notes*

1 Why does the student visit the professor?
- Ⓐ To submit a term paper
- Ⓑ To drop the professor's class
- Ⓒ To ask for an extension on her homework
- Ⓓ To get some advice

2 What does the professor do for the student?
- Ⓐ She tells the student a story.
- Ⓑ She lends the student a book.
- Ⓒ She gives the student extra credit.
- Ⓓ She signs the student's form.

3 What can be inferred about the professor?
- Ⓐ She disagrees with the student's choice.
- Ⓑ She is teaching three classes that semester.
- Ⓒ She has a high opinion of the student.
- Ⓓ She has never spoken to the student before.

4 Listen again to part of the conversation. Then answer the question.
Why does the professor say this:
- Ⓐ To protest the student's decision
- Ⓑ To suggest an alternative choice
- Ⓒ To give some encouragement
- Ⓓ To ask the student to repeat herself

Listen to part of a lecture in a history class. 1-27

> *Notes*

1 What aspect of Christopher Columbus does the professor mainly discuss?
   - (A) His voyages of discovery in the New World
   - (B) His legal problems and dealings with the king of Spain
   - (C) His early life in both Italy and Spain
   - (D) The problems he encountered trying to raise funds

2 Based on the information in the lecture, indicate which of Christopher Columbus's voyages to the New World the statements refer to.
   Click in the correct box for each statement.

	Second Voyage	Third Voyage
1 Columbus acquired both gold and slaves.		
2 Columbus was arrested on Hispaniola.		
3 The South American mainland was discovered.		
4 Seventeen ships accompanied Columbus on the trip.		

3 According to the professor, what happened on Columbus's fourth voyage to the New World?
   - (A) He discovered a large amount of gold.
   - (B) He lost more than half of his men.
   - (C) He discovered the island of Trinidad.
   - (D) He was shipwrecked on Jamaica for a year.

4 How is the lecture organized?
   - (A) The professor focuses only on Columbus's successful trips.
   - (B) Information about the voyages is told from Columbus's point of view.
   - (C) The voyages of Columbus are described in chronological order.
   - (D) The professor covers all four of Columbus's voyages to the New World.

10

Question Type 10 **Making Inferences**

Making Inferences questions focus on the implications that are made by the speakers in the passages. These questions appear after both lectures and conversations. These types of questions require the test taker to make inferences based upon the comments that the speakers make. Sometimes these are replay questions. So a short part of the lecture or conversation is played again.

Recognizing Making Inferences questions:

- What will the student probably do next?

- What can be inferred about X?

- What does the professor imply when he says this: (replay)

Helpful hints for answering the questions correctly:

- The speaker will often state what he or she intends to do next at the end of the passage. Listen carefully to determine what will happen next.

- Learn to identify when people are making statements in which they imply something.

- When there is a replay question, listen closely to the entire part that is replayed. Do not only focus on the sentence that is played a second time. The entire section is important in determining the correct answer.

Sample Making Inferences Question

Listen to part of a conversation between a student and a Registrar's office employee. 

> **W Student:** Good morning. I hope you can help me out. I have sort of a problem.
>
> **M Registrar's Office Employee:** I'll do my best. What is the nature of your problem?
>
> **W:** I need to transfer some credits. You see, um, I took a couple of classes at another university this summer. I have to transfer the credits here so that they're on my transcript. But I don't know what to do.
>
> **M:** Okay. It's really easy. First, which school did you attend?
>
> **W:** I went to City University. My advisor said that the school accepts transfer credits from City University.
>
> **M:** That's true. Uh . . . at least it's true most of the time. Okay, you should be fine with your choice of schools. Now, you need to provide me with a description of the course.
>
> **W:** Uh, sure. Should I tell you about the course or something?
>
> **M:** No, don't do that. I mean that you need to photocopy the class description from the City University course catalogue. You have a course catalogue, don't you?
>
> **W:** Er, no. I don't have one. What should I do?
>
> **M:** Look online. Use that computer over there. You should be able to get the class description. Print the description, and then come back here. I'll take care of the rest.

What will the student probably do next?
(A) Leave the Registrar's office
(B) Fill out a form
(C) Use a computer
(D) Give the man a course description

Answer Explanation

> The correct answer is Choice C. The employee needs a course description. He tells the student, "Look online. Use that computer over there." And then he tells the student to return to him with the course description. So it can be inferred that the student will use a computer next. Choices A, B, and D are all incorrect.

Listen to part of a conversation between a student and a professor. 1-29

> *Notes*

1   What does the student imply about her final report?
   (A) She will have no problem writing it.
   (B) She needs to do research on it at the library.
   (C) She has almost finished the paper.
   (D) She is trying to choose a topic for it.

2   According to the professor, what type of questions will the final exam mostly have?
   (A) Short answer questions
   (B) Multiple choice questions
   (C) True-false questions
   (D) Essay questions

3   What is the student's attitude toward the professor?
   (A) She is comfortable telling the professor about her personal life.
   (B) She appreciates the help the professor gives her.
   (C) She considers the professor her best instructor.
   (D) She is frustrated by the professor's answers.

4   Listen again to part of the conversation. Then answer the question.
   What is the purpose of the professor's response to the student:
   (A) To caution her
   (B) To compliment her
   (C) To inspire her
   (D) To instruct her

Listen to part of a lecture in an environmental studies class.  1-30

> *Notes*

1   What can be inferred about the professor?
   Ⓐ She gives frequent homework assignments.
   Ⓑ She expects the students to ask questions.
   Ⓒ She is going to give the students a test.
   Ⓓ She has just started lecturing for the day.

2   According to the professor, what was the Earth's first atmosphere formed of?
Click on 2 answers.
   1 Hydrogen
   2 Carbon dioxide
   3 Nitrogen
   4 Methane

3   Why does the professor discuss cyanobacteria?
   Ⓐ To note that they were the first organisms to evolve
   Ⓑ To explain the rise in free oxygen in the atmosphere
   Ⓒ To claim that they lived billions of years ago
   Ⓓ To state that they were expelled from volcanoes

4   Why does the professor tell the students about iron oxide?
   Ⓐ To explain how the atmosphere's past composition is known
   Ⓑ To ask the students to do their homework assignment on it
   Ⓒ To mention its connection with the Earth's first atmosphere
   Ⓓ To provide the students with its chemical formula

Unit 01

Task 1 The Best Trip You Have Ever Taken

Question

What was the best trip that you have ever taken? Include specific details and reasons in your response.

📁 **Brainstorming** Read over the ideas given in the box below. Decide which words are supporting ideas and which words are examples. Then use your choices to fill out the idea web.

▪ **Idea Box**

many museums and historical sites   studied the Italian language   enjoy history
visited them and took pictures   tried speaking Italian fun   communicating in foreign language

▪ **Idea Web**

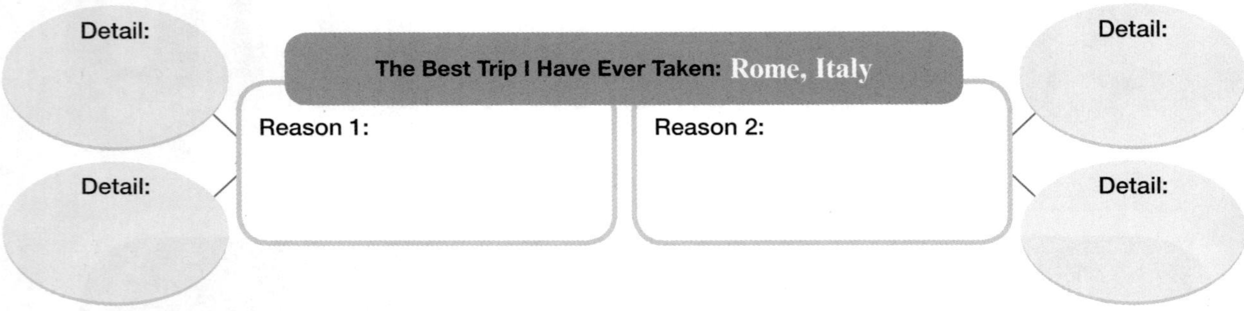

📁 **Organizing** Look back at the idea web. Use it to organize your response.

The Best Trip I Have Ever Taken:

First Reason:

Details:

Second Reason:

Details:

📁 **Speaking** Now give your spoken response for 45 seconds. You may use the guided response to assist you.

Guided & Sample Response 🎧 2-01

The best trip I _____________________ was my trip to Rome, Italy, last year. My family and
I went there for a week. _____________________, I enjoy history. There are many museums
_____________________ in Rome. My family and I spent several days visiting them. We took lots of
pictures and saw _____________________. In addition, I studied a little Italian when I was in school.
So I tried to speak Italian while I was in Rome. It was so much fun trying to communicate with people
_____________________.

Task 2 No Extracurricular Activities for University Freshmen

Question

> Do you agree or disagree with the following statement? University freshmen should not do
> any extracurricular activities. Include specific details and reasons in your response.

📁 **Brainstorming** Choose one of the two opinions you want to speak about. Then read over the
phrases below. Decide which phrases can be used to support your opinion. Finally, choose the correct
words to fill out the idea web.

▪ **Word List**

not all freshmen are the same	university is harder than high school	school is more important than clubs
no special rules for freshmen	shouldn't do too much	got all A's and wrote for student paper
get used to university life	no time to study if do other things	let freshmen decide for themselves
should treat all students the same	living away from home for first time	some can handle extra work

▪ **Idea Web**

Detail:

Detail:

**Should Not Do Any Extracurricular Activities
(Should Be Able to Do Extracurricular Activities)**

Reason 1:

Reason 2:

Detail:

Detail:

📁 **Organizing** Look back at the idea web. Use it to organize your response.

> My Choice:
>
> First Reason:
>
> Details:
>
> Second Reason:
>
> Details:

📁 **Speaking** Now give your spoken response for 45 seconds. You may use the guided response to assist you.

Guided & Sample Response 1: Should Not Do Any Extracurricular Activities 🎧 2-02

I agree that university freshmen shouldn't do any extracurricular activities. The first reason I support the statement is that freshmen need to get used ___________________. Many of them are living away from home ___________________. So they shouldn't try to do too much until they're used to school life. Another reason is that university ___________________ than high school. Freshmen who do extracurricular activities might not ___________________ to study. And their schoolwork is definitely more important than club memberships. So they shouldn't do any activities ___________________.

Guided & Sample Response 2: Should Be Able to Do Extracurricular Activities 🎧 2-03

I disagree with the statement. I support allowing freshmen to do extracurricular activities. Firstly, not all freshmen ___________________. Some can handle extracurricular activities while ___________________. As a freshman, I got all A's and wrote for the student newspaper. It was no problem for me. Next, ___________________ all of their students the same. Freshmen shouldn't have to live ___________________ that seniors don't have to follow. In my opinion, ___________________. So schools should let freshmen decide for themselves whether or not they want to do any extracurricular activities.

Task 3 All Ads to Be Removed from Academic Buildings

Reading Read the following announcement from the maintenance office.

No More Advertisements in Academic Buildings

This semester, people have been putting too many advertisements on the walls of the academic buildings. These advertisements are ruining the appearance of the buildings. Therefore, no more advertisements may be placed in academic buildings. Maintenance staff have been instructed to remove all advertisements that they find anywhere in the academic buildings. Advertisements may still be placed in all of the dormitories, the student center, and other approved locations around campus. Contact the maintenance office for more information.

Listening Listen to a short conversation related to the reading. Take notes about the woman's opinion. 2-04

Notes

The woman (agrees / disagrees) with the announcement.

Reason: ____

____

Key Words and Details: ____

____

Question

The woman expresses her opinion about the announcement by the maintenance office. Explain her opinion and the reasons she gives for holding it.

Speaking Now give your spoken response for 60 seconds. You may use the guided response to assist you.

Guided & Sample Response 2-05

The speakers are having a conversation about the decision to ___________________ from academic buildings on campus. The school administration believes that the ads are making the buildings look bad. The woman disagrees with the school administration. She gives two reasons for this belief. First, she says that there are ___________________ on the buildings. She feels that the ban ___________________ by the school. Second, the woman claims that ___________________. She has found out about ___________________ from the ads. And she ___________________ by reading an ad as well.

 # Marketing: Customer Lock-In

Reading Read the following passage about customer lock-in.

Customer Lock-In

Companies do not want to share their customers with other businesses. One way to avoid sharing customers is by using customer lock-in. This prevents customers from using one company's technology or products on another company's products. In this way, customers are locked in on a single company's goods. This guarantees that customers cannot use another company's products or services. This helps increase both sales and profits for the original manufacturer. And it helps reduce sales and profits for competing manufacturers.

Listening Listen to a short lecture related to the reading. Take notes on key words and specific information from the lecture.   2-06

Notes

Topic:

Detail 1:

Detail 2:

Key Words:

Question

The professor talks about her personal experiences while shopping. Explain how they are related to customer lock-in.

Speaking Now give your spoken response for 60 seconds. You may use the guided response to assist you.

Guided & Sample Response   2-07

The professor relates two of ______________________ while shopping. First, she mentions that she broke ______________________. She purchased a new one, but it wouldn't fit on her camera. The reason was that her camera could only use lenses that were made by the company ______________________.
The same thing happened to her with ______________________. She couldn't use a different company's battery on her laptop. The reason for both of these incidents was ______________________. This happens when companies make sure that the products of other companies ______________________ on their own products.

`Task 5` Taking a History Class

📁 **Listening** Listen to the following dialogue. Take notes as needed. 🎧 `2-08`

Notes

The Problem: ....

Solution 1: ....

....

Solution 2: ....

....

Speaking

Question

> **The students discuss two possible solutions to the man's problem. Describe the problem. Then state which of the two solutions you prefer and explain why.**

📁 **Speaking** Now give your spoken response for 60 seconds. You may use the guided response to assist you.

Guided & Sample Response 1: First Solution 🎧 `2-09`

The man has a problem concerning a class _______________________. He tried to _______________________, but he couldn't. The students propose two solutions to the man's problem. First, he could take the course with the professor _______________________. Second, he could take the same course but with _______________________. I think that the first choice is the better one. One reason is that the man wants to take the course with Professor Gilder. So he can do that during summer school. The second reason is that _______________________ during summer vacation. That way, he can make money. Then, he can afford _______________________.

Guided & Sample Response 2: Second Solution 🎧 `2-10`

The man has a problem concerning a class _______________________. He tried to _______________________, but he couldn't. The students propose two solutions to the man's problem. First, he could take the course with the professor _______________________. Second, he could take the same course but with _______________________. I think that the second choice is the better one. To begin with, the material, not the professor, _______________________. So the man can learn a lot by taking the class. Secondly, he can't afford to take summer school because tuition _______________________. So he should take the class during the regular semester.

📖 **Listening** Listen to a lecture on art history. Take notes on key words and concepts in the lecture.
🎧 2-11

Notes

Topic: ____

Detail 1: ____

____

Detail 2: ____

____

Key Words: ____

Question

> **Using points and examples from the talk, explain how photography has influenced artists.**

🗣 **Speaking** Now give your spoken response for 60 seconds. You may use the guided response to assist you.

Guided & Sample Response 🎧 2-12

In her lecture, the professor describes ___________________ on artists. She goes into detail about two effects. The first is that photography helped create the Realist Movement. Many artists, such as Gustave Courbet, tried to make paintings that ___________________. They focused on ___________________ that pictures provided. However, other artists moved away ___________________. They saw how detailed pictures taken by cameras were. And they didn't want to ___________________. They knew that they couldn't make more realistic pictures. So they created ___________________. This is art that doesn't look like anything real. Pablo Picasso and many others were abstract artists.

Unit 02

Task 1 **The Advantages of the Internet**

Question

> What are some advantages of the Internet? Include specific details and reasons in your response.

📁 **Brainstorming** Read over the ideas given in the box below. Decide which words are supporting ideas and which words are examples. Then use your choices to fill out the idea web.

- **Idea Box**

education	have telephone and video conversations	get university degrees online
	send email listen to online lectures	communication

- **Idea Web**

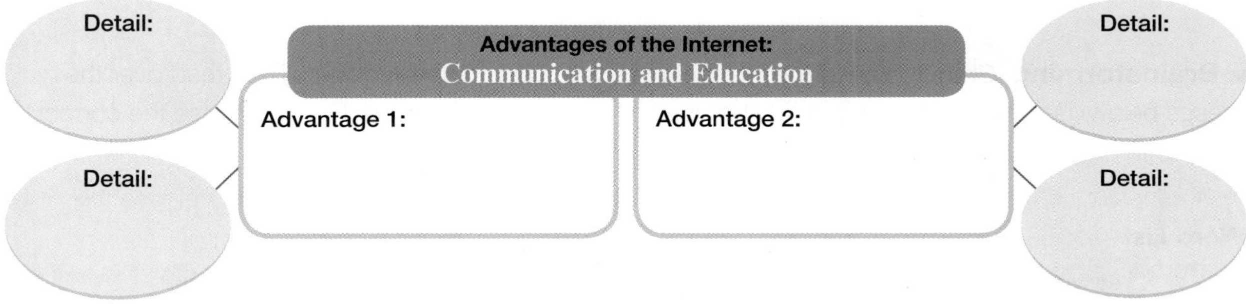

📁 **Organizing** Look back at the idea web. Use it to organize your response.

Advantages of the Internet:

First Advantage:

Details:

Second Advantage:

Details:

Speaking Now give your spoken response for 45 seconds. You may use the guided response to assist you.

Guided & Sample Response 2-13

The Internet has several advantages. But I think the two most important ones are ___________________. People all around the world ___________________ on the Internet. They send email messages to each other. And they have telephone and video conversations as well. People also benefit from the Internet because of ___________________ it provides. For instance, people can get university degrees online. There are also ___________________ that people can listen to. Many of these lectures are getting extremely popular. So the Internet is helping people around the world ___________________.

Task 2 Friendly Professors or Distant Professors

Question

> Is it better for a professor to be friendly with his or her students or to be distant from them? Include specific details and reasons in your response.

Brainstorming Choose one of the two opinions you want to speak about. Then read over the phrases below. Decide which phrases can be used to support your opinion. Finally, choose the correct words to fill out the idea web.

- **Word List**

easy to talk to	students confused by friendly profs.	distant teacher taught very well
not interested in being liked	didn't ask mean physics prof. questions	students eager to learn
only care about teaching	students and profs. aren't equals	comfortable lectures
shouldn't be friends	asked friend economics prof. questions	have better classes

- **Idea Web**

Detail:

Detail:

Friendly Professor (Distant Professor)

Reason 1:

Reason 2:

Detail:

Detail:

📁 Organizing Look back at the idea web. Use it to organize your response.

My Choice:

First Reason:

Details:

Second Reason:

Details:

📁 Speaking Now give your spoken response for 45 seconds. You may use the guided response to assist you.

Guided & Sample Response 1: Friendly Professor   🎧 2-14

It's definitely better for a professor to be friendly with his or her students. For one thing, _____________________ to a friendly professor. My economics professor was easy to talk to, so _____________________ him questions. My physics professor was mean, so I never asked him any questions. For another thing, friendly professors have better classes. Their lectures and discussions are _____________________. Most students _____________________ from these teachers. I always _____________________ in classes that had friendly teachers. I learned the least in classes that had mean teachers.

Guided & Sample Response 2: Distant Professor   🎧 2-15

Professors should always be distant from their students. That is _____________________ than being too friendly with the students. One reason is that professors and students aren't equals, so they _____________________. Students _____________________ about their relationships with professors who are too friendly. They won't have this problem with distant teachers. Next, distant teachers often _____________________ teaching the material. They aren't interested _____________________ by the students. The best teacher I ever had was distant. She wasn't friendly, but she taught the course material really well.

Task 3 Weekly Meetings in Dormitories

📁 **Reading** Read the following announcement by the student housing office.

Dormitories to Have Weekly Meetings

There will be weekly meetings in every dormitory on campus this semester. The students on each floor will have a meeting with their resident assistant. The meetings will be held in the lounges in the dormitories. These meetings may be held at any time, but they will take place once a week. They will provide the students with an opportunity to relax from their studies. In addition, they will allow the students to meet the others on the floors.

📁 **Listening** Listen to a short conversation related to the reading. Take notes about the man's opinion.

🎧 2-16

> ### *Notes*
>
> **The man (agrees / disagrees) with the announcement.**
>
> Reason: ____
>
> ____
>
> Key Words and Details: ______________________________________

Question

> **The man expresses his opinion about the announcement by the student housing office. Explain his opinion and the reasons he gives for holding it.**

📁 **Speaking** Now give your spoken response for 60 seconds. You may use the guided response to assist you.

Guided & Sample Response 🎧 2-17

The man and the woman are chatting about the announcement by _____________________. There will _____________________ in the school's dormitories. The man opposes these meetings. The first reason he is against them is that the meetings are _____________________. He likes to go home on the weekend. Then, he returns to school on Monday. But he can't _____________________ because of the meetings. He also has no interest in meeting _____________________ living in his dorm. He says that he doesn't like them, so he doesn't want to _____________________.

Task 4 Zoology: Communal Nutrition

Reading Read the following passage about communal nutrition.

Communal Nutrition

Many animals forage for food only for themselves. Yet others forage for an entire group. Animals that engage in communal nutrition are often those that live in large colonies. Insects sometimes display this behavior. They may find food that they themselves do not eat. Instead, the food is eaten by other members of the group. Thus all animals—especially those that cannot take care of themselves—are provided with food. By working together, the group can become much stronger.

Listening Listen to a short lecture related to the reading. Take notes on key words and specific information from the lecture. 🎧 2-18

> *Notes*
>
> Topic: ....
>
> Detail 1: ....
>
> ....
>
> Detail 2: ....
>
> ....
>
> Key Words: ....

Question

The professor talks about how ants forage for food. Explain how their behavior is related to communal nutrition.

Speaking Now give your spoken response for 60 seconds. You may use the guided response to assist you.

Guided & Sample Response 🎧 2-19

The professor tells the students about ___________________. He states that ants don't always eat the food they gather. The first reason is that ___________________ collect food. Many ants, such as the queen, males, and soldiers, don't. So other ants must gather food for them. In addition, ___________________ differ. ___________________ need protein while adults need sugar. So some ants collect food ___________________. This food goes to other ants. These actions relate to communal nutrition. In communal nutrition, animals forage ___________________. This helps the members of the group live long lives.

Listening Listen to the following dialogue. Take notes as needed. 🎧 2-20

Notes

The Problem: ....

Solution 1: ....

....

Solution 2: ....

Question

The students discuss two possible solutions to the woman's problem. Describe the problem. Then state which of the two solutions you prefer and explain why.

Speaking Now give your spoken response for 60 seconds. You may use the guided response to assist you.

Guided & Sample Response 1: First Solution 🎧 2-21

The woman tells the man about her problem. She is ___________________ to Costa Rica, but she needs someone to watch ___________________. They think of two solutions to her problem. The first is to ask her friend Janet to watch the bird for a week. The second is to take the bird ___________________. I feel that the first option is better. Janet has taken care of the bird ___________________. So she will know ___________________. Also, even though Janet is busy, taking care of a bird is simple. All Janet has to do is feed the bird and ___________________ every day.

Guided & Sample Response 2: Second Solution 🎧 2-22

The woman tells the man about her problem. She is ___________________ to Costa Rica, but she needs someone to watch ___________________. They think of two solutions to her problem. The first is to ask her friend Janet to watch the bird for a week. The second is to take the bird ___________________. I feel that the second option is better. The people ___________________ will take good care of the bird. That will keep the woman ___________________. In addition, Janet is busy and can't watch the bird. So the woman shouldn't ask her ___________________. That's not fair to Janet.

◼ Task 6 ◼ Environmental Studies: Carbon Dioxide Emissions

📁 **Listening** Listen to a lecture on environmental studies. Take notes on key words and concepts in the lecture. 🎧 2-23

Notes

Topic:

Detail 1:

Detail 2:

Key Words:

Question

> **Using points and examples from the talk, explain two ways that companies can reduce carbon dioxide emissions.**

📁 **Speaking** Now give your spoken response for 60 seconds. You may use the guided response to assist you.

Guided & Sample Response 🎧 2-24

The professor lectures about carbon dioxide emissions. He states that many people are ___________________ carbon dioxide emissions in the atmosphere. He gives the students two ways people are trying to do this. The first is ___________________. Filters remove carbon dioxide from the atmosphere. Some ___________________ into water and another gas. And other filters ___________________ to capture carbon dioxide. In addition, ___________________ near factories that emit carbon dioxide. The trees take the carbon dioxide and use it for photosynthesis. This gives the trees energy and provides oxygen ___________________. So both trees and animals gain in this way.

Unit 03

Task 1 Your Country's Strong Points

Question

What are some strong points about your country? Include specific details and reasons in your response.

Brainstorming Read over the ideas given in the box below. Decide which words are supporting ideas and which words are examples. Then use your choices to fill out the idea web.

■ **Idea Box**

students and adults constantly learn	emphasize education	country was once poor
many hardworking people	is rich country now	improves knowledge

■ **Idea Web**

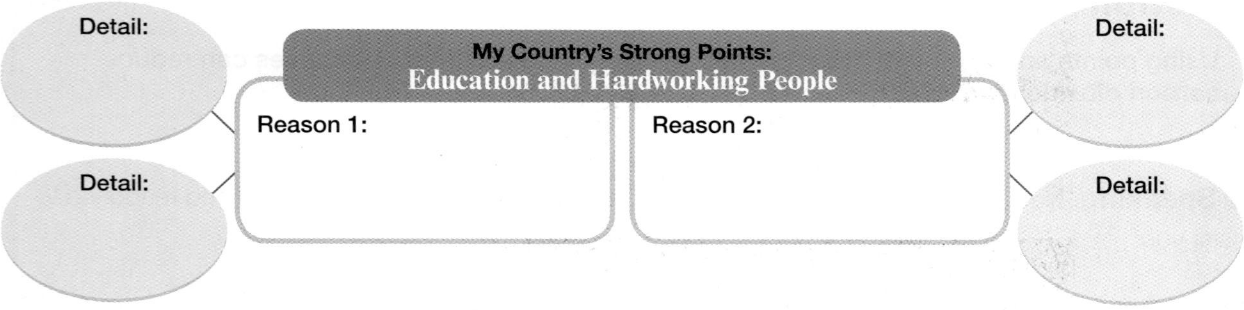

Organizing Look back at the idea web. Use it to organize your response.

My Country's Strong Points:

First Reason:

Details:

Second Reason:

Details:

Guided & Sample Response 🎧 2-25

In my opinion, my country has two major strong points. They are education and hardworking people. First of all, in my country, _____________________. So not only students but also adults are constantly learning. This improves _____________________ and makes them better employees. In addition, there are _____________________ in my country. A few decades ago, my country _____________________. But the citizens of my country all worked hard. They improved my country a lot. Today, my country is one of _____________________ in the world thanks to its hardworking people.

Task 2 Better Lives Now or 100 Years Ago

Question

> Do you agree or disagree with the following statement? People living in the present day have better lives than those who lived 100 years ago. Include specific details and reasons

Brainstorming Choose one of the two opinions you want to speak about. Then read over the phrases below. Decide which phrases can be used to support your opinion. Finally, choose the correct words to fill out the idea web.

■ **Word List**

healthier today	was clean and not polluted	people always in a hurry today
like jobs have today	people were relaxed	ive longer
slow pace of life	better medicine and health care	all kinds of jobs
disliked farming in the past	lived in countryside	cities today are dirty and overcrowded

■ **Idea Web**

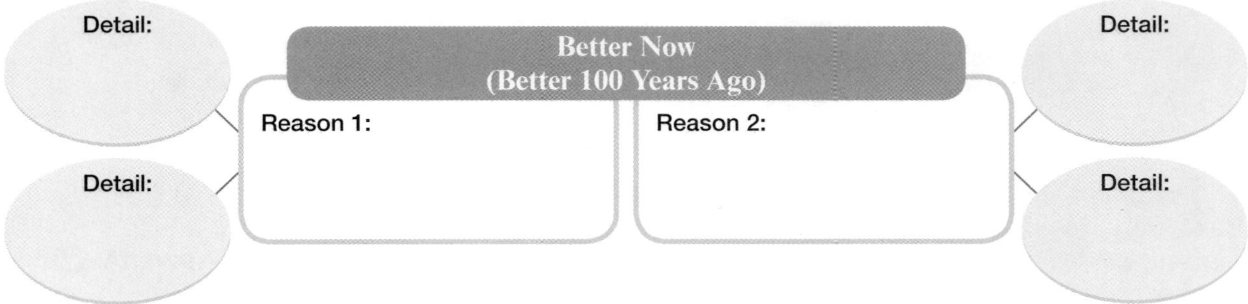

📁 **Organizing** Look back at the idea web. Use it to organize your response.

> My Choice: ....
>
> First Reason: ....
>
> Details: ....
>
> Second Reason: ....
>
> Details: ....

📁 **Speaking** Now give your spoken response for 45 seconds. You may use the guided response to assist you.

Guided & Sample Response 1: Better Now 🎧 2-26

I agree with the statement. It's true that people in the present day _____________________ than people who lived 100 years ago. The first reason _____________________. Nowadays, people have all kinds of jobs. These are jobs they often enjoy. 100 years ago, most people were farmers. Farming was very hard work that _____________________. Second, people living in modern times _____________________ people who lived 100 years ago. We have access to better _____________________, and we live much longer. So our lives are better than they used to be.

Guided & Sample Response 2: Better 100 Years Ago 🎧 2-27

I disagree with the statement. It's my belief that people _____________________ 100 years ago. Back then, most people lived _____________________. Today, most people live in cities. The countryside was clean and _____________________. But modern cities are dirty, polluted, and overcrowded. So modern-day people don't live in better places than people used to. Also, 100 years ago, the pace of life was slow. Therefore people _____________________. Nowadays, everyone is _____________________. People rush from one place to another. I don't think that's an improvement on life in the past.

Task 3 The School Directory

Reading Read the following announcement by the student services office.

New School Directory to Be Released

The school will release its new directory for the school year this Thursday. For the first time ever, the directory will not be printed on paper. Instead, it will be released only on the Internet. As a result, much more information than before will be placed in the directory. This year's directory will have the names and pictures of every student on campus. It will also have every student's email address. Students' phone numbers, however, will not be published.

Listening Listen to a short conversation related to the reading. Take notes about the woman's opinion. 2-28

> *Notes*
>
> **The woman (supports / does not support) the new student directory.**
>
> Reason:
>
> Key Words and Details:

Question

> **The woman expresses her opinion about the announcement by the student services office. Explain her opinion and the reasons she gives for holding it.**

Speaking Now give your spoken response for 60 seconds. You may use the guided response to assist you.

Guided & Sample Response 2-29

The man and the woman are talking about the new student directory. It will be released __________________________, so it will __________________________ than before. The woman likes that there will be more information in it. The first thing she mentions is that there will __________________________ in the directory. She says that she has called students by mistake before. But since there will be pictures of students, she won't __________________________ again. She also states that the online directory __________________________. She will be able to look up information anytime __________________________.

Task 4 Biology: Odor Defenses

📁 **Reading** Read the following passage about odor defenses.

Odor Defenses

Animals have many ways to defend themselves. They have sharp teeth and claws. Others run swiftly or use camouflage. And some animals have odor defenses. They use strong smells to defend themselves. Animals with odor defenses release foul-smelling scents when threatened. These smells may simply surround the animals. Or they may be directed toward an attacker. In both cases, the bad smells usually drive away the predator. Many predators learn to leave those animals alone in the future.

📁 **Listening** Listen to a short lecture related to the reading. Take notes on key words and specific information from the lecture.   🎧 2-30

<table>
<tr><td colspan="2">Notes</td></tr>
<tr><td>Topic:</td><td></td></tr>
<tr><td>Detail 1:</td><td></td></tr>
<tr><td></td><td></td></tr>
<tr><td>Detail 2:</td><td></td></tr>
<tr><td></td><td></td></tr>
<tr><td>Key Words:</td><td></td></tr>
</table>

Question

> The professor talks about skunks and stinkbugs. Explain how they are related to odor defenses.

📁 **Speaking** Now give your spoken response for 60 seconds. You may use the guided response to assist you.

Guided & Sample Response   🎧 2-31

During her lecture, the professor tells the class about the stinkbug and skunk. Both use
______________________. Odor defenses utilize scents _____________________. Animals release these
scents when ____________________ in some way. For instance, the stinkbug ___________________
that smells bad anytime it's threatened. And animals like birds don't eat stinkbugs because
of their bad smell. The professor also talks about the skunk. When a skunk sees an enemy, it
____________________ at the other animal. This liquid has a bad smell animals hate. It smells so bad
that ___________________ whenever they see a skunk.

Task 5 Driving a Friend Home

Listening Listen to the following dialogue. Take notes as needed. 2-32

Notes

The Problem: ____

Solution 1: ____

____

Solution 2: ____

____

Question

> **The students discuss two possible solutions to the man's problem. Describe the problem. Then state which of the two solutions you prefer and explain why.**

Speaking Now give your spoken response for 60 seconds. You may use the guided response to assist you.

Guided & Sample Response 1: First Solution 2-33

The man's problem is that _____________________ give his friend Andrew a ride home. However, he has a meeting _____________________ in thirty minutes. The man and woman discuss two solutions to the man's problem. The first is for the man to tell Andrew to find _____________________. The second is for the man to give Andrew a ride home and to _____________________ late. I like the first solution. The man's meeting is important, so he _____________________ for it. Also, it shouldn't be a problem for Andrew to find another way home. He probably knows other students with cars. Or he _____________________.

Guided & Sample Response 2: Second Solution 2-34

The man's problem is that _____________________ give his friend Andrew a ride home. However, he has a meeting _____________________ in thirty minutes. The man and woman discuss two solutions to the man's problem. The first is for the man to tell Andrew to find _____________________. The second is for the man to give Andrew a ride home and to _____________________ late. I like the second solution. The man promised Andrew a ride home, so he should _____________________. He can also call his advisor ahead of time. He can _____________________ and say that he'll be a few minutes late.

Listening Listen to a lecture on biology. Take notes on key words and concepts in the lecture.
2-35

Notes

Topic:

Detail 1:

Detail 2:

Key Words:

Question

Using points and examples from the talk, explain how elephants and fish engage in collective behavior.

Speaking Now give your spoken response for 60 seconds. You may use the guided response to assist you.

Guided & Sample Response 2-36

In her lecture, the professor tells the students about collective behavior by animals. She states that both _______________________ act collectively. First, she discusses elephants. She says that they _______________________ known as herds. Elephants do many activities together. They take care of their young, watch out for predators, and _______________________ while other elephants eat. These collective actions benefit _______________________. The professor mentions two types of fish behavior. Swordfish _______________________ large schools of fish and kill them. And schools of prey fish such as herring _______________________ to avoid getting killed by predators. Both swordfish and herring therefore use collective behavior.

Unit 04

Task 1 Your Favorite Teacher

Question

Who is your favorite teacher? Include specific details and reasons in your response.

📁 **Brainstorming** Read over the ideas given in the box below. Decide which words are supporting ideas and which words are examples. Then use your choices to fill out the idea web.

▪ **Idea Box**

| tells interesting stories | lets students contribute to class | students can give their opinions |
| has made me consider majoring in history | makes class fun | have class discussion every week |

▪ **Idea Web**

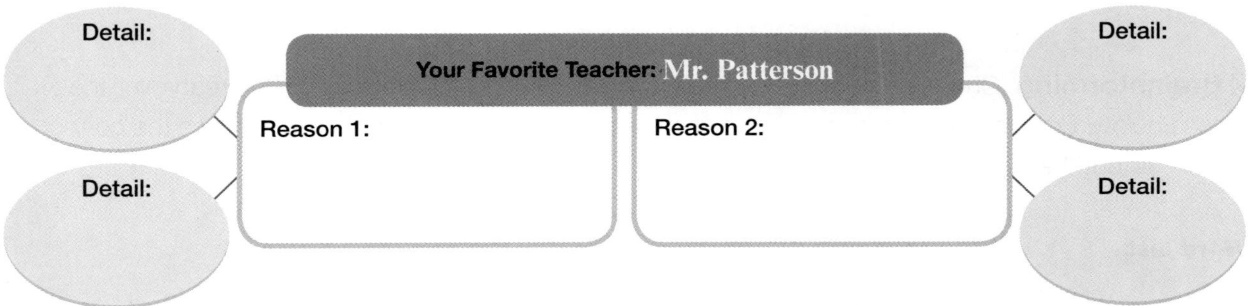

📁 **Organizing** Look back at the idea web. Use it to organize your response.

Your Favorite Teacher:

First Reason:

Details:

Second Reason:

Details:

Guided & Sample Response 🎧 2-37

My favorite teacher is Mr. Patterson. He teaches history at my school. He's my favorite teacher for two reasons. Firstly, he always _____________________. He tells stories that make history seem interesting. I never enjoyed history until _____________________. Now, I'm considering _____________________ at college. Secondly, he lets students contribute to class. Every week, we have _____________________ in one of our classes. Mr. Patterson asks us for our opinions. We get to speak about the past and what we think happened. Doing that is both _____________________.

Task 2 Students Should Take a Cooking Class at University

Question

> Do you agree or disagree with the following statement? Students should be required to take a cooking class at university. Include specific details and reasons in your response.

📁 **Brainstorming** Choose one of the two opinions you want to speak about. Then read over the phrases below. Decide which phrases can be used to support your opinion. Finally, choose the correct words to fill out the idea web.

■ **Word List**

can attend academy or take cooking lessons need skills to cook is important skill	
math and reading comprehension is nothing academic about cooking can apply skills learned at school	
couldn't cook well when lived alone can cook them in microwave not necessary skill anymore	
only teach academic courses many instant foods available wish had taken cooking class	

■ **Idea Web**

Detail:

Should Be Required (Should Not Be Required)

Reason 1:

Reason 2:

Detail:

Detail:

Detail:

📁 Organizing Look back at the idea web. Use it to organize your response.

> My Choice:
>
> First Reason:
>
> Details:
>
> Second Reason:
>
> Details:

📁 Speaking Now give your spoken response for 45 seconds. You may use the guided response to assist you.

Guided & Sample Response 1: Should Be Required 🎧 2-38

I think it's a great idea to require students to take a cooking class at university. For one, cooking is ____________________ everyone should know. I lived alone for two years after I graduated, but I ____________________. I wish I had taken a cooking class. Also, a lot of cooking requires a person to be exact and ____________________. So people need math and reading comprehension skills to cook. This makes cooking relevant ____________________. Students can ____________________ they learn at school to the kitchen while learning how to cook.

Guided & Sample Response 2: Should Not Be Required 🎧 2-39

I don't think students should be required to take a cooking class at university. To begin with, I believe that colleges should only ____________________. There's nothing academic about cooking. If students want to learn to cook, they can attend ____________________ or take cooking lessons. Another thing is that cooking skills ____________________. There are so ____________________ available these days. To cook them, just put them in the microwave for a minute or two. That's how I eat most of my meals. I can't cook, but that ____________________.

Reading Read the following announcement from the student activities office.

Premed Students to Do Shortened Internships

Next year, there will be a new policy for premed students. Students may no longer do internships lasting six months or a year. Instead, they will be restricted to internships lasting no more than three months. The dean of students has made this decision in response to complaints by both students and faculty members. Hopefully, this new policy will satisfy everyone involved. For more information, please contact the office of the dean of students or the Chemistry or Biology departments.

Listening Listen to a short conversation related to the reading. Take notes about the woman's opinion. 2-40

Notes

The woman (supports / does not support) the decision.

Reason: ....

....

Key Words and Details: ....

....

Question

> The woman expresses her opinion about the announcement by the dean of students.
> Explain her opinion and the reasons she gives for holding it.

Speaking Now give your spoken response for 60 seconds. You may use the guided response to assist you.

Guided & Sample Response 2-41

The speakers are talking about the announcement made by the dean of students. _____________________ may only have internships that _____________________. They cannot do internships longer than that. The woman agrees with the decision by the dean. She first states that her one-year internship _____________________ for her. She claims that she _____________________ while she was doing it. She also mentions that _____________________ while she had the internship. She didn't get all A's like she normally did. She _____________________ on the low grades that she received.

Task 4 Education: Behavior Contracting

📁 **Reading** Read the following passage about behavior contracting.

📁 **Listening** Listen to a short lecture related to the reading. Take notes on key words and specific information from the lecture. 🎧 2-42

Notes

Topic:

Detail 1:

Detail 2:

Key Words:

Question

The professor talks about her experience as a teacher. Explain how her experience is related to behavior contracting.

📁 **Speaking** Now give your spoken response for 60 seconds. You may use the guided response to assist you.

Guided & Sample Response 🎧 2-43

The professor tells the class about when she was an elementary school teacher. She had a student who never ___________________________. Instead, the student just yelled out questions and answers. The professor used ___________________________ to solve the problem. Behavior contracting involves two people ___________________________. One person will change his or her behavior. The other will ___________________________ for changing. This contract is for ___________________________. The professor agreed to give the student ___________________________ for good behavior. She took them away for bad behavior. Thanks to behavior contracting, the student's behavior improved.

📁 **Listening** Listen to the following dialogue. Take notes as needed. 🎧 2-44

<table>
<tr><td colspan="2">Notes</td></tr>
<tr><td>The Problem:</td><td></td></tr>
<tr><td>Solution 1:</td><td></td></tr>
<tr><td>Solution 2:</td><td></td></tr>
</table>

Question

> The students discuss two possible solutions to the woman's problem. Describe the problem. Then state which of the two solutions you prefer and explain why.

📁 **Speaking** Now give your spoken response for 60 seconds. You may use the guided response to assist you.

Guided & Sample Response 1: First Solution 🎧 2-45

The woman has a problem. She is supposed to lead ______________________, but her cousin is coming to school at the same time. The man and woman suggest two solutions to her problem. The first is for her to ______________________ to show her cousin around campus. The second is for her to ______________________. In my opinion, the first choice is better. By having a friend ______________________, the woman can lead the film discussion. So she ______________________ all of those students. Also, meeting a new person will be good for the woman's cousin. Maybe she can help ______________________ that way.

Guided & Sample Response 2: Second Solution 🎧 2-46

The woman has a problem. She is supposed to lead ______________________, but her cousin is coming to school at the same time. The man and woman suggest two solutions to her problem. The first is for her to ______________________ to show her cousin around campus. The second is for her to ______________________. In my opinion, the second choice is better. ______________________, so the woman should show her cousin around campus. In addition, since her cousin ______________________, it wouldn't be nice for the woman to ask a friend ______________________. That is something the woman should do herself.

📁 **Listening** Listen to a lecture on zoology. Take notes on key words and concepts in the lecture.

🎧 2-47

<table>
<tr><td colspan="2" align="center">Notes</td></tr>
<tr><td>Topic:</td><td></td></tr>
<tr><td>Detail 1:</td><td></td></tr>
<tr><td>Detail 2:</td><td></td></tr>
<tr><td>Key Words:</td><td></td></tr>
</table>

Question

> **Using points and examples from the talk, explain the two methods ants use when foraging.**

📁 **Speaking** Now give your spoken response for 60 seconds. You may use the guided response to assist you.

Guided & Sample Response 🎧 2-48

The professor lectures about the foraging habits of ants. She mentions that ants _____________________ of foraging. She describes two of them. The first concerns the direction ants move when _____________________. Ants will walk in _____________________ to find food. But, if there is no food, they will all move in a different direction. And no ants will continue moving in _____________________. Also, ants _____________________ to carry back large pieces of food. Ants don't break up the food into small pieces. Instead, _____________________ ants pick up a large piece of food and carry it back to their colony together.

05

Task 1 A Facility You Want Your School to Construct

Question

> Which type of facility would you like for your school to construct? Include specific details and reasons in your response.

📁 **Brainstorming** Read over the ideas given in the box below. Decide which words are supporting ideas and which words are examples. Then use your choices to fill out the idea web.

▪ Idea Box

rains a lot in city	could play them in gym	no basketball and volleyball
can't go outside in rain	play indoor sports	cancel P.E. when rains

▪ Idea Web

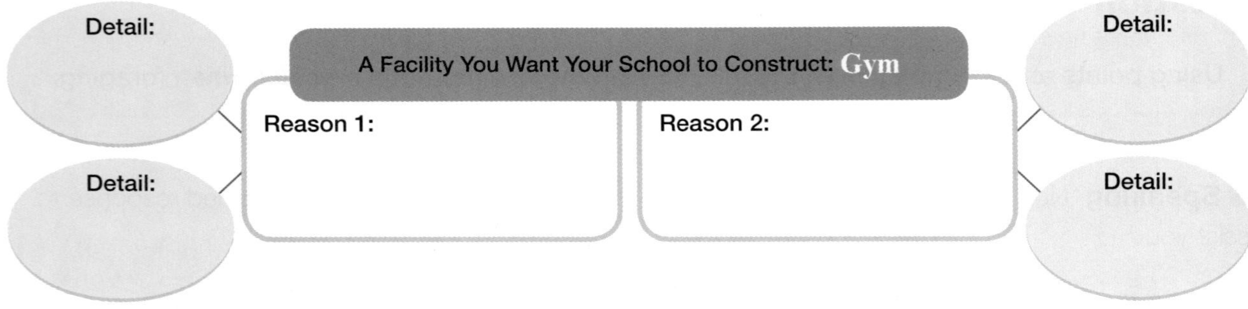

📁 **Organizing** Look back at the idea web. Use it to organize your response.

A Facility You Want Your School to Construct:

First Reason:

Details:

Second Reason:

Details:

📁 **Speaking** Now give your spoken response for 45 seconds. You may use the guided response to assist you.

Guided & Sample Response 🎧 2-49

I would really like for my school ________________________. There are two reasons that I want a gym. The first is that ________________________ in my city. When it rains, we have to ________________________ since we can't go outside. But if we have a gym, we ________________________ on rainy days. The second reason is that having a gym will let us ________________________ such as basketball and volleyball. We can't play either sport at my school now. However, we could play them if we had a gym.

Task 2 The Same Activities or Different Ones

Question

> **Is it better for people to do the same activities every day or to do different activities? Include specific details and reasons in your response.**

📁 **Brainstorming** Choose one of the two opinions you want to speak about. Then read over the phrases below. Decide which phrases can be used to support your opinion. Finally, choose the correct words to fill out the idea web.

■ **Word List**

play basketball every day	do different activities	is incredibly skilled
feels comfortable at theater	doing the same thing is boring	makes people feel comfortable
can learn new skills	best friend does something different daily	can become very skilled
am good basketball player	try to vary routine	friend watches movies every weekend

■ **Idea Web**

Do the Same Activities (Do Different Activities)

Detail:

Detail:

Reason 1:

Reason 2:

Detail:

Detail:

Organizing Look back at the idea web. Use it to organize your response.

My Choice:

First Reason:

Details:

Second Reason:

Details:

Speaking Now give your spoken response for 45 seconds. You may use the guided response to assist you.

Guided & Sample Response 1: Same Activities 2-50

In my opinion, it's better for people to do the same activities every day. The first reason is that this will let people become _______________________ these activities. For instance, I play basketball with my friends every day. Since I _______________________, I have become quite a good basketball player. The second reason is that familiar activities make people _______________________. One of my friends watches movies every weekend. I asked her why she does this. She responded that _______________________ at the movie theater. So she does an activity that _______________________.

Guided & Sample Response 2: Different Activities 2-51

I strongly believe that people should do different activities every day. One reason I feel this way is that always doing _______________________ is boring. I try to vary my routine. Some days, I meet my friends. Other days, I exercise or _______________________. Another reason I feel this way is that doing different activities _______________________ new skills. My best friend does _______________________ each day of the week. For example, he studies English on Mondays. He learns computer programming on Tuesdays. And he takes swimming lessons on Wednesdays. He's an incredibly _______________________.

Task 3 Free E-Readers for Students

📁 **Reading** Read the following announcement from the student services office.

All Students to Receive Free E-Readers

Due to the increasing popularity of e-books, the school will provide all students with free e-readers starting next semester. This will allow students to purchase electronic versions of their textbooks and other supporting materials. The e-readers are also able to surf the Internet and can do various other functions. Students will be given a choice between three different e-readers. The school will email students information about all three e-readers. Students may then inform the school about the e-reader they want.

📁 **Listening** Listen to a short conversation related to the reading. Take notes about the woman's opinion. 🎧 2-52

Notes

The woman (agrees / disagrees) with the decision.

Reason: ____

____

Key Words and Details: ____

____

Question

> **The woman expresses her opinion about the announcement by the student services office. Explain her opinion and the reasons she gives for holding it.**

📁 **Speaking** Now give your spoken response for 60 seconds. You may use the guided response to assist you.

Guided & Sample Response 🎧 2-53

The speakers are discussing the fact that the school will ________________________ to students next semester. This will let them ________________________. The woman supports this decision by the school. She tells the man two reasons that she is in favor of the school's decision. First, she states that the art books she must buy ________________________. However, the e-book versions are much less expensive. So she ________________________. She also notes that art books ________________________. Since she will have e-books in the future, she ________________________ around any heavy books.

Reading Read the following passage about short-term memory.

Short-Term Memory

People have both long-term memory and short-term memory. Long-term memories can stay with people for decades. Short-term memories disappear very quickly. Short-term memories may last only for a few seconds or minutes. Or they may last for a few hours or days. In most cases, short-term memories disappear because of the lack of importance of the memory. People keep their memories until they are no longer important. Then, their brains forget about the memories.

Listening Listen to a short lecture related to the reading. Take notes on key words and specific information from the lecture.   2-54

Notes

Topic:

Detail 1:

Detail 2:

Key Words:

Question

The professor talks about decay and interruption. Explain how they are related to short-term memory.

Speaking Now give your spoken response for 60 seconds. You may use the guided response to assist you.

Guided & Sample Response   2-55

The professor tells the students about how short-term memory can disappear. Short-term memories ___________________ long-term memories. ___________________ for a few seconds, minutes, hours, or days. Then, they disappear. One reason they disappear is decay. When you ___________________, it decays. The professor says that memories of ___________________ may decay. If you don't call a person for a while, you might forget that person's phone number. Interruption makes short-term memories disappear, too. ___________________, the professor received a text message. He read the message. However, because of the interruption, he forgot ___________________.

📁 **Listening** Listen to the following dialogue. Take notes as needed. 🎧 2-56

Notes

The Problem:

Solution 1:

Solution 2:

Speaking

Question

The students discuss two possible solutions to the woman's problem. Describe the problem. Then state which of the two solutions you prefer and explain why.

📁 **Speaking** Now give your spoken response for 60 seconds. You may use the guided response to assist you.

Guided & Sample Response 1: First Solution 🎧 2-57

The woman's problem is that she's having a party at her house, but _____________________.
_____________________, her house is going to be cold. The man and woman come up with two solutions to her problem. The first is for the woman to have the party _____________________ near her house. The second is for the woman to tell her guests to _____________________ to her house. I support the first solution because having the party at a restaurant will be _____________________. Secondly, the guests can help _____________________. If they do that, then the woman won't have to spend too much money.

Guided & Sample Response 2: Second Solution 🎧 2-58

The woman's problem is that she's having a party at her house, but _____________________.
_____________________, her house is going to be cold. The man and woman come up with two solutions to her problem. The first is for the woman to have the party _____________________ near her house. The second is for the woman to tell her guests to _____________________ to her house. I support the second solution because it _____________________ the woman money. She can't afford to go to a restaurant. Additionally, a party at a person's house is always fun. Even if it's cold, her guests will _____________________.

 # Psychology: Peer Reinforcement

Listening Listen to a lecture on history. Take notes on key words and concepts in the lecture.

2-59

Notes

Topic:

Detail 1:

Detail 2:

Key Words:

Question

Using points and examples from the talk, explain how peer reinforcement can improve students' behavior.

Speaking Now give your spoken response for 60 seconds. You may use the guided response to assist you.

Guided & Sample Response   2-60

In her lecture, the professor talks about peer reinforcement. She states that ___________________ to make some students behave. First, she explains how to do peer reinforcement. She tells the students ___________________ or say anything negative to bad students. Instead, they ___________________ who act properly. The bad students want ___________________. So they will begin behaving. The professor talks about her own personal experience. One girl never ___________________, but a boy did. She praised the boy and ___________________. Soon, the girl began to put her blocks away. So the professor praised her. The girl behaved well after that.

Chapter 4

Writing

Task 1 Sociology: The Shortage of Primary Care Doctors

Reading Read the passage carefully. Try to understand what the main argument of the passage is. You have 3 minutes to read.

The United States is suffering from a shortage of primary care doctors. In recent years, a large number of primary care doctors have been retiring. Unfortunately, they have not been replaced by the same number of doctors.

One reason for this shortage concerns the great expense of medical school. Recently, the cost of attending medical school has increased. Tuition at the top American medical schools is more than $50,000 a year. Students must also pay for their room and board and other expenditures. Since students typically do not work, most take out loans. After graduating, they have hundreds of thousands of dollars in loans to repay. Primary care doctors make lower salaries than other doctors. Thus few medical school students choose to become primary care doctors. It does not financially benefit them.

Another problem primary care doctors have is the large amount of paperwork they must do. These doctors see many patients each day. Because of insurance and other issues, they are constantly doing paperwork. This causes many doctors to work long hours. When doing paperwork, they are not earning any money. This makes being a primary care doctor unappealing to many people. Until the situation changes, the country will continue to have a shortage of these doctors.

Listening Now listen to part of a lecture on the topic you just read about. 3-01

Notes

📁 Tandem Note-Taking

<table>
<tr><td align="center">Reading</td><td align="center">Listening</td></tr>
<tr><td>

Main Idea:

First Supporting Argument:

Supporting Details:

Second Supporting Argument:

Supporting Details:

</td><td>

Main Idea:

First Supporting Argument:

Supporting Details:

Second Supporting Argument:

Supporting Details:

</td></tr>
</table>

Question

Summarize the points made in the lecture, being sure to explain how they cast doubt on specific points made in the reading passage.

📁 Writing Use this page to write your response. You have 20 minutes to complete your essay.

Task 2 Following Directions or Finding New Ways

Question

Some people think that employees who are good at following directions are ideal. Other people say that employees who try to find new ways to do something are better. What is your opinion? Use specific reasons and examples to support your answer.

📁 Planning

Following Directions	*Finding New Ways*
Thesis Statement:	Thesis Statement:
First Supporting Idea:	First Supporting Idea:
Supporting Examples:	Supporting Examples:
Second Supporting Idea:	Second Supporting Idea:
Supporting Examples:	Supporting Examples:
Conclusion:	Conclusion:

Unit 02

Task 1 Zoology: The American Burying Beetle

📁 **Reading** Read the passage carefully. Try to understand what the main argument of the passage is. You have 3 minutes to read.

The American burying beetle is a species of insect native to North America. It feeds on carrion—the bodies of dead animals. The beetle once lived all throughout North America. It was known to live in thirty-five American states. Yet, in the past century, the beetle population in the United States has declined dramatically. It is presently found in only five states.

Scientists suspect that the American burying beetle population has declined because humans have encroached on its territory. The beetle only eats carrion. So it needs dead animals in order to feed. Since humans have cut down forests and cleared fields, the beetle's habitats are being destroyed. So the beetle not only has less land to live on, but it also has fewer animals to feed on. Resultantly, its numbers have declined.

It is also possible that the beetles are being affected by chemicals used by farmers. The beetles have an acute sense of smell. They can detect dead animals from a great distance. They can also detect these animals soon after they die. But it is possible that certain chemicals farmers use interfere with their senses. These chemicals prevent the beetles from locating any food sources. So the beetles wind up starving to death.

📁 **Listening** Now listen to part of a lecture on the topic you just read about. 🎧 3-02

Notes

📁 Tandem Note-Taking

<table>
<tr><td>

Reading

Main Idea:

First Supporting Argument:

Supporting Details:

Second Supporting Argument:

Supporting Details:

</td><td>

Listening

Main Idea:

First Supporting Argument:

Supporting Details:

Second Supporting Argument:

Supporting Details:

</td></tr>
</table>

Writing

Question

Summarize the points made in the lecture, being sure to explain how they cast doubt on specific points made in the reading passage.

📁 Writing Use this page to write your response. You have 20 minutes to complete your essay.

 Helping Others

Question

Do you agree or disagree with the following statement? The young generation these days helps people more than previous generations did. Use specific reasons and examples to support your answer.

📁 Planning

Agree	Disagree
Thesis Statement:	Thesis Statement:
First Supporting Idea:	First Supporting Idea:
Supporting Examples:	Supporting Examples:
Second Supporting Idea:	Second Supporting Idea:
Supporting Examples:	Supporting Examples:
Conclusion:	Conclusion:

Writing

Unit 03

Task 1 Astronomy: The Ashen Light of Venus

Reading Read the passage carefully. Try to understand what the main argument of the passage is. You have 3 minutes to read.

Since 1643, observers of Venus have noticed something strange about the planet. The part of Venus that is unlit appears to emit a soft glowing light. This is known as the Ashen Light of Venus. No one is sure what causes it to occur.

One theory many believe is that lightning causes the glow on Venus. Venus has a very thick atmosphere. Thus storms often occur on its surface. In 2007, the satellite *Cassini* passed by Venus while going to Saturn. As it went by the planet, it made many observations. It detected some low-frequency waves that are sometimes caused by lightning. In addition, subsequent NASA missions have confirmed there is lightning on Venus. It may even get more lightning than Earth. So it is possible that lightning is causing the glow from Venus.

Others have suggested that the Ashen Light is not a product of Venus but comes from Earth instead. These people state that Earth's atmosphere distorts the light coming from Venus. For instance, high levels of humidity in the air can cause distortions in the atmosphere. So can precipitation such as rain or snow. When people observe Venus through telescopes during these weather conditions, they are seeing false images. So the Ashen Light may be merely an illusion.

Listening Now listen to part of a lecture on the topic you just read about. 3-03

Notes

📁 Tandem Note-Taking

<table>
<tr><th>Reading</th><th>Listening</th></tr>
<tr><td>Main Idea:</td><td>Main Idea:</td></tr>
<tr><td>First Supporting Argument:</td><td>First Supporting Argument:</td></tr>
<tr><td>Supporting Details:</td><td>Supporting Details:</td></tr>
<tr><td>Second Supporting Argument:</td><td>Second Supporting Argument:</td></tr>
<tr><td>Supporting Details:</td><td>Supporting Details:</td></tr>
</table>

Question

> Summarize the points made in the lecture, being sure to explain how they challenge specific arguments made in the reading passage.

📁 **Writing** Use this page to write your response. You have 20 minutes to complete your essay.

Task 2 Sharing Scientific Discoveries

Question

> Do you agree or disagree with the following statement? When scientists make a new discovery, they should share it with other people around the world. Use specific reasons and examples to support your answer.

📁 **Planning**

Agree	Disagree
Thesis Statement:	Thesis Statement:
First Supporting Idea:	First Supporting Idea:
Supporting Examples:	Supporting Examples:
Second Supporting Idea:	Second Supporting Idea:
Supporting Examples:	Supporting Examples:
Conclusion:	Conclusion:

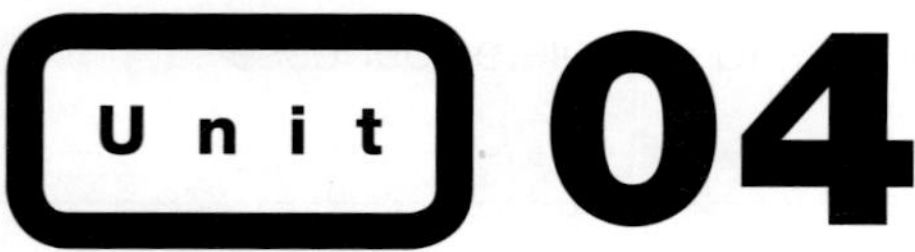

Task 1 Zoology: The Ivory-Billed Woodpecker

Reading Read the passage carefully. Try to understand what the main argument of the passage is. You have 3 minutes to read.

The ivory-billed woodpecker is a species of woodpecker that once lived in the Southeastern United States. Due to human expansion, the woodpecker population began declining in the 1800s. Today, it is considered an extinct species.

However, some people claim that the woodpecker is still alive. Recently, a person produced a picture of a bird that he claimed was an ivory-billed woodpecker. The bird in the picture is clearly a woodpecker. Yet the quality of the picture is bad. So it is difficult to get any details from the picture. Ivory-billed woodpeckers have distinct white and red markings that make them easy to recognize. However, the woodpecker in the picture does not appear to have those colors. So it most likely is not an ivory-billed woodpecker.

In the past few years, some researchers began looking for ivory-billed woodpecker nests yet found nothing. The birds make their nests in the trunks of dead trees. The researchers explored a large area of swampland. That is a preferred nesting location for the woodpeckers. Despite the extensive search, not a single ivory-billed woodpecker nest was found. There is simply no evidence that any ivory-billed woodpeckers are still alive. No one has seen any of them in years. In all likelihood, they are extinct.

Listening Now listen to part of a lecture on the topic you just read about. 3-04

Notes

📁 Tandem Note-Taking

Reading

Main Idea:

First Supporting Argument:

Supporting Details:

Second Supporting Argument:

Supporting Details:

Listening

Main Idea:

First Supporting Argument:

Supporting Details:

Second Supporting Argument:

Supporting Details:

Question

Summarize the points made in the lecture, being sure to explain how they challenge specific arguments made in the reading passage.

📁 **Writing** Use this page to write your response. You have 20 minutes to complete your essay.

Question

Do you agree or disagree with the following statement? It is important for the government to set aside land to protect wild animals and plants for future generations. Use specific reasons and examples to support your answer.

📁 Planning

Agree	*Disagree*
Thesis Statement:	Thesis Statement:
First Supporting Idea:	First Supporting Idea:
Supporting Examples:	Supporting Examples:
Second Supporting Idea:	Second Supporting Idea:
Supporting Examples:	Supporting Examples:
Conclusion:	Conclusion:

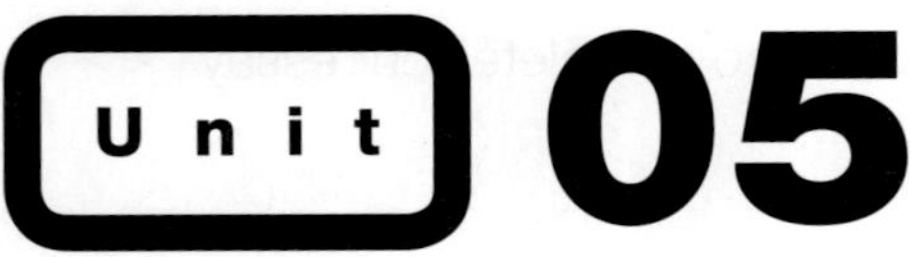

Task 1 Marine Biology: Turtle Exclusion Devices

Reading Read the passage carefully. Try to understand what the main argument of the passage is. You have 3 minutes to read.

Shrimpers—shrimp fishermen—often cast nets that reach the bottom of the ocean. These nets capture animals, such as sea turtles, other than shrimp. Therefore, the shrimpers utilize nets with turtle exclusion devices (TED). The TEDs enable turtles to escape from the net. Thus fewer turtles are being killed. Many TEDs do not work properly though. So the shrimpers' nets are still killing a lot of turtles.

Some people have suggested various ways to solve this problem. One idea is to make sure that all shrimpers bring their nets to the surface every few minutes. Turtles cannot breathe underwater. So they must surface to take in oxygen from the air. Many turtles drown when they get trapped in the nets. However, if shrimpers bring their nets above the surface soon after casting them, then fewer turtles will drown.

Another suggestion is that people make the TEDs larger. Many sea turtles grow to be quite large in size. For example, some loggerhead turtles can be more than 2.5 meters long. They may weigh more than 130 kilograms. These large turtles simply cannot escape from the TEDs. By making the devices larger, the turtles will be able to escape. And shrimpers will still be able to catch enough shrimp.

Listening Now listen to part of a lecture on the topic you just read about. 3-05

Notes

📁 Tandem Note-Taking

<table>
<tr><td>Reading</td><td>Listening</td></tr>
<tr><td>Main Idea:</td><td>Main Idea:</td></tr>
<tr><td>First Supporting Argument:</td><td>First Supporting Argument:</td></tr>
<tr><td>Supporting Details:</td><td>Supporting Details:</td></tr>
<tr><td>Second Supporting Argument:</td><td>Second Supporting Argument:</td></tr>
<tr><td>Supporting Details:</td><td>Supporting Details:</td></tr>
</table>

Writing

Question

Summarize the points made in the lecture, being sure to explain how they challenge specific claims made in the reading passage.

📁 Writing Use this page to write your response. You have 20 minutes to complete your essay.

Question

Some people think that the location is very important when they take a trip. Other people believe that it is more important to go on a trip with a good friend. What is your opinion? Use specific reasons and examples to support your answer.

📁 Planning

A Good Location	*A Good Friend*
Thesis Statement:	Thesis Statement:
First Supporting Idea:	First Supporting Idea:
Supporting Examples:	Supporting Examples:
Second Supporting Idea:	Second Supporting Idea:
Supporting Examples:	Supporting Examples:
Conclusion:	Conclusion:

Actual Test

Iceberg Formation

In the cold waters of the Arctic and North Atlantic oceans, ships' captains must be cautious. There are numerous large pieces of ice floating in the water. These icebergs can damage and sink any ships they hit.

2 → An iceberg resembles a small mountain in the ocean. It usually appears white on top and bluish on the bottom. This is due to how light reflects off its various surfaces. An iceberg may be any size and shape. Some are merely a few meters in size while others can extend for tens of kilometers. While some icebergs rise high out of the water, the bulk of their mass is found underwater.

Icebergs are always found in the oceans; however, they are not comprised of salt water. Instead, they are made of fresh water. In the Northern Hemisphere, the vast majority of icebergs come from glaciers or the edges of ice sheets in Greenland, Alaska, northern Canada, and parts of Scandinavia. Both glaciers and ice sheets tend to move or expand toward the ocean. When one of them reaches the ocean, its edge begins to float on the water. Then, both tides and waves start affecting the ice. This causes a process known as calving. Stress fractures appear in the ice. These widen and, eventually, result in a chunk of ice falling into the ocean. In that manner, an iceberg is formed.

4 → Experts believe that between 10,000 and 15,000 icebergs are created each year. Once the icebergs are floating freely in the ocean, they move with the tide, wind, and current. Many icebergs remain in the cold waters of the north. Others, however, find their way into warmer waters. As this happens, they melt and begin shrinking. Sometimes they break apart into smaller icebergs. Unfortunately, many icebergs drift into shipping lanes. The *Titanic* is the most famous ship sunk by an iceberg, but countless others have been lost because of them. Meanwhile, some icebergs reach land. These can obstruct harbors and clutter beaches. They remain problems until they melt entirely.

Glossary
chunk: a large piece
clutter: to make a mess; to fill up in a disorganized manner

1　The word extend in the passage is closest in meaning to
Ⓐ stretch
Ⓑ float
Ⓒ appear
Ⓓ last

2   Which of the sentences below best expresses the essential information in the highlighted sentence in the passage? Incorrect answer choices change the meaning in important ways or leave out essential information.

   Ⓐ The Northern Hemisphere has both glaciers and ice sheets in many different places.
   Ⓑ It is possible for icebergs to form from glaciers in the Northern Hemisphere.
   Ⓒ Most icebergs form in a number of different places in the Northern Hemisphere.
   Ⓓ In the Northern Hemisphere, there are many icebergs floating in the ocean.

3   In paragraph 2, the author's description of icebergs mentions all of the following EXCEPT:
   Ⓐ how large they may become
   Ⓑ how much they can weigh
   Ⓒ what colors they appear
   Ⓓ which appearance they have

4   In paragraph 4, why does the author mention The *Titanic*?
   Ⓐ To provide the ship's location when it went down
   Ⓑ To give the year when the ship was sunk
   Ⓒ To name a well-known ship sunk by an iceberg
   Ⓓ To explain exactly how the ship was hit

5   According to paragraph 4, which of the following is true of icebergs?
   Ⓐ They mostly remain near the glaciers that form them.
   Ⓑ They cause problems for people in a variety of ways.
   Ⓒ It can take several months for an iceberg to melt.
   Ⓓ In the past, they used to sink hundreds of ships a year.

The Radio and American Society

Italian inventor Guglielmo Marconi worked with radio waves in the late 1800s. He was chiefly interested in using them for communication. He was an early leader in the field. After Marconi, many others began working with radio waves as well. One result of their efforts was that public radio broadcasts started in the 1920s. They became very popular. By the 1930s, millions of people around the world were listening to the radio. Due to the high number of listeners, the radio greatly affected society during these two decades.

2 → In the 1920s, regular radio broadcasts began in the United States. Radio was an instant success. Radio stations swiftly appeared all over the country. They <u>aired</u> a variety of programs. These included news, sporting events, comedy shows, and dramas. Radio became one of the most popular forms of entertainment in the country. By the 1930s, it had become routine for Americans to sit around the radio to listen to the radio. These shared experiences helped bring the country together. For instance, millions of people were able to listen to live sporting events such as baseball games and boxing matches. No longer did they have to wait until the next day to read the results in the newspaper.

3 → In the 1930s, the United States was in the middle of the Great Depression. It caused severe problems to the national economy. In the early 1940s, the country was fighting World War II. This was a bleak time in the nation's history. President Franklin D. Roosevelt learned to use the radio to great effect. From 1933 to 1944, he gave a series of radio broadcasts. They were called fireside chats. His talks explained the problems facing the country. He provided comfort and support to the American people during these times of trouble.

People found uses for the radio in virtually all <u>facets</u> of society. The military used radio to send and receive messages. Ships and airplanes employed it, too. They were able to receive weather reports. And they used the radio to send messages when they had trouble.

Glossary
air: to broadcast on the radio or television
facet: an area; an aspect

---

6   The word They in the passage refers to
   Ⓐ Radio waves
   Ⓑ Their efforts
   Ⓒ Public radio broadcasts
   Ⓓ The 1920s

7 According to paragraph 2, radio made Americans feel closer to one another because
   (A) it allowed them to share certain experiences
   (B) they often listened to comedies and dramas on it
   (C) there were radio stations everywhere in the country
   (D) it increased the popularity of sporting events

8 The word bleak in the passage is closest in meaning to
   (A) disappointing
   (B) revealing
   (C) violent
   (D) miserable

9 The author discusses fireside chats in paragraph 3 in order to
   (A) note the information that they covered
   (B) describe an effective use of radio
   (C) mention a useful news broadcasting method
   (D) explain President Roosevelt's popularity

10 **Directions:** An introductory sentence for a brief summary of the passage is provided below. Complete the summary by selecting the THREE answer choices that express the most important ideas of the passage. Some sentences do not belong because they express ideas that are not presented in the passage or are minor ideas in the passage. **This question is worth 2 points.**

> Drag your answer choices to the spaces where they belong.
> To remove an answer choice, click on it. To review the passage, click on **View Text**.

The early years of radio broadcasts affected American society in many ways.
-
-
-

Answer Choices

1. President Roosevelt's fireside chats helped comfort many Americans.
2. The first public radio stations began to appear during the 1920s.
3. People listened to numerous shows on radio stations around the country.
4. Marconi did some of the most important work in radio wave transmissions.
5. It was possible for ships to transmit information over the radio.
6. Americans were brought together by listening to radio broadcasts.

The Orangutan

There are many primates, including gorillas, monkeys, chimpanzees, and humans. One of the most unique primates lives in parts of Indonesia and Malaysia. It is the orangutan. This animal is extremely intelligent. After the gorilla, it is the animal most closely related to humans. Unfortunately, it is an endangered species that faces extinction in the near future.

The orangutan is simple to identify due to its physical features. It has a thick neck, long and strong arms, and <u>bowed</u> legs. Unlike some primates, it lacks a tail. Its most easily identifiable feature is its hair. It has long reddish hair that covers its body except for the face. There are two types of orangutans. The first has a round face and dark hair. ■ The second has a narrow face and light hair. ■ Both, however, have hands with opposable thumbs. ■ And they have a lifespan ranging from thirty to fifty years. ■

3 → The orangutan makes its home in tropical rainforests. It prefers to stay high in the trees rather than to spend time on the ground. As a result, it has evolved to have strong arms. This makes climbing trees an easy task. The orangutan is <u>diurnal</u> rather than nocturnal. It sleeps at night in platforms or nests that it builds in trees. These are made from leaves and branches. An omnivore, it mainly eats plants, preferring fruit. But it also eats leaves, seeds, tree bark, flowers, and plant bulbs. It occasionally eats meat—mostly from small animals.

4 → Unlike many primates, the orangutan is not a social animal. Males tend to live alone. They only socialize with females for a few days each year. They do this for the purpose of mating. The females then raise their offspring alone. Baby orangutans remain with their mothers for about seven years until they reach maturity.

The orangutan's habitat is presently shrinking. One reason is that humans are cutting down the rainforests where it lives. Another is that many baby orangutans are being captured to be raised in captivity in zoos. Sadly, the orangutan is now endangered. And its numbers are decreasing every year.

Glossary
bowed: bent; curved outward
diurnal: awake and active during the day

---

11 Which of the following can be inferred from paragraph 3 about the orangutan?
    (A) It hunts some animals with other orangutans.
    (B) It is more active during the day than at night.
    (C) It uses vines to swing from tree to tree.
    (D) It lives in areas that lack a variety of foods.

12 In paragraph 3, the author's description of the food the orangutan eats mentions all of the following EXCEPT:

(A) It consumes more meat than vegetation.
(B) It enjoys a variety of plant products.
(C) Of all foods, it likes to eat fruit the most.
(D) It eats both meat and plant products.

13 According to paragraph 4, why do male orangutans spend time with female orangutans?

(A) To raise their babies together
(B) To mate in order to produce offspring
(C) To provide protection from predators
(D) To keep from becoming too lonely

14 The word captivity in the passage is closest in meaning to

(A) obedience
(B) perpetuity
(C) consideration
(D) custody

15 Look at the four squares [■] that indicate where the following sentence could be added to the passage.

These enable the orangutan to make use of simple tools, such as for hunting.

Where would the sentence best fit?
Click on a square [■] to add the sentence to the passage.

Measuring Earthquakes

The Earth's crust is comprised of numerous plates. Some cover an enormous amount of land. Others are smaller. These plates are not stationary but move toward or away from one another and sometimes even collide. When they move, the ground shakes. This is known as an earthquake, or seism. Earthquakes vary in their strength. Most are so weak that people cannot perceive them. Others can be felt by people and may cause minor damage. A few are so violent that they destroy entire cities. Due to the varied nature of earthquakes, scientists have devised ways to measure them. There are two methods they primarily utilize.

2 → The most well-known system for measuring earthquakes is the Richter scale. American scientist Charles Richter developed it in 1935. The Richter scale measures tremors by rating them with numbers starting at zero. It employs seismographs in doing so. These instruments have needles that vibrate during an earthquake. The needles make marks on paper. These marks record the intensity of the vibrations. There are seismographs located around the world. By taking measurements from different seismographs, scientists can determine exactly how powerful an earthquake is. ■ The weakest earthquakes are at the low end of the Richter scale. ■ Any tremor measuring two or less cannot be felt by people. ■ Earthquakes that can cause significant damage and deaths measure six or higher. ■ The most powerful earthquake ever recorded measured 9.5 on the Richter scale.

Some scientists do not utilize the Richter scale but instead measure earthquakes in another way. They rate tremors based upon how much damage they cause. After an earthquake, these scientists examine the damage done to the buildings and land in the affected area. Then, they rate the earthquake. This method is not as reliable as the Richter scale for two reasons. Firstly, uninhabited areas may be hit by powerful earthquakes yet receive low ratings since no buildings are damaged. Secondly, people in countries prone to earthquakes, such as Japan, construct earthquake-resistant buildings. Thus a strong earthquake may cause little damage in Japan while a less powerful one elsewhere may cause a tremendous amount of damage.

Glossary
perceive: to sense; to feel
tremor: an earthquake; a vibration

---

1 The word they in the passage refers to
   Ⓐ earthquakes
   Ⓑ scientists
   Ⓒ ways to measure them
   Ⓓ two methods

2 In paragraph 2, why does the author mention Charles Richter?
  (A) To credit him with inventing the Richter scale
  (B) To focus on his studies of earthquakes
  (C) To provide information about his personal life
  (D) To list some of his scientific achievements

3 The word uninhabited in the passage is closest in meaning to
  (A) undiscovered
  (B) unreported
  (C) unpopulated
  (D) unapproved

4 Look at the four squares [■] that indicate where the following sentence could be added to the passage.

For example, the San Francisco earthquake of 1906, which killed more than 3,000 people, measured about 7.8.

Where would the sentence best fit?
Click on a square [■] to add the sentence to the passage.

5 **Directions:** An introductory sentence for a brief summary of the passage is provided below. Complete the summary by selecting the THREE answer choices that express the most important ideas of the passage. Some sentences do not belong because they express ideas that are not presented in the passage or are minor ideas in the passage. **This question is worth 2 points.**

Drag your answer choices to the spaces where they belong.
To remove an answer choice, click on it. To review the passage, click on **View Text**.

Scientists have come up with two primary ways in which they measure the strength of earthquakes.

-
-
-

Answer Choices

1. The Japanese people construct buildings that can withstand earthquakes.
2. The Richter scale is the more accurate way to determine an earthquake's power.
3. Some consider the damage an earthquake causes when measuring its strength.
4. Most people use the Richter scale to measure earthquake intensity.
5. Plates in the Earth's crust move, which is what causes earthquakes to happen.
6. The majority of earthquakes on the planet are not felt by people at all.

Ponce de Leon

After Christopher Columbus discovered the New World in 1492, the Spanish began sending many expeditions across the Atlantic Ocean. Both members of the lower class and nobility made their way to the newly discovered continent. One nobleman who traveled there was Juan Ponce de Leon. Born in 1474, Ponce de Leon sailed with Christopher Columbus on his second trip to the New World. This was the beginning of a long career abroad.

On his voyage with Columbus, Ponce de Leon explored the island of Hispaniola. The next few years of his life are hazy. He may have remained in the New World the entire time, or he may have returned to Spain. By 1504, however, he was definitely in Hispaniola. At that time, he engaged in battle against the natives of the island. As a reward for his leadership, he was made a governor of a province there.

3 → In his role as governor, Ponce de Leon often met with members of native tribes. He heard many stories about a place that had both fertile land and extensive amounts of gold. In 1508, Ponce de Leon led an expedition of Puerto Rico in search of this place. He found some gold there and was subsequently named the governor of the island. While in Puerto Rico, he continued to hear stories from the natives. Some stories told of a land located to the northwest. And others concerned Bimini, an island in the Bahamas.

4 → According to legend, the Fountain of Youth was located on Bimini. The fountain supposedly had waters that would grant eternal youth to anybody who bathed in it. Intrigued, Ponce de Leon organized an expedition to find the fountain. It sailed in 1513, and Ponce de Leon and his men landed near the present-day city of St. Augustine, Florida. He and his men thought they were on an island but instead had arrived in North America. They explored Florida, as he called it, for eight months. Years later, in 1521, Ponce de Leon returned to Florida. There, he was wounded by natives in a battle and died soon afterward.

Glossary
subsequently: consequently; as a result
intrigued: interested in; curious about

---

6 Which of the sentences below best expresses the essential information in the highlighted sentence in the passage? Incorrect answer choices change the meaning in important ways or leave out essential information.

   Ⓐ People of various social standings sailed to the New World.
   Ⓑ More members of the lower class than the nobility went abroad.
   Ⓒ It was people from both social classes that discovered the New World.
   Ⓓ On the new continent, social classes were of little importance.

7　The word hazy in the passage is closest in meaning to
　　Ⓐ　ignored
　　Ⓑ　approved
　　Ⓒ　unclear
　　Ⓓ　distant

8　According to paragraph 3, Ponce de Leon went to Puerto Rico because
　　Ⓐ　the Spanish appointed him the island's governor
　　Ⓑ　he was searching for the Fountain of Youth
　　Ⓒ　the natives advised him to visit the island
　　Ⓓ　he wanted to find both fertile land and gold

9　The word it in the passage refers to
　　Ⓐ　legend
　　Ⓑ　the Fountain of Youth
　　Ⓒ　Bimini
　　Ⓓ　eternal youth

10　According to paragraph 4, which of the following is NOT true of the Fountain of Youth?
　　Ⓐ　Some stories claimed that it was in Florida.
　　Ⓑ　People believed that it had special powers.
　　Ⓒ　Ponce de Leon and his men searched for it.
　　Ⓓ　It was reported to be located on Bimini.

Plant Defenses against Herbivores

Many animals are herbivores. Therefore they obtain their nutrition from plants. Some consume fruit and nectar while others eat leaves or the plants themselves. In response to these animals, plants have evolved a number of defensive systems over time. There are three primary types of defenses that plants employ. They are physical defenses, chemical defenses, and mutual relationships with other organisms.

2 → Physical defenses—also known as mechanical defenses—are found on a plant's surface. For instance, thorns are one common physical defense. Plants such as blackberries and raspberries have <u>thorns</u>. These prevent animals from eating their fruits. Many animals are unwilling to be wounded by the thorns. So they leave plants with them alone. Other plants, particularly trees, have branches high above the ground rather than near it. This keeps animals such as deer from eating their leaves. Other plants have strong shells around their fruits or nuts. Two examples of these are walnuts and coconuts.

3 → Plant chemical defenses are those that involve chemical compounds. The chemicals utilized have nothing to do with a plant's growth or reproduction. They are secondary chemicals instead. A common chemical defense is one that makes the plant taste bad to herbivores. When a plant's leaves have large amount of <u>alkaloids</u>, for instance, they may taste bitter to animals. Thus animals learn not to eat these leaves. Other plants, such as poison ivy, can cause skin discomfort in animals. This makes them avoid these plants in the future. Some plants even have chemical defenses that can upset the digestive systems of animals.

The third primary type of plant defense is mutualism. This is a form of symbiosis. In mutualism, the plant and another organism—typically an animal—have a close relationship. The plant provides something, such as food or shelter, for the animal. In return, the animal offers protection. The acacia tree engages in this kind of relationship with a species of ant. The ant lives in the tree and eats its nectar. In return, the ant attacks and drives away other creatures that try to eat the leaves of the tree.

Glossary

thorn: a sharp spine on the branch of a plant
alkaloid: a compound that has a bitter taste

---

11 According to paragraph 2, which of the following is NOT true of plant physical defenses?
- Ⓐ They may offer protection to a plant's fruit.
- Ⓑ They can cause animals to fear some plants.
- Ⓒ They are located on the surfaces of plants.
- Ⓓ They can cause harm to some animals.

12 According to paragraph 3, animals avoid poison ivy because
   Ⓐ it gives them discomfort in their stomachs
   Ⓑ it can make some of them die
   Ⓒ it tastes bitter to most of them
   Ⓓ it causes them to develop skin problems

13 In paragraph 3, the author implies that mutualism
   Ⓐ happens more often between plants than animals
   Ⓑ lets both organisms benefit from their relationship
   Ⓒ is the most common of all types of plant defenses
   Ⓓ ends when one organism stops helping the other

14 In paragraph 3, the author's description of the acacia tree mentions which of the following?
   Ⓐ It has a mutual relationship with the acacia ant.
   Ⓑ It lets various species of ants live in its branches.
   Ⓒ It only grows in certain regions in the world.
   Ⓓ It provides nectar for the ants that protect it.

15 **Directions:** Select the appropriate statements from the answer choices and match them to the plant defense to which they relate. TWO of the answer choices will NOT be used. **This question is worth 3 points.**

Drag your answer choices to the spaces where they belong.
To remove an answer choice, click on it. To review the passage, click on **View Text**.

Answer Choices

1. Is the method employed by poison ivy
2. Makes animals avoid the plants at later times
3. Involves the acacia tree and a type of ant
4. Happens when branches grow high above the ground
5. May result in leaves tasting bad to animals
6. Takes place between two different organisms
7. Is utilized by walnut and coconut trees

INSECT

Physical (Select 2)
-
-

Chemical (Select 3)
-
-
-

Conversation 1~4: Listen to part of a conversation between a student and a professor.  4-01

1 Why does the student visit the professor?

(A) To show her the classes she wants to take

(B) To ask her about taking a trip abroad

(C) To find out what her major requirements are

(D) To talk about her previous semester

2 What is the professor's attitude toward the student?

(A) She thinks the student is bragging too much.

(B) She is complimentary of the student's actions.

(C) She wants the student to work a little harder.

(D) She believes the student has earned her grades.

3 What will the student probably do next?

(A) Show the professor some pictures of her trip

(B) Make a visit to the Registrar's Office

(C) Sign up for the professor's class

(D) Complete some work in her science class

4 Listen again to part of the conversation. Then answer the question.
What does the student imply when she says this:

(A) She plans to return to Spain one day.

(B) She is embarrassed about her behavior.

(C) She got back from Spain a few days ago.

(D) She wanted to stay in Spain longer.

Lecture 5~8: Listen to part of a lecture in a marine biology class. 

5   What is the lecture mainly about?
   - (A) The food the giant tortoise consumes
   - (B) The characteristics of the giant tortoise
   - (C) Where the giant tortoise usually lives
   - (D) The animals that hunt the giant tortoise

6   Why does the professor mention a giant tortoise that lived in an Australian zoo?
   - (A) To note that it can survive in captivity
   - (B) To show the students a picture of it
   - (C) To state that it successfully mated there
   - (D) To point out how many years it lived

7   In the lecture, the professor describes a number of facts about the giant tortoise. Indicate whether each of the following is a fact or not.
Click in the correct box for each statement.

	Fact	Not a Fact
1 It may weigh several hundred kilograms.		
2 It takes care of its young after they hatch.		
3 It has no need to drink water.		
4 It does not mate until it is at least twenty years old.		

8   According to the professor, which animals are noted for hunting and killing baby giant tortoises?
   - (A) Sharks
   - (B) Snakes
   - (C) Birds
   - (D) Rats

9 What is the main topic of the lecture?
  (A) Different types of complementary goods
  (B) The most well-known complementary goods
  (C) Complementary goods and the stores that sell them
  (D) Why people need complementary goods

10 Why does the professor tell the students that he never eats mustard?
  (A) To make sure that they know one of his personal preferences
  (B) To describe one of his shopping habits at the supermarket
  (C) To show that it is not always a complementary good for hotdogs
  (D) To explain why he dislikes one of the most popular condiments

11 What does the professor say about gas stations?
  (A) They make the greatest profits for oil companies.
  (B) They are the cheapest places to acquire gasoline.
  (C) They are mostly owned by various oil companies.
  (D) They sell a number of products that cars need to run.

12 How is the lecture organized?
  (A) The professor provides some demonstrations for the students.
  (B) The professor defines a term and then gives examples of it.
  (C) The professor shows a short film and then lectures on it.
  (D) The professor reads from prepared notes and asks for student input.

4-04

13 Why does the student visit the resident assistant?
  Ⓐ To complain about some students
  Ⓑ To request a change in roommates
  Ⓒ To ask to move to another floor
  Ⓓ To respond to an email he sent her

14 What does the student imply about Lewis and Walt?
  Ⓐ They sometimes go to her room to speak with her.
  Ⓑ They are first-year students at the school.
  Ⓒ They constantly listen to music in their room.
  Ⓓ They rarely do any studying in their room.

15 In the conversation, the student describes a number of facts about Lewis and Walt. Indicate whether each of the following is a fact or not.
Click in the correct box for each statement.

	Fact	Not a Fact
1 She lives in the dormitory room next to them.		
2 Both of them are majoring in the same field as her.		
3 They have too many late-night parties in their room.		
4 She has problems studying in her room because of them.		

16 What is the student's opinion of Lewis and Walt?
  Ⓐ She thinks that they are funny.
  Ⓑ She enjoys their company.
  Ⓒ She says they are both impolite.
  Ⓓ She cannot stand speaking with them.

17 What is the lecture mainly about?
- Ⓐ The healing properties of gemstones
- Ⓑ The scarcity and value of gemstones
- Ⓒ The various uses of gemstones
- Ⓓ The most valuable gemstones

18 What is a facet?
- Ⓐ A measurement of the size of a gemstone
- Ⓑ A gemstone that is considered very rare
- Ⓒ An industrial application used on gemstones
- Ⓓ A small, flat section cut into a gemstone

19 Based on the information in the lecture, indicate which gemstone the statements refer to. Click in the correct box for each statement.

	Diamond	Ruby
1 Is used on saws and other cutting tools		
2 Is utilized in some lasers		
3 Is the hardest known substance		
4 Is mostly used for jewelry in its natural form		

20 What is the professor's opinion of the theory that gemstones can affect people's bodies?
- Ⓐ He thinks that the theory is right.
- Ⓑ He does not know if it is true or not.
- Ⓒ He claims no evidence supports the theory.
- Ⓓ He believes that the theory is incorrect.

21 Which aspect of Australia does the professor mainly discuss?
- (A) Captain Cook and his voyage to the continent
- (B) Its discovery and colonization by the Europeans
- (C) The Aborigines and the culture they created there
- (D) The first settlement by the British at Botany Bay

22 Which country was the first ship that landed on Australia from?
- (A) Great Britain
- (B) Spain
- (C) the Netherlands
- (D) the United States

23 Why does the professor mention the American Revolution?
- (A) To explain why the British decided to colonize Australia
- (B) To note some of the key events that happened in that war
- (C) To state that many British convicts fought during it
- (D) To claim that Britain colonized Australia while fighting it

24 What will the professor probably do next?
- (A) Talk about Captain Cook
- (B) Discuss the first Australian colony
- (C) Detail the history of the Aborigines
- (D) Name some famous convicts

Conversation 1~4: Listen to part of a conversation between a student and a professor  4-07

---

1   What is the student's problem?
   (A) She is unhappy with a grade she received.
   (B) She cannot register for a certain class.
   (C) She dislikes the professor's teaching style.
   (D) She rarely speaks in class discussions.

2   What can be inferred about the student?
   (A) She is currently a sophomore.
   (B) She has to attend a class soon.
   (C) The professor is her favorite teacher.
   (D) She is majoring in history.

3   What does the professor offer to do for the student?
   (A) Allow her to enroll in the class
   (B) Put her on the class waitlist
   (C) Review her paper one more time
   (D) Let her take the test another time

4   Listen again to part of the conversation. Then answer the question.
   What can be inferred from the professor's response to the student:
   (A) She speaks too quickly at times.
   (B) The professor will consider her argument.
   (C) The student's assumption is wrong.
   (D) There is no way to help the student.

5   According to the professor, what physical characteristics do all birds of prey share?
Click on 2 answers.

- [1]   They have sharp talons and beaks.
- [2]   Their wings have the same shape.
- [3]   They prefer to hunt during the day.
- [4]   They are able to see very well.

6   How does the professor organize the information about the physical characteristics of birds of prey that he presents to the class?

- Ⓐ   By beginning with the differences and ending with the similarities
- Ⓑ   By focusing mainly on their wings and feathers
- Ⓒ   By showing the class slides of some birds
- Ⓓ   By talking mostly about eagles, owls, and condors

7   Why does the professor explain the term carrion?

- Ⓐ   Because a student misused the term when asking a question
- Ⓑ   Because he thinks that the class looks confused
- Ⓒ   Because a student does not know what it means
- Ⓓ   Because he believes the word is unknown to most students

8   Listen again to part of the lecture. Then answer the question.
What does the professor mean when he says this: 🎧

- Ⓐ   There are few elf owls in their region.
- Ⓑ   The elf owl weighs a very small amount.
- Ⓒ   Some elf owls can become quite large.
- Ⓓ   He has never seen an elf owl before.

9   What aspect of *The Canterbury Tales* does the professor mainly discuss?
- Ⓐ The stories told in it
- Ⓑ The process of writing it
- Ⓒ The language it was written in
- Ⓓ The background of the story

10 What is the professor's opinion of *The Canterbury Tales*?
- Ⓐ Many of its stories are not interesting.
- Ⓑ It is Geoffrey Chaucer's greatest work.
- Ⓒ No work in Middle English is better than it.
- Ⓓ The fact it is incomplete detracts from its value.

11 What are many of the themes of *The Canterbury Tales* about?
- Ⓐ Religion
- Ⓑ Chivalry
- Ⓒ Pilgrimages
- Ⓓ Social values

12 What does the professor imply about the students?
- Ⓐ They will enjoy most of the stories in the poems.
- Ⓑ They will have some trouble reading the poems.
- Ⓒ They will need a dictionary to understand some words.
- Ⓓ They will enjoy *The Canterbury Tales* more than other poems.

---

13 What are the speakers mainly discussing?
- Ⓐ Where the library's new books are
- Ⓑ How the student can make a library card
- Ⓒ How to get a book the student wants
- Ⓓ When the student's books are due

14 Why does the librarian explain how to put a hold on a book?
- Ⓐ To answer a question the student asks
- Ⓑ To say how quickly she can do it
- Ⓒ To encourage the student to get the book another way
- Ⓓ To mention that it might not be effective

15 What does the librarian ask the student to do?
Click on 2 answers.
- ☐1 Come back later in the day
- ☐2 Show his ID card to her
- ☐3 Return all of the books he has
- ☐4 Complete a form she gives him

16 What will the student probably do next?
- Ⓐ Fill out a form
- Ⓑ Leave the library
- Ⓒ Renew his books
- Ⓓ Check out a book

Lecture 17~20: Listen to part of a lecture in a physics class.  4-11

---

17 What is a swell?

   Ⓐ The highest point on a wave

   Ⓑ Wavelike motion in the absence of wind

   Ⓒ The energy that is produced by a wave

   Ⓓ The lowest point on a wave

18 Based on the information in the lecture, indicate which aspect of wave formation the statements refer to.

Click in the correct box for each statement.

	Wind	Fetch
1 Results in small waves on lakes and rivers		
2 Can make high waves when it blows quickly		
3 Is very concerned with distance		
4 Creates friction on the surface of the water		

19 What does the professor imply about monster waves?

   Ⓐ They are responsible for sinking many ships.

   Ⓑ They may kill people on occasion.

   Ⓒ They can form on some lakes and rivers.

   Ⓓ People near the coast must often watch for them.

20 Listen again to part of the lecture. Then answer the question.
What does the professor imply when he says this: 🎧

   Ⓐ He had not intended to talk about that topic.

   Ⓑ He thinks the topic he covered is interesting.

   Ⓒ He feels bad about going over a difficult topic.

   Ⓓ He wants the students to ask him some questions.

---

21 What is the main topic of the lecture?
- Ⓐ Adolf Hitler and Josef Stalin
- Ⓑ The division of Germany and Berlin
- Ⓒ The reasons the Cold War began
- Ⓓ The years between World War I and World War II

22 According to the professor, what took place after the Russian Revolution?
- Ⓐ World War I
- Ⓑ World War II
- Ⓒ The Russian Civil War
- Ⓓ The Korean War

23 Why does the professor discuss Winston Churchill?
- Ⓐ To give the years when he was prime minister
- Ⓑ To focus on his relationship with Josef Stalin
- Ⓒ To describe his role during the Cold War
- Ⓓ To note his creation of a popular term

24 What will the professor probably do next?
- Ⓐ Show some slides to the class
- Ⓑ Continue lecturing to the students
- Ⓒ Let a student give her presentation
- Ⓓ Allow the students to take a break

Task 1

What do you think of Internet shopping? Include specific details and reasons in your response.

Preparation time: 15 seconds
Response time: 45 seconds

Sample Response 4-13

Task 2

Do you agree or disagree with the following statement? Student evaluations of their teachers provide valuable information. Include specific details and reasons in your response.

Preparation time: 15 seconds
Response time: 45 seconds

Sample Response 1 4-14 / *Sample Response 2* 4-15

Reading

Reading time: 45 seconds

Payphones to Be Removed from Dormitories

All of the payphones in the university's dormitories will be removed this Saturday, October 3. The telephones are rarely used nowadays because most students have cellular phones. In addition, the university is losing money on the pay phones. It has to pay to install and maintain the phones. And it must pay monthly bills. Thus the administration has decided to save money by removing the phones. The payphones in academic buildings, however, will not be removed.

Listening

The woman expresses her opinion about the announcement by the school's management office. Explain her opinion and the reasons she gives for holding it.

Preparation time: 30 seconds
Response time: 60 seconds

Sample Response 

Reading

Reading time: 45 seconds

Animal Cooperation

Animals of the same species often cooperate with one another. They act together in many ways. They sometimes forage or hunt for food together. Adults often protect newborn or young animals from predators. When some animals are feeding, others may watch for predators or other forms of danger. By cooperating with one another, animals can be sure to get enough food and to keep themselves safe. This allows them to live longer lives.

Listening 

The professor talks about how monkeys behave around one another. Explain how their actions are related to animal cooperation.

Preparation time: 30 seconds
Response time: 60 seconds

Sample Response 4-19

Listening

The students discuss two possible solutions to the man's problem. Describe the problem. Then state which of the two solutions you prefer and explain why.

Preparation time: 30 seconds
Response time: 60 seconds

Sample Response 1  */ Sample Response 2* 

Listening

Using points and examples from the talk, explain the importance of the positions of birds' eyes.

Preparation time: 30 seconds
Response time: 60 seconds

Sample Response 4-24

Task 1

Reading

In North America, there are several species of pine beetles. These beetles kill enormous numbers of pine trees every year. In fact, they are responsible for killing more pine trees than anything else. Forests infested with pine beetles can suffer the deaths of thousands of trees. Fortunately, there are some defenses against pine beetles.

One defense for pine trees comes from nature itself: cold weather. Pine trees often grow in regions in North America that get cold weather. They may grow high in the mountains or in areas with cold winters. Pine beetles do not respond well to cold weather. This is especially true if the temperature remains cold for a long period of time. As insects, pine beetles cannot function in cold weather. When there are freezing temperatures, the beetles often die. Thus nature is responsible for killing large numbers of beetles.

Pine beetles tend to attack trees that are old and sickly. These trees are the most vulnerable. Young and mature trees can often protect themselves from pine beetles. As a result, there are efforts in some forests to cut down old and sick trees. This deprives pine beetles of ideal trees to attack. By cutting down vulnerable trees, people can get rid of pine beetles. Without any pine beetles, the entire forest will be safe from them.

Listening

Directions: You have 20 minutes to plan and write your response. Your response will be judged on the basis of the quality of your writing and on how well your response presents the points in the lecture and their relationship to the reading passage. Typically, an effective response will be 150 to 225 words.

Question

Summarize the points made in the lecture, being sure to explain how they challenge specific claims made in the reading passage.

Directions: Read the question below. You have 30 minutes to plan, write, and revise your essay. Typically, an effective response will contain a minimum of 300 words.

Question

Some people prefer to discuss an upsetting problem by email. Other people think that it is better to talk about an upsetting problem over the telephone. What is your opinion?

Use specific reasons and examples to support your answer.

Memo

Smart TOEFL® iBT Answers

Pre-Intermediate **2**

DARAKWON

Smart TOEFL® iBT Answers

Pre-Intermediate 2

DARAKWON

Answers, Scripts, and Translations

Chapter 1

Reading

Unit 01
p.10

Sample Factual Information Question

Translation

수 세기 동안, 사람들은 바다에서 자라는 다양한 식물들의 용도를 찾아내고 있다. 해초의 일종인 켈프가 그러한 것 중 하나이다. 여러 종의 켈프가 존재한다. 대부분은 식품이나 의약품으로서의 가치를 지니고 있다. 예를 들어, 일부 문화권에서는, 이를 오랫동안 섭취해 왔다. 이러한 점은 특히 아시아 국가의 사람들에게 사실이다. 주로 켈프를 건조시킨 다음, 생선과 같은 다른 음식들과 함께 이를 먹는다. 보다 최근에는, 켈프가 때때로 아이스크림의 재료에 포함되고 있으며, 또한 특정 음식에 있어서는 음식을 걸쭉하게 만드는 성분으로 사용되고 있다. 켈프는 의약품으로서도 가치가 높다. 켈프는 체내의 신진대사를 향상시켜 주는 호르몬을 생성시키기 때문에, 갑상선 문제를 가지고 있는 사람들이 주로 이것을 먹는다. 마지막으로, 켈프는 관절 통증을 완화시켜 줄 수 있기 때문에, 많은 노인들이 이를 가치 있게 여기고 있다. 관절염 환자들에게 매우 유익하다.

Mini Test 1

Answers

1. Ⓑ (Sentence Simplification Question)
2. Ⓐ (Factual Question)
3. Ⓓ (Inference Question)
4. 3, 5, 6 (Prose Summary Question)

Translation

토템폴

종종 미 원주민 부족들은 그들의 예술 작품으로 유명하다. 일부 경우, 이들은 아름다운 보석 제품들을 만든다. 몇몇 부족들은 암면 미술을 만드는 반면, 동굴 벽에 벽화를 그리는 부족들도 있다. 그러나, 논란의 여지는 있지만, 미 원주민 예술 중에 가장 인상적인 작품은 북아메리카의 태평양 연안 북서쪽 지역에서 나오는 것이다. 여기에는 워싱턴과 알래스카 주뿐만 아니라 캐나다의 브리티쉬 컬럼비아도 포함된다. 이들 지역에 있는 부족의 구성원들은 수 천년 동안 토템폴을 제작해 왔다.

토템폴은 나무의 몸통으로 만들어진 커다란 기념물이다. 크기가 다양하다. 일부는 1미터 정도의 높이이며, 12미터 이상의 높이까지 올라가는 것들도 있다. 토템폴에는 다양한 조각들이 새겨져 있다. 통상적으로 나무에 인간과 동물의 얼굴들이 새겨져 있다. 일부 토템폴에서는 새의 날개 모양을 한 부분이 튀어나와 있는 경우도 있다. 디자인 및 그 안에 새겨져 있는 대상들이 모두 다르기 때문에, 두 개의 토템폴이 똑같은 경우는 없다.

대부분의 토템폴은 붉은 삼나무로 만들어진다. 먼저, 나무를 필요한 길이로 자르고, 그 껍질을 벗겨낸다. 그런 다음 조각가가 토템폴에 기본적인 윤곽선을 그린다. 조각가가 위쪽으로 작업을 해나가기 때문에, 토템폴의 하단이 먼저 모양을 드러낸다. 조각이 완료되면, 그 다음에 토템폴을 색칠한다. 전체 과정에 2개월에서 8개월 정도가 소요될 수 있다. 그림이 마르면, 토템폴은 최종 위치에 세워지고, 이때 포틀래치라고 불리는 특별한 의식이 개최된다.

1700년대에 제임스 쿡 선상이 최초로 몇몇 토템폴을 발견한 후, 그는 이것이 "괴물 형상"이라고 생각했다. 하지만 그의 설명은 잘못된 것이었다. 토템폴은 아름다우며 중요한 기능을 수행한다. 종종 이야기를 말해 준다. 부족의 전설이나 혹은 각 가족들의 역사를 이야기해 줄 수도 있다. 한 부족의 문화적 신념을 나타낼 수도 있다. 그리고 중요한 인물들을 추모하기 위해 사용될 수도 있다. 하지만, 종교적 우상은 아니며, 그렇기 때문에 종교적인 의식과는 관련이 없다.

Mini Test 2

Answers

1. Ⓐ (Rhetorical Purpose Question)
2. Ⓒ (Inference Question)
3. Ⓑ (Vocabulary Question)
4. Ⓒ (Factual Question)
5. 3rd (Insert Text Question)

Translation

습지

해양, 바다, 호수, 강, 그리고 시내를 포함한 다양한 수역들이 존재한다. 습지도 그중 하나이다. 습지는 습지대지만, 한 가지 측면에서 다른 수역들과 다르다: 습지는 나무로 덮여 있다.

습지는 여러 지역에 존재하지만, 커다란 수역 근처, 특히 호수나 강 근처에 위치하는 경향을 보인다. 강이 저지대를 통과하면서 유속이 느려질 때 주로 형성된다. 미시시피 강, 아마존 강, 그리고 나일 강 근처 모두에 습지가 존재한다. 또한 해양이나 바다 근처에서 형성되는 습지들도 있다. 이러한 습지는 저지대의 해안가 지역에서 발견되며 바닷물을 포함하고 있거나 혹은 염분이 섞인 물을 포함하고 있다. (케냐에는 인도양 근처에 이러한 종류의 습지들이 많다.) 그리고 기타 커다란 수역 근처에서 발견되는 소수의 습지들도 있다. 이러한 습지들은 보통 계절에 따라 생기는데, 우기 때 형성되고 연중 다른 시기에는 말라 있다.

그처럼 많은 지역에서 습지를 찾아 볼 수 있다는 사실로 인해, 서로 다른 무수히 많은 종류의 습지가 존재한다. 가장 흔한 두 가지 유형은 산림 습지와 관목 습지이다. 산림 습지는 땅에 수분이 그렇게 많지 않은 지역에서 일반적이다. 산림 습지에는 두 가지 종류가 있다: 침엽수 습지와 활엽수 습지가 그것이다. 침엽수 습지에서는 소나무, 전나무, 그리고 삼나무가 지배적인 반면, 활엽수 습지에는 주로 단풍나무, 느릅나무, 자작나무, 그리고 참나무가 포함되어 있다. 관목 습지에 대해 말하자면, 이들은 지면이 연중 대부분 물로 덮여 있는 지역에서 확산된다. 또한 이곳에는 오리나무와 버드나무와 같이, 보다 작은 나무들이 있다. 기타 유형의 습지 중에서는, 염습지가 가장 일반적이다. 염수에서 생존할 수 있는 몇 안 되는 나무 중 하나인 맹그로브 나무가 여기에서 지배적이다.

습지는 생태계의 중요한 부분이다. 전형적으로 이들은 풍부한 생명체들을 공급해 준다. 어류 및 파충류들이 이곳에서 특히 번성하지만, 포유류뿐만 아니라 여러 종의 조류들도 습지에서 서식한다. 이들은 또한 많은 종의 식물들의 서식처이기도 한데, 이 중 일부는 희귀한 것이거나 멸종 위기에 처한 것들이다. 마지막으로, 이들은 인근의 범람하는 강으로부터 나오는 많은 양의 물을 흡수할 수 있기 때문에, 홍수를 예방하는데 도움이 될 수 있다.

Unit 02
p.16

Sample Vocabulary Question

Translation

오늘날, 신용 카드로 물건 및 서비스를 구매하는 것은 일반적인 일이다. 이는 몇 가지 혜택을 제공해 준다. 예를 들어, 많은 양의 현금을 수중에 가지고 다닐 필요가 없다. 이로써 도둑들로부터 자신을 보호하는데 도움이 된다. 또한, 신용 카드를 사용하면, 나중에 금액을 지불하더라도, 그 즉시 제품이나 서비스를 받아 볼 수 있다. 이러한 카드가 오늘날 빈번히 사용되고 있지만, 이들은 비교적 새로운 것이다. 신용이라는 개념은 수 세기 동안 존재해 왔다. 하지만 신용 카드는 1900년대에 처음으로 소개되었다. 이러한 카드는 몇 가지 방면에서 현재의 카드와 달랐다. 가장 분명한 것은 이들이 사용될 수 있는 장소이다. 최초의 신용 카드는 이를 발행한 상점이나 기업에서만 사용될 수 있었다. 하지만, 현대의 신용 카드는 전 세계 다수의 사업체에서 승인을 받고 있다.

Answers

1. (D) (Sentence Simplification Question)

2. (D) (Factual Question)

3. (B) (Vocabulary Question)

4. 2, 4, 6 (Prose Summary Question)

Translation

맨하튼 프로젝트

세계 1차 대전(1914–1918) 동안, 수백 만 명의 군인들이 유럽의 전쟁터에서 목숨을 잃었다. 하지만, 수많은 사람들을 사망시킬 수 있는 많은 무기를 가지고 있음에도 불구하고, 사람들은 보다 파괴적인 무기를 만들어 내기 위해 끊임없이 노력했다. 일부 과학자들은 원자를 분열시킴으로써 믿을 수 없을 정도로 강력한 폭탄을 만드는 일이 가능하다는 점을 깨달았다. 이로써, 그들이 깨달은 바에 의하면, 원자 폭탄을 만들 수 있게 되었다. 이는 세상에서 가장 강력한 무기가 될 것이었다.

1930년대, 아돌프 히틀러의 나치 독일을 위해 일하던 과학자들이 원자 폭탄을 제조하는 법을 연구하기 시작했다. 이러한 사실은 미국의 과학자들에게 알려졌다. 1939년, 알버트 아인슈타인과 기타 유명한 몇몇 물리학자들이 미국의 대통령인 프랭클린 D. 루즈벨트에게 편지를 썼다. 이들은 대통령에게 나치가 하고 있는 일에 대해 경고해 주었다. 더 나아가, 이들은 미국의 자체적인 원자 폭탄 프로젝트를 시작할 것을 촉구했다. 이로써 루즈벨트는 1942년에 맨하튼 프로젝트를 시작하게 되었다. 이러한 일은 세계 2차 대전의 중반부에 이루어졌다. 맨하튼 프로젝트의 목적은 원자 폭탄을 만드는 것이었다. 캐나다와 영국이 미국에 합류했다.

맨하튼 프로젝트로 3개국 30개 이상의 지역에서 시설이 갖추어졌다. 하지만 뉴멕시코의 로스앨러모스가 중심이었다. 레슬리 그로브즈 장군이 프로젝트의 군사적인 측면을 담당했다. 로버트 오펜하이머는 수석 과학자였다. 그는 프로젝트를 위해 일하는 민간인 과학자들을 이끌었다. 세계에서 가장 명석한 과학자 중 일부가 맨하튼 프로젝트에 관련되어 있었다. 여기에는 엔리코 페르미, 닐스 보아, 그리고 리차드 파인먼이 포함되었다.

3년 동안, 팀은 목적을 향해 나아갔다. 이들은 다양하고 복잡한 과학적 및 기술적 문제들을 해결해야 했다. 주요 난관은 무기에 필요한 핵 물질을 만드는 것이었다. 결국, 과학자들은 두 가지 종류의 폭탄을 만들어 냈다. 하나는 플루토늄을 사용한 것이었다. 다른 하나는 우라늄을 사용한 것이었다. 1945년 7월 16일, 원자 폭탄이 뉴멕시코에서 성공적으로 폭파되었다. 그 무렵, 독일은 패배를 했다. 하지만, 8월 초, 두 개의 원자 폭탄이 일본에 투하되었다. 이로써 일본은 항복할 수 밖에 없었고 세계 2차 대전은 종식되었다.

Answers

1. (C) (Vocabulary Question)

2. (B) (Vocabulary Question)

3. (D) (Factual Question)

4. (A) (Inference Question)

5. 4th (Insert Text Question)

Translation

앙리 마티스

앙리 마티스는 20세기의 가장 영향력 있는 화가 중 한 명으로서 널리 인정을 받고 있다. 미술과 관련된 경력은 1800년대에 시작되었지만, 그는 1900년대에 많은 작품을 만들었다. 평생 동안, 그는 200점 이상의 그림을 그렸다. 또한 많은 드로잉, 조각, 그리고 콜라주를 남겼다. 그의 작품들은 색의 생생한 사용으로 유명하며, 그는 야수파로 불리는 미술 사조와 종종 연관되고 있다.

마티스는 본래 법관이 될 의도를 가지고 있었다. 하지만 그는 심경의 변화를 겪었고,

그 대신 화가가 되기로 결심했다. 그래서 1989년에 미술 학교에서 공부를 하기 위해 파리로 갔다. 마티스의 초기 작품들은 주로 어둡고 우울한 편이었다. 이후, 그는 인상주의 화가인 존 피터 러셀을 만나게 되었다. 러셀은 마티스에게 빈센트 반 고흐와 다른 인상주의 화가들의 작품을 소개해 주었다. 그러한 결과로 마티스의 화풍은 급격한 변화를 겪었다. 그때부터 그는 보다 밝은 색으로 그림을 그리기 시작했다.

걸작으로 간주되는 마티스의 최초의 작품은 *저녁 식탁*인데, 그는 1897년에 이를 완성시켰다. 그는 1904년에 처음으로 개인전을 열었다. 바로 그 무렵에 그는 야수파와 관련을 맺게 되었다. 1905년경, 그는 그러한 미술 운동에서 가장 중요한 사람 중 한 명으로 여겨졌다. 마티스의 야수파 작품은 1904년에서 1908년까지만 계속되었는데, 하지만 이때는 그의 인생에서 매우 중요한 시기였다. 그의 야수파 작품들은 사실주의보다 생생한 색의 사용을 강조했다. 색들은 종종 하나의 색조로서, 다른 색이 섞이지 않은 것처럼 보였다. 또한 마티스는 이 기간 동안 상당히 많은 작품들을 만들었다. 처음에는, 많은 야수파 작품들이 조롱을 받았다. 하지만 시간이 지나면서, 사람들은 그 진가를 알게 되었다.

1920년대 동안과 그가 1954년 사망할 때까지, 마티스는 주로 전통적인 양식의 그림을 그렸다. 하지만, 나이가 들면서, 그림을 그리는 경우가 적어졌다. 대신, 종종 휠체어에 몸이 묶여 더 이상 그림을 그릴 수가 없었기 때문에, 그는 종이로 콜라주를 만들기 시작했다. (아마도 그중 가장 유명한 작품은 *푸른 누부 II*일 것이다.) 사망했을 당시, 그는 20세기 미술의 거장 중 한 명으로서 널리 추앙을 받았다.

Unit 03

p.22

Sample Inference Question

Translation

종종 엘리샤 오티스가 엘리베이터를 발명했다고 말해진다. 하지만 실제로는 그렇지가 않다. 사실, 최초의 엘리베이터는 2,000년 전에 발명되었다. 하지만, 1800년대가 되어서야 보다 뛰어난 엘리베이터가 만들어지기 시작했다. 이에 대한 한 가지 이유는, 1800년대 이전에는, 대부분의 건물들이 단 몇 층 높이에 불과했기 때문이었다. 따라서 엘리베이터가 필요하지 않았다. 하지만, 1800년대, 새로운 건축 재료들이 사용되기 시작했다. 이로써 사람들은 10층이나 그 이상의 건물들을 만들 수 있게 되었다. 하지만 사람들을 위아래 층으로 이동시키기 위한 기계적 장치가 없다면, 고층 건물을 세우는 일은 비현실적인 것이었다. 따라서 발명가들이 다양한 엘리베이터에 대해 연구를 했다. 엘리샤 오티스에 대해 말하자면, 그는 엘리베이터를 발명한 것이 아니었다. 대신, 1852년에 그에 대한 안전 제동 장치를 만들었다. 그 다음 해에, 그는 엘리베이터 판매 회사를 설립했다. 그 이후로, 전 세계 수백 만 명의 사람들이 Otis 엘리베이터를 타 왔으며 – 그리고 계속 사용하고 있다.

Answers

1. (A) (Rhetorical Purpose Question)

2. (C) (Inference Question)

3. (B) (Factual Question)

4. (B) (Vocabulary Question)

5. 2nd (Insert Text Question)

Translation

풍차

1700년대 산업 혁명 이전에는, 사람들이 이용할 수 있는 동력원이 거의 존재하지 않았다. 주로 동물이나 자신이 힘에 의존했다. 하지만, 몇몇 사람들은 수력을 이용했고, 동력을 공급받기 위해 풍력을 활용한 사람들도 있었다. 풍차를 건설함으로써 그렇게 했다.

풍차는 바람의 힘을 이용하여 기계를 작동시키는 구조물이다. 여러 종류의 풍차가 있지만, 가장 일반적인 것은 세로축 풍차이다. 여기에는 비행기 프로펠러의 외형과

같은, 4개의 기다란 날이 달려 있다. 바람이 불면 이러한 날이 바람을 받아서 중심축을 중심으로 회전하게 된다. 이들이 움직이면, 날이 풍차 자체 내의 기계와 연결되어 있는 구동축을 회전시키게 된다. 많은 경우, 풍차의 꼭대기 부분은 – 날이 달려 있는 부분은 – 돌아갈 수 있다. 이로써 날들이 바람을 받는 쪽으로 향하게 된다.

고대 이래로, 다양한 종류의 풍차들이 사용되어 왔다. 이들은 수 세기 전에 중동, 중국, 그리고 인도에서 만들어졌다고 알려져 있다. 유럽에는 1100년대에 풍차가 소개되었다고 생각된다. 초기 대부분의 풍차는 밀과 옥수수와 같은 곡물들을 빻는데 이용되었다. 곡물을 가루로 만드는 과정은, 손으로 하는 경우, 매우 힘든 일이었다. 하지만, 풍차는 기계가 그러한 일을 할 수 있도록 해주었다.

풍차를 세웠던 또 다른 이유는 물을 끌어올리기 위해서였다. 이로써 수천 개의 풍차들이 네덜란드에 세워졌다. 네덜란드는 북해 근처에 위치해 있는 저지대 국가이다. 그곳의 많은 지역이 바다로부터 개간한 땅이다. (실제로, 너무나 많은 토지를 간척했기 때문에, 그 나라의 약 1/4이 해수면 보다 낮은 위치에 있다.) 그렇게 하기 위해, 네덜란드 사람들은 제방을 쌓아서 일정 지역에 바닷물이 들어갈 수 없도록 했다. 그런 다음, 풍차를 이용하여 그처럼 제방으로 둘러 쌓인 지역으로부터 물을 빼내었다. 땅이 마르면, 네덜란드 사람들은 그 위에 곡식을 심거나 건물을 지을 수 있었다.

산업 혁명이 시작되자, 풍차가 사용되는 경우는 줄어들었다. 증기 엔진이 풍력으로 가동되던 기계류를 빠르게 대체했다. 오늘날, 풍차는 전기를 생산하기 위해 때때로 사용되고 있다. 하지만 예전만큼 널리 사용되고 있지는 않다.

Sample Negative Factual Information Question

Translation

사람들의 가장 일반적인 심리학적 성향 중 하나는 다른 사람들이 자신이 하는 것과 같은 방식으로 생각을 하고 믿게 된다고 가정하는 것이다. 이는 투사라고 불린다. 자신의 생각이나 감정을 다른 사람에게 투사하는 것이다. 대부분의 경우, 사람들은 부정적인 감정이나 의견을 다른 사람에게 투사한다. 이렇게 함으로써, 투사는 종종 사람들에게 방어 기제의 역할을 해준다. 예를 들어, 한 남성이 특정 국가 출신의 사람들에 대해 편견을 가지고 있다고 하자. 그는 그러한 점이 부정적인 측면이라고 생각할 수 있다. 따라서 이 사람은 다른 누군가가 그 나라에서 온 사람들에게 편견을 가지고 있다고 비난할 수 있다. 그렇게 함으로써, 이 사람은 편견에 사로 잡힌 자신의 생각을 또 다른 사람에게 투사하여, 실제로는 존재하지 않을 때에도 그러한 사람들이 존재한다고 상상을 하게 된다. 또한 긍정적인 측면에 투사를 이용하는 것도 가능하다. 아이스크림을 좋아하는 한 여성이 다른 사람들도 아이스크림을 좋아한다고 생각할 수 있다. 따라서 그녀는 자신의 감정을 다른 사람들에게 투사하고 있는 것이다.

Mini Test 1

Answers

1. Ⓓ (Vocabulary Question)

2. Ⓓ (Sentence Simplification Question)

3. Ⓑ (Negative Factual Question)

4. **Providing Food: 3, 7   Protecting Young: 2, 4, 5**
   (Fill in a Table Question)

Translation

동물의 양육

모든 동물들은 새끼를 낳고 기르도록 이끄는 본능을 가지고 있다. 하지만 짝짓기가 이루어지면, 동물들은 서로 다른 반응을 보인다. 일부 경우에는, 수컷들이 떠나서 새끼들과의 관계를 끊어 버린다. 이는 어류와 파충류 사이에서 흔한 행동이다. 종종, 새끼들이 태어나거나 부화할 때까지, 수컷들은 암컷과 함께 머무른다. 새끼들이 살아 남으면, 한쪽 혹은 양쪽 부모가 떠나 버릴 수도 있다. 하지만, 대부분의 조류와 포유류 종들은 새끼와 함께 지내면서 다 자랄 때까지 이들을 양육한다.

동물의 양육에 있어서 가장 중요한 두 가지 측면 중 하나는 먹이를 공급해 주는 것과 관련이 있다. 포유류가 태어나면, 암컷이 새끼에게 모유를 제공해 준다. 이후, 더 자라면, 새끼들은 모유 먹는 것을 중단하고 단단한 먹이를 섭취하게 된다. 그런 다음, 포유류들은 – 전형적으로 어미와 아비 모두가 – 새끼들에게 먹이를 공급해 준다. 동물을 잡아서 그 사체를 굴로 가지고 옴으로써 그렇게 한다. 혹은, 초식 동물의 경우, 이들은 새끼들에게 과일이나 야채를 가져다 주거나 자신들이 음식을 발견한 장소로 새끼들을 데리고 간다. 조류에 대해 말하자면, 이들은 먹이를 둥지로 가져와서 이를 새끼들에게 먹인다.

이러한 동물들이 나이를 먹으면, 부모들이 이들에게 먹이를 구하는 법을 가르쳐 준다. 동물들에게는 그렇게 할 수 있는 많은 방법들이 있다. 예를 들어, 치타는 죽은 동물을 새끼들에게 가지고 온다. 그러면 새끼 치타가 그러한 사체를 공격함으로써 사냥하는 법을 배우게 된다. 다른 동물들, 특히 고양이과의 동물들은 살아 있는 먹이를 가져와서 그 새끼들이 먹이를 죽이도록 한다. 많은 경우, 어린 동물들은 부모가 먹이를 찾아 다니는 동안 이들을 쫓아 다닌다. 지켜 봄으로써, 이들은 스스로 사냥하여 먹이를 획득하는 법을 알게 된다.

동물 양육에 있어서 중요한 두 번째 측면은 새끼를 보호해 주는 부모와 관련이 있다. 동물들은 둥지, 굴, 그리고 기타 안식처를 지어 새끼들을 보호한다. 포식자들로부터 알과 갓 태어난 새끼들을 보호하기 위해 경계를 선다. 많은 어린 동물들이 수 개월 혹은 수 년 동안 부모 곁에서 머무른다. 예를 들어, 수컷 새끼 사자는 약 2년 동안 어미 곁에 머무른다. 부모로부터 떨어져 살 수 있게 되면, 새끼 동물들은 혼자서 길을 떠나게 된다.

Mini Test 2

Answers

1. Ⓒ (Factual Question)

2. Ⓐ (Negative Factual Question)

3. Ⓑ (Inference Question)

4. **1, 5, 6** (Prose Summary Question)

Translation

중세 시대의 대학의 기원

800년, 샤를마뉴 대제가 신성 로마 황제의 자리에 올랐다. 그가 통치했던 지역은 신성 로마 제국으로 알려지게 되었다. 그의 제국은 중유럽과 서유럽의 넓은 지역에 걸쳐 있었다. 샤를마뉴는 선견지명이 있는 통치자였다. 따라서 사회의 여러 부분에서 개혁을 실시하려고 했다. 그러한 것 중의 하나가 교육이었다. 그는 교양이 있는 성직자들을 원했다. 그래서 자신의 제국 내에 있는 성당 및 수도원들에게 명령하여, 성직자가 될 소년들을 교육하기 위한 학교를 개설하도록 했다. 샤를마뉴는 814년에 사망했기 때문에, 그의 계획이 완전히 실행된 것은 아니었다. 하지만, 몇몇 장소에서 학교가 개설되었다. 이들은 차후 대학이 된 곳의 기원이 되었다.

샤르트르, 클뤼니, 랭스와 같은 지역에는 유명한 성당 학교들이 있었다. 교과 과정은 주로 종교적인 것이었다. 학생들은 라틴어, 문법, 수사학, 논리학, 그리고 신학을 배웠다. 시간이 지남에 따라, 교과 과정에 기타 과목들이 추가되었다. 여기에는 대수학, 기하학, 천문학, 그리고 음악이 포함되었다. 교사들은 성직자 및 수도사들이었다. 이들은 라틴어로 수업을 했는데, 그 이유는 라틴어가 가톨릭 교회 및 지식인들의 언어였기 때문이었다. 대부분의 학생들은 상류 계층 출신이었다. 여자 아이들은 사제직을 맡을 수가 없었으므로, 이러한 학교에서는 남자 아이들만을 가르쳤다.

시간이 지나면서, 이러한 학교들은 진화하기 시작했다. 이들로부터 최초의 대학이 생겨났다. 최초의 대학은 1088년 이탈리아의 볼로냐에 설립되었다. 파리 대학은 1150년에 대학으로 승인되었다. 그 다음 세기 동안, 서유럽의 여러 지역에서 대학이 설립되었다. 그중 대부분은 이탈리아, 프랑스, 스페인, 그리고 영국에 세워졌다. 중세 시대 동안, 이러한 학교들은, 가톨릭 교회를 포함하여, 외부의 간섭을 배제시켰다. 이로써 그들에게는 일정 정도의 자유가 생겼다. 이들은 자신이 가르치는 교과 과정을 확대시켰다. 새로운 수업에는 의학, 법학, 그리고 음악이 포함되었다. 다수의 젊은 사람들이 학구적인 미술 교육을 받았다. 따라서 이러한 대학들은 1400년대 르네상스가 시작되는데 도움이 되었다.

Answers

1. Ⓒ (Factual Question)
2. Ⓑ (Rhetorical Purpose Question)
3. Ⓒ (Inference Question)
4. Ⓓ (Vocabulary Question)
5. Ⓐ (Negative Factual Question)

Translation

신성 로마 제국

800년 성탄절에, 교황 레오 3세는 샤를마뉴를 신성 로마 황제로 임명했다. 교황에게는 다수의 적이 있었다. 그래서 그는 당시 유럽에서 가장 강력한 통치자의 보호를 받고자 했다. 샤를마뉴는 당시 가장 세력이 컸던 사람 중 한 명이었다. 하지만 그는 814년까지만 살았다. 신성 로마 제국은, 그의 영토는 그렇게 불렸는데, 그의 후손들에게 넘겨졌다. 하지만 그들은 한때 거대했던 제국을 분리시켜 놓았다. 따라서 신성 로마 제국은 그 세력과 이름 모두가 서서히 사라져 갔다.

샤를마뉴가 사망하고 거의 150년이 지난 후, 또 다른 교황이 자신이 위협받고 있다는 점을 깨닫게 되었다. 레오 3세가 했던 것과 마찬가지로, 그 교황은 적들로부터 자신을 보호하기 위해 게르만족 사람들에게 의지했다. 962년, 교황 요하네스 12세는 작센의 오토 1세에게 신성 로마 제국의 왕위를 수여했다. 오토는 자신의 통치 하에서 대부분의 게르만족들을 통일시켰다. 그는 또한 북부 이탈리아를 통치했다. 따라서 교황에게 이상적인 동맹 상대로 여겨졌다. 오토의 즉위로 인해, 신성 로마 제국은 다시 한 번 부흥하게 되었다.

오토와 이후 황제들은 가톨릭 교회의 일에 관여하기 시작했다. 그들은 종종 교황과 다툼을 벌였다. 자신들과 의견이 일치하지 않는 교황들은 해임시켰다. 그런 다음에는, 교황 직에 자신의 협력자들이 선출되도록 만들었다. 가톨릭 교회는 이와 같은 황제들의 간섭에 분개했다. 강력히 맞서 싸웠고, 따라서 이후 신성 로마 제국은 교회의 사안에 대한 개입을 중단했다.

시간이 지나면서 제국 자체도 변화했다. 영토 내의 지방 귀족들이 보다 많은 권력을 축적함에 따라, 황제는 서서히 권력을 잃어 갔다. 그 후 제국이 변화했다. 강력한 주, 작은 공국, 그리고 자유 도시 국가들로 이루어진 연합체가 되었다. 신성 로마 황제의 지위는 더 이상 세습되지 않았다. 대신, 선출되는 지위가 되었다. 수 세기에 걸쳐, 제국 내 각각의 주들은 대부분의 자체적인 사안들을 관할하게 되었다. 1700년대 무렵에는, 프러시아와 오스트리아가 제국을 지배했다. 1805년 나폴레옹이 오스트리아의 프란츠 2세를 패배시켰을 때, 신성 로마 제국은 쇠약한 존재가 되었다. 신성 로마 제국은 그 다음 해인 1806년에 소멸했다.

Unit 05

p.34

Sample Reference Question

Translation

밤하늘을 관찰하던 사람이 때때로 한 줄기의 광선을 볼 수도 있다. 통상적으로 이러한 빛은 하늘의 일정 부분을 가로지르다가 사라져 버린다. 이것은 유성이다. 유성은 먼지나 암석으로 된 입자일 수 있다. 빛이 생성되는 이유는 이것이 지구의 대기 내에서 타버리기 때문이다. 작은 크기로 인해, 손상되지 않은 채로 지구의 표면까지 도달하는 유성은 거의 없다. 대부분은 대기 내에서 완전히 소멸한다. 연중 몇 차례에 걸쳐, 태양 주위를 도는 도중, 지구는 성간 티끌 구름을 통과하게 된다. 그러한 결과로 유성우가 나타난다. 관찰하기에 이상적인 조건이라면, 유성우가 나타나는 동안에는 시간당 50개 이상의 유성을 볼 수가 있다. 페르세우스 유성우는 가장 유명한 유성우 중 하나이다. 통상 7월 하순에서 시작되어 8월 초순까지 계속된다. 또 다른 유성우로서 사자자리 유성우가 있는데, 이는 매년 11월에 나타난다.

Answers

1. Ⓐ (Factual Question)
2. Ⓑ (Reference Question)
3. Ⓓ (Rhetorical Purpose Question)
4. **1, 3, 4** (Prose Summary Question)

Translation

고속 열차

열차는 19세기 중반 이후로 사람과 화물 모두를 수송해 왔다. 당시로서는, 육상에서 가장 빠른 운송 수단이었다. 하지만 20세기 동안에, 주요 운송 수단으로서 자동차와 비행기가 열차를 대신하기 시작했다. 이에 대응하여, 기술자들은 열차의 이동 속도를 증가시키기 위해 연구해 왔다. 그 결과로서 고속 열차가 개발되었다.

고속 철도 시스템의 목적은 사람과 물건을 이곳에서 저곳으로 매우 빠르게 운송하는 것이다. 오늘날, 가장 빠른 속도의 열차는 시속 100킬로미터에서 300킬로미터 사이의 속도로 운행을 한다. 하지만, 일부는 시속 580킬로미터까지의 빠른 속도를 낼 수 있다. 기술자들은 미래에 이들이 훨씬 더 빠른 속도를 내도록 할 수 있을 것이라고 믿는다. 고속 열차에는 몇 가지 종류가 있다. 대부분은 전기로 작동되지만, 자기 부상 열차는 예외이다. 이들은 매우 빠른 속도로 이동을 하기 위해 자기 부상 기술을 이용한다.

대부분의 고속 열차는 그 용도에 맞게 특별히 설계된 선로에서 달린다. 이러한 선로는 용접으로 끊임없이 이어져 있는 레일로 구성되어 있는데, 따라서 레일 사이에 틈이 존재하지 않는다. 주로 곧게 뻗어 있으며 곡선인 부분은 매우 적다. 이로써 열차는 항상 높은 속도로 달릴 수 있는데, 그 이유는 곡선 구간을 지날 때 감속을 해야 하기 때문이다. 또한 그와 같은 곳에서의 고속 열차들은 정기 열차편이기 때문에, 건널목이 없다. 이 역시 교통 신호로 인해 열차가 속도를 줄이거나 정차를 해야 하는 경우를 차단시켜 준다. 열차 자체는 공기 역학적으로 설계되어 항력을 감소시킬 수 있는데, 항력은 속도를 감소시키는 것이다. 그 형태와 속도로 인하여, 이들은 종종 탄환 열차라고 불린다.

고속 철도 시스템의 주된 장점은 속도이다. 짧은 시간 내에 먼 거리를 횡단할 수 있다. 이로써 고속 철도 시스템은 비교적 서로 가까이에 있는, 인구가 많은 대도시 지역에서 인기가 높다. 예를 들어, 일본에는 광범위한 고속 열차 망이 연결되어 있다. 유럽도 그러하다. 현재, 중국에는 세계에서 가장 큰 규모의 고속 철도 연결 망이 갖춰져 있는데, 중국 전역에 6,000킬로미터의 선로가 이어져 있다.

Answers

1. Ⓓ (Reference Question)
2. Ⓐ (Negative Factual Question)
3. Ⓐ (Vocabulary Question)
4. Ⓒ (Factual Question)
5. **4th** (Insert Text Question)

Translation

단풍나무

매년 가을, 아시아, 유럽, 그리고 북아메리카 지역의 숲들은 초록색에서 밝은 빨간색, 오렌지색, 그리고 노란색으로 바뀐다. 이렇게 밝은 색을 내도록 만드는 나무 중 다수가 단풍나무이다. 단풍나무는 온대 기후에서 흔한 낙엽수이다. 전 세계에 걸쳐 125종의 단풍나무들이 자라고 있다. 단풍나무의 잎은 쉽게 알아볼 수 있는 독특한 모양을 가지고 있다: 하나의 기다란 줄기를 가지며 뻗어나 있는 세 개의 커다란 부분이 있는데, 여기에는 뾰족한 부분들이 많이 달려 있다.

단풍나무는 높이에 있어서 다양하다. 일반적으로 덩굴성 단풍나무는 불과 약 6미터 정도의 높이까지 성장하기 때문에, 관목으로 여겨진다. 사탕단풍은 높이가 약 25미터까지 자랄 수 있다. 그리고 은단풍과 기타 종들은 40미터 이상으로 자랄 수도 있다. 단풍나무는 주로 초봄에 피는 작은 꽃을 가지고 있다. 종에 따라, 이러한 꽃들은 오렌지색, 빨간색, 혹은 초록색을 띤다. 단풍나무의 잎 색깔은 봄에 진홍색으로 시작하여, 여름에는 초록색으로 바뀌고, 가을에는 빨간색, 오렌지색, 그리고 노란색으로 이루어진 멋진 색으로 변화한다. 단풍나무 씨앗은 날개처럼 생긴 특이한 모양으로 되어 있다. 씨앗은 날개의 한쪽 끝에 둘러 쌓여 있다. 씨앗의 모양으로 인하여 씨앗은 지면으로 떨어질 때 원을 돌며 떨어진다. 이처럼 원을 그리는 움직임으로 인해, 특히 바람이 부는 상황에서는, 씨앗이 나무에서 멀리 떨어져 나갈 수 있다. (이로써 단풍나무는 자신이 자라는 영역을 손쉽게 확장시킬 수 있다.)

단풍나무는, 특히 가을에, 보기가 아름답지만, 또한 많은 나무들이 상업적 가치를 지니고 있다. 일부 종은 공원 및 마당에 심어져서 아름다움을 더해 주고 있는데, 이로써 단풍나무를 전문으로 하는 원예장이 존재한다. 일부 단풍나무들은 목재용으로서 가치가 높다. 이들의 목재는 건설에서 사용되며, 또한 뛰어난 음향을 만들어내는 특성을 가지고 있기 때문에 악기를 만드는데도 이용된다. 사탕단풍은 수액으로 인해 가치가 높다. 수도꼭지를 이용하여 나무에서 수액을 빼낸다. 그러면 이를 끓여서 가공함으로써 메이플 시럽을 만들 수 있는데, 이는 감미료의 일종이다.

Unit 06

p.40

Sample Rhetorical Purpose Question

Translation

많은 사람들이 사업가로서의 존 D. 록펠러의 성공에 대해 잘 알고 있다. 1800년대 후반과 1900년대 초반에, 그는 세계에서 가장 부유한 사람 중 한 명이었다. 그의 회사인 스탠더드 오일은 석유 산업에서 주도적인 기업이었다. 하지만 많은 사람들이 그에 대해 알고 있지 못하고 있는 점은 그가 위대한 자선가였다는 것이다. 사람들은 종종, 그와 동시대 사람 중의 한 명인, 앤드류 카네기가 도서관을 세운 업적에 대해 알고 있다. 하지만 록펠러의 기부에 대해서는 알지 못한다. 그는 평생 동안 5억 달러 이상을 기부한 것으로 추측된다. 또한 그는 자신이 부유해 질 때까지 기부를 미루지 않았다. 그는 젊었을 때 소득의 10퍼센트를 자선 단체에 기부했다. 록펠러는 많은 단체에 기부금을 주었다. 그는 교육에 큰 관심을 가졌다. Chicago 대학에 8천만 달러 이상을 기부했다. 또한 의학 연구에도 많은 금액을 기부했다.

Mini Test 1

Answers

1. Ⓐ (Vocabulary Question)

2. Ⓓ (Reference Question)

3. Ⓓ (Factual Question)

4. Ⓑ (Negative Factual Question)

5. Ⓑ (Rhetorical Purpose Question)

Translation

블레즈 파스칼

블레즈 파스칼은 1623년부터 1662년까지 생존했던 프랑스인 과학자이자 철학자였다. 그가 살았던 당시에는, 과학자들이 여러 영역에서 일하는 것이 일반적이었다. 그러한 이유로, 파스칼은 몇 가지 영역에서 업적을 달성했다. 그는 주로 수학, 특히 기하학에 집중했다. 하지만 또한 기계식 계산기를 발명했고, 유체 역학에 관한 연구를 했으며, 그리고 진공에 대한 연구도 했다.

파스칼이 어렸을 때, 그는 굉장한 지능을 보였다. 그는, 특히 수학의 영역에서, 신동으로 여겨졌다. 안타깝게도, 그의 아버지는 가산을 탕진했다. 그래서 그는 세금을 징수하는 일을 해야 했다. 아버지를 돕는 일에 흥미를 갖게 되자, 파스칼은 불과 19세의 나이에 계산 기계를 발명해 냈다. 이것은 현대의 모든 계산기의 전신이었다. 파스칼린으로 알려진 이것은 상당히 복잡한 기계였다. 하지만 만들기가 어려웠으며 또한 값도 비쌌다. 파스칼은 총 20개의 기계를 만들었는데, 그중 일부는 오늘날까지 박물관에 남아 있다.

파스칼은 수학의 영역에서 많은 기여를 했다. 가장 유명한 것은 파스칼의 삼각형이라고 불리는 것이다. 이는 삼각형의 위쪽에 있는 숫자들이 합쳐지면 그 아래에 있는 숫자를 만들어 내는 삼각형이다. 파스칼은 카드 게임에서 나올 수 있는 가능한 모든 결과에 대해 생각해 보던 중, 이러한 삼각형을 고안해 냈다. 파스칼의 삼각형은 고대 중국인들에게도 알려져 있던 것이었다. 하지만 그것이 얼마나 중요한지를 깨달은 것은 그가 처음이었다. 삼각형에 관한 그의 연구는 확률 이론의 기반이 되었다.

유체 역학의 영역에서, 파스칼은 오늘날 파스칼의 법칙이라고 불리는 것에 이바지했다. 이는 한정된 공간 속의 액체에 가해진 압력은 모든 방향으로 동일하게 전달된다는 주장이다. 그는 또한 진공의 존재를 증명했다. 아리스토텔레스가 살았던 시대에는, 사람들이 진공 상태는 존재하지 않는다는 이론을 세웠다. 하지만, 파스칼은 그들 모두가 틀렸다는 점을 입증해 냈다. 안타깝게도, 파스칼은 젊은 나이에 사망했다. 그렇지 않았다면, 과학계에 대한 그의 기여는 훨씬 더 막대했을 것이다.

Mini Test 2

Answers

1. Ⓑ (Rhetorical Purpose Question)

2. Ⓓ (Vocabulary Question)

3. Ⓐ (Sentence Simplification Question)

4. **Jupiter: 1, 7   Saturn: 4, 5, 6** (Fill in a Table Question)

Translation

행성의 고리

1610년, 갈릴레오 갈릴레이는 토성 쪽으로 망원경을 돌렸다. 그는 자신이 본 것에 놀랐다. 토성의 각 측면에 튀어나와 있는 부분이 있는 것처럼 보였다. 수십 년 후인 1659년에, 천문학자인 크리스티안 호이겐스는 토성 전체를 둘러싸고 있는 것처럼 보이는 평평한 원반이 존재한다는 점을 관찰했다. 두 사람이 본 것은 토성의 고리였다.

태양계 내 8개의 행성은 두 개의 그룹으로 나누어진다: 지구형 행성과 목성형 행성이 그것이다. 수성, 금성, 지구, 그리고 화성은 지구형 행성이다. 보다 크기가 큰 목성형 행성은 목성, 토성, 천왕성, 그리고 해왕성이다. 목성형 행성들은 몇 가지 특성을 공유한다. 하나는 모든 행성에 그 주위를 둘러싸는 고리가 있다는 점이다. 토성이 가장 분명하다. 하지만 목성, 천왕성, 그리고 해왕성 또한 고리를 가지고 있다. 고리 자체는 빙정, 더스트, 그리고 암석으로 이루어져 있다. 이들을 구성하고 있는 대부분의 물질들은 상당히 작다. 하지만, 토성의 고리에는 직경이 수백 미터에 이르는 암석들이 있다. 또한, 고리 안에는 행성 주위를 도는 달들도 몇몇 있다.

천문학자들은 이러한 고리가 세 가지 방법 중 하나에 의해 생성되었다고 믿는다. 첫째, 행성이 처음으로 생성되었을 때 행성 주위를 계속해서 돌던 물질들로 인하여 만들어진 것일 수 있다. 둘째, 행성과 너무 가까운 궤도를 도는 달에서 나온 물질들로 일부 고리들이 만들어진 것일 수도 있다. 행성의 중력의 크기로 인해, 달이 쪼개져서, 중력의 결과로 생긴 파편들이 고리를 형성시켰다. 셋째, 일부 고리들은 유성체, 혜성, 혹은 소행성과 충돌한 근처의 달에서 생긴 파편들에 의해 형성된 것일 수 있다.

토성에 가장 큰 규모의 고리들이 있는데, 이들은 14개의 주요 그룹으로 이루어져 있다. 이러한 각 그룹 내에는 수천 개의 고리들이 존재한다. 이에 비해, 천왕성에는 13개의 뚜렷한 고리 그룹들이 있으며, 해왕성에는, 5개, 그리고 목성에는 4개가 있다. 목성의 고리는 가장 조밀하지 않으며, 주로 더스트로 이루어져 있다. 이로써 천문학자들은 주로 목성의 달에 가해진 다양한 충격으로 인해 이들이 생성되었을 것으로 믿고 있다. 해왕성의 고리는 그렇게 조밀하지 않다. 천왕성에 대해 말하지만, 천왕성의 고리는 주로 빙점으로 이루어져 있다.

Unit 07

p.46

Sample Insert Text Question

Translation

일부 문화들이 언제 그리고 왜 사라지는지는 종종 분명하다. 전쟁에서 하나의 문명이 다른 문명에 의해 패배를 당할 수도 있다. 혹은 질병이나 자연 재해로 인하여 수많은 사람들이 사망할 수도 있다. (많은 미 원주민 부족들은, 예를 들어, 1500년대 천연두의 확산으로 없어져 버렸다.) 하지만, 역사상 하나의 문명이 사라졌지만 그 소멸에 관한 어떠한 기록도 남아 있지 않은 경우가 많다. 아나사지의 경우가 그러하다. 이들은 미 원주민 부족이었다. 오늘날 미국의 포코너스 지역에 해당되는 곳에서 한때 생활을 했다. 약 200년에서 1300년까지 그곳에서 살았다. 고고학자들은 여러 아나사지 정착지에 관해 광범위한 연구를 해왔다. 그들의 문화에 대해 많은 것을 알게 되었다. 아나사지인들이 만들었던 일종의 공예에 대해서도 알고 있다. 그리고 아나사지인들이 어떤 작물을 재배했는지도 알게 되었다. 학자들이 알지 못하는 것은 왜 아나사지인들이 갑자스럽게 사라졌는가하는 점이다. 하지만, 이 문제에 대해 많은 이론들이 있다.

Mini Test 1

Answers

1. Ⓓ (Vocabulary Question)

2. Ⓑ (Negative Factual Question)

3. Ⓑ (Factual Question)

4. Ⓓ (Reference Question)

5. 1st (Insert Text Question)

Translation

남극의 공룡 화석

남극은 세계에서 가장 살기 힘든 기후 중 하나를 가지고 있다. 대부분이 얼음과 눈으로 덮여 있다. 그곳의 온도는 섭씨 마이너스 89도까지 내려갈 수 있다. 그 결과, 그곳은 과학자들이 공룡의 화석을 찾아낼 수 있을 것이라고 결코 예상하지 못했던 지역이었다. 그럼에도 불구하고, 1980년대, 일부 공룡들의 화석화된 유적들이 발견되었다. 그 후로, 최소 11개 종의 공룡들의 뼈가 그곳에서 발견되었다. 여기에는 초식 및 육식 공룡들 모두가 포함되어 있다. 이 모든 공룡들은 쥐라기 혹은 백악기 때 살았다. 이 두 기간은 2억 년 전부터 6천 5백만 년 전까지에 해당된다.

언뜻 보기에는, 공룡들이 한때 남극에서 살았다는 것이 이상하게 보일 수 있다. 어찌되었든, 공룡들은 따뜻하고 더운 기후에 적합했기 때문이다. 또한, 남극의 몹시 추운 기후에서는 거의 어떠한 식물도 자라지 않는다. 따라서 일부 사람들에게 초식 동물의 존재는 불가사의한 것으로 여겨진다. 하지만 이러한 사실들은 쉽게 설명될 수 있다. 남극이 항상 추웠던 것은 아니다. 실제로, 현재보다 훨씬 더 따뜻한 때가 있었다. 수백만 년 전, 남극은 현재의 위치에 있지 않았다; 훨씬 더 남쪽에 위치해 있었다. 그곳에서, 남극은 기타 모든 대륙들과 합쳐져서 적도 근처에 거대한 땅덩어리를 형성하고 있었다. (오늘날, 이는 과학자들에게 판게아라고 알려져 있는데, 판게아는 "모든 대륙"이라는 의미이다.) 이후, 이 초대륙은 보다 작은 두 개의 땅덩어리로 쪼개졌다. 하나는 북쪽에 있었다. 다른 하나는 남쪽에 있었다. 남쪽의 땅덩어리는 남아메리카, 인도, 호주, 아프리카, 그리고 남극을 형성하게 될 지역으로 이루어져 있었다.

남극이 이러한 두 개의 땅덩어리의 일부였을 때, 그곳의 기후는 상당히 달랐다. 보다 따뜻했으며, 그곳에서는 식물들이 자랐다. 따라서 많은 종의 공룡들에게 이상적인 서식지가 있었다. 현재의 위치로 이동하게 되었을 때에도, 일부 과학자들은 이곳이 한동안 상당히 따뜻했다고 믿고 있다. 이는 백악기 때였다. 백악기는 1억 4천 4백만 년과 6천 5백만 년 전 사이에 해당되었다. 따라서 공룡 및 기타 동물들이 수백 년 동안 남극에서 살았을 가능성이 높다. 그곳의 기후가 보다 혹독해 진 후에야 그곳의 대부분의 생물들이 소멸했다.

Mini Test 2

Answers

1. Ⓓ (Reference Question)

2. Ⓑ (Factual Question)

3. 2nd (Insert Text Question)

4. **1, 3, 4** (Prose Summary Question)

Translation

로큰롤 음악의 발전

몇몇 음악 장르는 미국에 그 기원을 두고 있다. 그중 하나가 로큰롤이다. 록 음악의 기원에 대해서는 몇 가지 논쟁이 존재한다. 하지만 대부분의 음악 연구가들은 그것의 발전에 두 개의 주요 요인이 관련되어 있었다는 점에 동의하고 있다. 첫 번째는 다양한 음악 장르가 혼합되었다는 것이다. 두 번째는 전자 악기 및 장비들이 만들어졌다는 것이다.

1940년대, 미국의 남부는 다양한 종류의 음악들이 풍부하게 존재하던 지역이었다. 그러한 기간 동안, 많은 음악가들이 음악을 가지고 실험을 했다. 이들은 다양한 장르의 요소들을 혼합시켰다. 이러한 장르에는 블루스, 컨트리, 재즈, 그리고 가스펠 음악이 포함되어 있었다. 이로써, 몇몇 음악가들은 혁신적인 소리를 만들어 냈다. 이러한 새로운 음악은 흑인 음악가들에 의해 더 많은 영향을 받았다. 이들은 음악에 재즈와 리듬 앤 블루스의 요소를 도입했다. 점프 블루스와 부기우기라고 불리는, 두 개의 새로운 형태의 음악으로 댄스 리듬을 연주했다. 이는 미국의 흑인과 백인 모두에게 높은 인기를 누렸다.

대략 비슷한 시기에, 보다 뛰어난 전자 기타, 전자 베이스 기타, 앰프, 그리고 마이크가 발명되었다. 이는 로큰롤의 발전을 가속화시켰다. 음악가들은 이러한 전자 장비들을 사용하여 그들이 만들어낸 새로운 소리를 들려 주었다. 곧, 기본적인 로큰롤 캄보가 등장하기 시작했다. 이는 한 명이나 두 명의 전자 기타 연주자, 한 명의 전기 베이스 기타 연주자, 한 명의 드럼 연주자, 그리고 때때로 한 명의 키보드 연주자를 갖추고 있는 악단이었다. 일부 밴드들은 호른과 어쿠스틱 장비를 사용했다. 하지만 이들은 인기가 보다 적었다.

1950년대 초, 이러한 두 개의 요인들이 로큰롤의 시작을 이끌어 냈다. 1951년, 클리블랜드의 라디오 디스크 자키였던 앨런 프리드가 이러한 새로운 음악을 정기적으로 틀어 주기 시작했다. 또한 그러한 음악 차제를 지칭하기 위해 "로큰롤"이라는 용어를 만들어 냈다. (새로운 음악을 위해 그가 생각해 낸 이름은 곧 사람들에게 큰 인기를 끌었다.) 1955년, '빌 헤일리 앤 더 코메츠'가 _락 어라운드 더 클락_ 음반을 녹음했다. 이는 로큰롤 음악에서 최초의 히트 음반이 되었다. 비슷한 시기에, 엘비스 프레슬리가 첫 녹음을 마쳤다. 그는 음악과 무대 퍼포먼스로 전 세계적인 센세이션을 일으켰다. 로큰롤은 곧 주류 형태의 음악이 되었다. 오늘날에는, 모든 음악 장르 중에서 가장 있기 있는 위치에 놓여져 있다.

Ⓤⓝⓘⓣ 08
p.52

Sample Sentence Simplification Question

Translation

1800년대, 미국의 많은 지역은 아직 사람이 살지 않는 곳이었다. 사람들은 그러한 많은 지역에 거의 가보지를 못했다. 이러한 점은 풍경화가들에게 좋은 기회를 제공해 주었다. 이들은 개척되지 않은 야생 지역을 그리고 색칠할 수 있었다. 대부분의 사람들이 미국에 그처럼 아름다운 곳이 존재한다는 점을 몰랐기 때문에, 미국의 대중은 이러한 화가들이 그린 그림에 종종 놀라워했다. 그 결과, 많은 화가들이 큰 명성을 얻었다. 그러한 화가 중 한 명이 토마스 모란이었다. 그는 1837년에 영국에서 태어났지만, 그의 가족들은 곧 미국으로 이주를 했다. 모란이 미술에 흥미를 갖게 된 것도 바로 이곳에서였다. 모란은 오대호 주변을 그리고 색칠하느라 얼마 간의 시간을 보냈다. 하지만, 그가 명성을 얻게 된 것은 이곳이 아니었다. 그가 명성을 얻은 곳은 옐로스톤에서였다. 1871년, 모란은 옐로스톤 원정대의 화가로서 고용이 되었다. 그 일이 그의 인생을 바꾸어 놓았다.

Mini Test 1

Answers

1. Ⓒ (Sentence Simplification Question)

2. Ⓐ (Vocabulary Question)

3. Ⓑ (Negative Factual Question)

4. **2, 4, 6** (Prose Summary Question)

Translation

쾌속선

사람들은 수천 년 동안 무역을 해왔다. 다른 사람들과 무역을 하기 위해, 육로나 해로로 상품들을 운송시켜 왔다. 상인들은 항상 선박으로서 보다 많은 상품을 운반할 수 있었다. 따라서, 수 세기 동안, 사람들은 상인들로 하여금 상품들을 보다 빠르게 이곳에서 저곳으로 이동시킬 수 있게 해주는, 보다 빠른 범선을 만들려고 시도했다. 1800년대, 바다를 항해하는 가장 빠른 선박이 만들어졌다: 바로 쾌속선이었다.

진정한 최초의 쾌속선은 1830년대 초반 미국에서 건조되었다. 그러한 설계는 곧 영국 및 그 밖의 지역에서 모방되었다. 1840년대경, 쾌속선은 전 세계 바다에서 흔히 볼 수 있는 광경이 되었다. 쾌속선은 빠르기 위해 설계된 것이었다. 대부분의 쾌속선에는 여러 개의 돛이 달린 세 개의 돛대가 있었다. 이러한 돛은 사각형 형태였는데, 이로써 많은 바람을 받을 수 있었다. 또한 이 선박들은 폭이 좁은 선체를 가지고 있었으며, 이로써 속력은 더욱 빨라졌지만 많은 양의 화물을 싣지는 못하게 되었다.

쾌속선이 최초로 만들어졌을 당시, 대부분의 뱃사람들은 약 240킬로미터를 항해하면 훌륭한 편이라고 생각했다. 하지만, 쾌속선은 하루에 평균 400킬로미터를 갔다. 가장 빠른 쾌속선은 단 하루에 600킬로미터 이상을 항해할 수도 있었다. 상품을 빨리 수송해야 할 필요가 있는 경우, 이처럼 굉장한 속도는 쾌속선을 매우 가치 있는 것으로 만들었다. 예를 들어, 쾌속선은 중국과 인도로부터 유럽과 미국으로 종종 차를 가져다 주었다. 이들은 열대 과일을 북쪽 지역으로 운송하고 동시에 다른 상인들이 북쪽 지역에서 보다 따뜻한 지역으로 얼음을 선적시켜 보내는데 활용되었다. 그리고, 캘리포니아 골드 러시 기간에는, 이는 1849년에 시작되었는데, 수천 명의 탐광자들이 쾌속선을 타고 항해를 했다. 이들은 육로로 미국을 가로질러 간 사람들보다 훨씬 더 빠르게 남아메리카의 최남단을 거쳐 먼 거리를 항해했다.

하지만 쾌속선의 시대는 갑작스러운 종말을 맞이했다. 1800년대 중반에 증기선이 사용되기 시작한 것이었다. 이들은 쾌속선보다 빠르게 이동했고, 나아가기 위해 바람에 의존하지 않았다. 1870년대 무렵, 바다를 가로질러 상품을 운송하던 쾌속선의 숫자는 얼마 되지 않았다.

Mini Test 2

Answers

1. Ⓐ (Vocabulary Question)

2. Ⓓ (Sentence Simplification Question)

3. Ⓒ (Reference Question)

4. Ⓒ (Rhetorical Purpose Question)

5. Ⓑ (Factual Question)

Translation

왕가의 계곡

고대 이집트에서, 파라오가 매장된 장소는 매우 중요한 곳이었다. 많은 파라오들이 자신들의 마지막 안식처로서 기능할 피라미드를 건설했다. 지하 무덤을 건설한 파라오도 있었다. 오늘날 룩소르 시 근처의 나일강 서쪽 강둑에는 왕가의 계곡이라고 알려진 지역이 있다. 수 세기 동안, 18번째, 19번째, 그리고 20번째 통치자에 해당했던 이집트 파라오들이 그곳에 자신들의 무덤을 건설했다. 그 후로, 고고학자들과 도굴꾼들은 숨겨져 있는 무덤을 찾기 위해 이러한 지역을 샅샅이 조사해 왔다.

대부분의 고고학자들은 왕족의 구성원들이 기원전 16세기에서 18세기 사이에 이 계곡에 매장되었다는데 의견을 같이 한다. 고대 도시인 테베가 – 오늘날의 룩소르인데 – 계곡의 입구에 위치해 있다. 파라오 및 그 가족들의 무덤은 계곡의 석회암 안쪽에 파져 있거나 그곳 땅속에 묻혀 있다. 침입자들로부터 안전한 곳으로 만들기 위해 무덤을 숨기기 위한 노력이 이루어졌다. 하지만 그중 다수가 발견되었다.

현재까지, 고고학자들은 63개의 무덤을 발견해 냈다. 일부는 단순한 방 형태이지만 수많은 방을 지니고 있는 것들도 있다. 전형적인 무덤 안에는 중앙 묘실로 이어지는 기다란 복도가 있다. 측면에 있는 방들은 종종 복도로부터 뻗어나 있다. 이집트인들은 보물뿐만 아니라 그들이 생각하기에 죽은 사람들이 사후 세계에서 필요로 할 물건들을 이러한 방에 놓아 두었다. 왕가의 계곡에 매장되어 있는 파라오 중에는 세티 1세, 람세스 2세, 그리고 투탕카멘이 있었다.

투탕카멘의 무덤은 1922년에 하워드 카터에 의해 발견되었다. 그는 크게 중요하지

않은 파라오였고 십대에 사망했다. 하지만 그의 무덤이 발견됨으로써 전 세계 모든 이들의 관심이 집중되었다. 그 이유는 투탕카멘의 무덤이 손상되지 않은 상태로 발견되었기 때문이었다. 그곳은 온갖 종류의 보물들로 가득 차 있었다. 고대 이후로, 약탈자들이 왕가의 계곡에 있는 무덤에서 보물들을 약탈해 갔기 때문에, 이는 드문 경우였다. 카터의 발견 이후로, 그곳에서 3개의 무덤이 더 발굴되었다. 더 많은 무덤이 존재하고 있을 가능성이 높다. 사막에서 누군가에 의해 발견되기를 기다리고 있을 뿐이다.

Ｕｎｉｔ 09

p.58

Sample Fill in a Table Question

Translation

고고학에서 가장 흥미로운 분야 중 하나는 육지에서 이루어지지 않는다. 물속에서 이루어진다. 바로 수중 고고학이다. 최근, 많은 난파선들이 발견되어 조사되고 있다. 하지만 이러한 종류의 고고학은 실행하기가 어렵다. 이에 대한 몇 가지 이유가 존재한다. 우선, 토사와 진흙으로 된 층에 매몰되어 있는 난파선을 발견해 내기가 힘들다. 많은 경우, 고고학자들은 발견물을 조사하기 위해 스쿠버 장비를 이용해야 한다. 이는 또한 위험성을 지닌다. 수 세기 동안 수중에 있던 유물들을 보존하는 것도 문제가 될 수 있다. 그리고, 마지막으로, 바다에서 발굴을 하는 비용이 높다.

다행스럽게도, 고고학자들은 이러한 문제에 대해 몇 가지 해결 방안을 고안해 냈다. 수중 음파 탐지기와 같은 현대 기술을 이용하여 난파선을 찾고 있다. 이렇게 함으로써, 난파선이 정확히 어디에 있는지를 알기 전까지, 잠수를 할 필요가 없다. 안전한 방법을 채택함으로써 물속에 있는 잠수부들의 안전을 보장할 수 있다. 그리고 실험실에서는 유물들이 표면으로 옮겨진 후 이들이 손상되는 것을 방지할 수 있다.

Mini Test 1

Answers

1. Ⓒ (Reference Question)

2. Ⓑ (Factual Question)

3. Ⓓ (Vocabulary Question)

4. Ⓐ (Sentence Simplification Question)

5. Ⓐ (Negative Factual Question)

Translation

조셉 콘래드

조셉 콘래드는 19세기 후반과 20세기 초의 가장 위대한 작가 중 한 명이었다. 폴란드에서 태어났지만, 20대 때 영국으로 이주했다. 그곳에서, 그는 영어로 말하고 쓰는 법을 배웠다. 여러 해 동안, 콘래드는 선원이었다. 항해를 함으로써 극동 지역, 남아메리카, 그리고 전 세계 기타 지역들을 가볼 수 있었다. 그의 개인적인 경험은 종종 자신의 모험 소설의 기반이 되었다.

콘래드가 살았던 당시, 많은 사람들이 전 세계의 특이한 지역으로 여행을 하고 있었다. 특히 작가들이 그러했다. 예를 들어, 허먼 멜빌은 자신의 경험을 기반으로 *모비딕*과 오무를 썼다. *황야의 부르짖음*의 작가인 잭 런던은 알래스카와 캐나다 북부를 여행했다. 루디야드 키플링은 자신이 인도에서 보냈던 시기에 대해 많은 소설을 썼다. 그의 작품에는 정글북과 킴이 포함되어 있었다. 그러한 점에 있어서 콘래드도 동시대의 사람들과 비슷했다. 그는 이국적인 장소로의 여행을 많은 소설의 기반으로서 활용했다.

콘래드는 1895년에 자신의 첫 번째 책을 출판했다. 제목은 올메이어의 우행이었다. 네덜란드령 동인도 제도를 배경으로 삼았는데, 이곳은 그가 이전에 방문했던 지역이었다. 콘래드 작품 중 다수는 이국적인 인물들로 가득한 해양 모험 소설이었다. 때때로 가상의 지역을 만들어 냈지만, 주로 그가 방문했던 지역에 기반해 있었다. 예를 들어, 그의 가장 뛰어난 작품 중의 하나인 노스트로모는 남미의 가상 국가를 그 배경으로 하고 있다.

일반적으로 콘래드의 작품들은 복잡한 편이며 많은 등장 인물들과 주제가 포함되어

있다. 그의 소설은 어조에 있어서 비관적인 경향을 보인다. 주인공은 종종 반영웅이다. 이러한 특성들 모두는 아마도 그의 가장 유명한 작품인 *어둠의 심장*에서 명백히 드러난다. 아프리카의 콩고가 배경인 이 책의 주제는 유럽의 백인들에 의해 아프리카가 식민지화되는 것이다. 정글에서 미쳐서 스스로가 왕과 같은 지도자가 되는 유럽 출신의 한 백인에 관한 이야기를 들려 준다.

모두 합해서, 콘래드는 1924년에 사망하기 전까지 18개의 소설을 썼다. 오늘날, 그의 소설 중 다수는 위대한 문학 작품으로서 여전히 추앙을 받고 있다.

Mini Test 2

Answers

1. Ⓓ (Factual Question)

2. Ⓑ (Inference Question)

3. Ⓒ (Rhetorical Purpose Question)

4. **Elliptical: 3, 6   Spiral: 1, 4, 7** (Fill in a Table Question)

Translation

은하의 종류

은하는 우주 내 다수의 항성들이 모여 있는 곳이다. 지구의 은하는 은하수이다. 천문학자들은, 확신하지는 못하지만, 은하수에 2천억 개에서 4천억 개의 항성들이 존재한다고 믿는다. 은하수는 우주에 있는 수십 억 개의 은하 중의 하나일 뿐이다. 이러한 은하들은 서로 같아 보이지 않는다. 다양한 형태를 가지고 있다. 1920년대에, 미국인 천문학자인 에드윈 허블이 그 형태에 기반하여 은하의 분류 체계를 만들었다. 그는 두 개의 기본적인 형태가 존재한다는 점을 알아냈다: 타원형과 나선형이 그것이다. 그는 또한 불규칙 은하라고 불리는, 세 번째 그룹도 확인해 냈다.

타원형 은하는 구 형태를 갖는다. 일부는 다른 것에 비해 보다 길쭉하다. 이러한 은하는 E0에서 E7까지의 범위로 분류된다. E0 은하는 거의 완전한 원형을 띤다. E7에 대해 말하자면, 이는 매우 길쭉한 타원형 형태를 갖기 때문에 다소 평평한 형태를 보인다. 타원형 은하에는 극도로 밝은 중심이 있으며 가장 자리는 희미하다. 주로, 이미 형성되어 있는 항성들로 이루어져 있다. 따라서 새로운 항성을 만드는데 필요한 성간 물질이 거의 포함되어 있지 않다. 타원형 은하는 우주에서 가장 크다. 일부에는 수조 개의 항성들이 포함되어 있다. 천문학자들은 이중 다수가 두 개 혹은 그 이상의 은하가 충돌했을 때 생성되었다고 믿고 있다.

나선형 은하에는 밝은 빛을 내는 중심 부풀음과, 부풀음에서 뻗어나 있는 팔이 있다. 또한 헤일로도 있는데, 여기에는 매우 오래된 항성들이 포함되어 있다. 중심 부풀음은 두 가지 형태를 띤다: 구 형태와 가로 무늬가 있는 형태이다. 부풀음에는 오래된 항성이 있는 반면, 보다 밝은 빛을 내는 팔에는 새로 생긴 항성이 포함되어 있다. 지구의 태양은 은하수의 팔 중 한 곳에 놓여져 있다. 이러한 은하는 S 혹은 SB 은하로 분류된다. S 은하는 구형인 중심 부풀음을 갖고 있는데 비해, SB 은하는 가로 무늬가 있는 중심 부풀음을 갖는다. 나선형 은하에는 그 팔의 형태와 외형에 따른 기타 하위 그룹들이 존재한다.

불규칙 은하에는 특정한 형태나 구조가 없다. 천문학자들은 이들을 Irr I과 Irr II 은하로 구분한다. 전자에는 매우 뜨거운 어린 항성들이 있다. 후자에는 너무나 많은 더스트가 포함되어 있기 때문에, 그 안에서 항성을 찾아내는 것이 불가능하다.

Unit 10
p.64

Sample Prose Summary Question

Translation

전 세계의 일부 지역들은 폭우가 내리는 시기를 겪게 된다. 또한 봄에 눈과 얼음이 녹아서 수위가 상승할 수도 있다. 두 경우 모두에 있어서, 홍수가 발생할 수 있다. 홍수에는 몇 가지 긍정적인 이점이 있다. 하지만 부정적인 영향이 더 많다. 가장 명백한 결과는 홍수가 인공 구조물에 야기하는 피해이다. 홍수는 건물과 도로를 파괴시키고 다리와 기타 구조물들을 유실되도록 만들 수 있다. 홍수는 – 특히 갑작스러운 홍수는 –

강이나 시내의 수위가 갑작스럽게 상승하는 경우, 사람들의 목숨을 앗아갈 수도 있다. 홍수는 또한 자연 환경에도 피해를 입힌다. 귀중한 표토를 유실시킬 수 있는데, 이로써 토지의 비옥도가 낮아지게 된다. 일부 지역에서는 침식을 일으킬 수도 있는데, 이로써 토지의 형태가 변하게 된다. 과도한 양의 물은 많은 식물 및 동물들을 죽일 수 있다. 마지막으로, 홍수는 전염병을 발생시킬 수 있다. 홍수의 여파로, 사람과 동물 모두가 다양한 질병에 걸리는 경우가 흔하다.

Mini Test 1

Answers

1. Ⓑ (Factual Question)

2. Ⓐ (Rhetorical Purpose Question)

3. **3ʳᵈ** (Insert Text Question)

4. **2, 4, 5** (Prose Summary Question)

Translation

새의 둥지

사실상 모든 조류의 종들이 일종의 둥지를 만든다. 새들이 둥지를 짓는 주된 이유는 알을 낳고 그런 다음에 알을 품기 위한 장소를 마련하기 위해서이다. 또한, 새들은 종종 둥지에서 잠을 자며, 포식자들로부터 몸을 피할 수 있는 장소로 둥지를 활용한다. 하지만 모든 새의 둥지들이 똑같은 것은 아니다; 새들은 다양한 장소에 둥지를 짓고 다양한 재료들로 둥지를 만든다.

전형적으로 새의 둥지의 위치는 매우 중요하다. 비록 많은 새들이 나뭇가지에 둥지를 틀지만, 보다 창의적인 새들도 있다. 예를 들어, 바다새는 종종 해안가 근처의 절벽에서 발견되는, 천연 동굴에 둥지를 짓는다. 많은 종의 딱따구리들은 나무에 굴을 파서 나무 안에 둥지를 짓는다. 펭귄과 같이 날지 못하는 새들은 지상에 둥지를 짓는다. (타조는, 날지 못하는 또 다른 새인데, 똑같은 행동을 한다.) 많은 새들은 인공 구조물에 둥지를 지음으로써 인간의 존재에 적응해 오고 있다. 제비들은 때때로 주택의 처마나 축사 내에 둥지를 틀며, 반면 송골매와 매는 대도시 지역의 고층 건물 중 튀어 나와 있는 부분에 둥지를 짓는다.

또한 둥지를 만드는데 사용하는 재료에 있어서도 새들은 창의적일 수 있다. 대부분의 새들은 그것이 무엇이던 자신들이 찾아 낼 수 있는 천연 재료들을 이용한다. 대부분의 경우, 나뭇가지, 잎, 그리고 풀로 둥지를 짓는다. 보다 단단한 나뭇가지가 둥지의 지주 역할을 하며, 따라서 내구성과 견고함을 제공해 준다. 그런 다음, 새들은 둥지를 부드럽게 만들고 빈 곳을 채우기 위해 나뭇잎과 풀을 추가시킨다. 몇몇 새들은 또한 돌, 이끼, 진흙, 그리고 깃털로 둥지를 만들기도 한다. 또한 새의 둥지에서 인간이 만든 다양한 물건들을 보게 되는 것도 특이한 일이 아니다. 본질적으로, 새들은 이용할 수 있는 모든 것을 이용하여, 알을 낳으면 알을 보관할 수 있고 그 후에는 갓 부화한 새끼들을 놓아둘 수 있는 둥지를 만든다.

Mini Test 2

Answers

1. Ⓒ (Vocabulary Question)

2. Ⓓ (Reference Question)

3. Ⓑ (Factual Question)

4. Ⓒ (Factual Question)

5. Ⓐ (Inference Question)

Translation

합금

수천 년 동안, 선사 시대의 사람들은 석기 시대에 살았다. 이들은 돌로부터 원시적인 도구를 만들었다. 그런 다음, 기원전 약 3300년경, 인간은 청동을 만드는 방법을 알아냈고, 청동기 시대에 진입했다. 청동은 기초 금속이 아니었다; 주석과 구리의 합성 물질이었다. 청동으로 인해, 사람들은 보다 강력하고 보다 날카로운 도구를 만들 수 있었다. 이로써 문명이 훨씬 더 빠르게 발전할 수 있었다.

청동은 합금이다. 합금이란 두 개 이상의 원소들이 합쳐져서 새로운 금속이 만들어진 것이다. 합금에는 항상 하나의 모재가 존재한다. 더해지는 첨가 원소는 금속일 수도 있고 금속이 아닐 수도 있다. 청동은 인류가 발명한 최초의 합금이었다. 하지만 다른 것들도 많다. 황동은 구리와 아연의 합성 물질이다. 일렉트럼은 은과 구리의 합성 물질이다. 강철은 또 다른 합금이다. 이는 철과 탄소로 만들어진다. 이들은 잘 알려져 있는 세 개의 합금이다.

합금에서 주된 금속은 모재라고 불린다. 다른 것들은 용질이다. 합금은 일반적으로 원소들을 녹여서 이들을 합성시킴으로써 만들어진다. 이때 매우 높은 열이 요구될 수도 있는데, 그 이유는 모든 원소들이 서로 다른 용해점을 갖기 때문이다. 새롭게 만들어진 합금은 종종 각 금속들의 용해점을 유지한다. 따라서 합금의 일부가 어떤 온도에서 녹기 시작할 수 있는 반면, 전체를 녹이기 위해서는 보다 높은 온도가 요구된다. 하지만, 원소들이 특정한 비율로 결합되면, 합금은 통상 새로운 용해점을 갖게 된다.

합금의 매력은 그것의 물리적 특성이 원래 원소들의 특성과 다르다는 점이다. 합금은 그 성분이 되는 금속들보다 더 딱딱하고, 더 가볍고, 혹은 더 단단할 수 있다. 열에 견디는 능력과 전기를 전도시킬 수 있는 능력 또한 바뀔 수 있다. 강철은 각 성분들보다 더 단단하고 더 딱딱한 합금의 한 예이다. 오늘날, 많은 합금들이 특별한 목적을 위해 만들어지고 있다. 예를 들어, 비행기, 로켓, 그리고 우주선은 특별한 합금을 필요로 한다. 가볍지만 강하고 열과 압력 모두를 견딜 수 있어야 한다. 티타늄은 – 알루미늄, 철, 그리고 기타 원소로 이루어진 합성 물질인데 – 항공 우주 산업에서 흔한 합금이다.

Chapter 2

Listening

Unit 01

p.72

Sample Gist-Content Question

Translation

M Professor: 사람들은 수천 년 동안 서로 간에 거래를 해왔습니다. 최초의 거래는 자신의 이웃들과 교환을, 어, 아시다시피 물물 교환을 한 사람들에 의해 이루어졌습니다. 아마도 어떤 사람이 또 다른 사람이 가지고 있던 고기를 얻기 위해 곡식을 거래했을 수도 있습니다. 혹은 동물의 가죽을 얻기 위해 누군가가 무기를 거래했을 수도 있고요. 누가 알겠습니까? 저는 사람들이 온갖 종류의 거래를 했을 것이라고 확신합니다.

시간이 지나면서, 사람들은 보다 멀리 떨어져 있는 다른 사람들과 거래를 하기 시작했습니다. 상인들은, 음, 자신들의 상품을 팔거나 거래하기 위해 새로운 지역으로 이동을 하기 시작했습니다. 이러한 상인들은 여행을 하면서 무역 루트를 만들었습니다. 무역 루트는, 흠… 상인들이 이곳에서 저곳으로 상품을 운송할 때 사용했던 길이라고 말씀을 드려야 할 것 같군요. 무역 루트는 육로나 수로일 수 있습니다. 최초의 무역 루트 중 다수는 사실상 수로를 통한 것이었습니다. 그 이유는 말이나 마차보다 배로써 많은 양의 상품을 운송하는 것이 보다 용이하기 때문입니다.

역사를 통해, 수상 무역 루트가 존재해 왔습니다. 일부는 단순한 것이었습니다. 단지 뗏목에 상품을 싣고 하류로 뗏목을 흘려 보낸 것과 관련된 것이었습니다. 바다를 건너는 항해와 관련된 것들도 있었습니다. 예를 들면, 어, 유럽인들은 아프리카 남쪽으로 항해를 함으로써, 인도에 이르는 무역 루트를 발견해 냈습니다. 또한 북미와 남미에 이르는 무역 루트도 개척했습니다. 물론, 육상 무역 루트 또한 존재합니다. 아마도 실크로드가 그중 가장 유명할 것입니다. 이는 중국에서 시작되어, 인도를 거쳐, 그리고 로마에서 끝이 났습니다.

아마도 여러분들께서는 왜 사람들이 무역 루트를 건설했는지에 대해 궁금해 하실 것 같군요. 이에 대해서는 많은 이유가 존재합니다. 그리고 그것이 제가 지금 여러분과 함께 논의하고 싶은 것이기도 합니다. 여러분 중에 알고 계신 분이 있나요? 어떻게 생각하시나요? 왜 사람들이 무역 루트를 건설했을까요…?

Mini Test 1 : Conversation

Answers

1. Ⓑ (Gist-Content Question)

2. Ⓓ (Detail Question)

3. Ⓑ (Understanding Function Question)

4. Ⓐ (Making Inferences Question)

Script 🔊 1-02

W Student: Greetings, Professor Nelson. I'm here to see you like you requested.

M Professor: Ah, thank you for dropping by, Alice. I know you're busy today, but I hope you can spare a few minutes to speak with me.

W: Of course, sir. I don't have to go to my next class until three. So I've got an hour of free time.

M: Excellent, excellent.

W: So, uh, what do you want to talk to me about?

M: It's about the paper you need to write. I'm talking about the one that's due in two weeks.

W: Ah, sure. I haven't started writing it yet. I'm kind of busy at the moment. So, um, I probably won't begin until, hmm . . . next week I guess.

M: Well, if you don't mind, I'd like you to turn in your paper a week early. I'd like you to submit it by November 23.

W: By next week? B-b-but . . . How come I need to turn it in before everyone else?

M: Excuse me. Well, to be honest, Alice, your grade in this class is rather low. So, um, I'd like to help you out a bit. If you turn in the paper early, I will grade it immediately. I will return it to you two days after I receive it. Then, you can make any changes that I suggest and fix your paper. Once you do that, you can resubmit the paper.

W: Oh, I see. That way, I'll have a chance to get a higher grade. Okay, sure, that's a cool idea. I can go for that.

M: Wonderful. So get started on that paper right away, please. If you do that, you should be able to get your grade up from a C to a B. That would make both of us happy.

Translation

W Student: 안녕하세요. Nelson 교수님. 말씀하신 대로 교수님을 뵙기 위해 여기에 왔습니다.

M Professor: 아, 들려 줘서 고마워요, Alice. 학생이 오늘 바쁜 것은 알고 있지만, 저와 이야기를 나누기 위해 몇 분간 시간을 내줄 수 있기를 바라요.

W: 물론이에요, 교수님. 3시까지는 다음 수업에 가지 않아도 되거든요. 그래서 한 시간 동안은 한가하죠.

M: 잘 되었군요, 잘 되었어요.

W: 그러면, 어, 저와 무엇에 대해 이야기하고 싶으신가요?

M: 학생이 써야 할 보고서에 관해서요. 2주일 후에 마감인 보고서를 말씀드리고 있는 거에요.

W: 아, 그래요. 쓰는 것을 아직 시작도 못했어요. 지금은 바쁜 때라서요. 그래서, 음, 아마도, 흠… 제 생각에는 다음 주까지는 시작하지 못할 것 같아요.

M: 음, 괜찮다면, 학생이 1주일 빨리 보고서를 제출해 주었으면 해요. 11월 23일까지 제출해 주었으면 해요.

W: 다음 주까지요? 하–하–하지만… 왜 제가 다른 사람들보다 먼저 제출해야 하나요?

10

M: 미안해요. 음, 솔직히 말하면, Alice, 이번 수업에서 학생의 성적은 다소 낮은
편이에요. 그래서, 음, 제가 학생에게 약간의 도움을 주고 싶어요. 보고서를 빨리
제출하면, 제가 바로 성적을 매길 거예요. 보고서를 받고 이틀 후에 다시 돌려 주도록
할게요. 그러면, 학생은 제가 제안한 대로 보고서를 고쳐서 수정을 할 수 있을 거예요.
그렇게 한 다음에는, 보고서를 다시 제출할 수 있고요.

W: 오, 알겠어요. 그렇게 하면, 보다 높은 성적을 받을 수 있는 기회를 얻게 되겠군요.
좋아요, 물론이에요. 멋진 아이디어군요. 그렇게 할 게요.

M: 잘 되었군요. 그러면 지금 바로 보고서 작성을 시작하세요. 그렇게 하면, C에서 B까지
성적을 올릴 수 있게 될 거예요. 그러면 우리 둘 모두에게 좋을 것 같군요.

Mini Test 2 : Lecture

Answers

1. Ⓒ (Gist-Content Question)

2. **Temperate Zone:** 1 , 3 , 4   **Tropical Zone:** 2
   (Connecting Content Question)

3. Ⓑ (Understanding Organization Question)

4. Ⓐ (Detail Question)

Script 1-03

W Professor: I'd like to turn your attention to the various climate zones on the planet. The Earth has three distinct climate zones. They are the polar zones, the temperate zones, and the tropical zone. Roughly speaking, the polar zones are located north of sixty degrees latitude and south of sixty degrees latitude. Uh, remember that there are polar zones in both the Northern and Southern hemispheres. The same is true of the temperate zones. They are located between twenty-three and sixty degrees north and south latitude. There is just one tropical zone. It's found between twenty-three degrees north latitude and twenty-three degrees south latitude. Please understand that these numbers are just rough guides. It's not like the climate changes abruptly at a certain degree of latitude. Nature simply doesn't work like that.

Within each zone, there is a standard climate. For example, the weather in the polar zones is mostly cold and icy except for during the very short summers they experience. The temperate zones, however, get a variety of temperatures and weather. They experience rainy, dry, sunny, cloudy, hot, cold, and . . . well, you get the point. The temperate zones get all kinds of weather. Note that the temperate zones are warmer than the polar zones yet cooler than the tropical zone. As for the tropical zone, it's characterized by high temperatures, high humidity, and plenty of rainfall.

There are, however, exceptions to these norms. For example, there are deserts in both the temperate and tropical zones that get very little water. Think about the Sahara Desert. It's mostly situated in the northern temperate zone. Some of the highest recorded temperatures on the planet have been recorded there. Also, some high mountain ranges in both the temperate and tropical zones have snow and freezing temperatures. There's even a mountain range in tropical Uganda that has snow on its highest peaks.

There are other factors that also affect the climate in these zones. Let's see . . . The coastlines of continents and their interiors often have very different climates. This is true even if the regions are at the same degree of latitude. Ocean currents can affect the climate as well. Think about the role that the Gulf Stream plays. It keeps the weather in parts of Northern Europe much warmer than it really should be.

Another factor is the tilt of the Earth's axis. Because of that, we have seasons. This causes the weather in each climate zone to vary throughout the year. This variation is most pronounced in the temperate zones. So they have four distinct seasons. The polar zones and tropical zone experience smaller changes though. The polar zones, for instance, heat up a bit in summer. Some places even become green. But the ice caps in the far north and south don't melt. As for the tropical zone, it gets slightly cooler or hotter. But most people don't notice the difference.

Translation

W Professor: 지구 상의 다양한 기후대로 관심을 돌리고 싶군요. 지구에는 서로 구별되는 세 개의 기후대가 존재합니다. 한대 지방, 온대 지방, 그리고 열대 지방이 그것이죠. 대략적으로 말씀을 드리면, 한대 지방은 북위 60도와 남위 60도에 위치해 있습니다. 어, 북반구와 남반구 모두에 한대 지방이 존재한다는 점을 기억해 주세요. 온대 지방에 있어서도 마찬가지입니다. 이들은 북위 및 남위 23도와 60도 사이에 위치해 있습니다. 열대 지방은 단 한 곳에만 있습니다. 북위 23도와 남위 23도 사이에서 발견됩니다. 이러한 수치들은 대략적인 가이드용일 뿐이라는 점을 이해해 주십시오. 특정 위도에서 갑작스러운 기후 변화가 일어나는 것은 아닙니다. 자연에서는 그와 같은 일이 일어나지 않습니다.

각각의 지방에서는, 표준적인 기후가 존재합니다. 예를 들면, 한대 지방의 날씨는, 그곳에서 나타나는 매우 짧은 여름 기간을 제외하면, 대부분 쌀쌀하고 매우 추운 편입니다. 하지만, 온대 지방에는 다양한 기온 및 날씨가 존재합니다. 이곳에서는 비가 많고, 건조하고, 화창하고, 구름이 많이 끼고, 덥고, 춥고, 그리고… 음, 무슨 말인지 아실 것입니다. 온대 지방에는 모든 종류의 날씨가 존재합니다. 온대 지방은 한대 지방보다 더 따뜻하지만 열대 지방보다는 더 서늘하다는 점을 주목해 주세요. 열대 지방에 대해 말씀을 드리면, 이곳은 높은 기온, 높은 습도, 그리고 많은 양의 강우를 그 특징으로 삼습니다.

하지만, 이러한 기준에 있어서 예외가 존재합니다. 예를 들면, 온대 지방과 열대 지방 모두에는 비가 거의 내리지 않는 사막이 존재합니다. 사하라 사막에 대해 생각해 보세요. 이는 주로 온대 지방의 북쪽에 위치해 있습니다. 지구에서 가장 높았던 기온 중 몇몇은 그곳에서 기록되었습니다. 또한, 온대 지방과 열대 지방 모두에 있는 몇몇 높은 산맥에서는 눈이 내리며 매우 낮은 온도를 보입니다. 열대에 있는 우간다에서는 산정상에 눈이 있는 산맥이 존재하기도 합니다.

이러한 지역의 기후에 영향을 미치는 또 다른 요인들도 존재합니다. 봅시다… 종종 대륙의 해안가와 그 내륙에서 서로 매우 다른 기후가 나타납니다. 심지어 같은 위도 상에 있는 지역들에서도 그렇습니다. 해류 또한 기후에 영향을 미칠 수 있습니다. 멕시코 만류가 하고 있는 역할에 대해 생각해 보세요. 이는 북부 유럽 지역의 날씨를 과도할 정도로 따뜻하게 만듭니다.

또 다른 요인은 지축의 기울기입니다. 이 때문에, 계절이 나타납니다. 이로써 각각의 기후대는 연중 다양한 날씨를 갖게 됩니다. 이러한 다양성은 온대 지방에서 가장 분명하게 나타납니다. 따라서 여기에서는 서로 뚜렷이 구분되는 4개의 계절이 존재합니다. 하지만 한대 지방과 열대 지방은 보다 작은 변화만을 겪습니다. 한대 지방은, 예를 들어, 여름에 약간만 열을 받습니다. 일부 지역들은 심지어 푸르게 됩니다. 하지만, 극북과 극남의 만년설은 녹지 않습니다. 열대 지방에 대해 말하자면, 약간 더 춥거나 약간 더 덥습니다. 하지만 대부분의 사람들은 그 차이를 알아차리지 못합니다.

Unit 02
p.76

Sample Gist-Purpose Question

Translation

W1 Student Housing Office Employee: 네? 제가 도와 드릴 일이라도 있나요?

W2 Student: 그렇게 해주셨으면 좋겠어요. 기숙사 방을 바꾸기에는 시간이 너무 늦었나요?

W1: 아니에요. 너무 늦지는 않았어요. 바꿀 수 있는 기한은 내일 모레까지죠. 하지만, 그렇게 하기 위해서는 충분한 사유가 있어야 해요. 왜 다른 곳으로 방을 옮기고자 하나요?

W2: 제 기숙사 방이 너무 시끄러워서요. 제 말은, 어, 학생들이 항상 음악을 틀고, 복도 주변을 뛰어다니고, 그리고… 음, 너무 시끄럽게 굴어요.

W1: 알겠어요. 그러면 어디로 방을 옮기고자 하나요?

W2: 캠퍼스 내에 조용한 기숙사가 있다고 들었어요. 사실인가요?

W1: 네, 그래요. Deacon Hall이 조용한 기숙사예요. 그곳에서 학생들은 어느 때라도 음악을 틀거나 시끄러운 소리를 내지 못하도록 되어 있죠.

W2: 오, 완벽할 것 같군요. 제 성적에 문제가 생기기 전에 그곳으로 방을 꼭 옮겨야 할 것 같아요. Deacon Hall에 적어도 하나의 빈 방이 있다고 말씀해 주셨으면 해요.

W1: 확인해 볼게요… 음, 운이 좋으시군요. 그 기숙사에 들어갈 수 있는 방이 세 개가 있네요. 선호하는 층이 있나요?

W2: 흠… 가능하면 가장 높은 층이었으면 해요. 지상에서 가까운 아래층에 있는 것은 좋아하지 않거든요. 몇 번째 층을 주실 수 있나요?

Mini Test 1 : Conversation

Answers

1. (A) (Gist-Purpose Question)

2. (B) (Detail Question)

3. (B) (Understanding Function Question)

4. (D) (Making Inferences Question)

Script 🎧 1-05

M Student: Good afternoon. Would you happen to be Ms. Samantha Whittaker?

W Bursar's Office Employee: That's right. I'm Samantha. And you are?

M: My name is Eric Gilbert. I called you yesterday and made an appointment with you for today. I'm here to speak with you now.

W: Ah, right. I scheduled you for two thirty. I wasn't expecting you to be here so early. Anyway, uh, please take a seat . . . Now, why don't you tell me what you're here about?

M: Sure thing. Um, two weeks ago, I received this letter from your office. Here it is . . . Basically, uh, the letter reads that I haven't paid my tuition.

W: Okay. We send out a lot of these. So I don't know the exact reason we sent you a letter like this. Well, hold on. Of course I know the reason: You haven't paid your tuition. That's why we mailed you the letter. But I'd like to know your reason for not paying it.

M: Ah, right. That's what I am here to discuss with you.

W: Sure. Go on.

M: I have a scholarship from a local charity. It pays half of my tuition. And my family pays the other half. If you'll notice, my family paid half of my tuition a while ago. However, the charity hasn't paid the other half yet.

W: That's not good. Is the charity going to send the money sometime soon?

M: Yes, it is. I have another letter here . . . Take a look. The charity had some problems, but now they're solved. So the money will be sent by this Friday. Is that acceptable?

W: It should be. Let me read this letter more closely. Hold on a second.

Translation

M Student: 안녕하세요. 혹시 Samantha Whittaker 선생님이신가요?

W Bursar's Office Employee: 맞아요. 제가 Samantha예요. 그러면 학생은요?

M: 제 이름은 Eric Gilbert예요. 어제 제가 전화를 드려서 오늘 선생님과의 약속을 잡았죠. 선생님과 말씀을 나누기 위해 지금 이곳에 온 것이고요.

W: 아, 맞아요. 학생과 2시 30분에 만나기로 시간을 정했죠. 이렇게 일찍 여기에 오리라고는 예상을 하지 못했네요. 어쨌든, 어, 앉으세요… 자, 무엇 때문에 학생이 여기에 왔는지 제게 말씀해 주시겠어요?

M: 물론 그럴게요. 음, 2주 전에, 선생님 사무실로부터 이 편지를 받았어요. 여기에 있어요… 기본적으로, 어, 편지에는 제가 등록금을 내지 않았다고 쓰여 있더군요.

W: 알겠어요. 저희는 이러한 편지들을 많이 발송하고 있죠. 그래서 이와 같은 편지를 학생에게 보낸 정확한 이유는 잘 모르겠어요. 음, 잠시만요. 그래요, 이유를 알겠네요: 학생이 등록금을 지불하지 않았군요. 그것이 바로 저희가 편지를 발송한 이유예요. 하지만 등록금을 지불하지 않은 학생의 이유를 알고 싶군요.

M: 아, 맞아요. 그것이 바로 선생님과 논의하기 위해 제가 여기에 온 이유예요.

W: 그래요. 말씀해 보세요.

M: 저는 지역 자선 단체로부터 장학금을 받고 있어요. 학비의 절반을 대주죠. 그리고 제 가족들이 나머지 절반을 대주고요. 확인해 보시면, 제 가족들은 얼마 전에 학비의 절반을 지급해 주었어요. 하지만, 자선 단체에서 아직 나머지 반을 지급해 주지 않았어요.

W: 좋지 않군요. 자선 단체에서 빠른 시간 내에 학비를 보내 줄 예정인가요?

M: 네, 그래요. 여기에 또 다른 편지가 있어요… 보세요. 자선 단체에 약간의 문제가 있었지만, 이제 해결되었어요. 그래서 이번 주 금요일까지 송금이 될 거예요. 괜찮을까요?

W: 그럴 거예요. 제가 이 편지를 보다 자세히 읽어 볼게요. 잠시만 기다려 주세요.

Mini Test 2 : Lecture

Answers

1. (B) (Gist-Content Question)

2. (C) (Gist-Purpose Question)

3. (A) (Detail Question)

4. (A) (Making Inferences Question)

Script 🎧 1-06

W Professor: In today's lecture, I'd like to discuss some aspects of animal territorialism. This refers to the space that an animal or, uh, a group of animals occupies. Basically, the animals mark an area as their own. They do this for a few reasons. The main one is that their food sources are in that territory. For instance, um, predatory animals such as lions and wolves often mark off a large area of land. That's where they get their food. As for other animals, their territory might contain their breeding grounds. In addition, newborn animals often hide in a group's territory. There, the parents and other adults can protect them from various dangers.

M Student: How do animals know where another animal's territory begins? And how do they know how large the territory is? Could you talk about that, please?

W: It would be my pleasure. Animals have three main ways of indicating to other animals that they have, um, claimed a certain area as their territory. The first way is by using noises. Some birds, for instance, make sounds that tell other birds that they shouldn't enter a certain area. The second way that animals mark their territory is simply through their physical presence. Some animals patrol the edges of their territory.

If other animals try to enter it, they may act in an aggressive manner. For instance, some animals rely on visual displays to frighten off trespassers. The hippopotamus does this. If an animal goes too near a riverbank that a hippo considers its own, it will open its mouth wide and display its teeth. If the animal moves closer, the hippo will respond physically. It will charge and attack the invading animal. The third way that many animals mark their territory is by using scents. They might urinate on trees or bushes. Others have special glands in their bodies. These glands secrete liquids that animals can smell and identify as territory markers.

In many cases, when an animal comes too close or tries to enter another's territory, the animal claiming the area will defend it. As I just mentioned, the hippo does that. Many others behave the same way. Some make aggressive visual displays. If the intruder leaves, they won't pursue it. However, if an animal goes far into another's territory, the defending animal will attack it. Wolves are known for doing this. So are lions. They do this because a lot is at stake. The animals are defending their food supply. By letting in other animals—even members of their own species—they run the risk of having less food to eat. The animals also need to protect their young. This is especially true of birds. Some birds have to wait a long time for their eggs to hatch. So they behave rather aggressively when an animal invades their territory.

Now, let's check out some individual species and see how they behave. We'll start with some well-known predators. First up is the wolf . . .

Translation

W Professor: 오늘 강의에서는, 동물의 영역성에 관한 몇 가지 측면에 대해 논의해 보고자 합니다. 이는 동물이나, 어, 동물의 무리가 차지하고 있는 공간을 지칭합니다. 기본적으로, 동물들은 일정 지역을 자신의 영토로 표시합니다. 몇 가지 이유 때문에 그렇게 하는 것이죠. 주된 이유는 그들의 먹이가 그 영역 안에 있기 때문입니다. 예를 들어, 음, 사자 및 늑대와 같은 포식 동물들은 종종 넓은 지역에 표시를 해둡니다. 그들이 먹이를 얻는 장소인 것입니다. 다른 동물들에 대해 말하지만, 그들의 영토에는 새끼를 기르는 장소가 포함되어 있을 수 있습니다. 또한, 새끼 동물들은 종종 무리의 영역 내에서 몸을 숨기기도 합니다. 그곳에서는, 어미와 기타 성숙한 개체들이 다양한 위험으로부터 새끼들을 보호해 줄 수 있습니다.

M Student: 어디에서 또 다른 동물의 영역이 시작된다는 점을 동물들이 어떻게 아나요? 그리고 그러한 영역이 얼마나 큰지를 어떻게 알죠? 그에 대해 말씀해 주실 수 있으신가요?

W: 물론 말씀해 드리죠. 동물들에게는 자신들이, 음, 특정 지역을 자신의 영역으로 차지하고 있다는 점을 다른 동물들에게 알려 줄 수 있는 세 가지 주요한 방법이 있습니다. 첫 번째 방법은 소리를 이용하는 것입니다. 몇몇 새들은, 예를 들면, 다른 새들이 특정 영역으로 들어오지 못하도록 소리를 냅니다. 동물들이 자신의 영역을 나타내는 두 번째 방법은 물리적으로 그곳에 존재하는 것입니다. 몇몇 동물들은 영토의 가장자리를 돌아다닙니다. 다른 동물들이 그곳에 진입하려고 하면, 그들은 공격적인 태도로 행동을 하게 될 것입니다. 예를 들어, 일부 동물들은 침입자들을 위협하여 쫓아내기 위해 시각적인 모습에 의존합니다. 하마가 그렇게 합니다. 자신의 영토라고 생각하는 강둑 주변에 어떤 동물이 너무 가까이 다가오면, 하마는 입을 크게 벌려 이빨을 내보입니다. 그러한 동물이 보다 가까이 다가오면, 하마는 신체적으로 반응을 합니다. 돌격해서 침입한 동물을 공격할 것입니다. 많은 동물들이 영역을 표시하는 세 번째 방법은 냄새를 이용하는 것입니다. 이들은 나무나 수풀에 소변을 볼 수도 있습니다. 신체 내에 특별한 분비선을 가지고 있는 동물들도 있습니다. 이러한 분비선에서는 액체가 분비되는데, 이로써 동물들은 그 냄새를 맡고 이를 영역 표시 장치로 인식하게 됩니다.

많은 경우, 어떤 동물이 다른 동물의 영토에 너무 가까이 다가가거나 여기에 진입하려고 할 때, 그 지역을 차지하고 있는 동물은 방어를 하게 됩니다. 조금 전에 말씀을 드렸듯이, 하마가 그렇게 합니다. 다른 많은 동물들도 동일한 방식으로 행동을 합니다. 일부는 시각적으로 공격적인 자세를 취합니다. 침입자가 떠나는 경우에는 이를 쫓지 않을 것입니다. 하지만, 어떤 동물이 또 다른 동물의 영역으로 너무 깊이

들어간다면, 방어하는 동물이 공격을 하게 될 것입니다. 늑대들이 그러한 행동을 하는 것으로 알려져 있습니다. 사자들도 마찬가지고요. 많은 것의 성패가 달려 있기 때문에 그렇게 합니다. 동물들은 먹이 공급원을 보호합니다. 다른 동물들을 안에 들여놓음으로써 – 심지어 같은 종의 동물이라도 – 먹을 수 있는 먹이가 줄어들 위험을 겪게 됩니다. 또한 동물들은 자신의 새끼를 보호해야 합니다. 이는 특히 새에 있어서 사실입니다. 일부 새들은 알이 부화하기까지 오랜 시간을 기다려야 합니다. 따라서 어떤 동물이 자신의 영역에 침입하면, 이들은 보다 공격적으로 행동을 합니다.

자, 몇몇 개별적인 종에 대해 확인해 보고 그들이 어떻게 행동하는지를 알아보도록 합시다. 잘 알려져 있는 몇몇 포식자들에 대한 이야기로 시작해 보죠. 첫 번째는 늑대로서…

Unit 03 p.80

Sample Detail Question

Translation

M Professor: 좋아요, 음, 몬테소리식 교육법에 대해서는 충분히 다루어 본 것 같군요. 또 다른 종류의 대안 학습법으로 넘어가 보도록 하겠습니다. 이는 매년 보다 많은 인기를 얻고 있습니다. 그리고 그러한 점은 전혀 놀라울 것이 없습니다. 어쨌거나, 수 세기 동안 선호되어 온 학습법이었으니까요. 바로 홈스쿨링을 말씀드리고 있는 것입니다.

오늘날 우리에게 있는 학교는 비교적 새로 만들어진 것이라는 점을 기억해 주십시오. 대중 교육은 1800년대 이후에 나타났을 뿐입니다. 그 전에는, 대부분 두 가지 방법으로 학습을 했습니다: 교회나 기타 종교적인 기관의 소규모 학교에 다녔습니다. 혹은 가정에서 교육을 받았습니다.

1800년대와 1900년대에는, 대부분의 부모들이 아이들을 공립이나 사립 학교에 보냈습니다. 하지만, 과거, 오, 과거 수십 년 전부터, 많은 미국인 부모들이 집에서 아이들을 가르치기 시작했습니다. 여러 가지 이유 때문에 그렇게 하고 있습니다. 먼저, 아이들이 학교에서 받는 교육에 대해 부모들이 만족하지 못합니다. 많은 부모들은 자신들이 집에서 아이들을 더 잘 가르칠 수 있다고 생각합니다. 종교적인 이유 때문에 아이들을 집에서 가르치는 부모들도 있습니다. 집단 따돌림을 예방하기 위해 그렇게 하는 부모들도 있고요. 그 이유가 무엇이던 간에, 홈스쿨링을 하는 아이들은 집에 머무르면서 집에서 배웁니다.

자, 이러한 아이들이 교육을 제대로 받지 못하고 있다고 생각하실 수도 있겠군요. 음, 전혀 그렇지가 않습니다. 실제로, 홈스쿨링을 하는 많은 아이들이 우수한 교육을 받고 있습니다. 오늘날 부모들은 아이들을 가르치는데 도움이 되는, 다양한 출처들에 접근을 하고 있습니다. 예를 들어, 부모들이 이용할 수 있는 교육 도구들이 있습니다. 인터넷에서 강의를 다운로드할 수 있습니다. 홈스쿨링용 소프트웨어 프로그램을 구입할 수 있습니다. 일부 과목에 대해서는 특정 가정 교사를 고용할 수 있습니다. 많은 경우, 홈스쿨링을 하는 아이들은 고등 교육을 받는 동시에 더 적은 시간 동안만 공부를 합니다. 상당히 인상적이죠, 그렇지 않나요? 홈스쿨링의 몇몇 교과 과정에 대해 알려 드리도록 하겠습니다. 여러분들께서 상당히 흥미로워 하실 것이라고 생각합니다.

Mini Test 1 : Conversation

Answers

1. Ⓒ (Gist-Content Question)

2. Ⓑ (Detail Question)

3. Ⓑ (Making Inferences Question)

4. ②, ④ (Detail Question)

Script 🎧 1-08

M Student: Good afternoon. I need to talk to someone here about my bill.

W Student Housing Office Employee: A bill? I'm sorry, but you've got the wrong office. We don't handle bills here. You need to go to the Bursar's office. The people there handle all financial matters at this school.

M: Uh . . . Actually, I was just at the Bursar's office a few minutes ago. I spoke to a woman there, and, um, she told me to come here. But you're telling me to go back there. I'm kind of confused about this.

W: Hmm . . . Okay, she must have had a reason for sending you here. Why don't you tell me what your problem is?

M: Okay, I can do that. Take a look at this bill, please . . .

W: Yeah . . . It's a bill for a single room. That's the rate you should pay. It's the correct amount.

M: Yes, that's right. However, I currently live in a double room.

W: Aha . . . Okay, then we have a problem. And now I know why the woman at the Bursar's office sent you here. You're probably listed on the computer system as having a single room. May I see your ID card, please?

M: Of course. Here it is.

W: Thank you . . . Elliot Martin . . . You live in room 211 in Robinson Hall?

M: No, ma'am. That's the room next to mine. I live in room 210 . . . Ah, I get it. Room 211 is a single. That's what the problem is.

W: Yeah. I'm so sorry about that. Let me change your room listing on the computer. Then, I'll print a form up for you. You can take it back to the Bursar's office. The person there will charge you the proper amount then. This will take just a couple of minutes, so please be patient.

M: No problem. Thanks so much for helping me.

Translation

M Student: 안녕하세요. 고지서에 관해서 이곳 누군가와 이야기를 해야 해서요.

W Student Housing Office Employee: 고지서요? 죄송하지만, 사무실을 잘못 찾아오셨군요. 이곳에서는 고지서를 취급하지 않아요. 재무과로 가셔야 하죠. 그곳 사람들이 여기 학교의 모든 재정적인 문제들을 담당하고 있거든요.

M: 어… 실은, 몇 분 전에 재무과에 이미 갔다 왔어요. 그곳의 한 여자 선생님과 이야기를 했는데, 음, 저보고 이리로 가라고 하시더군요. 하지만 선생님께서는 저에게 다시 그곳으로 가라고 말씀하시네요. 이에 대해 당황스럽군요.

W: 흠… 좋아요, 틀림없이 학생을 이곳으로 보낸 이유가 있을 것 같군요. 문제가 무엇인지 제게 말씀해 주시는 것이 어떨까요?

M: 그래요, 그럴 수 있어요. 이 고지서를 봐 주시면…

W: 예… 1인실에 대한 고지서군요. 학생이 지불해야 하는 비용이네요. 정확한 금액이고요.

M: 네, 맞아요. 하지만, 저는 현재 2인실에 살고 있어요.

W: 아하… 좋아요, 그러면 문제가 있군요. 그리고 이제 재무과의 여자 선생님께서 왜 학생을 이리로 보냈는지도 알겠어요. 아마도 학생이 컴퓨터 시스템에 1인실에 있다고 입력되어 있는 것 같군요. 제가 학생증을 봐도 될까요?

M: 물론이에요. 여기 있어요.

W: 고마워요… Elliot Martin… Robinson Hall의 211호에 살죠?

M: 아니에요, 선생님. 그건 제 옆 방이에요. 저는 210호에 살고 있어요… 아, 알겠어요. 211호는 1인실이에요. 문제가 바로 그것이었군요.

W: 예. 그 점에 대해서는 정말 유감이에요. 컴퓨터에서 학생의 방 호수를 바꾸어 놓을게요. 그리고 난 뒤, 학생을 위해 양식을 한 장 출력해 드릴게요. 그것을 다시 재무과로 가지고 가세요. 그러면 그곳 담당자가 학생에게 적절한 요금을 부과해 줄 거예요. 단 몇 분 간의 시간이 걸릴 테니, 잠시만 기다려 주시고요.

M: 물론이에요. 도와주셔서 정말 고맙습니다.

Mini Test 2 : Lecture

Answers

1. B (Making Inferences Question)

2. C (Understanding Organization Question)

3. C (Detail Question)

4. A (Understanding Attitude Question)

Script 🎧 1-09

W Professor: After the Renaissance, the first major period of music was the Baroque Period. Music historians date it from around 1600 to 1750. The Baroque Period began in Northern Italy as well as in some of the northern German states at the same time. Of course, the term Baroque wasn't used back then. It was applied by later music historians. In fact, the term was first used to refer to a style of architecture that was popular in the 1600s and 1700s. The word "baroque" comes from the Italian word *barocco*. That word translates as both "bizarre" and "exuberant."

As for me, I'd say that exuberant is a more apt description. The reason is that the music of this time was quite exuberant or, uh, lively. This is especially true when comparing Baroque music to music from earlier periods. We're going to listen to some Baroque music in a bit. And I think you'll understand exactly what I'm talking about once you hear it. [4]**Now, uh, the Baroque Period was clearly the child of the Renaissance. During the Renaissance, musicians began exploring more secular forms of music. They moved away from the religious music that had dominated previous eras. Baroque musicians did the same thing.** But that's not to say that Baroque musicians abandoned religious music entirely. On the contrary, Johann Sebastian Bach, one of the greatest of all Baroque composers, wrote a great deal of church music. Yet he also composed secular music, um, as did many others. For instance, Bach's *Brandenburg Concertos* are some of the greatest works from the entire period.

There's another reason that Baroque music was often secular. Baroque composers frequently had patrons. A patron was a rich person—usually a noble—who financially supported the composer. In the past, many patrons had connections to the Church. Yet, starting in the Renaissance, secular patrons became more common. This trend continued during the Baroque Period. These patrons greatly influenced the composers they sponsored. After all, the patrons wanted composers to write music that they enjoyed. This helped make the music more secular in nature.

During the Baroque Period, there was a move toward tonality. Additionally, chords, rather than individual notes, were used. Many musicians began using a key, which was a central tone for their music. Bach was instrumental at developing the use of a central key for various compositions. Finally, there was a slow move away from creating music that used singers in a chorus along with an orchestra. Instead, Baroque music usually focused only on the instrumental sounds of an orchestra.

I should point out that singing roles were not abandoned entirely though. Choral groups remained an essential part of the religious compositions of Bach and many others. And the rise of opera is an important theme in Baroque music. In fact, many famous composers of the era wrote operas as well as instrumental compositions. Antonio Vivaldi of Italy, for example, composed more than ninety operas in his lifetime.

Translation

W Professor: 르네상스 이후, 음악에 있어서 첫 번째 주요한 시기는 바로크 시대였습니다. 음악사가들은 그 기원을 약 1600년에서 1750년까지로 보고 있습니다. 바로크 시대는 북부 이탈리아뿐만 아니라 독일 북부의 일부 주에서 동시에 시작되었습니다. 물론, 바로크라는 용어는 당시에 사용되지 않았습니다. 이후 음악사가들에 의해 적용이 되었죠. 사실, 그러한 용어는 1600년대와 1700년대에 인기가 있었던 건축 양식을 지칭하기 위해 처음으로 사용되었습니다. "바로크"라는 단어는 이탈리아어 단어인 *barocco*에서 유래되었습니다. 이 단어는 "특이한"과 "활기찬"이라는 뜻 모두로 번역이 됩니다.

저로서는, '활기차다'란 뜻이 보다 적합한 설명이라고 말씀드리고 싶군요. 그 이유는 이 시기의 음악이 상당히 활기차거나, 어, 생동감이 있기 때문입니다. 바로크 음악과 그 이전 시기의 음악을 비교해 볼 때 특히 그렇습니다. 잠시 바로크 음악을 들어보도록 하죠. 그리고 여러분들께서 한번 들어 보시면, 제가 무엇을 말씀드리고 있는지를 정확히 이해하실 것이라고 생각합니다. 자, 어, 바로크 시대는 분명 르네상스의 산물이었습니다. 르네상스 기간에, 음악가들은 보다 세속적인 형태의 음악을 탐구하기 시작했습니다. 이들은 이전 시대를 지배했던 종교적인 음악으로부터 벗어났습니다. 바로크 시대의 음악가들도 마찬가지였습니다. 하지만 바로크 시대의 음악가들이 종교 음악을 완전히 포기했다는 말은 아닙니다. 반대로, 요한 세바스찬 바흐는, 바로크 시대의 가장 위대한 작곡가 중 한 명인데, 많은 교회 음악을 만들었습니다. 하지만 그 또한 다른 사람들과 마찬가지로, 세속적인 음악도 작곡했습니다. 예를 들어, 바흐의 *브란덴부르크 협주곡*은 전 시대를 통틀어 가장 위대한 작품 중의 하나입니다.

바로크 음악이 종종 세속적이었던 또 다른 이유가 있습니다. 바로크 시대의 작곡가들에게는 후원자가 있는 경우가 많았습니다. 후원자는 부유한 사람으로서 – 보통은 귀족이었는데 – 재정적으로 작곡가를 지원해 주었습니다. 과거에는, 많은 후원자들이 가톨릭 교회와 관련되어 있었습니다. 하지만 르네상스 시대를 시작으로, 세속적인 후원자들이 보다 일반적이게 되었습니다. 이러한 경향은 바로크 시대 동안 계속되었습니다. 이 후원자들은 자신들이 후원해 주었던 작곡가들에게 막대한 영향을 끼쳤습니다. 어찌되었던, 후원자들은 자신이 좋아하는 음악을 작곡가들이 만들어 주기를 원했으니까요. 이로써 그 특성상 음악이 보다 세속적으로 되었습니다.

바로크 시대 동안, 조성을 지향하는 움직임이 있었습니다. 또한, 각각의 음보다는 화음이 사용되었습니다. 많은 음악가들이 조성을 사용하기 시작했는데, 이는 음악에 있어서 중심이 되는 곡조였습니다. 바흐는 다양한 작곡에 있어서 중심이 되는 조성을 사용하는 것에 많은 영향을 끼쳤습니다. 마지막으로, 오케스트라와 함께 합창 단원을 이용하는 음악을 만드는 것은 점차 기피되었습니다. 그 대신, 바로크 음악은 통상적으로 오케스트라의 악기 소리에만 초점을 맞추었습니다.

하지만 노래를 하는 역할이 없어진 것은 아니었다는 점을 지적해야 할 것 같군요. 바흐 및 기타 많은 사람들의 종교적인 작곡에 있어서 합창단은 필수적인 부분으로 남아 있었습니다. 그리고 바로크 음악에서는 오페라의 성장이 중요한 주제였습니다. 실제로, 당대의 많은 유명 작곡가들이 기악곡뿐만 아니라 오페라를 썼습니다. 이탈리아의 안토니오 비발디는, 예를 들면, 생전에 90개 이상의 오페라를 작곡했습니다.

Unit 04

p.84

Sample Detail Question

Translation

W Professor: 역사상 비범했던 인물 중 한 명이 줄리어스 시저입니다. 이번 학기에 우리가 공부하게 될 가장 중요한 사람 중 한 명입니다. 그는 로마 공화국의 멸망과 관련이 있었습니다. 또한 로마 제국의 출범과도 연관이 있었습니다. 물론, 그러했을 때, 그가 생존해 있지는 않았습니다. 로마 제국이 설립되기 전에 로마 의회에서 암살을 당했죠. 어쨌든, 음, 로마의 역사에서 줄리어스 시저가 얼마나 중요했는지는 과소평가할 수 없을 것입니다.

시저는 기원전 102년과 100년 사이에 태어났습니다. 귀족 가문에서 태어났죠. 부유하지는 않았지만, 상류 계급에 속했습니다. 따라서 시저는 특권 계층의 교육을

받았습니다. 이는 그가 로마 군단에서 장교로 복무해야 한다는 점을 의미했습니다. 이는 시저가 널리 알려지게 된 계기가 되었습니다. 군단에서 복무를 할 당시, 시저는 갈리아를 정복하는 책임을 맡았습니다. 어, 오늘날 프랑스가 있는 지역입니다.

시저 덕분에 갈리아에서 어떤 일이 있었는지에 대해 우리는 많은 것을 알고 있습니다. 아시다시피, 어, 대부분의 사람들은 시저를 독재자나 장군으로서만 알고 있습니다. 하지만 그는 그 이상이었습니다. 명석한 연설가였습니다. 또한 뛰어난 작가이기도 했고요. 그의 작품인 *갈리아 전기*는 그로 하여금 갈리아를 정복하게 해주었던 군사 행동에 대해 설명해 주었습니다. 그 책에 있는 그의 자세는 단순하고 간단합니다. 실제로, 인생 전체를 통해, 그는 기억에 남는 수많은 글을 썼습니다. 예를 들어, 압도적이었던 한 번의 승리 후에… 어, 갈리아가 아니라 다른 곳에서의… 그는 로마로 말을 전했습니다. *Veni vidi vici*라고 적었습니다. 이 라틴어 구절은 "왔노라, 보았노라, 점령했노라"로 번역이 됩니다. 간결하며 직접적으로 요점을 전달합니다. 그렇지 않나요? 어쨌든, 그가 한 말 대신에 시저의 생애에 대한 이야기로 되돌아 가도록 하겠습니다.

Mini Test 1 : Conversation

Answers

1. Ⓑ (Gist-Purpose Question)

2. Ⓒ (Understanding Function Question)

3. **Fact:** 2 , 3   **Not a Fact:** 1 , 4 (Detail Question)

4. Ⓐ (Understanding Attitude Question)

Script 🎧 1-11

W Professor: Brad, you look like you've got something on your mind. Is there anything you want to talk about?

M Student: Actually, yes, there is something, Professor Goodman. I've got a minor dilemma now.

W: What is it?

M: I'm trying to make up my mind about something. Do you mind if I tell you about it?

W: I'm all ears.

M: Thanks. Okay, I signed up for one more class than normal this semester. It's a psychology class. The first class of the semester meets this Wednesday afternoon.

W: Is there a problem with the class?

M: Not exactly. This is my problem: I got offered an internship at a consulting company yesterday. It's a pretty good opportunity. Uh, no . . . It's actually an incredible opportunity. But I'm afraid I might have to reject the offer.

W: Let me guess . . . The company wants you to do your internship on Wednesday afternoon, right?

M: Precisely. If I do the internship, I have to go there every Wednesday and Friday afternoon. My Friday afternoon schedule is clear. So that's not a problem. But I've got the psychology class on Wednesday. What do you think I should do?

W: You're not a psychology major, so I assume the class is an elective. Hmm . . . I would definitely rate the internship as more important. I mean, you've told me before that you want to work at a consulting company after you graduate. So here's your chance. This internship will provide you with a great deal of experience. It could be, uh, it could be invaluable for getting a job later.

M: Even if it's not a paid internship? I won't make anything from it. Does that matter?

W: Not really. Get experience now. You'll make money later. Do the internship. You won't regret that choice.

M: Okay, Professor. You've convinced me. Thanks for the advice.

Translation

W Professor: Brad, 무언가에 대해 고민하고 있는 것처럼 보이는군요. 이야기하고 싶은 것이 있나요?

M Student: 실은, 그래요, 있어요, Goodman 교수님. 저는 지금 사소한 딜레마에 빠져 있어요.

W: 그것이 무엇인가요?

M: 무언가에 대해 결정을 내리려고 하고 있어요. 그에 대해 교수님께 말씀을 드려도 될까요?

W: 물론 들을게요.

M: 고맙습니다. 좋아요, 저는 이번 학기에 평소보다 하나 더 많은 수업에 등록을 했어요. 심리학 수업이죠. 학기의 첫 수업은 이번 수요일 오후에 있고요.

W: 그 수업에 문제라도 있나요?

M: 그런 것은 아니에요. 제 문제는 바로 이것이에요: 어제 한 컨설팅 회사로부터 인턴쉽 제의를 받았어요. 상당히 좋은 기회이죠. 어, 아니에요… 정말로 굉장한 기회에요. 하지만 그 제안을 거절해야 할 것 같아서 안타까워요.

W: 짐작해 볼게요… 그 회사에서 학생이 수요일 오후에 인턴쉽에 참여하기를 바라나요, 그런가요?

M: 정확해요. 제가 인턴쉽에 참여한다면, 매주 수요일과 금요일 오후마다 그곳으로 가야 하죠. 제 금요일 오후 시간표는 비어 있어요. 그래서 그것은 문제가 되지 않죠. 하지만 수요일에는 심리학 수업이 있어요. 제가 어떻게 해야 한다고 생각하시나요?

W: 학생은 심리학 전공이 아니기 때문에, 그 수업은 선택 과목일 것이라고 생각되는군요. 흠… 저는 분명 인턴쉽이 더 중요하다는 평가를 내리겠어요. 제 말은, 학생이 졸업을 한 다음에는 컨설팅 회사에서 일을 하고 싶다고 예전에 말했잖아요. 그러니 이번이 학생에게는 기회예요. 이번 인턴쉽은 학생에게 많은 경험을 가져다 줄 거예요. 그것은, 어, 그것은 이후 일자리를 구하는데 매우 중요할 거예요.

M: 급여가 없는 인턴쉽이라도요? 저는 그로부터 어떤 것도 받지 못할 거에요. 그것이 문제가 되나요?

W: 꼭 그렇지는 않아요. 경험을 얻으세요. 돈은 나중에 벌 수 있어요. 인턴쉽에 참여하세요. 그러한 선택을 후회하지는 않을 거에요.

M: 좋아요, 교수님. 저를 설득시키셨군요. 조언에 감사드립니다.

Mini Test 2 : Lecture

Answers

1. ⓒ (Gist-Content Question)

2. **Fact:** 1 , 2   **Not a Fact:** 3 , 4 (Detail Question)

3. Ⓑ (Understanding Organization Question)

4. Ⓑ (Understanding Attitude Question)

Script 🎧 1-12

M Professor: We're studying Islamic architecture today. When I use the term Islamic architecture, by the way, I'm referring to the architecture of the Middle East. I'm not referring to places such as Indonesia or Africa, which both have large Muslim presences. Islamic architecture has a wide variety of styles. I intend to show you several buildings in detail today. But let me give you a brief overview of some common aspects of Islamic architecture before doing so.

To begin with, there are several types of buildings common in Islamic architecture. The mosque, of course, is by far the most dominant. A mosque is a place of worship for Muslims. As you can see here on the screen, mosques are built in many styles. Most are rectangular in shape . . . like this . . . and this one, too . . . They have a large central prayer hall . . . which is usually domed. Please note that domes were not common in early Islamic architecture. The oldest surviving mosques instead have flat roofs with many columns . . . As for domes, the Ottomans started using them in the fifteenth century. See this . . . and this . . . Some mosques even have more than one dome . . . You can see the large central dome and several smaller ones around it . . . A dome may be slight in size and curvature . . . or large, prominent, and bulging . . .

Mosques have minarets. You've all seen them even if you don't know their names. They are large towers . . . Minarets are almost always the highest points of the mosque . . . Most mosques have two minarets . . . or four . . . The number varies depending on both the culture and the branch of Islam that the people who built the mosque practice.

Another common aspect of Islamic architecture is the central courtyard. This is found in mosques . . . and secular buildings . . . The courtyard is an inner sanctum of sorts. It's a peaceful place in which people can relax. It typically has many plants . . . and may have a fountain as well . . . Courtyards are common in private homes, too . . . They are one of the few places where women who live in strict Islamic countries can move about with their faces uncovered.

One more interesting aspect of Islamic architecture is the patterns of the designs on the walls, columns, and ceilings. They're often done in intricate patterns . . . and can be quite colorful as well . . . We call this pattern arabesque. One common theme in arabesque designs is floral patterns . . . You can often see the leaves of plants or flowers entwined around each other. An arabesque design may be drawn . . . done in a mosaic with colored tiles . . . or carved directly into the stone of a building . . .

Ah, before we look at any buildings in detail, let me mention one important thing: There are no depictions of animals or people in Islamic buildings. The use of such images is forbidden in Islam. Now, that having been said, let's look at what I consider some of the finest examples of Islamic architecture. I think you'll be impressed by what you see.

Translation

M Professor: 오늘은 이슬람 건축에 대해서 공부해 보려고 합니다. 그건 그렇고, 제가 이슬람 건축이라는 용어를 사용할 때는, 중동의 건축을 지칭하는 것입니다. 인도네시아나 아프리카와 같은, 두 곳 모두에서 많은 이슬람 교도들이 있지만, 그러한 지역을 지칭하는 것은 아닙니다. 이슬람 건축에는 다양한 양식이 존재합니다. 오늘은 몇몇 건물들을 상세하게 여러분께 보여 드리고자 합니다. 하지만 그렇게 하기 전에, 이슬람 건축의 몇 가지 공통적인 측면에 대해 간략히 검토해 보도록 하겠습니다.

우선, 이슬람 건축에는 몇 가지 공통적인 유형의 건물들이 있습니다. 물론, 모스크가 가장 지배적입니다. 모스크란 이슬람 교도들을 위한 예배 공간입니다. 여기 스크린에서 볼 수 있듯이, 모스크는 여러 가지 양식으로 지어져 있습니다. 대부분은 형태에 있어서 직사각형인데… 이것처럼요… 그리고 이것도 마찬가지입니다… 중앙에는 커다란 예배당이 있으며… 이는 보통 돔으로 되어 있습니다. 돔은 초기 이슬람 건축에서 일반적인 것이 아니었다는 점에 주목해 주십시오. 그 대신 현존하는 가장 오래된 모스크에는 많은 기둥이 달려 있는 평평한 지붕이 있습니다… 돔에 대해 말씀을 드리면, 15세기에 오스만 사람들이 이를 사용하기 시작했습니다. 이것을 보시면… 그리고 이것도요… 일부 모스크에는 한 개 이상의 돔이 있습니다… 중앙에 있는 커다란 돔과 그 주변에 있는 몇 개의 작은 돔 보실 수 있으실 것입니다… 돔은 크기가 작고 구부러져 있을 수도 있으며… 혹은 커다랗고, 돌출되어 있으며, 불룩한 모양을 가지고 있을 수도 있습니다…

모스크에는 뾰족탑이 있습니다. 그 이름은 모르실지라도, 여러분 모두가 본 적이 있으실 것입니다. 이들은 커다란 탑입니다… 뾰족탑은 모스크에서 거의 항상 가장 높은 부분이며… 대부분의 모스크에는 두 개나… 네 개의 뾰족탑이 있습니다… 그러한 숫자는 모스크를 만든 사람들의 문화 및 이슬람 분파에 따라 달라집니다.

이슬람 건축의 또 다른 일반적인 측면은 중앙에 있는 뜰입니다. 이는 모스크와… 세속적인 건물에서 발견됩니다… 뜰은 일종의 지성소입니다. 사람들이 평정을 찾을 수 있는 평화로운 장소입니다. 그곳에는 전형적으로 많은 식물들이 있으며… 또한 분수가 있을 수도 있습니다… 뜰은 개인 주택에 있어서도 일반적인 것입니다… 엄격한 이슬람 국가에서 사는 여성들이 얼굴을 가리지 않고서도 돌아다닐 수 있는 몇 안 되는 장소 중의 하나입니다.

이슬람 건축의 또 다른 흥미로운 측면 중 하나는 벽, 기둥, 그리고 천장에 있는 디자인 문양입니다. 종종 복잡한 문양으로 되어 있으며… 그리고 또한 상당히 다채로울 수 있습니다… 우리는 이러한 문양을 아라베스크라고 부릅니다. 아라베스크 디자인의 한 가지 공통적인 주제는 꽃 문양입니다… 식물의 잎과 꽃이 서로 휘감고 있는 것을 종종 보실 수 있을 것입니다. 아라베스크 디자인은… 색깔이 있는 타일로 모자이크식으로 그려질 수도 있고… 혹은 건물의 석재에 직접적으로 새겨질 수도 있습니다…

아, 건물들을 자세히 살펴보기에 앞서서, 한 가지 중요한 점을 말씀드리도록 하겠습니다: 이슬람 건물에는 동물이나 사람에 대한 묘사가 없습니다. 그러한 이미지를 사용하는 것은 이슬람교에서 금지되어 있습니다. 자, 말씀을 드렸으므로, 제가 생각하기에 이슬람 건축에서 가장 멋진 사례들을 살펴보도록 합시다. 여러분들께서 보시는 것에 깊은 인상을 받게 될 것이라고 생각합니다.

Unit 05

p.88

Sample Understanding the Function of What Is Said Question

Translation

W1 Student: McDaniel 교수님, 지금 사무실에서 나가실 건가요?

W2 Professor: 어, 네, Patricia. 오늘 수업은 다 끝났어요. 그래서 집에 가려고 준비 중이죠. 무언가에 대해 저와 이야기를 해야 하나요?

W1: 네, 그래요. 저를 위해 일이 분 정도 시간을 내어 주실 수 있나요?

W2: 물론 그럴 수 있죠. 무슨 일인가요?

W1: 교수님께 정말로 큰 부탁을 드려야 해서요. 저는, 어, 저는 교수님께서 저를 위해 추천서를 써 주셨으면 해요. 면접이 다가 오고 있는데, 회사의 담당자 분이 제가 두어 개의 추천서를 가지고 올 것을 요청하더군요.

W2: 이번 면접이 내일은 아니겠죠, 그런가요?

W1: 오, 아니에요, 교수님. 다음 주 화요일이에요.

W2: 다행이군요. 오늘 밤에 써야 할 지도 모른다고 생각했거든요. 하지만 화요일은 괜찮아요. 그렇게 할 수 있어요.

W1: 정말 감사합니다. 제게 안 된다고 말씀하실까봐 걱정했어요.

W2: 아, 그런 일은 없을 거에요. 하지만 학생이 제게 큰 도움을 줄 수 있어요. 제가 학생의 추천서를 쓸 때 도움이 될 거에요. 제게 이메일을 보내 주는 것이 어떨까요? 이메일에, 제가 추천서에서 언급하기를 바라는 모든 것을 적어 주세요. 그러면 그러한 것들을 포함시키려고 노력해 볼게요.

Mini Test 1 : Conversation

Answers

1. Ⓑ (Gist-Purpose Question)

2. ③ , ④ (Detail Question)

3. Ⓐ (Making Inferences Question)

4. Ⓒ (Understanding Function Question)

Script 🎧 1-14

W1 Registrar's Office Employee: Next? Number seventy-three? Come to counter four, please.

W2 Student: Ah, hi. I've got number seventy-three. Here you are.

W1: Thank you. And good afternoon to you. How may I be of assistance?

W2: I'm here to get some copies of my transcript. I already filled out the form. So, uh, here it is.

W1: Thank you for doing that. Most students don't fill out the form until they get up to the counter.

W2: Er, yeah, I didn't do that the last time I was here. The man who helped me out wasn't very happy though. So, uh, I decided not to make the same mistake again.

W1: I hope he wasn't too hard on you. But, uh, anyway . . . Let me take a look at the form, please. And may I see your student ID as well?

W2: Yes, of course. Here it is. Um, I hate to ask, but is it possible to get my transcripts by the end of the day?

W1: Hmm . . . It's one thirty now . . . And we close at six o'clock . . . Let me think for a second . . . ⁴Yeah, I think they can be ready by then. How many copies do you need?

W2: Ten, please.

W1: **Ten? Why so many?**

W2: Uh, I'm applying to a bunch of graduate schools this year. I figure that, uh, by applying to so many, I have a good chance of getting accepted to at least one. In this economy, I really don't want to have to look for a job. You know what I mean?

W1: Totally. You're doing a smart thing. It's tough out there. Anyway, it costs four dollars per transcript. Would you like to pay now or when you pick them up?

W2: I'll pay now. I've got enough cash on me. Hold on a moment while I get in my purse.

Translation

W1 Registrar's Office Employee: 다음 분? 73번이요? 4번 카운터로 와 주세요.

W2 Student: 아, 안녕하세요. 제가 73번을 뽑았어요. 여기 있어요.

W1: 고마워요. 그리고 안녕하세요. 어떻게 도와드릴까요?

W2: 성적표 사본을 몇 장 얻기 위해 왔어요. 양식에는 이미 내용을 기입했고요. 그래서, 어, 여기에 있어요.

W1: 그렇게 해주시다니 고맙네요. 대부분의 학생들은 카운터에 오기 전까지 양식에 내용을 기입하지 않거든요.

W2: 어, 예. 저도 지난 번에 여기에 왔을 때에는 그렇게 하지 않았어요. 저를 도와 주었던 남자 분이 그다지 기분 좋아 보이지 않았죠. 그래서, 어, 같은 실수를 다시 하지 않기로 결심했어요.

W1: 그분이 학생에게 너무 심하게 대하지는 않았기를 바라요. 하지만, 어, 어쨌든… 양식을 제가 볼게요. 그리고 학생의 학생증도 볼 수 있을까요?

W2: 네, 물론이에요. 여기 있어요. 음, 여쭤 보기는 싫지만, 오늘 업무 시간이 끝날 때까지 성적표를 받는 것이 가능할까요?

W1: 흠… 지금이 1시 30분이고… 우리는 6시 정각에 문을 닫는데… 잠시 생각해 볼게요… 예, 그때쯤에는 준비가 될 수 있을 거에요. 몇 장이 필요한가요?

W2: 10장이요.

W1: 10장이요? 왜 그렇게 많이 필요하죠?

W2: 어, 올해 여러 군데의 대학원에 지원을 하고 있어요. 저는, 어, 그처럼 많은 곳에 지원을 해야, 적어도 한 곳에서 입학 허가가 날 가능성이 크다는 점을 알았어요. 지금의 경제 상황에서, 정말로 일자리를 찾고 싶지는 않거든요. 무슨 말씀인지 아시죠?

W1: 그럼요. 현명하게 행동하고 있군요. 그쪽은 상황이 힘들죠. 어쨌든, 성적표 1매당

4달러에요. 지금 지불하실 건가요, 아니면 찾으러 오실 때 지불하실 건가요?

W2: 지금 지불할게요. 수중에 현금이 충분히 있거든요. 지갑을 꺼내는 동안 잠시만 기다려 주세요.

Mini Test 2 : Lecture

Answers

1. ⓒ (Gist-Content Question)

2. 1 , 3 (Detail Question)

3. ⓓ (Making Inferences Question)

4. ⓐ (Understanding Function Question)

Script 🎧 1-15

M Professor: The term megafauna refers to animals that are larger than normal ones. Uh, please don't misunderstand though. I'm not talking about large felines such as lions and tigers or elephants and giraffes. [4]Instead, what I'm talking about are huge species of animals. These are animals that, um, that pretty much no longer exist. Hmm . . . Some of you look confused. **Let me give you some examples . . .** About 400 years ago on Madagascar, there was a bird that was three meters in height and laid enormous eggs. In North America, there used to be massive lions, huge mammoths, big saber-toothed tigers, giant sloths, large dire wolves, humungous bears, and really big horses. Hmm . . . I think I used just about every adjective for "large" that I know. Anyway, those animals are all examples of megafauna. Interestingly, there were at least 135 species of megafauna in North America. However, they all became extinct prior to the arrival of the Europeans in the late 1400s.

The question I want to answer now is this . . . Why did they die out . . . ? There are several theories. One is that an ice age killed them. Scientists have found many fossilized remains of megafauna dating back 15,000 years. That, by the way, was during the time of the last ice age. This theory is a strong possibility. However, remember that there have been many ice ages in Earth's history. And the earlier ice ages didn't kill the megafauna. So, um, let's think. What happened in North America around 15,000 years ago . . . ? Anyone . . . ?

W Student: I know. That's when humans crossed a land bridge from Asia and arrived in North America.

M: Bingo. You got it, Sue. Nowadays, it's believed that most megafauna in North American were killed off by these early human settlers. No one knows for sure, but most people agree that the first humans arrived in North America between 13,000 and 15,000 years ago. They arrived on a pristine continent unspoiled by human activity. The megafauna had not had any previous interactions with humans. Therefore, they didn't know that they should fear humans. The humans were hungry and often hunted these animals. In many cases, they hunted the megafauna to extinction.

Of course, humans didn't hunt all of them to extinction. However, they did something else that caused many megafauna to become extinct: They intruded into the animals' territories. As humans settled more land, this left the animals with increasingly smaller territories. This caused their numbers to decline. Over time—in some cases, in just a few centuries—many of these megafauna became extinct.

W: Is it really possible for some animals to become extinct in a few hundred years? That seems sort of extreme.

M: Yes, Sue, it is possible. Let me tell you about the moa. It was a large flightless bird that lived in New Zealand. It went extinct in just a hundred years. Here's what happened . . .

Translation

M Professor: 거대 동물이라는 용어는 일반적인 동물보다 더 커다란 동물을 지칭합니다. 어, 하지만 오해하지는 마세요. 사자와 호랑이 같은 커다란 고양이나 코끼리와 얼룩말을 말씀드리는 것이 아닙니다. 대신, 제가 말씀드리고 있는 것은 거대한 동물의 종입니다. 이들은, 음, 결코 더 이상 존재하지 않는 동물들입니다. 흠… 여러분 중 몇 분께서 혼란스러워 하시는 것 같군요. 몇 가지 예를 들어 드리죠. 약 400년 전의 마다가스카르에서는, 높이가 3미터에 이르고 수많은 알을 낳았던 새가 있었습니다. 북아메리카에서는 한때 육중한 사자, 거대한 매머드, 덩치가 큰 검치호, 커다란 나무늘보, 몸집이 큰 이리, 엄청난 크기의 곰, 그리고 정말로 큰 말들이 있었습니다. 흠… 제가 아는 "커다란"이란 뜻의 거의 모든 형용사를 다 사용한 것 같군요. 어쨌든, 이러한 동물들이 모두 거대 동물의 예입니다. 흥미롭게도, 북아메리카에는 최소 135종의 거대 동물들이 존재했습니다. 하지만, 1400년대 후반 유럽인들이 도착하기 전에, 모두 멸종하게 되었죠.

지금 제가 답하고자 하는 질문은 이렇습니다… 왜 이들이 소멸했을까요…? 몇 가지 이론들이 존재합니다. 그 하나는 빙하기로 인해 이들이 모두 죽었다는 것입니다. 과학자들은 그 기원이 15,000년 전으로 거슬러 올라가는 많은 화석화된 유적들을 발견해 냈습니다. 그건 그렇고, 이는 마지막 빙하기 때였습니다. 이 이론은 가능성이 높은 이론입니다. 하지만, 지구 역사상 많은 빙하기가 있었다는 점을 기억해 주세요. 그리고 그 이전에 있었던 빙하기 때는 거대 동물들이 죽지 않았습니다. 그러면, 음, 생각해 봅시다. 약 15,000년 전에 북아메리카에서 어떤 일이 일어났을까요…? 누구 없나요…?

W Student: 제가 알고 있습니다. 인간들이 아시아로부터 육교를 건너 북아메리카에 도착했던 때입니다.

M: 맞습니다. 학생이 맞췄군요, Sue. 오늘날, 북아메리카 대부분의 거대 동물들은 그러한 초기 정착민들에 의해 사라졌다고 생각됩니다. 아무도 확실하게는 모르지만, 대부분의 사람들은 13,000년과 15,000년 전 사이에 인간이 처음으로 북아메리카에 도착했다는 점에 동의하고 있습니다. 이들은 인간의 활동으로 훼손되지 않은 자연 그대로의 대륙에 도착했습니다. 거대 동물들은 그 이전에 인간들과 접촉을 해본 적이 없었습니다. 따라서, 자신들이 인간을 두려워해야 한다는 점을 알지 못했습니다. 인간들은 굶주려 있었고 종종 이러한 동물들을 사냥했습니다. 많은 경우, 인간들은 거대 동물들을 사냥하여 멸종으로 몰고 갔습니다.

물론, 인간들이 이들 모두를 사냥하여 멸종에 이르게 한 것은 아닙니다. 하지만, 많은 거대 동물들이 멸종하는데 원인이 된 무엇인가를 했습니다: 바로 그러한 동물들의 영역을 침범했던 것입니다. 인간들이 보다 넓은 지역에 정착함에 따라, 동물들의 영토는 점차 줄어들게 되었습니다. 이로써 그 숫자가 감소하게 되었습니다. 시간이 지나면서 – 일부 경우에는 단지 몇 세기 만에 – 이러한 거대 동물 중 다수가 멸종했습니다.

W: 수백 년 만에 몇몇 동물들이 멸종하는 것이 정말로 가능한가요? 극단적인 경우처럼 보이는데요.

M: 네, Sue, 가능합니다. 모아에 대해 말씀해 드리죠. 이는 뉴질랜드에서 살았던, 날지 못하는 커다란 새였습니다. 모아는 단지 수백 년 만에 멸종을 했습니다. 어떤 일이 있었는지를 말씀해 드리면…

Unit 06　　　　　　　　　　p.92

Sample Understanding the Speaker's Attitude Question

Translation

W Professor: Jeff, 이제 다음 학기 수업에 대한 결정을 내렸나요?

M Student: 거의요. 전에 말씀을 드렸던 네 개의 수업은 수강할 거예요. 상기시켜드리면… 생물학, 경제학, 수학, 그리고 영문학 수업이죠.

W: 아, 맞아요. 기억나요. 좋은 선택이라고 생각해요. 그리고 학생이 수업에서 잘 할

것이라고 확신하고요.

M: 저도 그랬으면 좋겠어요.

W: 저도 그래요. 자, 어, 마지막 남은 수업은 어떻게 할 건가요? 기억을 떠올려 보면… 두 수업 중에서 어떤 것을 선택하려고 하나요?

M: 천문학과의 수업을 수강하는 것에 대해 생각해 보고 있어요. 천문학 102수업이죠. 기초 수준의 개론 수업이에요. 제가 생각하고 있는 또 다른 수업은 역사 1150이고요. 초기 미국 역사에 관한 수업이죠.

W: 그러면 왜 결정을 내릴 수가 없는 건가요?

M: 음, 어, 기본적으로… 두 수업 모두를 좋아해요. 그리고, 경제학이 전공이기 때문에, 두 수업 모두가 필수 과목이고요. 그래서 다른 것 대신에 하나의 수업을 들음으로써 더 이익이 되는 것은 아니에요. 어떻게 해야 할지 잘 모르겠어요.

W: 흠… 제가 알기로는, 천문학 수업은 매 학기 마다 개설되죠. 하지만, 역사 수업은 3년 동안 개설이 된 적이 없었어요. 그리고 학생은 2학년이니까…

M: 아, 알겠어요. 좋아요. 그러면 천문학 수업은 다음으로 미루어야 할 것 같군요.

Mini Test 1 : Conversation

Answers

1. (A) (Gist-Purpose Question)

2. (C) (Making Inferences Question)

3. (D) (Detail Question)

4. (D) (Understanding Attitude Question)

Script ∩ 1-17

M Professor: Kimberly, thanks for dropping by my office. You're, uh, you're probably wondering why I didn't give you your test back in class, right?

W Student: Yes, sir. I am kind of curious about that. Did I fail the test or something?

M: You didn't fail. But you got a C+ on the exam.

W: Oh . . . That's not good.

M: What happened, Kimberly? This is our third test of the semester. You got a 95 on the first one. And you got a, uh, a 98 on the second I believe.

W: That's correct.

M: But you got a 78 on this one. Didn't you study for the test?

W: I studied for the test. But I guess I didn't study enough, sir. I'm sorry about my grade. I'll make sure I do better on the last test.

M: Is everything all right, Kimberly? I'm a little concerned. [4]I mean, um, you were outstanding in the first half of the semester. You were active in the class discussions. And your two tests were very well done. **But, um, since about three weeks ago, the quality of your work has slipped.** Do you know what I'm saying?

W: Yes, sir. I understand. It's just . . .

M: Yes?

W: About three weeks ago, I had to start working a second job. My father got fired from his job, so my parents can't afford to pay my tuition anymore. If I want to stay here, I have to earn more money. I guess I'm, uh, I'm just not used to working so much.

M: I understand, Kimberly. You may not know this . . . but, um, you can apply for a hardship scholarship. The school offers them to students in situations like yours. Would you like some

more information on them?

W: I'd love that, sir. Getting any kind of help now would be incredible.

Translation

M Professor: Kimberly, 사무실에 들려 줘서 고마워요. 학생은, 어, 학생은 아마도 제가 수업 시간에 학생의 시험지를 돌려주지 않은 것에 대해서 궁금해 할 것 같군요. 맞나요?

W Student: 네, 교수님. 그 점에 대해 궁금해하고 있어요. 제가 시험에 통과하지 못했거나 혹은 다른 일이 있나요?

M: 통과를 못한 것은 아니에요. 하지만 학생은 시험에서 C+를 받았어요.

W: 오… 좋지 않군요.

M: 무슨 일이 있었나요, Kimberly? 이번 시험은 학기 중 세 번째 시험이에요. 학생은 첫 번째 시험에서 95점을 받았어요. 그리고, 어, 두 번째 시험에서는 98점을 받을 것으로 알고 있고요.

W: 맞아요.

M: 하지만 이번 시험에서는 78점을 받았어요. 시험 공부를 하지 않았나요?

W: 시험 공부를 했어요. 하지만 충분히 하지는 못한 것 같아요, 교수님. 제 성적에 대해서는 죄송해요. 마지막 시험에서는 반드시 더 잘하도록 할게요.

M: 별일 없는 거죠, Kimberly? 약간 걱정이 되는군요. 제 말은, 음, 학생은 학기 초반에 두각을 나타내었어요. 수업 토론에서도 적극적이었죠. 그리고 두 번의 시험은 매우 잘 보았고요. 하지만, 음, 약 3주 전부터, 학업 성적이 떨어지고 있어요. 제가 무슨 말을 하는지 알겠나요?

W: 네, 교수님. 알아요. 단지…

M: 네?

W: 약 3주 전에, 부업을 시작해야 했어요. 아버님께서 직장에서 해고되셔서, 부모님들께서 더 이상 제 학비를 대실 수가 없거든요. 이곳에 계속 머물러 있고 싶지만, 돈을 더 많이 벌어야만 해요. 제가, 어, 제가 그렇게 많은 일을 하는데 익숙하지 않은 것 같네요.

M: 이해가 가는군요, Kimberly. 학생이 이러한 점은 모를 수도 있는데… 하지만, 음, 가계 곤란 장학금을 신청할 수도 있어요. 학교측은 학생과 같은 상황에 처해 있는 학생들에게 그러한 장학금을 지급해 주고 있죠. 그에 대한 정보를 더 원하나요?

W: 정말로 원해요, 교수님. 현재로서는 어떤 형태의 도움을 받더라도 정말 좋을 것 같아요.

Mini Test 2 : Lecture

Answers

1. (B) (Detail Question)

2. (B) (Understanding Attitude Question)

3. **Generation Ship:** [1], [4] **Wormhole:** [2], [3]
   (Connecting Content Question)

4. (C) (Understanding Organization Question)

Script ∩ 1-18

M1 Professor: Since the space age began decades ago, humans have traveled in space. Sadly, we haven't gone very far. Mostly, we send people up into low-Earth orbit. Yes, we've sent a few men to the moon. But that's the farthest anyone has been from Earth. I consider that to be a real shame. Of course, we've sent satellites vast distances. Many have visited both the inner and outer planets, and, um, the *Voyager* satellites are at the edge of the solar system as I speak. But humans haven't ventured far at all.

In space terms, however, even those satellites have traveled short distances. Space is so vast that we use the term light year to express how much time it takes light to reach distant objects, such as, uh, stars. Because of the enormity of space, human travel even to the closest stars seems impossible. Yet that hasn't stopped some people from thinking of how to travel to the stars. Oh, we call that interstellar travel by the way. Writers of science fiction have come up with numerous ideas for interstellar travel. Can anyone give me an example? Brian . . . ?

M2 Student: There's warp drive, like in *Star Trek*. And people use hyperspace drives in *Star Wars*.

M1: Ah, yes. Those are two examples from movies. Warp drives and hyperspace drives are essentially the same. They are engines that enable spacecraft to move faster than the speed of light. These engines often have unique mechanisms. Or they may rely on a special type of fuel to run. At the present time, these engines are strictly science fiction. There are some scientists and engineers trying to figure out how to make them. But no one has succeeded yet.

There are some other ideas for interstellar travel though. One is the generation ship. This is an enormous ship that moves slower than the speed of light. It would have many humans on board and would carry large stores of food, plants, animals, oxygen, and water. Basically, people would live their entire lives on the ship as it slowly moves through space. These people would grow old and die. Then, their children would take over. After centuries perhaps, the descendants of the original colonists would reach their destination. I'm not so sure that's an appealing idea though. No matter how big the ship, imagine spending your entire life on it. I sure can't picture myself doing that.

Here's another potential method to achieve interstellar travel: wormholes. These are places in space that allow ships to, um, to jump far distances. A wormhole is sort of like a, hmm . . . a tube or tunnel. A ship enters it and then exits a wormhole elsewhere in the galaxy. Travel through a wormhole would be instantaneous. Imagine being in our solar system one moment and then suddenly appearing several hundred light years away. Here's the interesting part: Some scientists believe that wormholes exist. They have proven mathematically that there are wormholes. Now, uh, all we have to do is find them.

Translation

M1 Professor: 수십 년 전 우주 시대가 시작된 이래로, 인간은 우주를 여행해 왔습니다. 안타깝게도, 그렇게 멀리까지 가지는 못했습니다. 주로, 저지구 궤도로 사람들을 보내고 있습니다. 그래요, 몇몇 사람들을 달로 보내기도 했습니다. 하지만 그것이 지구를 떠나 가장 멀리 간 경우였습니다. 정말로 안타까운 일이라고 생각합니다. 물론, 매우 먼 거리로 인공위성들을 보내고 있습니다. 다수는 내행성과 외행성 모두를 방문했으며, 음, *보이저* 위성들은 제가 말씀드리는 이 순간에도 태양계의 가장자리에 있습니다. 하지만 인간은 결코 멀리까지 가본 적이 없습니다.

하지만, 우주 용어로, 그러한 위성들 조차 짧은 거리를 여행했습니다. 우주는 너무도 방대하기 때문에 우리는 광년이라는 용어를 사용하여, 예컨대, 어, 항성과 같이 멀리 떨어져 있는 물체에 빛이 도달하는 시간을 표현합니다. 우주의 광대함 때문에, 가장 가까운 항성까지 여행하는 것도 불가능한 것처럼 보입니다. 하지만 그러한 점이 사람들로 하여금 항성까지 여행하는 방법을 생각하지 못하도록 하는 것은 아닙니다. 오, 그건 그렇고 우리는 그러한 것을 성간 여행이라고 부릅니다. 공상 과학 소설의 작가들은 성간 여행에 대한 수많은 아이디어들을 제시해 왔습니다. 누가 제게 예를 들어 주실 수 있나요? Brian…?

M2 Student: *스타트렉*에 있는 것과 같은, 공간 이동 추진이 있습니다. 그리고 *스타워즈*에서는 초공간 항해가 사용됩니다.

M1: 아, 네. 그것들은 영화에서 나온 두 가지 사례입니다. 공간 이동 추진과 초공간 항해는 본질적으로 동일한 것입니다. 우주선을 빛의 속도보다 빠르게 이동할 수 있도록

해주는 엔진인 것이죠. 그러한 엔진은 종종 특별한 기계입니다. 혹은 작동하기 위해서 특정한 유형의 연료에 의존하고 있는 것일 수도 있고요. 현재로서, 그러한 엔진은 공상 과학에서만 나타납니다. 어떻게 만들 수 있는지를 알아내려고 노력 중인 몇몇 과학자 및 엔지니어들도 있습니다. 하지만 아직 아무도 성공을 하지는 못했습니다.

하지만 성간 여행에 대한 또 다른 아이디어들이 있습니다. 그 하나가 세대 우주선입니다. 이는 빛의 속도보다 느리게 움직이는 거대한 우주선입니다. 많은 인간들이 탑승할 수 있으며 막대한 양의 식량, 식물, 동물, 산소, 그리고 물을 저장해서 다닐 수 있습니다. 기본적으로, 우주선이 천천히 우주를 돌아다니는 동안, 사람들은 일생을 우주선에서 보내게 될 것입니다. 이러한 사람들은 나이가 들어 죽게 될 것입니다. 그 후, 그들의 아이들이 임무를 넘겨 받게 됩니다. 아마도 수세기가 지나면, 원래의 식민지 사람들의 후손들이 목적지에 도달하게 될 것입니다. 하지만 이것이 매력적인 아이디어인지는 잘 모르겠군요. 우주선이 얼마나 크던 간에, 그곳에서 일생을 보낸다고 상상해 보십시오. 제 자신이 그렇게 하는 것은 상상할 수가 없을 것 같습니다.

성간 여행을 할 수 있는 가능한 방법이 또 하나 있습니다: 바로 웜홀입니다. 이것은 우주선이, 음, 먼 거리를 점프할 수 있도록 해주는, 우주에 있는 장소입니다. 웜홀은 일종의, 흠… 관이나 터널과 같은 것입니다. 우주선이 그 안으로 들어가면 은하계의 다른 곳에 있는 웜홀로 빠져 나오게 됩니다. 웜홀을 통과하는 여행은 순식간에 이루어집니다. 어느 순간 우리 태양계 내에 있다가 갑자기 수백 광년 떨어진 곳에서 나타난다고 상상해 보십시오. 제가 흥미로운 점을 알려 드리겠습니다: 일부 과학자들은 웜홀이 존재한다고 믿습니다. 수학적으로 웜홀이 존재한다는 점을 입증해 냈죠. 자, 어, 우리가 해야 할 일은 그것을 찾아내는 것뿐입니다..

p.96

Sample Understanding Organization Question

Translation

W Professor: 태양계에서 가장 특이한 천체 중의 하나는 혜성입니다. 혜성은 행성 및 달보다 훨씬 더 작습니다. 전형적으로는 소행성의 크기와 비슷합니다. 어, 하지만 케레스와 베스타 같은 소행성보다는 크지 않습니다. 대부분의 혜성들은 직경이 1킬로미터에서 10킬로미터 정도입니다. 소수의, 음, 직경이 80킬로미터에 이르는 슈퍼 혜성이 발견된 적도 있습니다. 하지만 이는 극히 드문 경우입니다.

혜성은 기본적으로 얼음과 더스트로 이루어진 커다란 원형 물체입니다. 얼음은 얼려진 물과 기타 얼려진 기체로 구성된 혼합체입니다. 태양계 내의 혜성들 중 다수가 주기 혜성입니다. 이는 200년 이하의 주기로 태양을 돈다는 점을 의미합니다. 하지만, 다른 혜성들은 매우 긴 궤도를 갖습니다. 종종 태양계 외부의 깊은 곳까지 돌아다닙니다. 이러한 혜성들은 수백 년 혹은 심지어는 수천 년에 걸쳐서 태양 주변을 한 차례 돌 수도 있습니다.

가장 유명한 혜성은 핼리 혜성입니다. 76년마다 궤도를 한 바퀴 도는 주기 혜성입니다. 마지막으로 모습을 드러냈던 때는 1986년이었습니다. 안타깝게도, 다소 인상적이지 못한 모습이었습니다. 1910년과 1835년에 훨씬 더 밝았습니다. 실제로, 핼리 혜성은 2,000년 이상 동안 알려져 있었습니다. 중국인들은 기원전 240년에 이를 알아차렸습니다. 이 혜성은 천문학자인 에드문트 핼리의 이름을 따서 이름이 지어졌습니다. 그는 혜성의 궤도를 계산하여 그것이 언제 태양계로 다시 들어오게 될 것인지를 예측했습니다. 불행하게도, 핼리는 혜성이 돌아오기 전에 사망했습니다. 그래서 자신의 예측이 맞았는지 혹은 그렇지 않았는지를 결코 알지 못했습니다.

어쨌든, 일반적인 혜성에 대한 이야기로 되돌아 갑시다. 모든 혜성들은 서로 구별되는 몇 개의 부분을 지니고 있습니다. 가장 중요한 세 개의 부분은 핵, 코마, 그리고 꼬리입니다. 이 셋 중에서는 꼬리가 가장 장관입니다. 하지만 핵은 혜성 자체를 구성하고 있습니다. 따라서 우선 핵에 대해서 검토해 보도록 합시다.

Mini Test 1 : Conversation

Answers

1. Ⓐ (Gist-Purpose Question)

2. ③, ④ (Detail Question)

3. Ⓒ (Understanding Attitude Question)

4. Ⓑ (Understanding Function Question)

Script 🎧 1-20

M Computer Laboratory Employee: Good afternoon. Um, are you here for a lab class? There aren't any more lab classes scheduled for today.

W Student: Uh, no. I'm not here to attend a class. I'm looking for Daniel Porter.

M: That's me. I'm Daniel. What can I do for you?

W: Oh, hi. My name is Clarice Weathers. I just got hired to work in the lab as an assistant here. Uh, I've got a letter from Professor Jackson in my purse. Hold on a second . . .

M: Sure.

W: Aha, I've got it. Here you go . . .

M: Hmm . . . Okay, it looks like you're my newest student employee. It's a pleasure to get a chance to work with you.

W: Thanks for saying that. So, uh, what exactly do I need to do? My first shift is tomorrow morning at nine o'clock. However, if you want to show me a few things now . . . uh, if you're not busy that is . . . that would be fine with me. My schedule is free for the next two hours.

M: Okay, that sounds good. Let me show you around the lab for about ten minutes. I can point out where we keep the supplies and chemicals. And I can tell you about a few of the duties you're going to have. How about that?

W: That's great. That way, I can be ready to start bright and early tomorrow. Uh, I have a question though . . . I'm not going to have to teach any lab classes or anything, am I? I mean, uh, I'm only a junior, so I don't think I'm qualified.

M: [4]Don't worry about that. Only graduate students teach lab classes. **There will be a lab class during your shift tomorrow, but I'll be teaching it.** All you will have to do is help me in various ways.

W: Okay. That's good to know.

Translation

M Computer Laboratory Employee: 안녕하세요. 음, 실험실 수업 때문에 오신 건가요? 오늘 예정된 실험실 수업은 더 이상 없는데요.

W Student: 어, 아니에요. 수업을 들으려고 온 것은 아니에요. 저는 Daniel Porter 선생님을 찾고 있어요.

M: 바로 저예요. 제가 Daniel이죠. 무엇을 도와 드릴까요?

W: 오, 안녕하세요. 제 이름은 Clarice Weathers에요. 여기 실험실에서 조교로 근무하도록 채용이 되었죠. 어, 제 가방에 Jackson 교수님의 서한이 있어요. 잠시만 기다려 주세요…

M: 물론 그럴게요.

W: 아하, 여기에 있네요. 보세요…

M: 흠… 좋아요. 새로운 학생 직원인 것 같군요. 함께 일할 기회를 갖게 되어 기쁘네요.

W: 그렇게 말씀해 주시다니 감사합니다. 그러면, 어, 제가 정확히 무엇을 해야 하나요? 첫 번째 근무는 내일 오전 9시에 있어요. 하지만, 지금 몇 가지 일들을 알려 주시고자 한다면… 어, 그렇게 바쁘지 않으시다면… 저로서는 좋을 것 같아요. 제 시간표 상 다음 두 시간 동안은 비어 있어요.

M: 그래요, 좋아요. 약 10분 동안 실험실을 안내해 드릴게요. 비품 및 화학 물질들을 어디에 보관하는지도 알려 드릴 수 있어요. 그리고 학생의 몇 가지 업무에 대해서도 말씀을 드릴 수 있고요. 어떤가요?

W: 좋아요. 그렇게 하면, 내일 일찍 희망차게 시작할 준비가 될 것 같아요. 어, 하지만

질문이 하나 있는데… 실험실 수업 같은 것을 맡거나 하지는 않겠죠, 그런가요? 제 말은, 어, 저는 3학년일 뿐이라서, 제가 그럴 자격이 있다고는 생각하지 않거든요.

M: 그 점에 대해서는 걱정하지 말아요. 대학원생들만 실험실 수업을 맡을 수 있죠. 내일 학생의 근무 시간 동안에 실험실 수업은 있겠지만, 그 수업은 제가 맡을 거예요. 학생이 해야 할 일은 여러 방면으로 저를 도와 주는 것뿐이에요.

W: 그렇군요. 알게 되어 기쁘네요.

Mini Test 2 : Lecture

Answers

1. Ⓓ (Gist-Content Question)

2. Ⓐ (Detail Question)

3. Ⓓ (Understanding Organization Question)

4. Ⓑ (Understanding Attitude Question)

Script 🎧 1-21

M Professor: Today, we're going to talk about animation. I'm sure all of you have seen different types of animation, or cartoons, as people sometimes call them. Nowadays, lots of animation is done on computers. However, the first animated shorts and feature films were all drawn by hand. So, uh, we're going to discuss the early years of animation today. Animation originated in early drawings and paintings. Sometimes these were done in sequence. This enabled the pictures to tell stories. Later, mechanical viewers were invented. These had pictures drawn inside a cylinder. When the pictures were rotated and viewed through a narrow slit, they created the illusion of movement. Everyone knows what I'm talking about, right . . . ? Good.

So that was a primitive sort of animation. But, in the late 1800s, motion picture cameras and projectors were invented. As a result, it wasn't long before animation made it to film. Most early versions of animated films were quite short. I'm going to show you a few in a bit, so you'll see just how brief they were. But let me get through my lecture first. Uh, anyway . . . uh, as I was saying, most early animated films were short. The reason was that the pictures were all hand drawn. That's an incredibly labor-intensive process. Thus it makes sense that the films were short if you think about it.

So, uh, each picture was photographed, and the film was made one frame at a time. In the early days, each frame was a separate drawing. Even the background had to be redrawn for each frame. Can you imagine having to do that again and again . . . ? It must have been incredibly tiresome. Now, around, um . . . 1914, the use of clear celluloid sheets became the norm. These clear sheets allowed animators to use the same background each time a frame was photographed. They simply drew the characters and other elements on other celluloid sheets and placed them on top of one another. [4]Stacking celluloid sheets gave the illusion of depth to animation. Oh, uh, the word for these celluloid sheets is cel. **That's C-E-L, not C-E-L-L.**

By the 1920s, many small animation studios had sprung up in the United States and other countries. They used an assembly-line process to produce cheap animated shorts. Some people wrote the stories . . . Others drew the cels . . . Others colored them . . . And then the cels were photographed. Once the sound era began, though, the process changed. In most animation that has sound, the dialogue is recorded first. This is done so that the characters' mouths can be drawn to match the words they're saying. In case you're curious, *Steamboat Willie*, which starred Mickey Mouse and was released in 1928, was one of the first animated movies to use sound.

The first animated films were photographed in black and white. Gradually, color photography became more accessible. In 1931, Walt Disney made one of the first animated films in color. He also released *Snow White and the Seven Dwarves* in 1937. It was the first successful feature-length animated film in color. Now, um, about Walt Disney . . .

Translation

M Professor: 오늘은, 애니메이션에 대해 이야기할 것입니다. 여러분 모두가 다양한 종류의 애니메이션, 혹은 사람들이 때때로 만화라고 부르는 것을 본 적이 있으리라고 확신합니다. 오늘날, 많은 애니메이션은 컴퓨터로 작업이 되고 있습니다. 하지만, 최초의 단편 및 장편 애니메이션 영화는 모두 손으로 그려졌습니다. 그래서, 어, 오늘은 애니메이션의 초창기에 대해 논의해 보도록 하겠습니다. 애니메이션은 초기 드로잉 및 회화에서 기원했습니다. 때때로 이들은 순서대로 그려졌습니다. 이로써 그림들이 이야기를 전할 수 있게 되었습니다. 이후, 슬라이드를 보기 위한 기계 장치가 발명되었습니다. 여기에는 실린더 안에 그려진 그림이 있었습니다. 그림이 회전을 하며 좁은 틈으로 보여지면, 운동 착시가 일어났습니다. 제가 말하고 있는 바를 모두들 아시겠죠, 그렇죠…? 좋습니다.

그래서 바로 그것이 원시적인 형태의 애니메이션이었습니다. 하지만 1800년대 후반, 영화 촬영기와 영사기가 발명되었습니다. 그 결과, 얼마 되지 않아 애니메이션은 영화화되었습니다. 애니메이션 영화의 대다수 초기 작품들은 상당히 짧았습니다. 잠시 몇 개를 여러분들께 보여 드리면, 얼마나 짧은지를 알게 되실 것입니다. 하지만 먼저 강의를 계속하도록 하겠습니다. 어, 어쨌든… 말씀드린 바와 같이, 대부분의 초기 애니메이션 영화는 짧았습니다. 그 이유는 그림들이 모두 손으로 그려졌기 때문이었습니다. 매우 많은 노동력이 들어가는 작업입니다. 따라서 그 점에 대해 생각해 보시면 영화가 짧은 것이 이해가 되실 것입니다.

그래서, 어, 각각의 그림들이 촬영되었고, 영화는 한 번에 한 프레임씩 만들어졌습니다. 초창기에, 각각의 프레임은 독립적인 그림이었습니다. 심지어 각각의 프레임들을 위해 배경을 다시 그려야만 했습니다. 그런 일을 반복해서 해야만 했다는 점에 상상이 가시나요…? 틀림없이 매우 성가신 일이었을 것입니다. 자, 약, 음… 1914년경, 투명한 셀룰로이드 종이의 사용이 일반화되었습니다. 이러한 투명한 종이는 애니메이션 제작자로 하여금 한 프레임이 촬영될 때마다 동일한 배경을 사용할 수 있도록 해주었습니다. 또 다른 셀룰로이드 종이에 등장 인물 및 기타 요인들을 그리고 이들을 또 다른 종이 위에 올려 놓았습니다. 겹쳐진 셀룰로이드 종이는 애니메이션에 깊이감을 주었습니다. 오, 어, 이러한 셀룰로이드 종이에 대한 명칭은 셀입니다. C-E-L입니다. C-E-L-L이 아니고요.

1920년경, 미국 및 다른 나라에서 많은 소규모 애니메이션 스튜디오들이 생겨났습니다. 조립 라인을 사용하여 저렴한 애니메이션 단편 영화들을 생산해 냈습니다. 몇몇 사람들이 스토리를 작성했고… 일부는 셀을 그렸으며… 그것을 색칠한 사람도 있었고… 그리고 나서 셀이 촬영되었습니다. 하지만, 유성 영화 시대가 시작되자 그러한 과정은 바뀌었습니다. 소리가 들어가는 대부분의 애니메이션에서는, 대화가 먼저 녹음됩니다. 등장 인물들이 말하는 단어와 그 입 모양이 일치하도록 등장 인물의 입을 그려야 하기 때문입니다. 궁금해 하시는 경우를 위해 말씀을 드리면, *증기선 윌리*, 이는 미키 마우스가 등장하는 1928년에 개봉된 작품인데, 소리를 사용한 최초의 애니메이션 영화 중 하나였습니다.

최초의 애니메이션 영화들은 흑백으로 촬영이 되었습니다. 점차적으로, 컬러 사진술을 이용할 수 있게 되었습니다. 1931년, 월트 디즈니가 최초의 컬러 애니메이션 영화 중 하나를 만들었습니다. 그는 또한 1937년에 *백설 공주와 일곱 난장이*를 개봉시켰습니다. 컬러로 된 장편 애니메이션 영화 중 최초로 성공적인 것이었습니다. 자, 음, 월트 디즈니에 대해서는…

Sample Connecting Content Question

Translation

W Professor: 그러면, 어, 몇 개의 서로 다른 계기들을 언급했으므로, 정말로 빠르게 정리를 해보도록 합시다. 여러분들이 반드시 기억해야 할 세 가지의 계기가 있습니다. 물론, 첫 번째는 온도계입니다. 우리는 이를 이용하여 온도를 측정합니다. 그 다음은 기압계입니다. 이는 기압을 측정해 줍니다. 세 번째는 풍속계입니다. 이 계기는 바람의 속도를 측정해 줍니다. 다른 계기들도 중요하기 때문에, 그 역시 기억하고 계셔야 합니다. 하지만 이제, 그 외의 다른 것에 대해 이야기하고자 합니다.

제가 검토해 보고자 하는 것은 바로 이것입니다: 기상학자들이 날씨를 예측하는데 도움을 주는 도구들입니다. 아시겠지만, 어, 온도계와 풍속계는 날씨를 예측해 주지 않습니다. 그들이 할 수 있는 일은 현재의 기상 상태에 대해 이야기해 주는 것이 전부입니다. 음, 어, 기압계가 날씨를 예측해 줄 수도 있다고 생각합니다. 어찌되었든, 기압계를 사용하여 곧 비가 내릴지 혹은 그렇지 않을지를 알 수 있으니까요.

하지만 오늘날 기상학자들이 보유하고 있는 첨단 장비들은 어떨까요? 첨단 기술을 가지고 있기 때문에 우리는 매우 운이 좋습니다. 날씨를 예측하는데 도움을 주죠. 물론, 항상 맞는 것은 아닙니다. 날씨는, 어… 너무나도 예측하기가 어렵습니다. 어쨌든, 제가 언급하고 있는 이러한 장비들은 무엇일까요…? 첫 번째는 위성입니다. 수많은 기상 위성들이 궤도를 돌고 있습니다. 이들은 사실상 지구 전체의 이미지를 제공해 줍니다. 어디에서 폭풍이 형성되고 어떤 곳으로 향하는지에 대해 알려 주는 것과 같은 일을 합니다. 도플러 레이더는 또 다른 중요한 장비입니다. 폭풍의 강도 및 어느 지역에 비가 내릴 것인지를 알려 줍니다. 또한, 수많은 장비를 갖춘 기구가 공중으로 보내집니다. 이들은 기온과 기압을 측정합니다. 따라서 날씨가 변하고 있다는 점을 나타내 주는 대기 상의 변화에 대해 알려 줍니다. 봅시다. 그 밖에 어떤 것이 있을까요…?

Mini Test 1 : Conversation

Answers

1. **B** (Detail Question)

2. **B** (Making Inferences Question)

3. **A** (Connecting Content Question)

4. **C** (Understanding Attitude Question)

Script   1-23

M1 Librarian: You look like you could use some assistance. Is there something I can do for you, young man?

M2 Student: Yes, sir. I'm trying to find a couple of books for an English literature paper I'm writing. But, uh, the library doesn't seem to have them in its collection.

M1: I see. Do you have the titles?

M2: Yes, I do. Here . . . Let me type the title of the first one onto the computer . . .

M1: Ah, okay. We don't have that book. How about the other one you're looking for . . . ?

M2: Sure. I can type it in as well . . . But, when I did that a moment ago, I got the same result . . . See . . . Nothing. I really need those books to write my paper. I don't know what I'm going to do without them.

M1: Well, you shouldn't get discouraged. Have you considered going to the interlibrary loan desk?

M2: Um . . .

M1: Okay. I see you don't know what I'm talking about. Let me explain. Using interlibrary loan allows you to check out books from other colleges and universities. All you need to do is visit the desk over there . . . See it . . . ?

M2: Yes, I do.

M1: Great. Go there and fill out a request-book form. Then, the person will get the book from another library for you.

M2: That's great. But, um, how long does it take?

M1: It depends. If the book comes from a local library, it might just take one or two days. If it comes from a library in another state, it could take up to a week. Oh, just so you know . . . You can use interlibrary loan to get copies of articles from journals as well.

M2: Cool. That was my next question. You've been a big help, sir. Thanks so much for telling me what to do.

Translation

M1 Librarian: 도움이 필요한 것 같아 보이네요. 제가 도와 드릴 일이 있을까요, 학생?

M2 Student: 네, 선생님. 저는 지금 쓰고 있는 영문학 보고서를 위해 두어 권의 책을 찾고 있는 중이에요. 하지만, 어, 도서관에 소장되어 있는 책이 없는 것 같아요.

M1: 그렇군요. 제목이 있나요?

M2: 네, 있어요. 여기 있는데… 첫 번째 책 제목을 컴퓨터에 입력해 드릴게요…

M1: 아, 그래요. 그 책을 가지고 있지 않네요. 찾고 있는 또 다른 책은 어떤가요…?

M2: 물론이에요. 마찬가지로 입력해 드릴 수 있어요… 하지만, 제가 조금 전에 해보았을 때, 똑같은 결과를 얻었어요… 보세요… 없어요. 보고서를 쓰기 위해서는 정말로 그 책들이 필요해요. 책이 없다면 어떻게 해야 할지 잘 모르겠어요.

M1: 음, 낙담하지는 마세요. 도서관 상호 대출 데스크로 가보려는 생각은 했나요?

M2: 음…

M1: 그래요. 제가 무엇에 대해 말하고 있는지 학생이 모르고 있는 것 같군요. 설명해 드리죠. 도서관 상호 대출을 이용하면 다른 대학 및 대학교에서 책을 대출할 수가 있어요. 학생이 해야 할 일은 저쪽에 있는 데스크로 가는 것이 전부이죠… 보이나요…?

M2: 네, 그래요.

M1: 좋아요. 그곳으로 가서 도서 요청 양식에 내용을 기입하세요. 그러면, 담당자가 다른 도서관에서 책을 구해다 줄 거에요.

M2: 잘 되었군요. 하지만, 음, 시간이 얼마나 걸리나요?

M1: 경우에 따라 달라요. 해당 도서가 인근 도서관에 있으면, 하루나 이틀 정도만 걸려요. 다른 주에 있는 도서관에 있다면, 1주일 까지 걸릴 수도 있고요. 오, 아시다시피… 도서관 상호 대출을 이용하여 잡지 기사들에 대한 사본도 얻을 수 있어요.

M2: 잘 되었네요. 그것이 제 다음 번 질문이었어요. 큰 도움이 되었습니다. 선생님. 제가 어떻게 해야 할 지를 알려 주셔서 정말 고맙습니다.

Mini Test 2 : Lecture

Answers

1. (B) (Gist-Content Question)

2. (A) (Making Inferences Question)

3. (C) (Connecting Content Question)

4. (B) (Detail Question)

Script 🎧 1-24

M Professor: Early humans were hunter-gatherers. So they spent a large amount of their time searching for food. They either killed animals for their meat or collected various types of fruits, vegetables, and nuts. Some of this food lasted a long time without spoiling. For instance, various fruits, vegetables, and grains could last for several days, uh, or even weeks, without going bad. But meat and fish spoiled quickly. Early humans moved around a lot, so they were accustomed to finding new sources of food. However, once humans began farming the land and living in villages, towns, and cities, preserving food became vital. Why's that . . . ? Well, the people needed to preserve the crops they had harvested. These crops gave them a food supply during winter and times when there were crop failures or famines.

As you can imagine, the earliest methods of food storage were quite, uh, primitive. For instance, people often dug pits in the ground. They buried the food in the pits and then covered them with dirt. Other people put food in caves. Both the pits and caves were cool and usually dry. They also kept the food out of the sun. Of course, humans had to prevent animals from eating the food. This was a particular problem for food stored in caves.

Later, the invention of pottery proved to be extremely useful for food preservation. Large amounts of food could be stored in clay pots. Grain, as well as liquids such as wine and beer, was frequently stored in these containers. Another early method was fermentation. Grapes fermented and became wine while hops and other grains fermented and turned into beer. Thus wine and beer were two staple drinks for humans up until modern times.

As civilization became more advanced, better food preservation methods were developed. One was the silo. This is a large, dry, and dark building that grain is stored in. Silos keep grain from getting wet, which makes it rot. They also prevent rats and other vermin from eating the grain. Silos are important since many types of grains won't spoil for years if they're stored properly. Both the ancient Egyptians and Romans made great use of grain silos. People also learned to dry food. Thousands of years ago, humans realized that dried fruits and vegetables lasted much longer than fresh ones. So they often put their food out in the sun to dry it. Thus they could eat the dried food at a later time.

The methods I've given you have all been for fruits and vegetables. But, um, what about meat and fish preservation methods? Sure, um, some people dried them. But there were other ways to preserve them. In cold climates, people simply left meat and fish outside, where they would freeze. Others relied upon smoking or pickling them. But the main type of preservation for meat and fish was salting. The reason was that salted meat could last a long time without spoiling.

Translation

M Professor: 초기 인류는 수렵 · 채집인이었습니다. 따라서 음식을 찾는데 많은 시간을 보냈죠. 고기를 얻기 위해 동물들을 죽이거나 다양한 종류의 과일, 채소, 그리고 견과류들을 수집했습니다. 이러한 음식 중 일부는 부패하지 않고 오랫동안 남아 있었습니다. 예를 들어, 여러 가지의 과일, 채소, 그리고 곡물들은 수일 동안, 어, 혹은 심지어 수주 동안 상하지 않고 남아 있었습니다. 하지만 고기와 생선은 빨리 상했습니다. 초기 인류는 많이 돌아다녔는데, 그래서 새로운 식량을 찾는데 익숙해져 있었습니다. 하지만, 인류가 농사를 짓고 마을, 소도시, 그리고 대도시에 거주하기 시작하자, 음식을 보존하는 일은 매우 중요해졌습니다. 왜 그럴까요…? 음, 사람들은 수확한 곡식들을 보존해야 했습니다. 이러한 곡물들은 겨울과 흉작 및 기근이 들었을 때, 식량이 되어 주었습니다.

짐작하실 수 있듯이, 음식을 저장하는 최초의 방법은 상당히, 어, 원시적이었습니다. 예를 들어, 사람들은 종종 땅에 구덩이를 팠습니다. 구덩이에 음식을 묻고 흙으로 그 위를 덮었습니다. 동굴에 음식을 저장해 두었던 사람들도 있었습니다. 구덩이와 동굴 모두는 온도가 낮고 보통 건조한 편이었습니다. 또한 햇빛이 비추지 않는 곳에 음식을 보관했습니다. 물론, 인간들은 동물들이 음식을 먹지 않도록 해야 했습니다. 이는 동굴 속에 음식을 저장하는 경우에 특히 문제가 되었습니다.

이후, 도기의 발명은 음식 저장에 매우 유용한 것으로 판명되었습니다. 많은 양의 음식이 토분에 저장될 수 있었습니다. 곡물은, 포도주와 맥주 같은 액체뿐만 아니라, 종종 이러한 용기에 저장되었습니다. 또 다른 초기의 방법은 발효였습니다. 포도는 발효되어 포도주가 되었고, 호프와 기타 곡물들은 발효되어 맥주가 되었습니다. 따라서 포도주와 맥주는 현대에 이르기까지 인간에게 주요한 음료 중 일부가 되어 왔습니다.

문명이 보다 발전할수록, 보다 뛰어난 음식 저장 방법이 개발되었습니다. 그 하나가 사일로였습니다. 이것은 곡물을 저장하는, 커다랗고, 건조하고, 그리고 어두운 건물입니다. 사일로는 곡물에 습기가 차는 것을 방지해 주었는데, 습기가 차면 곡물이 썩습니다. 이들은 또한 쥐나 다른 해충들이 곡물을 먹는 것을 예방해 주었습니다. 제대로만 저장된다면 많은 종류의 곡물들이 수년 동안 썩지 않을 것이기 때문에, 사일로는 중요합니다. 고대 이집트인들 및 로마인들 모두가 곡물 저장용 사일로를 잘 활용했습니다. 또한 사람들은 음식을 건조시키는 법을 알아내었습니다. 수천 년 전, 인간은 건조시킨 과일과 채소가 신선한 것보다 훨씬 더 오래 지속된다는 점을 깨달았습니다. 그래서 종종 건조를 시키기 위해 음식을 햇빛에 놔두었습니다. 따라서 차후에 건조시킨 음식을 먹을 수 있었습니다.

제가 여러분께 알려 드린 방법들은 모두 과일과 채소에 관한 것이었습니다. 하지만, 음, 고기나 생선을 보전시키는 방법은 어떨까요? 물론, 음, 일부 사람들은 그것들을 건조시켰습니다. 하지만 이들을 보존하는 다른 방법들이 있었습니다. 추운 기후에서, 사람들은 고기와 생선을 야외에 두었는데, 여기에서는 냉동이 되었습니다. 연기를 쏘이거나 절이는 방법에 의존했던 사람들도 있었습니다. 하지만 고기와 생선을 보존시키는 주된 방식은 염장이었습니다. 그 이유는 염장한 고기가 부패하지 않고 오랜 시간 동안 지속될 수 있었기 때문이었습니다.

Unit 09

p.104

Sample Connecting Content Question

Translation

M Professor: 귀중한 광물을 채광하기에 앞서, 먼저 그것들을 찾아내야 합니다. 과거에는, 첨단 도구를 이용할 수가 없었습니다. 따라서 주로 운에 의해서 광물을 발견해 냈습니다. 우리에게는 다행스러운 일인데, 오늘날에는 운에 의존할 필요가 없습니다. 대신 지질학자들이 여러 가지의 특별한 장비들을 활용하고 있습니다.

우리가 사용하는 특별한 장비에는 어떤 것들이 있을까요…? 봅시다… 가이거 계수기, 중력계, 자력계, 그리고, 어, 특히 폭파 장치들이 있습니다. 각각에 대해 말씀 드리죠. 여러분 책의 82페이지를 봐 주세요. 윗부분의 왼쪽 코너에 있는 그림을 확인해 주십시오. 그것이 가이거 계수기입니다. 가이거 계수기는 우라늄과 같은 방사선 물질을 찾는데 효과적입니다. 우라늄은, 음, 여러분들도 알고 있으리라 확신하는데, 원자력 발전과 원자 폭탄 모두에 사용되는 중요한 원소입니다.

가이거 계수기 옆에 있는 그림은 중력계를 나타냅니다. 이 기계들은 다양한 암석층에 대한 밀도의 차이를 나타내 줍니다. 왜 그러한 점이 중요할까요…? 음, 지질학자들은 지하 암석의 밀도를 살펴보고, 그런 다음에 그들이 무엇으로 이루어져 있는지를 알아낼 수 있습니다. 그럼으로써 실제로 흙을 파고 암석을 가까이에서 살펴봐야 하는 수고를 덜게 됩니다. 여러분 책에 있는 세 번째 그림을 봐 주시면… 어, 가이거 계수기 아래쪽에 있는 그림입니다. 그것이 자력계입니다. 그 이름에서 알 수 있듯이, 이는 자력으로 작동됩니다. 기본적으로, 어, 철광을 발견하는데 도움을 주는 자기장을 만들어냅니다. 마지막으로, 폭파 장치는 어떨까요? 이들을 가지고 작업을 하는 것은 실제로 꽤 재미있습니다. 어쨌든, 폭발물은 지하 깊숙이 들어가서 다시 튀어나오는 충격파를 발생시킵니다. 이들이 이동하는 속도에 따라 지하에 있는 암석의 유형을 알 수 있습니다. 폭발물은 석탄, 석유, 그리고 가스를 찾는데 유용합니다.

Mini Test 1 : Conversation

Answers

1. Ⓑ (Gist-Purpose Question)

2. Ⓓ (Detail Question)

3. Ⓒ (Making Inferences Question)

4. Ⓑ (Understanding Function Question)

Script 🎧 1-26

W1 Student: Good morning, Professor Martin. It's a beautiful day, isn't it?

W2 Professor: Oh, hi, Alexandra. Are you here to turn in your paper? You're a couple of days early you know. It's not due until Friday.

W1: Ah, actually, no, I'm not here to do that.

W2: Really? Then what brings you here so early in the morning?

W1: Uh . . . I hate to say this, but I am going to have to drop your class.

W2: You are?

W1: Yes, ma'am. I'd love to keep taking it, but I'm totally overwhelmed with all of my other classes this semester. You see, uh, I'm taking twenty-four hours this semester.

W2: Twenty-four? That's a lot.

W1: [4]It is. I thought I could handle it, but . . . um, I can't. I'm simply exhausted trying to go to all of my classes. And I'm starting to fall behind in my class work, too.

W2: Why not stop taking another class?

W1: I'd love to, but all of the other classes I'm taking are requirements. This is my only elective. You see, uh, I'm trying to graduate a semester early. If I drop a required class, I won't be able to do that. I'm so sorry. I love your class, but I simply can't stay in it.

W2: That's fine. I understand. So, um, did you bring the form for me to sign?

W1: Yes, I did. I've got it right here. If you don't mind signing it . . .

W2: Not at all. All right . . . Well, Alexandra, I enjoyed having you in my class. You're always welcome to sit in on it anytime. Not for credit of course. But come to one of my lectures if you have the time.

Translation

W1 Student: 안녕하세요, Martin 교수님. 날씨가 좋네요, 그렇지 않나요?

W2 Professor: 오, 안녕하세요, Alexandra. 보고서를 제출하기 위해 이곳에 왔나요? 알겠지만 이틀 정도 빠르군요. 마감일은 금요일이에요.

W1: 아, 실은, 아니에요, 그렇게 하려고 온 것은 아니에요.

W2: 정말인가요? 그러면 무엇 때문에 이처럼 아침 일찍 여기에 왔나요?

W1: 어… 이렇게 말씀드리고 싶지는 않지만, 교수님 수업에 대한 수강 신청을 취소해야 해서요.

W2: 취소한다고요?

W1: 네, 교수님. 계속 수강하고 싶지만, 이번 학기의 다른 수업으로 인해 어찌할 바를 모르겠어요. 아시다시피, 어, 저는 이번 학기에 24학점을 수강하고 있거든요.

W2: 24학점이요? 많군요.

W1: 그래요. 감당할 수 있을 것 같았는데, 하지만… 음, 그럴 수가 없네요. 모든 수업을 들으려고 하다가 지쳐 버렸어요. 그리고 학업에서도 뒤쳐지기 시작했고요.

W2: 다른 수업을 포기하는 것은 어떤가요?

W1: 그렇게 하고 싶지만, 제가 수강하고 있는 다른 수업들은 모두 필수 과목이에요. 이 수업만이 선택 과목이죠. 아시겠지만, 어, 저는 한 학기 일찍 졸업을 하려고 노력하고 있어요. 필수 과목의 수강을 취소하면, 그럴 수가 없게 될 거에요. 정말로 죄송해요. 교수님 수업은 좋아하지만, 수업에 계속 남아 있을 수가 없어요.

W2: 괜찮아요. 이해해요. 그러면, 음, 제가 서명할 양식을 가지고 왔나요?

W1: 네, 가지고 왔어요. 바로 여기에 있어요. 서명하는 것을 꺼리신다면…

W2: 전혀 그렇지 않아요. 좋아요… 음, Alexandra, 제 수업에 학생이 있어서 즐거웠어요. 학생이 수업에 들어오는 것은 언제라도 환영이에요. 물론 학점을 위해서가

아니고요. 하지만 시간이 있으면 제 강의 중 하나에 들어오도록 해요.

Answers

1. Ⓐ (Gist-Content Question)

2. **Second Voyage:** ☐1, ☐4 **Third Voyage:** ☐2, ☐3
   (Connecting Content Question)

3. Ⓓ (Detail Question)

4. Ⓒ (Understanding Organization Question)

Script 🎧 1-27

M Professor: Once Christopher Columbus returned to Spain from his first voyage to the New World, he began making plans for a second trip. It didn't take him long to arrange everything. On September 24, 1493, he set sail with seventeen ships and about 1,200 men. In early November, the expedition reached the Caribbean Sea. Columbus and his men visited many islands that he hadn't seen on his first voyage. They spent time exploring Cuba, Hispaniola, and Jamaica. Columbus still, however, erroneously believed that those islands were somewhere off the coast of China. On that voyage, Columbus found a small amount of gold. To help pay for the expedition, Columbus tried bringing hundreds of captured natives back to Spain. He intended to sell them as slaves. Many of them died on the voyage home though. After establishing a few small settlements on Hispaniola, Columbus set sail for home. He returned to Spain in the fall of 1494.

So Columbus had completed two trips to the New World. But his investors hadn't seen very much in terms of profit. All he brought back was a bit of gold and a few slaves. Oh, he also brought some samples of tobacco and other plants that were unknown in Europe. But that didn't satisfy anyone. Nevertheless, Columbus started planning a third trip. This time, though, he could only get six ships. And it took him a while to find backers. His tiny fleet left Spain on May 30, 1498. There were two objectives: to resupply some Spanish settlements and to look for the mainland of what he, um, he still thought was Asia. On the trip, Columbus sent three ships to Hispaniola. He sailed south with the other three. In July, he found the island of Trinidad. In August, he discovered the South American mainland. Columbus then turned north to the colony on Hispaniola. When he arrived, he encountered trouble. The governor of Hispaniola had Columbus arrested. Columbus's two brothers, who had gone on the trip, were arrested as well. Then, they were sent to Spain as prisoners.

Columbus was arrested mainly because the colonists on Hispaniola were upset with him. They thought Columbus had lied to them. They hadn't found any of the riches that he had promised. So they accused Columbus of committing various atrocities. There, um, may have been some truth to the accusations. After all, Columbus could be a cruel man at times. Anyway, Columbus and his brothers appealed to the Spanish king, who released them.

Columbus then began planning a fourth trip. He raised enough funds for four ships. They set sail on May 12, 1503. This time, Columbus had both good and bad luck. He made some discoveries along the coast of Central America. However, he also got shipwrecked on Jamaica. He and his men were stranded there for a year. They were rescued and returned to Spain in November of 1504. Columbus died in 1506, so he was never able to make another voyage to the Americas.

Translation

M Professor: 크리스토퍼 콜럼버스가 신세계로의 첫 번째 항해로부터 스페인으로 돌아왔을 때, 그는 두 번째 여행에 대한 계획을 세우기 시작했습니다. 모든 것을 준비하는데 많은 시간이 걸리지는 않았습니다. 1493년 9월 24일, 그는 17척의 선박과 약 1,200명의 사람들과 함께 출항을 했습니다. 11월 초, 원정대는 카리브 해에 도착했습니다. 콜럼버스와 그의 선원들은 첫 번째 항해에서 보지 못했던 많은 섬을 방문했습니다. 쿠바, 히스파니올라, 그리고 자메이카를 탐험하며 시간을 보냈습니다. 하지만, 콜럼버스는 그러한 섬들이 중국의 해안에서 약간 떨어져 있는 곳이라고 잘못 생각하고 있었습니다. 항해에서, 콜럼버스는 적은 양의 금을 발견했습니다. 원정대의 비용을 대기 위해, 콜럼버스는 수백 명의 원주민 포로들을 스페인으로 데리고 오려고 했습니다. 노예로서 이들을 팔 의도였습니다. 하지만 그중 다수는 고국으로 가는 도중 목숨을 잃었습니다. 히스파니올라에 몇 개의 작은 정착촌을 설립한 후, 콜럼버스는 고향으로의 항해를 시작했습니다. 1494년 가을에 그는 스페인으로 돌아왔습니다.

그래서 콜럼버스는 신세계로의 두 차례 여행을 마쳤습니다. 하지만 이윤이라는 관점에서 투자자들이 많은 것을 얻지는 못했습니다. 그가 가지고 온 것은 약간의 금과 몇 명의 노예뿐이었습니다. 오, 또한 몇 개의 담배 표본과 유럽에 알려져 있지 않았던 기타 식물들도 가지고 왔습니다. 하지만, 그것은 누구도 만족시키지 못했습니다. 그럼에도 불구하고, 콜럼버스는 세 번째 여행을 계획하기 시작했습니다. 하지만 이번에는, 6척의 선박만을 구할 수 있었습니다. 그리고 지원자들을 찾는데 얼마 간의 시간이 걸렸습니다. 그의 소규모 선단은 1498년 5월 30일에 스페인을 떠났습니다. 두 가지 목적이 있었습니다: 몇 군데의 스페인 정착촌에 물자를 공급해 주는 것과 그가, 음, 그가 여전히 아시아라고 생각했던 곳의 본토를 찾는 것이었습니다. 여행에서, 콜럼버스는 세 척의 배를 히스파니올라에 보냈습니다. 그는 다른 세 척의 선박과 함께 남쪽으로 항해를 했습니다. 7월에, 그는 트리니다드 섬을 발견했습니다. 8월에는, 남아메리카의 본토를 발견했습니다. 이후 콜럼버스는 히스파니올라에 있는 식민지를 향해 북쪽으로 방향을 돌렸습니다. 그가 도착했을 때, 그는 문제에 부딪치게 되었습니다. 히스파니올라의 총독이 콜럼버스를 체포했던 것입니다. 콜럼버스의 두 형제들도, 이들도 여행을 떠났는데, 체포되었습니다. 그 후, 이들은 죄수로서 스페인으로 보내졌습니다.

콜럼버스는 주로 히스파니올라의 식민지 주민들이 그에 대해 화가 나 있었다는 이유로 체포되었습니다. 그들은 콜럼버스가 자신들에게 거짓말을 했다고 생각했습니다. 그들은 그가 약속했던 어떠한 부도 발견하지 못했습니다. 따라서 콜럼버스가 여러 가지의 악행을 저질렀다고 비난했습니다. 음, 그러한 비난에는 어느 정도의 진실이 있었을 수도 있습니다. 어찌되었던, 콜럼버스는 때때로 잔인한 사람이 되기도 했으니까요. 어쨌든, 콜럼버스와 그의 형제들은 스페인 국왕에게 호소를 했고, 그는 이들을 풀어 주었습니다.

그 후 콜럼버스는 네 번째 여행을 계획하기 시작했습니다. 4척의 선박에 대한 충분한 자금을 마련했습니다. 이들은 1503년 5월 12일에 출항을 했습니다. 이번에는, 콜럼버스에게 행운과 악운이 동시에 있었습니다. 그는 중앙 아메리카의 해안을 따라 몇 차례의 발견을 이루어 냈습니다. 하지만, 또한 자메이카에서는 난파를 당했습니다. 그와 그의 선원들은 1년 동안 그곳에서 발이 묶여 있었습니다. 이들은 구조되어 1504년 11월에 스페인으로 돌아왔습니다. 콜럼버스는 1506년에 사망을 했기 때문에, 아메리카 대륙으로의 항해는 더 이상 할 수 없었습니다.

Unit 10

p.108

Sample Making Inferences Question

Translation

W Student: 안녕하세요. 저를 도와 주실 수 있었으면 좋겠어요. 제게 일종의 문제가 있거든요.

M Registrar's Office Employee: 최선을 다해 드릴게요. 어떤 성격의 문제인가요?

W: 학점을 이전해야 해서요. 아시다시피, 음, 저는 이번 여름에 다른 대학에서 두어 과목의 수업을 들었어요. 이곳으로 학점을 이전해야만 그것들이 제 성적표 상에 나타나거든요. 하지만 어떻게 해야 할지 잘 모르겠어요.

M: 좋아요. 정말로 간단한 일이죠. 먼저, 어떤 학교에 다니셨나요?

W: City 대학에 다녔어요. 제 지도 교수님께서 City 대학에서 받은 학점을 이곳 학교에서 인정해 준다고 말씀하셨죠.

M: 맞아요. 어… 적어도 대부분의 경우에 그렇죠. 좋아요, 학교 선택은 잘 하신 것 같군요. 자, 제게 교과 개요를 주셔야 해요.

W: 어, 물론 그렇게요. 제가 선생님께 교과에 관한 것 등을 말씀드리면 되나요?

M: 아니에요, 그렇게 하지는 마세요. 제 말은 학생이 City 대학의 대학 요람에서 강의 개요 부분을 복사해야 한다는 뜻이었어요. 대학 요람은 가지고 있죠, 그렇지 않나요?

W: 어, 아니에요. 가지고 있지 않아요. 어떻게 해야 하죠?

M: 인터넷을 보세요. 저쪽에 있는 컴퓨터를 사용하시고요. 강의 개요를 얻으실 수 있을 거에요. 개요를 출력하셔서 다시 이쪽으로 오세요. 나머지는 제가 처리해 드릴게요.

Mini Test 1 : Conversation

Answers

1. Ⓐ (Making Inferences Question)

2. Ⓓ (Detail Question)

3. Ⓑ (Understanding Attitude Question)

4. Ⓑ (Understanding Function Question)

Script 🎧 1-29

W1 Professor: So that's how you should write your final report. Do you understand everything clearly now, Claire?

W2 Student: Yes, ma'am, I do. Thank you so much for the explanation. Oh, uh, the due date is next week, right?

W1: That's correct. You need to submit your report before five in the evening next Thursday.

W2: That won't be a problem. Now that I know what to do, I can write six pages quickly.

W1: That's good to hear. I'm looking forward to reading it.

W2: I'll do my best . . . Uh, before I leave, I have one more thing to talk about. That is, uh, if you don't mind.

W1: I don't mind at all, Claire. What else do you want to ask me?

W2: [4]It's about the final exam. I know we won't take the exam until two weeks from now. But, uh, to be honest, I'm not pleased with my grade. I want to make sure I do well on the test. That way, uh, I'll hopefully get a better grade.

W1: That's the right attitude. So, um, what about the test do you want to know?

W2: Basically, is it going to be the same type of test as the midterm?

W1: Not exactly. There were lots of short answer questions on the midterm. There were also some multiple choice questions. But the bulk of the final exam will be essay questions. You see, uh, I want you to think about everything we've studied this semester. So the essay questions will ask about broad topics. You'll be expected to write on several subjects.

W2: Oh, I see. It's a good thing I asked. I wasn't planning on studying any material we learned before the midterm.

W1: You'd better study that information. For the final, I expect you to know everything we've covered since the first day of class.

Translation

W1 Professor: 그래서 학생은 기말 보고서를 그러한 방식으로 써야 해요. 이제 모든

것이 확실하게 이해가 되었나요, Claire?

W2 Student: 네, 교수님, 이해가 되었어요. 설명해 주셔서 정말 고맙습니다. 오, 어, 마감일이 다음 주죠, 그렇죠?

W1: 맞아요. 다음 주 목요일 오후 5시 전까지 보고서를 제출해야 하죠.

W2: 문제가 없을 거에요. 어떻게 해야 할지를 알았으니까, 6페이지는 빨리 쓸 수 있어요.

W1: 그런 말을 들으니 기분이 좋군요. 읽게 되기를 고대하고 있을게요.

W2: 최선을 다 할게요… 어, 자리에서 일어나기 전에, 이야기해야 할 것이 하나 더 있어요. 그게, 어, 교수님께서 괜찮으시다면요.

W1: 물론 괜찮아요, Claire. 그 밖의 어떤 것을 묻고자 하나요?

W2: 기말 시험에 관해서요. 지금부터 2주 내로는 시험을 보지 않을 것이라는 점은 알고 있어요. 하지만, 어, 솔직히 말씀드리면, 저는 제 성적에 만족하고 있지 않아요. 이번 시험에서 확실히 좋은 성적을 얻기를 원해요. 그렇게 되면, 어, 아마도 더 좋은 성적을 얻을 수 있을 거에요.

W1: 좋은 태도로군요. 그러면, 음, 시험의 어떤 부분에 대해 알고자 하나요?

W2: 기본적으로, 중간 고사와 동일한 유형의 시험이 되는 건가요?

W1: 꼭 그렇지는 않아요. 중간 고사 때는 짧게 답하는 문제들이 많았죠. 또한 복수의 답을 고르는 문제들도 있었고요. 하지만 대부분의 기말 고사에는 에세이를 쓰는 문제가 나와요. 아시다시피, 어, 저는 이번 학기에 우리가 공부한 모든 것에 대해 학생이 생각해 보았으면 해요. 그래서 에세이 문제는 광범위한 주제를 묻는 것이 될 거에요. 몇 가지 사안에 대한 글을 쓰게 될 것이죠.

W2: 오, 그렇군요. 여쭤 보기를 잘 했네요. 중간 고사 전에 배운 수업 내용은 공부할 계획을 하지 않았거든요.

W1: 그러한 내용을 공부해 두는 것이 좋을 거에요. 기말 고사에서, 저는 수업 첫 날부터 우리가 다루어 본 모든 내용을 학생이 알고 있었으면 해요.

Mini Test 2 : Lecture

Answers

1. Ⓓ (Making Inferences Question)

2. ①, ④ (Detail Question)

3. Ⓑ (Understanding Organization Question)

4. Ⓐ (Understanding Function Question)

Script 🎧 1-30

W Professor: Okay, has everyone handed in their homework . . . ? Great. Settle down, please, everyone. We have a lot of material to cover in today's class . . . Earth's atmosphere is seventy-eight percent nitrogen, roughly twenty-one percent oxygen, and tiny percentages of carbon dioxide and other gases. Interestingly, these numbers have not always been the same. In fact, the composition of the atmosphere changed several times in Earth's early years.

At first, the atmosphere was mostly comprised of methane and hydrogen along with some carbon. But solar winds stripped the planet of its first atmosphere. Later, as the planet cooled, there was a great deal of volcanic activity. This vented many of the gases that were inside the Earth. These gases were primarily carbon dioxide, sodium dioxide, and hydrogen sulfide. Oh, and in addition to those gases, there was a great deal of water vapor. So there was oxygen in the atmosphere, but it wasn't free standing. It was bound to other elements in the guise of various gases.

Then, around 3.7 billion years ago, the level of free oxygen began to increase. This was caused by algae in the oceans. Around that time, a type of blue-green algae, called, uh, cyanobacteria, became more common in the oceans. The algae utilized photosynthesis to make energy. So they took carbon dioxide and used the sun's heat to make energy. One byproduct of photosynthesis is that free oxygen atoms . . . uh, you know, those not bound to other elements . . . were created. Slowly, the oxygen level in the atmosphere started rising. Much of this oxygen was absorbed by rocks in the planet. But the rocks reached their saturation point about 2.4 billion years ago. Then, the atmosphere we have today gradually formed. Please note, though, that the oxygen level has varied over time. Sometimes it has been higher. Other times, um, it has been lower. But free oxygen has always been present. And its presence enabled oxygen-breathing life forms to evolve. Do you have a question for me? You in the back row . . . ?

M Student: Yes, ma'am. I'm curious . . . How do we know all of this? I mean, uh, you're talking about events that happened billions of years in the past.

W: That's a good question. Let me answer it for you. We mostly know this because of the Earth's rocks. We can date rocks back billions of years. Certain sedimentary rocks contain layers of red rocks. These red rocks are iron oxide. We call rocks with these layers, um, banded iron formations. If you don't know, iron oxide is a compound formed by iron and oxygen atoms. So the presence of iron oxide indicates high levels of free oxygen in the atmosphere. The oxygen levels were so high that the element combined with the iron to form iron oxide. I hope that answers your question.

Translation

W Professor: 좋아요, 모두들 과제를 제출하셨나요…? 좋아요. 모두 앉아 주시고요. 오늘 수업에서 다루어야 할 내용들이 많습니다… 지구의 대기는 78%가 질소이며, 약 21%가 산소이고, 그리고 약간의 퍼센트가 이산화탄소와 기타 기체로 되어 있습니다. 흥미롭게도, 이러한 수치가 항상 동일한 것은 아니었습니다. 실제로, 대기의 성분은 초기 지구에서 수 차례의 변화를 겪었습니다.

처음에는, 대기가 약간의 탄소와 함께 메탄과 수소로 주로 구성되어 있었습니다. 하지만 태양풍이 지구로부터 최초의 대기를 벗겨 내었습니다. 이후, 지구가 식어 감에 따라, 막대한 화산 활동이 일어났습니다. 이로써 지구 내부에 있던 많은 기체들이 밖으로 빠져 나왔습니다. 이러한 기체들은 주로 이산화탄소, 이산화나트륨, 그리고 황화수소였습니다. 오, 그리고 그러한 기체와 함께, 막대한 양의 수증기도 존재했습니다. 따라서 대기에는 산소가 있었지만, 독립적으로 존재하지는 못했습니다. 다양한 형태의 기체들 내부에 있는 다른 원소들과 결합이 되어 있었죠.

이후, 약 37억년 전에, 유리산소의 수치가 증가하기 시작했습니다. 바다의 해조류가 그 원인이 되었습니다. 당시, 일종의 남조 식물들, 소위, 어, 시아노박테리아가 바다에서 흔해졌습니다. 이 해조류들은 광합성을 이용하여 에너지를 생성했습니다. 따라서 이산화탄소를 흡수했고 태양열을 이용하여 에너지를 만들었습니다. 광합성의 부산물 중 하나는 유리산소의 원자가… 어, 아시다시피, 다른 원소와 결합되지 않은 것들인데… 생성되었다는 점이었습니다. 서서히, 대기 내 산소의 수치는 증가하기 시작했습니다. 이러한 산소의 상당 부분은 지구의 암석에 의해 흡수되었습니다. 하지만 암석들은 약 24억년 전에 포화점에 이르게 되었습니다. 이후, 오늘날 존재하는 대기가 점차적으로 형성되었습니다. 하지만, 산소 수치는 시간에 따라 다양했다는 점에 주목해 주세요. 때때로 보다 높았던 적도 있었습니다. 다른 경우, 음, 보다 낮은 적도 있었고요. 하지만 유리산소는 항상 존재했습니다. 그리고 그것의 존재로 인해 산소로 호흡하는 생명체들이 진화할 수 있었죠. 질문이 있나요? 뒷줄에 있는 학생…?

M Student: 네, 교수님. 궁금한데요… 어떻게 그런 모든 것에 대해 어떻게 알죠? 제 말은, 어, 교수님께서 과거 수십 억년 전에 일어났던 사건들에 대해 말씀하고 계시잖아요.

W: 좋은 질문이군요. 대답을 해 드리죠. 보통은 지구의 암석 때문에 그러한 점을 알고 있습니다. 수십 억년 전까지 암석의 연대를 측정할 수가 있죠. 특정 퇴적암에는 붉은 암석의 층이 포함되어 있습니다. 이러한 붉은 암석은 산화철입니다. 우리는 이러한 층이 있는 암석을, 음, 호상철광층이라고 부릅니다. 모르시는 경우를 위해 말씀을 드리면, 산화철은 철과 산소 원자에 의해 결합된 화합물입니다. 따라서 산화철이 존재한다는 것은 대기 중에 유리산소가 높은 수치로 있다는 점을 나타내 줍니다. 산소 수치가 매우 높았기

때문에 그러한 원소가 철과 결합하여 산화철이 형성된 것이죠. 학생의 질문에 대답이 되었기를 바랍니다.

Chapter 3

Speaking

Unit 01 p.114

Task 1 The Best Trip You Have Ever Taken

📁 Brainstorming

Idea Web

The Best Trip I Have Ever Taken: Rome, Italy

Reason 1: *enjoy history*

Detail: *many museums and historical sites; visited them; took pictures; saw impressive artifacts*

Reason 2: *studied the Italian language*

Detail: *tried speaking Italian; fun communicating in foreign language*

📁 Organizing

The Best Trip I Have Ever Taken: Rome, Italy

First Reason: *enjoy history*

Details: *many museums and historical sites; visited them and took pictures*

Second Reason: *studied Italian in school*

Details: *tried speaking Italian in Rome; was fun trying to communicate in foreign language*

📁 Speaking

Guided & Sample Response 🎧 2-01

The best trip I <u>have ever taken</u> was my trip to Rome, Italy, last year. My family and I went there for a week. <u>To begin with,</u> I enjoy history. There are many museums <u>and historical sites</u> in Rome. My family and I spent several days visiting them. We took lots of pictures and saw <u>many impressive artifacts</u>. In addition, I studied a little Italian when I was in school. So I tried to speak Italian while I was in Rome. It was so much fun trying to communicate with people <u>in a foreign language</u>.

Translation

내가 해본 최고의 여행은 작년 이탈리아의 로마에 갔던 여행이었다. 내 가족과 나는 일주일을 머물기 위해 그곳에 갔다. 우선, 나는 역사를 좋아한다. 로마에는 박물관과 역사적인 장소들이 많다. 내 가족과 나는 그러한 곳들을 방문하느라 며칠을 보냈다. 우리는 많은 사진을 찍고 많은 인상적인 유물들을 보았다. 또한, 나는 학교에 다닐 때 이탈리아어를 약간 배웠다. 그래서 로마에 있을 때 이탈리아어로 대화를 시도해 보았다. 외국어로 사람들과 의사소통을 하는 것은 매우 재미있는 일이었다.

Task 2　No Extracurricular Activities for University Freshmen

📁 Brainstorming

Idea Web

Should Not Do Any Extracurricular Activities // Should Be Able to Do Extracurricular Activities

Reason 1: get used to university life // not all freshmen are the same

Detail: living away from home for first time; shouldn't do too much // some can handle extra work; got all A's and wrote for student paper

Reason 2: university is harder than high school // should treat all students the same

Detail: no time to study if do other things; school is more important than clubs // no special rules for freshmen; let freshmen decide for themselves

📁 Organizing

My Choice: Should Not Do Any Extracurricular Activities // Should Be Able to Do Extracurricular Activities

First Reason: get used to university life // not all freshmen are the same

Details: living away from home for first time; shouldn't do too much // some can handle school and extracurricular activities; got all A's and wrote for student paper

Second Reason: university is harder than high school // should treat all students the same

Details: no time to study if do extracurricular activities; school more important than clubs // no special rules for freshmen; not fair; let freshmen decide for themselves

📁 Speaking

Guided & Sample Response 1: Should Not Do Any Extracurricular Activities　🎧 2-02

I agree that university freshmen shouldn't do any extracurricular activities. The first reason I support the statement is that freshmen need to get used to university life. Many of them are living away from home for the first time. So they shouldn't try to do too much until they're used to school life. Another reason is that university is harder academically than high school. Freshmen who do extracurricular activities might not have enough time to study. And their schoolwork is definitely more important than club memberships. So they shouldn't do any activities other than studying.

Translation

나는 대학 신입생들이 어떠한 과외 활동도 해서는 안 된다는 점에 동의한다. 내가 그러한 진술을 지지하는 첫 번째 이유는 신입생들이 대학 생활에 적응해야 하기 때문이다. 신입생 중 다수는 처음으로 집에서 멀리 떨어져 있게 된다. 따라서 학교 생활에 적응하기 전까지, 너무 많은 활동을 해서는 안 된다. 또 다른 이유는 고등학교보다 대학이 학업 면에서 더 힘들기 때문이다. 과외 활동을 하는 신입생들은 공부할 시간이 충분하지 않을 수도 있다. 그리고 학업은 분명 동아리 회원 일보다 더 중요하다. 따라서 공부 이외의 다른 활동을 해서는 안 된다.

Guided & Sample Response 2: Should Be Able to Do Extracurricular Activities　🎧 2-03

I disagree with the statement. I support allowing freshmen to do extracurricular activities. Firstly, not all freshmen are the same. Some can handle extracurricular activities while keeping their grades up. As a freshman, I got all A's and wrote for the student newspaper. It was no problem for me.

Next, universities should treat all of their students the same. Freshmen shouldn't have to live by special rules that seniors don't have to follow. In my opinion, that's not fair. So schools should let freshmen decide for themselves whether or not they want to do any extracurricular activities.

Translation

나는 그러한 진술에 동의하지 않는다. 나는 신입생에게 과외 활동을 허가하는 것을 지지한다. 먼저, 모든 신입생들이 똑같은 것은 아니다. 일부는 성적을 유지하면서 과외 활동을 감당해 낼 수가 있다. 신입생일 때, 나는 전과목에서 A를 받았고 학생 신문에 글을 썼다. 나에게는 전혀 문제가 되지 않았다. 다음으로, 대학은 모든 학생들을 똑같이 대우해야 한다. 4학년생들이 따라야 할 필요가 없는 특별한 규칙을 신입생이라고 준수해야 할 필요는 없다. 내 생각으로, 그것은 공정하지 않다. 따라서 학교는 과외 활동을 하고자 하는지 혹은 그렇지 않은지에 대해 신입생 스스로가 결정을 내리도록 해야 한다.

Task 3　All Ads to Be Removed from Academic Buildings

📁 Reading

Translation

대학 건물에 더 이상 광고를 붙여서는 안 됩니다

　이번 학기에, 사람들이 학과 건물 벽에 너무나 많은 광고를 붙이고 있습니다. 이러한 광고들은 건물의 외관을 해칩니다. 따라서, 대학 건물에 광고를 부착하는 것은 더 이상 허용되지 않습니다. 관리처 직원들은 대학 건물에서 찾아낼 수 있는 모든 광고들을 제거하도록 지시를 받았습니다. 모든 기숙사, 학생 회관, 그리고 캠퍼스 내의 기타 승인된 장소에서는 광고물을 부착할 수 있습니다. 더 많은 정보를 얻기 위해서는 관리처로 연락해 주십시오.

📁 Listening

> _Notes_
>
> The woman (agrees / **disagrees**) with the announcement.
>
> **Reason:** aren't too many ads; ban isn't needed; reads the ads a lot; news about events on campus; found job from ad
>
> **Key Words and Details:** aren't that many ads in most of the buildings; administration is overreacting; no need for the ban; always read them; learned about a lot of various events on campus; found my part-time job from one of those ads

Script　🎧 2-04

W Student: I'm not very happy about the new ban on advertisements.

M Student: Are you talking about the school's decision to ban ads in academic buildings?

W: That's right. I think the school is making a bad decision.

M: I disagree with you. All of those ads make the buildings look ugly.

W: I don't think so. There actually aren't that many ads in most of the buildings. I think that someone in the administration is overreacting. There's no need for the ban. At least, um, that's what I believe.

M: Okay, but tell me something . . .　Have you ever read any of those ads?

W: Sure, I have. Haven't you?

M: No, I've never done that before. I can't say that I have ever read a single ad on campus. I just don't see the point.

W: You might not have done that. But I always read them. I have learned about a lot of various events on campus from them. And I found my part-time job from one of those ads as well.

M: Hmm . . . Maybe I should try reading them sometimes.

Translation

W Student: 광고에 대한 새로운 금지 조치는 그다지 만족스럽지가 않아.

M Student: 대학 건물에 광고를 금지시키는 학교 측의 결정에 대해 말하는 거니?

W: 맞아. 학교 측이 좋지 못한 결정을 내리고 있다고 생각해.

M: 네 말에 동의하지 않아. 그러한 모든 광고들이 건물들을 지저분하게 보이도록 만들고 있잖아.

W: 나는 그렇게 생각하지 않아. 대부분의 건물에 실제로 그렇게 많은 광고들이 있는 것은 아니야. 나는 행정 당국의 누군가가 과잉 반응을 보이고 있다고 생각해. 금지 조치를 내릴 필요는 없어. 적어도, 음, 내가 생각하기로는.

M: 그래, 하지만 말해 봐… 그러한 광고를 읽어 본 적이 있어?

W: 물론, 있지. 너는 읽어 본 적이 없어?

M: 어, 한 번도 읽어본 적이 없어. 교내에서 한 번이라도 광고를 읽어본 적이 있다고 말할 수는 없을 것 같아. 요점을 알지 못하겠는걸.

W: 본 적이 없을 수도 있겠지. 하지만 나는 항상 읽어 봐. 캠퍼스에서 일어나는 여러 다양한 행사들에 대해 그로부터 알 수가 있어. 그리고 내 아르바이트도 또한 그러한 광고 중 하나에서 찾아냈어.

M: 흠… 나도 가끔은 읽어 봐야겠군.

Speaking

Guided & Sample Response 🎧 2-05

The speakers are having a conversation about the decision to <u>remove all advertisements</u> from academic buildings on campus. The school administration believes that the ads are making the buildings look bad. The woman disagrees with the school administration. She gives two reasons for this belief. First, she says that there are <u>not too many ads</u> on the buildings. She feels that the ban <u>is an overreaction</u> by the school. Second, the woman claims that <u>the ads are useful</u>. She has found out about <u>events on campus</u> from the ads. And she <u>got her job</u> by reading an ad as well.

Translation

화자들은 교내 대학 건물에서 모든 광고를 제거하겠다는 결정에 관해 대화를 나누고 있다. 학교 행정 당국은 광고들이 건물을 지저분하게 보이도록 만든다고 생각한다. 여자는 학교 행정 당국의 주장에 동의하지 않는다. 이러한 생각에 대해 그녀는 두 가지 이유를 제시한다. 첫째, 그녀는 건물에 그렇게 많은 광고가 있는 것은 아니라고 말한다. 그녀는 금지 조치가 학교 당국의 과잉 반응이라고 생각한다. 둘째, 여자는 광고가 유용하다고 주장한다. 그녀는 광고로부터 교내의 행사들에 대해 알 수 있었다. 그리고 광고를 읽음으로써 일자리도 얻었다.

Task 4 Marketing: Customer Lock-In

Reading

Translation

고객 고착

　기업들은 다른 사업체들과 자신의 고객을 공유하고 싶어하지 않는다. 고객을 공유하지 않을 수 있는 한 가지 방법은 고객 고착을 이용하는 것이다. 이는 고객들로 하여금 한 기업의 기술 혹은 제품을 다른 기업의 제품에서는 사용할 수 없도록 만드는 것이다. 이렇게 함으로써, 고객들은 하나의 기업 제품만을 쓸 수 있게 된다. 이는 정규 제조업자의 판매량 및 이윤 모두를 증가시키는데 도움이 된다. 그리고 경쟁 업체의 판매량 및 이윤을 감소시키는데도 도움이 된다.

Listening

Script 🎧 2-06

W Professor: Manufacturers are very competitive. They often do their best to prevent other companies from gaining access to their customers. They can do this by using customer lock-in. Let me tell you about it by relating two of my personal experiences.

　Photography is one of my hobbies. I love taking pictures. A couple of months ago, I broke a camera lens. I liked the original lens for my camera. But I decided to buy a lens made by a different company. So I bought the lens, but I couldn't attach it to the camera. You see, uh, the camera company had designed the camera so that only lenses it made could be attached to it. I had to return the other lens and buy one from the company that had made my camera.

　Here's something else that happened to me. There's a new laptop battery that just got released on the market. It lasts for a really long time. Uh, it lasts much longer than other batteries. Unfortunately, I can't use it on my current laptop. Why not? Well, the computer maker designed my laptop only to take the batteries that it makes. Once again, because of customer lock-in, my purchasing choices are restricted.

Translation

W Professor: 제조업체들은 매우 경쟁적입니다. 종종 최선을 다해 다른 기업들이 자신의 고객에 접근하는 것을 막으려고 하죠. 고객 고착을 이용하여 그렇게 할 수가 있습니다. 저의 개인적인 두 차례의 경험을 언급함으로써 그에 대해 말씀드리도록 하겠습니다.

　사진은 제 취미 중 하나입니다. 사진을 찍는 것을 매우 좋아하죠. 두 달 전, 카메라 렌즈가 고장이 났습니다. 저는 제 카메라의 원래 렌즈를 좋아했습니다. 하지만 다른 기업에서 만든 렌즈를 구입하기로 결정을 했습니다. 그래서 그러한 렌즈를 구입했지만, 그것을 카메라에 부착시킬 수가 없었습니다. 아시겠지만, 어, 카메라 회사는 자신이 만든 렌즈만이 카메라에 부착되도록 카메라를 설계했던 것입니다. 저는 렌즈를 반품시켰고 제 카메라를 만들었던 기업의 렌즈를 구입했습니다.

　제게 있었던 또 다른 일을 알려 드리죠. 얼마 전에 시장에 출시된, 신제품인 노트북용 배터리가 있습니다. 정말로 오랫동안 지속이 됩니다. 어, 다른 배터리보다 훨씬 더 오래 갑니다. 안타깝게도, 저는 그것을 현재의 제 노트북에 사용할 수가 없습니다. 왜 없을까요? 음, 컴퓨터 제조업체가 자신들이 만든 배터리만을 사용할 수 있도록 노트북을 설계했기 때문입니다. 또 다시, 고객 고착 때문에, 저의 구매 선택은 제한을 받고 있습니다.

Speaking

Guided & Sample Response 🎧 2-07

The professor relates two of <u>her personal experiences</u> while shopping. First, she mentions that she broke <u>a camera lens</u>. She purchased a new one, but it wouldn't fit on her camera. The reason was that her camera could only use lenses that were made by the company <u>that made her camera</u>. The same thing happened to her with <u>a laptop battery</u>. She couldn't use a different company's battery on her laptop. The reason for both of these incidents was <u>customer lock-in</u>. This happens when companies make sure that the products of other companies <u>cannot be used</u> on their own products.

Translation

교수는 쇼핑을 하면서 개인적으로 겪었던 두 차례의 경험에 대해 이야기하고 있다. 먼저, 그녀는 자신의 카메라 렌즈가 고장이 났다고 언급한다. 새로운 렌즈를 구입했지만, 그것은 그녀의 카메라에 맞지 않았다. 그 이유는 그녀의 카메라에 그 카메라를 만든 기업이 생산한 렌즈만을 사용할 수 있었기 때문이었다. 똑같은 일이 노트북 배터리에 있어서도 일어났다. 그녀는 자신의 노트북에 다른 기업의 배터리를 사용할 수가 없었다. 이러한 두 번의 일 모두가 일어난 이유는 고객 고착 때문이었다. 이는 기업들이 다른 기업의 제품을 자신의 제품에 사용할 수 없도록 만들고자 할 때 발생한다.

Task 5 · Taking a History Class

Listening

> *Notes*
>
> **The Problem**: the man could not register for a class, so he needs to take it later
>
> **Solution 1**: take the class during summer school
>
> **Solution 2**: take the same class but with a different professor

Script · 2-08

W Student: Dave, did you manage to sign up for that ancient history class? Uh, you know, the one with Professor Gilder?

M Student: No, I didn't. It was full by the time I tried to register. I am so upset about that. I was looking forward to taking his class.

W: I'm sorry to hear that. What are you going to do? You've been talking about taking his class for weeks.

M: Well, Professor Gilder is going to teach the same class this summer. It's an intensive class in summer school. I suppose I could sign up for that.

W: Cool. Go for it.

M: But there's a problem. Summer school costs $1,000, and I don't have that kind of money. It's already difficult for me to pay my tuition. Paying even more money would be hard for me to do.

W: Then why don't you take the ancient history class with Professor Reed? He's teaching the same class, isn't it?

M: He is. But . . .

W: But what?

M: Even though I love the material, I don't like Professor Reed. He's such a boring lecturer. If I take his class, I might be bored all semester long.

Translation

W Student: Dave, 고대사 수업에 대한 수강 신청을 했니? 어, 알겠지만, Gilder 교수님 수업을?

M Student: 아니, 못했어. 내가 등록하려고 했을 무렵에는 인원이 다 차있더군. 그에 대해 매우 기분이 좋지 않아. 그분의 수업을 듣게 되기를 고대하고 있었는데.

W: 그런 말을 들으니 유감이구나. 이제 어떻게 할 거니? 몇 주 동안 그 분의 수업을 듣는 것에 대해 이야기했잖아.

M: 음, Gilder 교수님께서 이번 여름에 같은 수업을 맡게 되실 거야. 여름 계절 학기의

집중적인 코스지. 그 수업에 등록할 수 있을 것이라고 생각해.

W: 잘 되었구나. 신청해 봐.

M: 하지만 문제가 하나 있어. 여름 계절 학기 수업은 1,000달러의 비용이 드는데, 나는 그 정도의 돈을 가지고 있지 않아. 학비를 대느라 이미 충분히 힘들거든. 돈을 더 지불하게 되면 어려워질 거야.

W: 그러면, Reed 교수님의 고대사 수업을 수강하는 것은 어때? 그분도 같은 수업을 담당하실 거야. 그렇지 않니?

M: 그럴 거야. 하지만…

W: 하지만 뭐?

M: 내가 그러한 수업 내용을 좋아할 지라도, 나는 Reed 교수님을 좋아하지 않아. 그분께서는 강의를 매우 지루하게 하셔. 그분의 수업을 듣는다면, 나는 학기 내내 지루해질 거야.

Speaking

Guided & Sample Response 1: First Solution  2-09

The man has a problem concerning a class <u>he wants to take</u>. He tried to <u>register for it</u>, but he couldn't. The students propose two solutions to the man's problem. First, he could take the course with the professor <u>during summer school</u>. Second, he could take the same course but with <u>a different professor</u>. I think that the first choice is the better one. One reason is that the man wants to take the course with Professor Gilder. So he can do that during summer school. The second reason is that <u>the man can work</u> during summer vacation. That way, he can make money. Then, he can afford <u>the summer school tuition</u>.

Translation

남자는 자신이 수강하고자 하는 수업에 관련된 문제를 가지고 있다. 그는 그 수업에 등록을 하려고 했지만, 그럴 수가 없었다. 남자의 문제에 대해 학생들은 두 가지 해결 방안을 제시하고 있다. 첫째, 그는 여름 계절 학기 기간에 그 교수의 수업을 수강할 수 있다. 둘째, 그는 동일한 과목을 수강할 수 있지만, 다른 교수의 수업을 들어야 한다. 나는 첫 번째 방안이 더 좋은 선택이라고 생각한다. 한 가지 이유는 남자가 Gilder 교수의 수업을 듣고 싶어한다는 점 때문이다. 따라서 그는 여름 계절 학기에서 그렇게 할 수 있다. 두 번째 이유는 남자가 여름 방학 동안 일을 할 수 있기 때문이다. 그렇게 함으로써, 그는 돈을 벌 수가 있다. 그러면, 여름 계절 학기에 대한 비용을 마련할 수 있을 것이다.

Guided & Sample Response 2: Second Solution  2-10

The man has a problem concerning a class <u>he wants to take</u>. He tried to <u>register for it</u>, but he couldn't. The students propose two solutions to the man's problem. First, he could take the course with the professor <u>during summer school</u>. Second, he could take the same course but with <u>a different professor</u>. I think that the second choice is the better one. To begin with, the material, not the professor, <u>is more important</u>. So the man can learn a lot by taking the class. Secondly, he can't afford to take summer school because tuition <u>is too expensive</u>. So he should take the class during the regular semester.

Translation

남자는 자신이 수강하고자 하는 수업에 관련된 문제를 가지고 있다. 그는 그 수업에 등록을 하려고 했지만, 그럴 수가 없었다. 남자의 문제에 대해 학생들은 두 가지 해결 방안을 제시하고 있다. 첫째, 그는 여름 계절 학기 기간에 그 교수의 수업을 수강할 수 있다. 둘째, 그는 동일한 과목을 수강할 수 있지만, 다른 교수의 수업을 들어야 한다. 나는 두 번째 방안이 더 좋은 선택이라고 생각한다. 우선, 교수가 아니라, 수업 내용이 더 중요하다. 따라서 남자는 그 수업을 수강함으로써 더 많이 배울 수 있다. 둘째, 학비가 너무 비싸기 때문에, 그에게는 여름 계절 학기 수업을 들을 여유가 없다. 따라서 그는 정규 학기 동안에 수업을 들어야 한다.

Task 6 Art History: Photography

📁 Listening

> **Notes**
>
> **Topic:** art history; how photography influenced artists in the past
>
> **Detail 1:** artists tried to imitate details of pictures
>
> photos show great detail; tried to imitate; Realist Movement started; Gustave Courbet
>
> **Detail 2:** artists began making abstract art
>
> couldn't compete on details with cameras; began making abstract art; is unrealistic
>
> **Key Words:** photographs capture a single moment in time; tried to imitate; Realist Movement was born; tried to paint their pictures to look just like snapshots; drove some artists away from realist art; try a different form of art; abstract art; images don't resemble physical things

Script 🎧 2-11

W Professor: Photography was invented in 1835. Early photographs were fairly crude. But the technology rapidly improved. And here's something interesting about cameras: They greatly influenced the world of art. Allow me to give you a couple of examples.

First of all, photographs capture a single moment in time. They also show a great amount of detail. Well, um, early artists noticed this. And they tried to imitate it. Thus the Realist Movement was born. In France, one of the leaders was Gustave Courbet. He usually painted pictures of everyday scenes from regular people's lives. Photography greatly influenced Courbet and other European Realists. They tried to paint their pictures to look just like snapshots. Take a look at this painting . . . and this photograph . . . Do you see how similar they are?

Interestingly, the camera also drove some artists away from realist art. You see, uh, many artists recognized that a picture taken with a camera was always going to look more realistic than a painting made by an artist. This caused some artists to try a different form of art. I'm talking about abstract art. For centuries, artists made realistic-looking paintings. But, in the early 1900s, some artists began making abstract art. Abstract art is not painted realistically. The images don't resemble actual physical things. Pablo Picasso and Georges Braque did work in Cubism. Other abstract artists soon followed. And many of them painted that way because of the camera.

Translation

W Professor: 사진은 1835년에 발명되었습니다. 초기의 사진은 꽤 조잡스러웠죠. 하지만 사진 기술은 빠르게 향상되었습니다. 그리고 카메라에 관해 흥미로운 점을 알려 드리겠습니다: 이들은 미술계에 많은 영향을 끼쳤습니다. 두 가지 예를 들어 드리죠.

먼저, 사진은 시간상 한 순간을 포착해 냅니다. 또한 막대한 양의 세부적인 것들을 보여 줍니다. 저기, 음, 초기 화가들은 이러한 점에 주목했습니다. 그리고 그를 모방하기 위해 노력했습니다. 따라서 사실주의가 태동했던 것입니다. 프랑스에서는, 주도적인 화가 중 한 명으로 귀스타브 쿠르베가 있었습니다. 그는 통상 일반적인 사람들의 삶에서 나온 일상적인 장면들을 그렸습니다. 사진은 쿠르베 및 기타 유럽의 사실주의 화가들에게 막대한 영향을 미쳤습니다. 그들은 자신의 그림을 스냅 사진과 똑같이 보이도록 그리려고 했습니다. 이 그림을 보시고… 그리고 이 사진을 봐 주세요… 이들이 얼마나 비슷한지 아시겠죠?

흥미롭게도, 카메라는 또한 몇몇 화가들이 사실주의 미술에서 멀어지도록 만들었습니다. 아시다시피, 어, 많은 화가들은 카메라로 찍은 사진이 화가가 그린 그림보다 항상 더 사실적으로 보일 것이라는 점을 깨달았습니다. 이로써 몇몇 화가들은 다른 형태의 미술을 시도하게 되었습니다. 추상 미술에 대해 말씀드리고 있는 것입니다. 수 세기 동안, 화가들은 실제처럼 보이는 그림을 그렸습니다. 하지만, 1900년대 초반, 일부 화가들은 추상 미술을 만들기 시작했습니다. 추상 미술은 사실적으로 그려지는 것이 아닙니다. 이미지들이 실제 물리적인 것들과 닮아 있지 않습니다. 파블로 피카소와 조르주 브라크는 입체파 작품을 만들었습니다. 곧 다른 추상 화가들이 그 뒤를 따랐습니다. 그리고 그중 다수는 카메라 때문에 그런 식으로 그림을 그린 것이었습니다.

📁 Speaking

Guided & Sample Response 🎧  2-12

In her lecture, the professor describes <u>the effects of photography</u> on artists. She goes into detail about two effects. The first is that photography helped create the Realist Movement. Many artists, such as Gustave Courbet, tried to make paintings that <u>looked like pictures</u>. They focused on <u>the extreme details</u> that pictures provided. However, other artists moved away <u>from realist art</u>. They saw how detailed pictures taken by cameras were. And they didn't want to <u>compete with cameras</u>. They knew that they couldn't make more realistic pictures. So they created <u>abstract art</u>. This is art that doesn't look like anything real. Pablo Picasso and many others were abstract artists.

Translation

강의에서, 교수는 사진이 화가들에게 미친 영향에 대해 설명한다. 그녀는 두 가지 영향에 대해 세부적으로 다루고 있다. 첫째는 사진이 사실주의가 탄생하는데 도움이 되었다는 점이다. 귀스타브 쿠르베와 같은 많은 화가들은 사진처럼 보이는 그림을 그리고자 했다. 이들은 사진이 제공해 주는 극단적인 세부 양식에 초점을 맞추었다. 하지만, 다른 화가들은 사실주의 미술에서 멀어져 갔다. 이들은 카메라에 의해 촬영된 사진들이 얼마나 세부적인지를 알게 되었다. 그리고 카메라와 경쟁하는 것을 원하지 않았다. 이들은 자신들이 보다 사실적인 그림을 그릴 수는 없다는 점을 알았다. 따라서 추상 미술을 만들었다. 이는 실제의 것처럼 보이지 않는 미술이다. 파블로 피카소 및 기타 많은 화가들이 추상주의 화가였다.

Unit 02

p.121

Task 1 The Advantages of the Internet

📁 Brainstorming

Idea Web

Advantages of the Internet: Communication and Education

Advantage 1: communication

Detail: send email; have telephone and video conversations

Advantage 2: education

Detail: get university degrees online; listen to online lectures

📁 Organizing

Advantages of the Internet: communication and education

First Advantage: communication

Details: talk to others around the world; send email; have telephone and video conversations

Second Advantage: education

Details: many opportunities; get university degrees online; listen to online lectures; getting popular; people becoming more education

📁 Speaking

Guided & Sample Response 🎧 2-13

The Internet has several advantages. But I think the two most important ones are <u>communication and education</u>. People all around the world <u>communicate with others</u> on the Internet. They send email messages to each other. And they have telephone and video conversations as well. People also benefit from the Internet because of <u>the educational opportunities</u> it provides. For instance, people can get university degrees online. There are also <u>numerous online lectures</u> that people can listen to. Many of these lectures are getting extremely popular. So the Internet is helping people around the world <u>become more educated</u>.

Translation

인터넷에는 몇 가지 장점이 있다. 하지만 나는 가장 중요한 두 개의 장점이 의사소통과 교육이라고 생각한다. 전 세계의 사람들은 인터넷으로 서로 의사소통을 할 수가 있다. 서로에게 이메일 메시지를 보낸다. 그리고 전화 및 영상 통화도 한다. 또한 인터넷이 제공하는 교육적 기회 때문에, 사람들은 인터넷으로부터 혜택을 받는다. 예를 들어, 온라인으로 대학 학위를 얻을 수 있다. 또한 수강할 수 있는 많은 온라인 강의들도 존재한다. 이러한 강의 중 많은 것들이 높은 인기를 얻고 있다. 따라서 인터넷은 전 세계 사람들이 보다 많은 교육을 받는데 도움을 주고 있다.

Task 2 Friendly Professors or Distant Professors

📁 Brainstorming

Idea Web

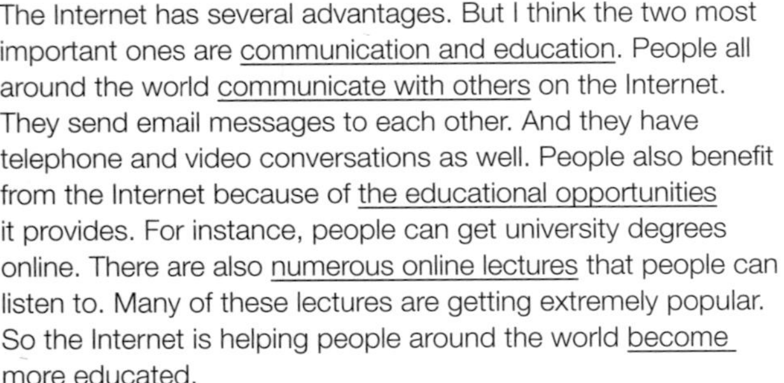

Friendly Professor // Distant Professor

Reason 1: *easy to talk to // students and profs. aren't equals*

Detail: *asked friendly economics prof. questions; didn't ask mean physics prof. questions // shouldn't be friends; student confused by friendly profs.*

Reason 2: *have better classes // only care about teaching*

Detail: *comfortable lectures; students eager to learn // not interested in being liked; distant teacher taught very well*

📁 Organizing

My Choice: *Friendly Professor // Distant Professor*

First Reason: *easy to talk to // students and profs. aren't equals*

Details: *asked friendly economics prof. question; didn't ask mean physics prof. questions // shouldn't be friends; students can be confused by friendly profs.*

Second Reason: *have better classes // only care about teaching*

Details: *lectures are comfortable; students eager to learn; learned the most from friendly profs.; learned the least from mean profs. // not interested in being liked; distant teacher taught very well*

📁 Speaking

Guided & Sample Response 1: Friendly Professor 🎧 2-14

It's definitely better for a professor to be friendly with his or her students. For one thing, <u>it's easy to talk</u> to a friendly professor. My economics professor was easy to talk to, so <u>I always asked</u> him questions. My physics professor was mean, so I never asked him any questions. For another thing, friendly professors have better classes. Their lectures and discussions are <u>always comfortable</u>. Most students <u>are eager to learn</u> from these teachers. I always <u>learned the most</u> in classes that had friendly teachers. I learned the least in classes that had mean teachers.

Translation

자신의 학생들에게 친절한 교수가 분명 더 낫다. 우선, 친절한 교수에게는 말을 거는 것이 쉽다. 내 경제학 교수님은 말을 건네기가 쉬워서, 나는 항상 그분에게 질문을 했다. 내 물리학 교수님은 성격이 좋지 못하셔서, 그분에게는 어떤 질문도 하지 않았다. 다음으로, 친절한 교수가 수업을 더 잘 한다. 그들의 강의와 토론은 항상 편안하다. 대부분의 학생들은 이러한 교수로부터 배우고 싶어한다. 나는 항상 친절한 교수들이 있는 수업에서 가장 많이 배웠다. 성격이 좋지 못한 교수가 있는 수업에서는 가장 적게 배웠다.

Guided & Sample Response 2: Distant Professor 🎧 2-15

Professors should always be distant from their students. That is <u>a better policy</u> than being too friendly with the students. One reason is that professors and students aren't equals, so they <u>shouldn't be friends</u>. Students <u>can get confused</u> about their relationships with professors who are too friendly. They won't have this problem with distant teachers. Next, distant teachers often <u>only care about</u> teaching the material. They aren't interested <u>in being liked</u> by the students. The best teacher I ever had was distant. She wasn't friendly, but she taught the course material really well.

Translation

교수는 항상 학생들로부터 거리를 두어야 한다. 이는 학생들에게 너무 친절하게 대하는 것보다 좋은 방책이다. 한 가지 이유는 교수들과 학생들이 동등하지 않기 때문이며, 따라서 그들은 친구가 될 수 없다. 학생들은 너무 친절한 교수와의 관계에서 혼란을 겪을 수 있다. 거리를 두는 교수와는 그러한 문제를 겪지 않게 될 것이다. 다음으로, 거리를 두는 교수는 종종 수업 내용을 가르치는 것에만 신경을 쓴다. 학생들이 자신을 좋아하는지에 대해서는 관심이 없다. 내가 만난 가장 뛰어난 교수는 학생들과 거리를 두었다. 친절하지는 않았지만, 수업 내용을 정말로 잘 가르쳐 주었다.

Task 3 Weekly Meetings in Dormitories

📁 Reading

Translation

기숙사에서 매주 모임을 갖습니다

이번 학기 교내 모든 기숙사에서는 매주 모임이 열리게 될 것입니다. 각 층의 학생들은 기숙사 조교와 함께 모임을 하게 될 것입니다. 모임은 기숙사 내의 라운지에서 열리게 될 것입니다. 이러한 모임은 어느 때라도 열릴 수 있지만, 일주일에 한 차례만 열리게 될 것입니다. 모임에서 학생들은 학업으로부터 휴식을 취할 수 있는 기회를 얻게 될 것입니다. 또한, 학생들은 같은 층에 있는 다른 학생들도 만나 볼 수 있을 것입니다.

📁 Listening

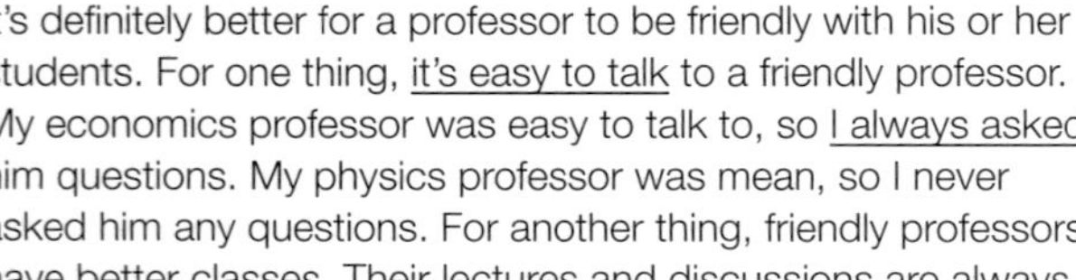

Notes

The man (agrees / disagrees) with the announcement.

Reason: *meetings on Sunday nights; likes to return to school on Monday morning; can't do that now; doesn't want to meet some neighbors; dislikes some students in dorm*

Key Words and Details: *like to visit my parents' on the weekend; usually come back to school on Monday morning; have to be at school for meetings; not fair; don't want to meet everyone in the dorm; don't like some of the other students; don't want to hang out with them*

Script 🎧 2-16

W Student: Are you going to the dorm meeting on Sunday at eight?

M Student: I don't have a choice, do I? Of course I'm going to go.

W: I get the feeling that you aren't happy about it.

M: You're right about that. To be honest, I'm quite upset about these meetings. For one thing, we have these meetings on Sunday night.

W: That's not too bad.

M: Maybe not for you. But I like to visit my parents' home on the weekend. I usually come back to school on Monday morning. But now I have to be at school on Sunday for these meetings. That's not fair.

W: Okay, but don't you want to meet your neighbors? That's one of the points of these meetings.

M: There are other ways to meet our neighbors. We don't need the school to help us out.

W: Uh-huh.

M: Besides, I don't want to meet everyone in the dorm. I don't like some of the other students. So I don't want to hang out with them. But the school is forcing us to do that. That's just not right.

Translation

W Student: 일요일 8시의 기숙사 모임에 갈 거니?

M Student: 선택권이 없잖아. 그렇지 않나? 물론 가게 되겠지.

W: 그러한 것에 대해서 기분이 별로인 것 같네.

M: 그 점에 대해서는 네 말이 맞아. 솔직히 말하면, 나는 이러한 모임에 대해 매우 기분이 나빠. 우선, 우리는 일요일 밤에 모임을 갖게 되어 있어.

W: 그렇게 나쁜 것은 아니잖아.

M: 너에게는 그럴 수도 있겠지. 하지만 나는 주말에 부모님 댁을 방문하는 것을 좋아해. 보통은 월요일 아침에 학교로 돌아오지. 하지만 이제는 모임을 위해서 일요일에는 학교에 있어야 해. 그건 공정하지 않아.

W: 그래, 하지만 이웃들을 만나 보고 싶지 않니? 그것이 이번 모임의 의도 중 하나야.

M: 이웃들을 만날 수 있는 다른 방법들도 있어. 학교 측의 도움은 필요 없어.

W: 그렇군.

M: 게다가, 기숙사 내의 모든 사람들을 만나 보고 싶지는 않아. 나는 몇몇 학생들을 좋아하지 않아. 그래서 그들과 함께 어울리고 싶지가 않고, 하지만 학교 측이 우리에게 그렇게 하도록 강요하고 있어. 그것은 옳은 일이 아니야.

📁 Speaking

Guided & Sample Response 

The man and the woman are chatting about the announcement by <u>the student housing office</u>. There will be <u>be weekly meetings</u> in the school's dormitories. The man opposes these meetings. The first reason he is against them is that the meetings are <u>on Sunday night</u>. He likes to go home on the weekend. Then, he returns to school on Monday. But he can't <u>do that anymore</u> because of the meetings. He also has no interest in meeting <u>some of the students</u> living in his dorm. He says that he doesn't like them, so he doesn't want to <u>socialize with them</u>.

Translation

남자와 여자는 학생 주거 사무실의 공지 사항에 대해 이야기를 나누고 있다. 학교의 기숙사에서 매주 모임이 열리게 될 것이다. 남자는 이러한 모임에 반대한다. 그가 반대하는 첫 번째 이유는 모임이 일요일 밤에 열리기 때문이다. 그는 주말에 집에 가는 것을 좋아한다. 그리고 월요일에 학교로 돌아온다. 하지만 모임 때문에 그는 더 이상 그렇게 할 수가 없다. 그는 또한 자신의 기숙사에서 살고 있는 몇몇 학생들을 만나 보는 것에 관심이 없다. 그들을 좋아하지 않기 때문에, 그는 그들과 어울리고 싶지 않다고 말한다.

Task 4 Zoology: Communal Nutrition

📁 Reading

Translation

집단 영양

많은 동물들이 자신만을 위해서 먹이를 찾아 다닌다. 하지만 무리 전체를 위해 먹이를 찾아 다니는 동물들도 있다. 집단 영양과 관계된 동물들은 종종 커다란 군락을 이루어 살아간다. 곤충들이 때때로 이러한 행동을 보인다. 이들은 자신이 먹지 않는 먹이를 찾으려고 할 수도 있다. 대신, 그러한 먹이는 무리의 다른 구성원들이 먹는다. 따라서 모든 동물들이 – 특히 스스로를 돌볼 수 없는 동물들이 – 먹이를 공급받게 된다. 협력을 함으로써, 그러한 무리는 보다 강해질 수 있다.

📁 Listening

Notes

Topic: communal nutrition

Detail 1: not all ants forage
queen, males, and soldiers don't forage; workers gather food; share with others

Detail 2: ants nutritional needs differ
adults and babies need different food; ants gather; food is divided

Key Words: not all ants forage for food; queen ant doesn't forage; nor do the males; worker ants have the task of gathering food; share this food; different ants need different types of nutrition; search for different types of food; take the food back; divided according to what each ant needs

Script 🎧 2-18

M Professor: When you watch ants forage, you'll notice that they take all kinds of food to their colonies. They bring back leaves, fruit, vegetables, and even the bodies of other animals. Individual ants don't always eat the food that they find. Instead, they, uh, they gather it to serve their entire community. This is known as communal nutrition.

Ants behave this way for a couple of reasons. The first is that not all ants forage for food. For instance, the queen ant doesn't forage. Nor do the males. Their duty instead is to reproduce. Likewise, certain ants, uh, the soldiers, defend the colony. Therefore worker ants have the task of gathering food. They then share this food with all of the other ants.

In addition, different ants need different types of nutrition. For example, adult ants need food that has a high sugar content. Baby ants require food with lots of protein in it. The ants that forage thus search for different types of foods. When they take the food back to the colony, it is divided according to what each ant needs. As a result, all of the ants are able to eat thanks to the actions of a few.

Translation

M Professor: 개미가 먹이를 찾아 돌아다니는 모습을 지켜보면, 그들이 온갖 종류의 먹이를 개미집으로 가지고 가는 것에 주목하게 됩니다. 나뭇잎, 과일, 채소, 그리고 심지어는 다른 동물의 사체도 가지고 가죠. 개개의 개미들이 자신이 발견한 먹이를 항상 먹는 것은 아닙니다. 대신, 그들은, 어, 그들은 집단 전체에 먹이를 공급하기 위해 먹이를 모읍니다.

두 가지 이유로 인해 개미들이 이러한 방식으로 행동을 합니다. 첫 번째는 모든 개미들이 먹이를 찾아 돌아다니는 것은 아니기 때문입니다. 예를 들어, 여왕 개미는 먹이를 찾으러 돌아다니지 않습니다. 수개미들도 마찬가지고요. 대신 이들의 임무는 번식을 하는 것입니다. 마찬가지로, 특정 개미들, 어, 병정 개미는 개미집을 방어합니다. 따라서 일개미들이 먹이를 모으는 일을 담당하게 됩니다. 이들은 이후 그러한 먹이를 다른 모든 개미들과 공유하게 됩니다.

또한, 서로 다른 개미들은 서로 다른 종류의 영양분을 필요로 합니다. 예를 들면, 다

자란 개미는 당분이 높은 먹이를 필요로 합니다. 새끼 개미들은 많은 단백질이 포함되어 있는 먹이를 필요로 하고요. 따라서 먹이를 찾아 돌아다니는 개미들은 다양한 종류의 먹이를 찾습니다. 먹이를 개미집으로 가지고 오면, 먹이는 각각의 개미들의 필요에 따라 나누어집니다. 그 결과, 소수의 행동 덕분에 모든 개미들이 먹이를 먹을 수 있게 됩니다.

📁 Speaking

Guided & Sample Response 🎧 2-19

The professor tells the students about <u>how ants forage</u>. He states that ants don't always eat the food they gather. The first reason is that <u>only a few ants</u> collect food. Many ants, such as the queen, males, and soldiers, don't. So other ants must gather food for them. In addition, <u>ants' nutritional needs</u> differ. <u>Baby ants</u> need protein while adults need sugar. So some ants collect food <u>they don't need</u>. This food goes to other ants. These actions relate to communal nutrition. In communal nutrition, animals forage <u>for an entire group</u>. This helps the members of the group live long lives.

Translation

교수는 학생들에게 개미들이 어떻게 먹이를 찾아 돌아다니는지에 대해 이야기한다. 그녀는 개미들이 항상 자신이 모은 먹이를 먹는 것은 아니라고 말한다. 첫 번째 이유는 소수의 개미들만이 먹이를 모으기 때문이다. 여왕 개미, 수캐미, 그리고 병정 개미와 같은 다른 개미들은 그렇게 하지 않는다. 따라서 다른 개미들이 이들을 위해 먹이를 모아야 한다. 또한, 개미의 영양학적인 필요성은 서로 다르다. 다 자란 개미들은 당분을 필요로 하는 반면, 새끼 개미들은 단백질을 필요로 한다. 따라서 일부 개미들은 자신이 필요로 하지 않는 먹이를 모은다. 이 먹이는 다른 개미들에게로 간다. 이러한 행동은 집단 영양과 관련이 있다. 집단 영양에서, 동물들은 무리 전체를 위해 먹이를 찾아 돌아다닌다. 이는 무리 구성원들이 보다 오래 사는데 도움이 된다.

Task 5　Taking Care of a Bird during Vacation

📁 Listening

> #### Notes
> **The Problem**: the woman is going on vacation and needs someone to take care of her bird
> **Solution 1**: ask her friend Janet to watch her bird
> **Solution 2**: take her bird to a pet hotel

Script 🎧 2-20

W Student: I can't wait for spring break to arrive. I'm going to visit Costa Rica for an entire week.

M Student: That sounds like fun. But, uh, what are you going to do about your bird? Is someone going to take care of it?

W: Hmm . . . I'm not sure yet. I was thinking of asking Janet to take care of Polly for me. She has done that for me in the past.

M: Yeah, I remember that. But Janet is pretty busy trying to finish her senior thesis. She might not have time to watch Polly during spring break.

W: Oh . . . I didn't know that about Janet.

M: Why don't you drop Polly off at a pet hotel? I believe that there's one near the school. My dog stayed there once, and the people there took great care of him. He loved it there.

W: I might do that. But there's just one problem with a pet hotel.

M: What's that?

W: Even though the service is great, the price is expensive. I don't know if I can afford to pay for an entire week.

M: Hmm . . . You're correct. It is rather costly.

Translation

W Student: 빨리 봄 방학이 왔으면 좋겠어. 나는 일주일 동안 코스타리카에 가 있을 거야.

M Student: 재미있을 것 같구나. 하지만, 어, 너의 새에 대해서는 어떻게 할 거니? 누군가가 돌봐 주기로 했어?

W: 흠… 아직 잘 모르겠어. Janet에게 Polly를 돌봐달라고 부탁할까 생각 중이었어. 이전에 그렇게 해준 적이 있거든.

M: 응, 나도 기억이 나. 하지만 Janet은 졸업 논문을 완성하기 위해 매우 바빠. 봄 방학 동안 Polly를 봐 줄 시간이 없을 수도 있어.

W: 오… Janet에 대해 그러한 점은 모르고 있었네.

M: Polly를 애완 동물용 호텔에 맡기는 것은 어때? 학교 근처에 한곳이 있다고 알고 있어. 내 개도 한번 그곳에 머물렀는데, 그곳 사람들이 개를 잘 돌보아 주었지. 걔가 그곳을 좋아하더군.

W: 그렇게 할 수도 있겠지. 하지만 애완 동물용 호텔에는 한 가지 문제가 있어.

M: 그것이 뭔데?

W: 서비스가 뛰어날 지라도, 가격이 비싸. 내가 일주일 동안의 비용을 감당할 수 있을지 잘 모르겠어.

M: 흠… 네 말이 맞아. 상당히 비싸지.

📁 Speaking

Guided & Sample Response 1: First Solution 🎧 2-21

The woman tells the man about her problem. She is <u>taking a trip</u> to Costa Rica, but she needs someone to watch <u>her pet bird</u>. They think of two solutions to her problem. The first is to ask her friend Janet to watch the bird for a week. The second is to take the bird <u>to a pet hotel</u>. I feel that the first option is better. Janet has taken care of the bird <u>in the past</u>. So she will know <u>what to do</u>. Also, even though Janet is busy, taking care of a bird is simple. All Janet has to do is feed the bird and <u>give it water</u> every day.

Translation

여자는 남자에게 자신의 문제에 대해 말하고 있다. 그녀는 코스타리카로 여행을 갈 것이지만, 자신의 애완용 새를 돌보아 줄 누군가를 필요로 한다. 그녀의 문제에 대해 그들은 두 가지 해결 방안을 생각해 보고 있다. 첫 번째는 그녀의 친구인 Janet에게 일주일 동안 새를 돌보아 달라고 부탁하는 것이다. 두 번째는 새를 애완 동물용 호텔에 데리고 가는 것이다. 나는 첫 번째 방안이 더 낫다고 생각한다. Janet은 과거에 새를 돌봐 준 적이 있다. 따라서 어떻게 해야 할지를 알고 있을 것이다. 또한, Janet이 바쁘더라도, 새를 돌보는 일은 간단하다. Janet이 해야 할 일은 매일 새에게 먹이와 물을 주는 것이 전부이다.

Guided & Sample Response 2: Second Solution 🎧 2-22

The woman tells the man about her problem. She is <u>taking a trip</u> to Costa Rica, but she needs someone to watch <u>her pet bird</u>. They think of two solutions to her problem. The first is to ask her friend Janet to watch the bird for a week. The second is to take the bird <u>to a pet hotel</u>. I feel that the second option is better. The people <u>at the pet hotel</u> will take good care of the bird. That will keep the woman <u>from worrying</u>. In addition, Janet is busy and can't watch the bird. So the woman shouldn't ask her <u>for a big favor</u>. That's not fair to Janet.

Translation

여자는 남자에게 자신의 문제에 대해 말하고 있다. 그녀는 코스타리카로 여행을 갈 것이지만, 자신의 애완용 새를 돌보아 줄 누군가를 필요로 한다. 그녀의 문제에 대해 그들은 두 가지 해결 방안을 생각해 보고 있다. 첫 번째는 그녀의 친구인 Janet에게 일주일 동안 새를 돌보아 달라고 부탁하는 것이다. 두 번째는 새를 애완 동물용 호텔에 데리고 가는 것이다. 나는 두 번째 방안이 더 낫다고 생각한다. 애완 동물용 호텔의 사람들은 새를 잘 돌보아 줄 것이다. 그럼으로써 여자는 걱정을 하지 않아도 될 것이다. 또한, Janet은 바빠서 새를 돌볼 수가 없다. 따라서 여자는 그녀에게 어려운 부탁을 해서는 안 된다. 그것은 Janet에게 공정한 일이 아니다.

Task 6 Environmental Studies: Carbon Dioxide Emissions

📁 Listening

Notes

Topic: *environmental studies; two ways to reduce carbon dioxide emissions*

Detail 1: *filters*

capture carbon dioxide; turn it into water and a gas; charcoal filters absorb it

Detail 2: *planting trees*

trees need carbon dioxide; use for photosynthesis; create oxygen; animals can breathe

Key Words: *capture carbon dioxide; create a chemical reaction; breaks down the carbon dioxide; charcoal; absorbs the carbon dioxide; planting many trees around factories; trees take carbon dioxide from the atmosphere; free oxygen; reduce carbon dioxide and provide us with oxygen to breathe*

Script 🎧 2-23

M Professor: Nowadays, many people are concerned about reducing various emissions into the atmosphere. This includes pollutants. It also includes carbon dioxide. Some people are convinced that carbon dioxide is contributing to the heating of the Earth's atmosphere. So scientists are devising ways to reduce the amount of carbon dioxide emissions. Here are two methods.

Lots of factories release carbon dioxide into the atmosphere. Carbon dioxide is frequently created as a byproduct of certain manufacturing processes. However, scientists have managed to make carbon dioxide filters. Some filters capture carbon dioxide. Then, they create a chemical reaction. This reaction breaks down the carbon dioxide. As a result, water and a harmless gas are created. Uh, thus carbon dioxide emissions are reduced. That's how some popular types of filters work. Additionally, other filters use charcoal. The charcoal absorbs the carbon dioxide. This keeps it from being, um, being released into the atmosphere. As you can likely tell, there are numerous ways to filter carbon dioxide.

Here's another interesting method. Lately, people have begun planting many trees around factories. As you know, trees need carbon dioxide to use photosynthesis. In using photosynthesis, trees take carbon dioxide from the atmosphere. Then, they create energy for themselves as well as free oxygen. All animals on the planet—including humans—need oxygen to survive. So trees can reduce carbon dioxide and provide us with oxygen to breathe. When they're near factories, they have easy access to carbon dioxide.

Translation

M Professor: 오늘날, 많은 사람들이 대기로 배출되는 다양한 배기 가스들을 줄이는데 관심을 가지고 있습니다. 여기에는 대기 오염 물질이 포함됩니다. 또한 이산화탄소도 포함되고요. 몇몇 사람들은 이산화탄소가 지구의 대기 온도 상승에 일정한 기여를 하고 있다고 확신합니다. 따라서 과학자들이 이산화탄소의 방출량을 줄이기 위한 방법들을 고안해 내고 있습니다. 두 가지 방법을 알려 드리겠습니다.

많은 공장들이 대기 중으로 이산화탄소를 배출합니다. 이산화탄소는 종종 특정 제조 과정 상의 부산물로서 생성됩니다. 하지만, 과학자들이 이산화탄소 여과 장치를 만들고 있습니다. 몇몇 여과 장치들은 이산화탄소를 가두어 놓습니다. 그런 다음, 화학 반응을 일으킵니다. 이러한 반응으로 이산화탄소가 분해됩니다. 그 결과, 물과 해롭지 않은 기체가 생성됩니다. 어, 따라서 이산화탄소 방출량이 줄어듭니다. 이것이 바로 몇몇 유명한 종류의 여과 장치들이 작동되는 방식입니다. 또한, 다른 여과 장치들은 숯을 이용합니다. 숯은 이산화탄소를 흡수합니다. 이로써 이산화탄소가, 음, 대기로 방출되는 것을 막을 수 있습니다. 아마 여러분들도 알고 계시겠지만, 이산화탄소를 여과시키는 수많은 방법들이 존재합니다.

또 다른 흥미로운 방법이 있습니다. 최근, 공장 주변에 많은 나무들을 심기 시작했습니다. 아시겠지만, 나무들이 광합성을 이용하기 위해서는 이산화탄소를 필요로 합니다. 광합성을 이용함에 있어서, 나무들은 대기로부터 이산화탄소를 흡수합니다. 그런 다음, 유리산소뿐만 아니라 자기 자신을 위한 에너지를 생성해 냅니다. 지구 상의 모든 동물들은 – 인간을 포함해서 – 살아가기 위해 산소를 필요로 합니다. 따라서 나무들은 이산화탄소를 줄여 주고 우리가 호흡할 수 있도록 산소를 제공해 줄 수 있습니다. 공장 주변에 있는 경우, 이들은 이산화탄소를 쉽게 얻을 수 있습니다.

📁 Speaking

Guided & Sample Response  2-24

The professor lectures about carbon dioxide emissions. He states that many people are <u>trying to reduce</u> carbon dioxide emissions in the atmosphere. He gives the students two ways people are trying to do this. The first is <u>by using filters</u>. Filters remove carbon dioxide from the atmosphere. Some <u>break it down</u> into water and another gas. And other filters <u>use charcoal</u> to capture carbon dioxide. In addition, <u>people plant trees</u> near factories that emit carbon dioxide. The trees take the carbon dioxide and use it for photosynthesis. This gives the trees energy and provides oxygen <u>for animals to breathe</u>. So both trees and animals gain in this way.

Translation

교수는 이산화탄소 방출에 대한 강의를 하고 있다. 그는 많은 사람들이 대기로 배출되는 이산화탄소의 양을 경감시키기 위해 노력하고 있다고 말한다. 그는 학생들에게 그렇게 하기 위해 사람들이 하고 있는 두 가지 방법을 제시해 준다. 첫째는 여과 장치를 이용하는 것이다. 여과 장치는 대기로부터 이산화탄소를 제거시킨다. 일부는 이산화탄소를 분해시켜 물과 또 다른 기체로 만들어 놓는다. 그리고 다른 여과 장치들은 숯을 이용하여 이산화탄소를 가둔다. 또한, 사람들은 이산화탄소를 방출하는 공장 근처에 나무를 심고 있다. 나무들은 이산화탄소를 섭취하여 이를 광합성에 이용한다. 이로써 나무들은 에너지를 얻게 되며 동물들은 호흡을 할 수 있는 산소를 제공받는다. 따라서 이러한 방법으로 나무와 동물 모두가 이익을 얻는다.

Unit 03 p.128

Task 1 Your Country's Strong Points

📁 Brainstorming

Idea Web

My Country's Strong Points: Education and Hardworking People

Reason 1: *emphasize education*

Detail: *students and adults constantly learn; improves knowledge*

Reason 2: *many hardworking people*

Detail: *country was once poor; is rich country now*

📁 Organizing

My Country's Strong Points: education and hardworking people

First Reason: emphasize education

Details: students and adults constantly learn; improves knowledge; better employees

Second Reason: many hardworking people

Details: country was once poor; citizens worked hard; improved country; is rich country now

📁 Speaking

Guided & Sample Response  2-25

In my opinion, my country has two major strong points. They are education and hardworking people. First of all, in my country, <u>we emphasize education</u>. So not only students but also adults are constantly learning. This improves <u>people's knowledge</u> and makes them better employees. In addition, there are <u>many hardworking people</u> in my country. A few decades ago, my country <u>was very poor</u>. But the citizens of my country all worked hard. They improved my country a lot. Today, my country is one of <u>the richer countries</u> in the world thanks to its hardworking people.

Translation

내 의견으로, 우리 나라는 두 개의 주요한 강점을 가지고 있다. 그것은 교육과 근면한 사람들이다. 우선, 우리 나라에서는, 교육을 강조한다. 따라서 학생들뿐만 아니라 성인들도 끊임없이 배운다. 이로써 사람들의 지식이 증가되고 그들을 보다 뛰어난 직원들로 만든다. 또한, 우리 나라에는 근면한 사람들이 많다. 수십 년 전, 우리 나라는 매우 가난했다. 하지만 우리 나라 국민들은 모두 열심히 일을 했다. 우리 나라를 많이 발전시켰다. 오늘날, 근면한 사람들 덕분에 우리 나라는 부유한 나라 중의 하나가 되었다.

Task 2 Better Lives Now or 100 Years Ago

📁 Brainstorming

Idea Web

Better Now // Better 100 Years Ago

Reason 1: all kinds of jobs // lived in countryside

Detail: like jobs have today; disliked farming in the past // was clean and not polluted; cities today are dirty and overcrowded

Reason 2: healthier today // slow pace of life

Detail: better medicine and health care; live longer // people were relaxed; people always in a hurry today

📁 Organizing

My Choice: Better Now // Better 100 Years Ago

First Reason: all kinds of jobs // lived in countryside

Details: people today have many jobs; enjoy them; people in past were farmers; disliked farming // country was clean; not polluted; people now live in cities; are dirty, polluted, and overcrowded

Second Reason: healthier today // slow pace of life

Details: better medicine and health care; live longer // people were very relaxed; people always in a hurry today; rush around; no improvement

📁 Speaking

Guided & Sample Response 1: Better Now  2-26

I agree with the statement. It's true that people in the present day <u>have better lives</u> than people who lived 100 years ago. The first reason <u>has to do with jobs</u>. Nowadays, people have all kinds of jobs. These are jobs they often enjoy. 100 years ago, most people were farmers. Farming was very hard work that <u>most people disliked</u>. Second, people living in modern times <u>are healthier than</u> people who lived 100 years ago. We have access to better <u>medicine and health care</u>, and we live much longer. So our lives are better than they used to be.

Translation

나는 그러한 진술에 동의한다. 현재의 사람들이 100년 전에 살았던 사람보다 더 나은 삶을 살고 있다. 첫 번째 이유는 직업과 관련이 있다. 오늘날, 사람들은 온갖 종류의 직업을 가지고 있다. 사람들이 좋아하는 직업들이 종종 있다. 100년 전에는, 대부분의 사람들이 농부였다. 농사는 대부분의 사람들이 좋아하지 않는 매우 힘든 일이었다. 둘째, 현대에 사는 사람들은 100년 전에 살았던 사람보다 더 건강하다. 우리는 보다 나은 의학과 건강 보험을 이용할 수 있으며, 훨씬 더 오래 살고 있다. 따라서 우리의 삶이 예전보다 더 낫다.

Guided & Sample Response 2: Better 100 Years Ago

 2-27

I disagree with the statement. It's my belief that people <u>lived better lives</u> 100 years ago. Back then, most people lived <u>in the country</u>. Today, most people live in cities. The countryside was clean and <u>not polluted</u>. But modern cities are dirty, polluted, and overcrowded. So modern-day people don't live in better places than people used to. Also, 100 years ago, the pace of life was slow. Therefore people <u>were very relaxed</u>. Nowadays, everyone is <u>always in a hurry</u>. People rush from one place to another. I don't think that's an improvement on life in the past.

Translation

나는 그러한 진술에 동의하지 않는다. 나는 100년 전의 사람들이 더 나은 삶을 살았다고 믿는다. 당시, 대부분의 사람들은 시골에서 살았다. 오늘날, 대부분의 사람들은 도시에서 산다. 시골은 깨끗하고 오염이 되지 않았다. 하지만 현대의 도시들은 더럽고, 오염되었으며, 그리고 사람들로 붐비고 있다. 따라서 현대의 사람들은 예전 사람들보다 더 나은 곳에서 살고 있지 않다. 또한, 100년 전에는, 삶의 속도가 느렸다. 그렇기 때문에 사람들은 매우 여유로웠다. 오늘날에는, 모든 사람들이 항상 바쁘다. 이곳에서 저곳으로 사람들이 몰려 다닌다. 나는 그러한 것이 과거의 삶이 개선된 결과라고 생각하지 않는다.

Task 3 The School Directory

📁 Reading

Translation

새로운 학교 안내 책자가 발간될 것입니다

학교 측에서 이번 주 목요일에 새로운 학교 안내 책자를 발간할 예정입니다. 처음으로, 안내 책자는 종이로 인쇄되지 않을 것입니다. 대신, 인터넷으로만 발간이 될 것입니다. 따라서, 이전보다 훨씬 더 많은 정보들이 안내 책자에 담겨질 것입니다. 올해의 안내 책자에는 교내 모든 학생들의 이름과 사진이 들어가게 될 것입니다. 또한 모든 학생들의 이메일 주소도 들어있을 것입니다. 하지만, 학생들의 전화 번호는 공개되지 않을 것입니다.

📁 Listening

Script 🎧 2-28

M Student: I am pretty upset about what the school is doing with the directory this year.

W Student: What are you so mad about? The new directory is going to be wonderful.

M: I disagree. I don't want all of my personal information published online.

W: But I think the school is doing a good thing. You know, a few times in the past, I contacted the wrong students. However, now that the directory will have pictures of students, I won't make that mistake anymore.

M: But what about the email addresses?

W: I think having them will be great. Now, it will be easier than ever to contact other students.

M: It seems like a violation of my privacy.

W: I disagree. Oh, and there's one more thing that I like about the new directory.

M: What's that?

W: Since the directory will be online, it will be simple to access. I won't have to go back to my dorm room to get information on other students. Now, I can just use my smartphone to look up the information whenever I need it. I think that's great.

Translation

M Student: 올해 안내 책자에 관해서 학교 측이 하고 있는 일에 대해서는 몹시 기분이 언짢군.

W Student: 무엇 때문에 그렇게 기분이 안 좋니? 새로운 안내 책자는 굉장할 거야.

M: 나는 동의하지 않아. 개인적인 내 모든 정보가 온라인으로 공개되는 것은 원치 않거든.

W: 하지만 나는 학교 측이 잘 하고 있다고 생각해. 알겠지만, 과거 몇 차례, 나는 학생들의 잘못된 연락처로 연락을 했어. 하지만, 안내 책자에 학생들의 사진이 있게 되어서, 그와 같은 실수는 더 이상 하지 않게 될 거야.

M: 하지만 이메일 주소에 대해서는?

W: 이메일 주소를 얻게 된다면 좋을 것 같아. 이제, 다른 학생들과 연락을 취하는 것이 그 어느 때보다 더 쉬워 질 거야.

M: 그것은 사생활 침해인 것으로 보여.

W: 네 말에 동의하지 않아. 오, 그리고 새로운 안내 책자에 대해서 마음에 드는 것이 하나 더 있어.

M: 그것이 뭔데?

W: 안내 책자가 온라인으로 발간될 것이기 때문에, 이용하기가 더 간편해 질 거야. 다른 학생들에 관한 정보를 얻기 위해 기숙사 방으로 돌아가야 할 필요가 없게 될 거고. 이제, 스마트폰을 이용해서 필요할 때마다 정보를 찾을 수 있어. 멋진 일이라고 생각해.

📁 Speaking

Guided & Sample Response 🎧 2-29

The man and the woman are talking about the new student directory. It will be released <u>on the Internet</u>, so it will <u>contain more information</u> than before. The woman likes that there will be more information in it. The first thing she mentions is that there will <u>be pictures of students</u> in the directory. She says that she has called students by mistake before. But since there will be pictures of students, she won't <u>make that mistake</u> again. She also states that the online directory <u>will be convenient</u>. She will be able to look up information anytime <u>with her smartphone</u>.

Translation

남자와 여자는 새로운 학생용 안내 책자에 관해 이야기하고 있다. 인터넷으로 발간이 될 것이기 때문에, 이전보다 더 많은 정보를 포함하게 될 것이다. 여자는 그곳에 더 많은 정보가 있게 될 것이라는 점에 만족해한다. 그녀가 언급하는 첫 번째 사항은 안내 책자에 학생들의 사진이 있게 될 것이라는 점이다. 그녀는 자신이 전에 학생들에게 잘못 전화를 했다고 말한다. 하지만 학생들의 사진이 있게 될 것이므로, 그러한 실수는 다시 하지 않게 될 것이다. 그녀는 또한 온라인 안내 책자가 편리할 것이라고 주장한다. 그녀는 스마트폰으로 언제라도 정보를 찾을 수 있을 것이다.

Task 4 Biology: Odor Defenses

📁 Reading

Translation

냄새를 이용하는 방어 수단

동물들은 스스로를 방어할 수 있는 여러 가지 방법을 가지고 있다. 날카로운 이빨과 발톱을 가지고 있다. 빨리 달리거나 위장을 이용하는 동물들도 있다. 그리고 일부 동물들은 냄새를 이용하는 방어 수단을 가지고 있다. 이들은 강력한 냄새를 이용하여 스스로를 방어한다. 냄새를 이용하는 방어 수단을 지닌 동물들은 위협을 받는 경우에 역겨운 냄새를 배출한다. 이러한 냄새는 해당 동물의 주위를 둘러쌀 수도 있다. 혹은 공격하는 동물 쪽으로 향할 수도 있다. 두 경우 모두에 있어서, 통상 역한 냄새가 포식자를 내쫓는다. 많은 포식자들은 차후 그러한 동물들을 가만히 나두어야 한다는 점을 알게 된다.

📁 Listening

Script 🎧 2-30

W Professor: One unique way some animals defend themselves is by creating bad smells. Both the stinkbug and the skunk do this.

There are countless species of stinkbugs. They all defend themselves similarly. When a stinkbug is threatened, it secretes a liquid. This liquid smells awful. Anything the liquid touches smells bad as well. I'm sure some of you are familiar with this smell. What did you do when you smelled it . . . ? You ran away from the stinkbug, right? Well, that's what many animals do. Many won't eat it either. Most birds, for instance, spit out a stinkbug as soon as they put it in their mouths. That's quite an effective defense.

Skunks also use odor to defend themselves. When a skunk is threatened, it turns away from its enemy. It puts its body in a position where its head is lowered but its back and tail are raised. Then, it shoots a foul-smelling spray at the attacker. Skunks can shoot this spray at least two meters. It smells horrible. It's hard to remove as well. Animals hate it. Most animals flee merely at the sight of a skunk. They have no desire to get sprayed.

Translation

W Professor: 일부 동물들이 <u>스스로를</u> 방어하는데 사용하는 독특한 한 가지 방법은 악취를 풍기는 것입니다. 방귀벌레와 스컹크 모두가 그렇게 합니다.

무수히 많은 종의 방귀벌레들이 있습니다. 이들 모두는 유사한 방식으로 <u>스스로를</u> 보호합니다. 방귀벌레는 위협을 받으면, 액체를 분비합니다. 이러한 액체에서는 끔찍한 냄새가 납니다. 그것이 무엇이던 간에 액체가 닿는 것에서도 악취가 나고요. 여러분 중 몇 분께서는 이러한 냄새에 익숙하시리라 확신합니다. 냄새를 맡았을 때 어떻게 하셨나요…? 방귀벌레로부터 달아나셨을 것입니다. 그렇죠? 음, 그것이 바로 많은 동물들이 하는 행동입니다. 또한 다수의 동물들이 그것을 잡아먹지 않습니다. 예를 들어, 대부분의 새들은 방귀벌레를 입 속에 넣자마자 그것을 뱉어냅니다. 매우 효과적인 방어 수단인 것이죠.

스컹크 또한 냄새를 이용하여 <u>스스로를</u> 방어합니다. 스컹크는 위협을 받으면, 상대편 반대쪽으로 몸을 돌립니다. 머리를 낮추고 등과 꼬리를 들어 올리는 자세를 취합니다. 그런 다음, 공격자를 향해 악취가 나는 분무를 뿌립니다. 스컹크는 최소 2미터까지 이러한 분무를 뿌릴 수가 있습니다. 냄새가 끔찍합니다. 또한 제거하기도 어렵고요. 동물들은 그 냄새를 싫어합니다. 대부분의 동물들이 스컹크를 보면 달아나 버립니다. 분무가 발사되기를 원하지 않는 것이죠.

 Speaking

Guided & Sample Response 🎧 2-31

During her lecture, the professor tells the class about the stinkbug and skunk. Both use <u>odor defenses</u>. Odor defenses utilize scents <u>that smell terrible</u>. Animals release these scents when <u>they're threatened</u> in some way. For instance, the stinkbug <u>releases a liquid</u> that smells bad anytime it's threatened. And animals like birds don't eat stinkbugs because of their bad smell. The professor also talks about the skunk. When a skunk sees an enemy, it <u>sprays some liquid</u> at the other animal. This liquid has a bad smell animals hate. It smells so bad that <u>animals run away</u> whenever they see a skunk.

Translation

강의에서, 교수는 방귀벌레와 스컹크에 대해 학생들에게 이야기하고 있다. 둘 모두는 냄새를 이용하는 방어 수단을 사용한다. 냄새를 이용하는 방어 수단은 끔찍한 악취가 나는 냄새를 활용한다. 어떠한 방식으로 위협을 받는 경우에 동물들은 이러한 냄새를 배출한다. 예를 들어, 방귀벌레는 위협을 받는 경우마다 고약한 냄새가 나는 액체를 분비한다. 그리고 새와 같은 동물들은 그들의 악취 때문에 방귀벌레를 잡아먹지 않는다. 교수는 또한 스컹크에 대해서도 말한다. 스컹크는 적을 발견하면, 그 동물을 향해 액체를 뿌린다. 이러한 액체에서는 동물들이 싫어하는 악취가 난다. 냄새가 너무 역겨워서 동물들은 스컹크를 볼 때마다 도망쳐 버린다.

Task 5 Driving a Friend Home

📁 Listening

> *Notes*
>
> **The Problem:** the man's friend wants a ride home, but the man has a meeting soon
>
> **Solution 1:** tell the friend to find his own way home
>
> **Solution 2:** take the friend home and be late for the meeting

Script 🎧 2-32

W Student: Stuart, I think that Andrew is waiting outside for you. He told me that you're going to give him a ride home in a few minutes.

M Student: Whoops. That totally slipped my mind.

W: What? Is there some kind of a problem? Don't you and Andrew live on the same street?

M: Yeah, he's my next-door neighbor. The problem is that I've got a meeting with my advisor in half an hour. The meeting is going to last at least an hour. We're supposed to talk about a big project I'm going to do this summer.

W: What are you going to do about Andrew?

M: Hmm . . . I might just apologize and tell him to find another way home.

W: But you guys live twenty minutes away from school. Walking home might be tough on Andrew.

M: True. I guess that I could give him a ride home. But then I'd be at least ten minutes late for the meeting with my advisor.

W: That doesn't sound too bad.

M: Actually, my advisor gets really upset when people are just one minute late. He's quite strict about that. He'd be pretty angry with me.

Translation

W Student: Stuart, Andrew가 밖에서 너를 기다리고 있는 것 같아. 잠시 후에 네가 자신을 집까지 태워 줄 것이라고 내게 말했어.

M Student: 이런. 완전히 잊고 있었군.

W: 뭐라고? 무슨 문제라도 있어? 너와 Andrew는 같은 동네에서 살고 있지 않니?

M: 응, 그는 바로 옆집에서 살아. 문제는 내가 30분 후에 지도 교수님과 만나기로 했다는 점이야. 만나면 최소 1시간은 걸릴 거고. 이번 여름에 내가 하게 될 중요한 프로젝트에 대해 이야기하기로 되어 있거든.

W: Andrew에 대해서는 어떻게 할 거니?

M: 흠… 그에게 사과하고 다른 방법으로 집에 가라고 말해 줘야 할 것 같아.

W: 하지만 너희들은 학교에서 20분 떨어진 거리에서 살고 있잖아. 집까지 걸어가는 것은 Andrew에게 힘든 일이 될 거야.

M: 맞아. 그를 집까지 태워 줄 수도 있을 거라고 생각해. 하지만 그러면 지도 교수님과의 약속에 최소한 10분 정도 늦게 될 거야.

W: 그렇게 나빠지는 않을 것 같은데.

M: 실은, 지도 교수님께서 사람들이 단 1분만 늦어도 정말로 화를 내서. 그 점에 대해서는 매우 엄격하시지. 내게 화를 많이 내실 거야.

📁 Speaking

Guided & Sample Response 1: First Solution 🎧  2-33

The man's problem is that <u>he's supposed to</u> give his friend Andrew a ride home. However, he has a meeting <u>with his advisor</u> in thirty minutes. The man and woman discuss two solutions to the man's problem. The first is for the man to tell Andrew to find <u>another way home</u>. The second is for the man to give Andrew a ride home and to <u>go to his meeting</u> late. I like the first solution. The man's meeting is important, so he <u>shouldn't be late</u> for it. Also, it shouldn't be a problem for Andrew to find another way home. He probably knows other students with cars. Or he <u>can walk home</u>.

Translation

남자의 문제는 그가 친구인 Andrew를 집까지 태워 주기로 했다는 점이다. 하지만, 그는 30분 후에 지도 교수와 만나기로 약속을 했다. 남자의 문제에 대해 남자와 여자는 두 가지 해결 방안에 대해 논의한다. 첫째는 남자가 Andrew에게 집에 갈 다른 방법을 찾아보라고 말하는 것이다. 두 번째는 남자가 Andrew를 집까지 태워 주고 약속에 늦게 가는 것이다. 나는 첫 번째 방안을 좋아한다. 남자의 약속은 중요하기 때문에, 늦어서는 안 된다. 또한, Andrew가 집에 갈 다른 방법을 찾는 것은 문제가 되지 않을 것이다. 아마도 그는 차가 있는 다른 학생들을 알고 있을 수도 있다. 혹은 집까지 걸어갈 수도 있다.

Guided & Sample Response 2: Second Solution  2-34

The man's problem is that <u>he's supposed to</u> give his friend Andrew a ride home. However, he has a meeting <u>with his advisor</u> in thirty minutes. The man and woman discuss two solutions to the man's problem. The first is for the man to tell Andrew to find <u>another way home</u>. The second is for the man to give Andrew a ride home and to <u>go to his meeting</u> late. I like the second solution. The man promised Andrew a ride home, so he should <u>keep his promise</u>. He can also call his advisor ahead of time. He can <u>explain the situation</u> and say that he'll be a few minutes late.

Translation

남자의 문제는 그가 친구인 Andrew를 집까지 태워 주기로 했다는 점이다. 하지만, 그는 30분 후에 지도 교수와 만나기로 약속을 했다. 남자의 문제에 대해 남자와 여자는 두 가지 해결 방안에 대해 논의한다. 첫째는 남자가 Andrew에게 집에 갈 다른 방법을 찾아보라고 말하는 것이다. 두 번째는 남자가 Andrew를 집까지 태워 주고 약속에 늦게 가는 것이다. 나는 두 번째 방안을 좋아한다. 남자는 Andrew에게 집까지 태워다 주겠다고 약속을 했기 때문에, 그는 약속을 지켜야 한다. 또한 그는 미리 자신의 지도 교수에게 전화를 걸 수 있다. 상황을 설명해서 잠시 늦을 것이라고 말할 수 있을 것이다.

Task 6 Biology: Collective Behavior

Listening

> *Notes*
>
> **Topic:** biology; collective behavior in animals
>
> **Detail 1:** elephants
> live in herds; take care of babies; watch for predators; protect while foraging
>
> **Detail 2:** fish
> swordfish hunt other fish together; prey fish avoid predators together
>
> **Key Words:** very social animals; look after baby animals and the younger members of the herd; provides protection; help each other when foraging for food; while some forage, others watch out for danger; swordfish pursue large schools of fish; kill them; return together to eat; prey fish; move in unison in different directions; hard for predators to kill them

Script 2-35

W Professor: You might believe that elephants and fish have nothing in common. But you'd be wrong about that. Both elephants and many kinds of fish engage in collective behavior. This refers to actions that animals do together in groups.

Let me tell you about elephants first. Elephants are very social animals. They live in groups called herds. When a herd is together, the elephants take care of one another. For instance, adult elephants look after baby elephants and the younger members of the herd. The herd also provides protection against predators. Of course, not many animals hunt elephants. But it sometimes happens. Elephants even help each other when foraging for food. While some forage, others watch out for danger. Then, when the elephants are finished eating, they stand guard as the others eat.

As for fish, well, they also exhibit collective behavior. Groups of swordfish often hunt other types of fish. The swordfish pursue large schools of fish and kill them with their long bills. Then, after they are done hunting, they return together to eat the fish they killed. Many schools of prey fish act collectively as well. Oh, uh, when I say prey fish, I am referring to fish such as herring, shad, and smelt. Anyway, um, when predators are pursuing them, they seem to move in unison in different directions. This makes it hard for predators to kill them. In this way, collective behavior keeps many fish alive.

Translation

W Professor: 코끼리와 물고기 사이에는 아무런 공통점도 없을 것 같다고 생각하실 수도 있겠군요. 하지만 그 점에 대해서는 잘못 생각하고 계신 것일 수도 있습니다. 코끼리 및 여러 종류의 물고기들은 모두 집단 행동을 합니다. 이는 동물들이 무리를 지어 함께 하는 행동을 말합니다.

먼저 코끼리에 대해 말씀을 드리죠. 코끼리는 매우 사회적인 동물입니다. 코끼리 떼라고 불리는 무리를 지어서 생활합니다. 코끼리 떼가 모여 있으면, 코끼리들은 서로를 돌보아 줍니다. 예를 들어, 다 자란 코끼리들은 아기 코끼리 및 무리 내 보다 어린 구성원들을 돌봅니다. 코끼리 떼는 또한 포식자들로부터 보호를 해줍니다. 물론, 코끼리를 사냥하는 동물들은 많지 않습니다. 하지만 때때로 그런 경우가 발생하기도 합니다. 코끼리들은 심지어 음식을 찾을 때에도 서로에게 도움을 줍니다. 몇몇 코끼리들이 음식을 찾기 위해 돌아다니는 동안, 다른 코끼리들은 위험을 경계해 줍니다. 그런 다음, 이 코끼리들이 식사를 끝내면, 다른 코끼리들이 먹이를 먹는 동안 이들이 경계를 서 줍니다.

물고기에 대해 말씀을 드리면, 이들 역시 집단 행동을 보입니다. 황새치 무리는 종종 다른 종류의 물고기들을 사냥합니다. 황새치들은 커다란 물고기 떼를 쫓아다니며 긴 주둥이로 이들을 죽입니다. 그런 다음, 사냥을 마치면, 함께 돌아와서 자신들이 잡은 먹이를 먹습니다. 먹잇감이 되는 많은 물고기 떼들도 집단적으로 행동을 합니다. 오, 어, 제가 먹잇감이 되는 물고기라고 말씀을 드릴 때는, 정어리, 청어, 그리고 빙어를 언급하는 것입니다. 어쨌든, 음, 포식자들에게 쫓기는 경우, 이들은 일제히 서로 다른 방향으로 움직이는 것처럼 보입니다. 이로써 포식자들은 그들을 죽이는 것이 어렵게 됩니다. 이러한 방식으로, 집단 행동은 많은 물고기들을 생존할 수 있도록 만듭니다.

Speaking

Guided & Sample Response  2-36

In her lecture, the professor tells the students about collective behavior by animals. She states that both <u>elephants and fish</u> act collectively. First, she discusses elephants. She says that they <u>live in groups</u> known as herds. Elephants do many activities together. They take care of their young, watch out for predators, and <u>stand guard</u> while other elephants eat. These collective actions benefit <u>the entire herd</u>. The professor mentions two types of fish behavior. Swordfish <u>collectively hunt</u> large schools of fish and kill them. And schools of prey fish such as herring <u>move as one</u> to avoid getting killed by predators. Both swordfish and herring therefore use collective behavior.

Translation

강의에서, 교수는 학생들에게 동물들의 집단 행동에 대해 말하고 있다. 그녀는 코끼리와 물고기들 모두가 집단적으로 행동한다고 말한다. 먼저, 그녀는 코끼리에 대해 논의한다. 그녀는 이들이 코끼리 떼라고 알려진 무리 속에서 생활한다고 말한다. 코끼리들은 함께 여러 가지의 일들을 한다. 새끼들을 돌보고, 포식자들을 감시하며, 다른 코끼리들이 먹이를 먹는 동안 경계를 선다. 이러한 집단 행동은 무리 전체에 이익이 된다. 교수는 두 종류의 물고기들의 행동에 대해 언급을 한다. 황새치는 거대한 물고기 떼를 집단적으로 사냥하여 이들을 죽인다. 그리고 정어리와 같이 먹잇감이 되는 물고기 떼는 포식자에 의해 목숨을 잃지 않기 위해 하나처럼 행동한다. 따라서 황새치와 정어리 모두 집단 행동을 이용한다.

Unit 04

Task 1 Your Favorite Teacher

📁 Brainstorming

Idea Web

> Your Favorite Teacher: Mr. Patterson
>
> **Reason 1:** makes class fun
>
> **Detail:** tells interesting stories // has made me consider majoring in history
>
> **Reason 2:** lets students contribute to class
>
> **Detail:** have class discussion every week // students can give their opinions

📁 Organizing

> Your Favorite Teacher: Mr. Patterson
>
> **First Reason:** makes class fun
>
> **Details:** tells stories that make history interesting; never enjoyed history before; thinking of majoring in it now
>
> **Second Reason:** lets students contribute to class
>
> **Details:** have class discussion every week; asks for our opinions; students can speak about past; entertaining and educational

📁 Speaking

Guided & Sample Response 🎧 2-37

My favorite teacher is Mr. Patterson. He teaches history at my school. He's my favorite teacher for two reasons. Firstly, he always <u>makes class fun</u>. He tells stories that make history seem interesting. I never enjoyed history until <u>I took his class</u>. Now, I'm considering <u>majoring in it</u> at college. Secondly, he lets students contribute to class. Every week, we have <u>a big discussion</u> in one of our classes. Mr. Patterson asks us for our opinions. We get to speak about the past and what we think happened. Doing that is both <u>entertaining and educational</u>.

Translation

내가 가장 좋아하는 선생님은 Patterson 선생님이다. 그는 학교에서 역사를 가르친다. 두 가지 이유에서 그는 내가 가장 좋아하는 선생님이다. 첫째, 그는 항상 수업을 재미있게 만든다. 역사가 흥미로워 보이도록 해주는 이야기를 말해 준다. 그의 수업을 듣기 전까지는 역사가 전혀 재미있지 않았다. 현재, 나는 대학에서 역사를 전공하는 것에 대해 생각해 보고 있다. 둘째, 그는 학생들이 수업에 참여할 수 있도록 한다. 매주, 우리는 한 수업에서 토론을 한다. Patterson 선생님은 우리에게 의견을 묻는다. 우리는 과거에 대해, 그리고 우리가 생각하기에 어떤 일이 있었는지에 대해 말하게 된다. 그렇게 하는 것은 재미있기도 하고 교육적이기도 하다.

Task 2 Students Should Take a Cooking Class at University

📁 Brainstorming

Idea Web

> Should Be Required // Should Not Be Required
>
> **Reason 1:** is important skill // only teach academic courses
>
> **Detail:** couldn't cook well when lived alone; wish had taken cooking class // is nothing academic about cooking; can attend academy or take cooking lessons

> **Reason 2:** need skills to cook // not necessary skill anymore
>
> **Detail:** math and reading comprehension; can apply skills learned at school // many instant foods available; can cook them in microwave

📁 Organizing

> **My Choice:** Should Be Required // Should Not Be Required
>
> **First Reason:** is important skill // only teach academic courses
>
> **Details:** lived alone for two years; couldn't cook well; wish had taken cooking class // is nothing academic about cooking; can attend academy or take cooking lessons
>
> **Second Reason:** need skills to cook // not necessary skill anymore
>
> **Details:** math and reading comprehension skills; apply skills learned at school when cooking // many instant foods available; can cook them in microwave

📁 Speaking

Guided & Sample Response 1: Should Be Required 🎧 2-38

I think it's a great idea to require students to take a cooking class at university. For one, cooking is <u>an important skill</u> everyone should know. I lived alone for two years after I graduated, but I <u>couldn't cook well</u>. I wish I had taken a cooking class. Also, a lot of cooking requires a person to be exact and <u>to follow directions</u>. So people need math and reading comprehension skills to cook. This makes cooking relevant <u>as a college course</u>. Students can <u>apply the skills</u> they learn at school to the kitchen while learning how to cook.

Translation

나는 대학에서 학생들에게 요리 수업을 수강하도록 하는 것이 멋진 아이디어라고 생각한다. 우선, 요리는 모든 사람이 알고 있어야 하는 중요한 기술이다. 나는 졸업 후에 2년 동안 혼자 살았지만, 요리를 잘하지 못한다. 요리 수업을 들었으면 좋았을 것이다. 또한, 많은 요리는 개인으로 하여금 정확성과 지시 사항을 따를 것을 요구한다. 따라서 요리를 하기 위해서는 수학과 독해 실력이 필요하다. 이로써 요리는 대학 수업으로서 적절한 것이 된다. 학생들은 요리하는 법을 배우면서 학교에서 배운 기술을 주방에서 적용해 볼 수 있을 것이다.

Guided & Sample Response 2: Should Not Be Required 🎧 2-39

I don't think students should be required to take a cooking class at university. To begin with, I believe that colleges should only <u>teach academic courses</u>. There's nothing academic about cooking. If students want to learn to cook, they can attend <u>a private academy</u> or take cooking lessons. Another thing is that cooking skills <u>aren't necessary anymore</u>. There are so <u>many instant foods</u> available these days. To cook them, just put them in the microwave for a minute or two. That's how I eat most of my meals. I can't cook, but that <u>hasn't hurt me</u>.

Translation

나는 대학에서 학생들에게 요리 수업을 수강하도록 해야 한다고 생각하지 않는다. 우선, 나는 대학이 학문과 관련된 과목을 가르쳐야 한다고 생각한다. 요리에는 어떠한 학문적인 것도 없다. 학생들이 요리를 배우고자 한다면, 사설 학원에 다니거나 혹은 요리 강좌를 수강하면 된다. 또 다른 이유는 요리 능력이 더 이상 필요하지 않기 때문이다. 오늘날 이용할 수 있는 인스턴트 식품들이 너무나 많다. 이를 요리하기 위해서는, 단지 일이 분간 이들을 전자레인지에 넣어 두면 된다. 내가 대부분의 식사를 해결하는 방법이다. 나는 요리를 못하지만, 그로 인해 내가 피해를 입은 적은 없다.

Task 3 — Premed Internships

📁 Reading

Translation

의예과 학생들은 단기 인턴쉽에 참여해야 합니다

　내년에, 의예과 학생들을 위한 새로운 방침이 적용될 예정입니다. 학생들은 더 이상 6개월이나 1년 동안 지속되는 인턴쉽에 참여할 수 없습니다. 대신, 3개월을 넘지 않는 인턴쉽으로 제한이 될 것입니다. 학생 및 교수진 모두의 불만 사항에 대응하여, 학생처장님께서 이러한 결정을 내리셨습니다. 아마도, 이번 새 방침으로 인해, 관련된 모든 사람들이 만족해할 것입니다. 보다 많은 정보를 원하시는 경우, 학생처장님이나 화학과 혹은 생물학과 학과장님 사무실로 연락하시기 바랍니다.

📁 Listening

> **Notes**
>
> The woman (**supports** / does not support) the decision.
>
> **Reason:** *did one-year internship; had hard year; physically tired; got low grades*
>
> **Key Words and Details:** *did a twelve-month internship last year; was the hardest year I've ever gone through; physically wore me down; got worn out; first time that I didn't get all A's; didn't have enough time to study; didn't study at all*

Script 🎧 2-40

M Student: This is totally annoying. I just got accepted by a company to do a six-month internship. But since I'm a premed student, I can't do it now.

W Student: That's too bad. But I think that the school is making the right decision.

M: How come?

W: I did a twelve-month internship last year. My junior year was the hardest year I've ever gone through.

M: What was so hard about it?

W: It physically wore me down. I was constantly going to my internship. And I worked really hard at the hospital. I simply got worn out.

M: Hmm . . . How about your grades?

W: Last year, my grades went down. It was the first time that I didn't get all A's. I didn't have enough time to study.

M: Because of your internship?

W: Pretty much. Many times after I got home from my internship, I went to bed immediately. I didn't study at all. But, uh, this year, I'm not doing an internship. I have more time to study. So my grades have gone back up again.

Translation

M Student: 이번 일은 정말로 화나게 만드는군. 얼마 전 나는 한 기업의 6개월짜리 인턴쉽 제의를 수락했어. 하지만 내가 의예과 학생이기 때문에, 이제는 그렇게 할 수가 없어.

W Student: 안 되었구나. 하지만 나는 학교 측이 올바른 결정을 내리고 있다고 생각해.

M: 어째서?

W: 나는 작년에 12개월짜리 인턴쉽에 참가했어. 3학년은 내가 겪어본 것 중 가장 힘든 해였지.

M: 그에 관해 어떤 점이 가장 힘들었는데?

W: 신체적으로 매우 피곤했어. 나는 항상 인턴쉽에 참가했지. 그리고 병원에서 정말로 열심히 일을 했거든. 그냥 지쳐버렸어.

M: 흠… 성적은 어땠는데?

W: 작년에, 내 성적은 떨어졌어. 처음으로 전 과목에서 A를 받지 못했지. 공부할 시간이 충분히 없었거든.

M: 인턴쉽 때문에?

W: 거의 그런 셈이야. 여러 차례 인턴쉽을 마치고 집에 돌아오면, 나는 곧바로 잠을 자러 갔어. 전혀 공부를 하지 못했지. 하지만, 어, 올해, 나는 인턴쉽에 참여하고 있지 않아. 공부할 시간을 더 많이 갖게 되었지. 그래서 성적이 다시 회복되고 있어.

📁 Speaking

Guided & Sample Response 🎧 2-41

The speakers are talking about the announcement made by the dean of students. <u>Premed students</u> may only have internships that <u>last for three months</u>. They cannot do internships longer than that. The woman agrees with the decision by the dean. She first states that her one-year internship <u>was physically difficult</u> for her. She claims that she <u>was always tired</u> while she was doing it. She also mentions that <u>her grades went down</u> while she had the internship. She didn't get all A's like she normally did. She <u>blames her internship</u> on the low grades that she received.

Translation

화자들은 학생처장이 발표한 공지 사항에 대해 이야기하고 있다. 의예과 학생들은 3개월 동안 지속되는 인턴쉽에만 참여할 수 있다. 그보다 오래 지속되는 인턴쉽에는 참여할 수가 없다. 여자는 학생처장의 결정에 찬성한다. 그녀는 먼저 1년 동안의 인턴쉽으로 자신이 신체적으로 힘들었다고 언급한다. 그렇게 하는 동안 항상 자신이 피곤했다고 주장한다. 그녀는 또한 인턴쉽에 참가하는 동안 자신의 성적이 하락했다고 언급한다. 그녀는 평상시와 달리 전과목에서 A를 받지 못했다. 그녀는 자신이 받은 낮은 성적에 대해 인턴쉽을 탓하고 있다.

Task 4 — Education: Behavior Contracting

📁 Reading

Translation

행동 계약

　몇몇 어린 아이들은 행동 장애를 가지고 있다. 이를 해결할 수 있는 한 가지 방법은 행동 계약을 이용하는 것이다. 이 방법에서는, 한 명의 아이와 한 명의 어른이 계약을 맺게 된다. 아이는 나쁜 행동을 그만두는 것에 동의한다. 그리고 어른은 아이에게 보상을 해주는데 동의한다. 이러한 계약은 통상 1주일이나 2주일 정도의 단기간을 위한 것이다. 계약이 종료되면, 새로운 계약이 성립될 수 있다. 새로운 계약에서는 종종 더 바람직한 행실에 대해 보다 많은 보상이 제공된다.

📁 Listening

> **Notes**
>
> **Topic:** *behavior contracting*
>
> **Detail 1:** *student named Tina never raised hand*
> *yelled questions and answers; couldn't get her to stop*
>
> **Detail 2:** *use behavior contracting on Tina*
> *got gold star for raising hand; lost gold star for not raising hand; worked well*
>
> **Key Words:** *bad habit; never raised her hand; said whatever she was thinking; tried many ways to get her to stop; nothing worked; agreement; raised her hand before speaking, I would give her a gold star; if she spoke without raising her hand, I would take one gold star away; changed; would constantly raise her hand; definitely worked for her*

Script 🎧 2-42

W Professor: We often have to get creative when dealing with problem students. There are many methods you can use to improve their behavior. I recommend behavior contracting.

When I taught at an elementary school, I used behavior contracting. It was effective in many cases. I had a student named Tina. Tina had one bad habit. She never raised her hand during class. Instead, she just said whatever she was thinking. She yelled out questions as well as answers. It was so annoying. I tried many ways to get her to stop. But nothing worked.

Then, I came to an agreement with her. Anytime that she raised her hand before speaking, I would give her a gold star. But, if she spoke without raising her hand, I would take one gold star away from her. We agreed to do this for one week. The way she changed was amazing. She really wanted those gold stars. So she would constantly raise her hand. Of course, she forgot to do that sometimes. But she ended the first week with twelve gold stars. Then, we made a new contract for two weeks. She didn't lose a single gold star during that time. Behavior contracting definitely worked for her.

Translation

W Professor: 문제 학생들을 다룰 때는 종종 창의적이어야 합니다. 그들의 행동을 개선시키기 위해 사용할 수 있는 많은 방법들이 있습니다. 저는 행동 계약을 추천합니다.

초등학교에서 교편을 잡았을 때, 저는 행동 계약을 이용했습니다. 많은 경우에 효과적이었죠. Tina라는 이름의 학생이 있었습니다. Tina는 나쁜 버릇 하나를 가지고 있었습니다. 수업 중에 결코 손을 들지 않았습니다. 대신, 그것이 무엇이든, 자신이 생각하는 바를 말할 뿐이었습니다. 소리를 지르면서 답을 말하고 질문을 했습니다. 매우 골치 아픈 일이었습니다. 저는 그녀를 저지하기 위해 많은 방법을 시도해 보았습니다. 하지만 어떤 것도 효과가 없었죠.

그리고 나서, 저는 그녀와 협정을 맺었습니다. 말을 하기 전에 그녀가 손을 들으면, 저는 언제라도 그녀에게 작은 금별을 주었습니다. 하지만, 손을 들지 않고 말을 하는 경우에는, 그녀에게서 금별 하나를 빼앗았습니다. 우리는 1주일 동안 그렇게 하는 것에 동의했습니다. 그녀가 변화된 방식은 놀라운 것이었습니다. 그녀는 정말로 그러한 금별을 원했습니다. 그래서 항상 손을 들고자 했습니다. 물론, 때때로 그렇게 하는 것을 잊기도 했죠. 하지만 첫 주가 끝났을 때, 그녀는 12개의 금별을 가지고 있었습니다. 그리고 나서, 우리는 2주간의 새로운 계약을 맺었습니다. 그때는 한 개의 금별도 잃지 않았습니다. 분명 행동 계약이 그녀에게 효과가 있었던 것이었죠.

Speaking

Guided & Sample Response  2-43

The professor tells the class about when she was an elementary school teacher. She had a student who never <u>raised her hand</u>. Instead, the student just yelled out questions and answers. The professor used <u>behavior contracting</u> to solve the problem. Behavior contracting involves two people <u>making a contract</u>. One person will change his or her behavior. The other will <u>reward that person</u> for changing. This contract is for <u>a short amount of time</u>. The professor agreed to give the student <u>gold stars</u> for good behavior. She took them away for bad behavior. Thanks to behavior contracting, the student's behavior improved.

Translation

교수는 학생들에게 자신이 초등학교 교사였을 때에 대해서 이야기하고 있다. 그녀에게는 결코 손을 들지 않았던 한 학생이 있었다. 대신, 그 학생은 소리를 지르면서 질문을 하고 대답을 했다. 교수는 그러한 문제를 해결하기 위해 행동 계약을 이용했다. 행동 계약은 계약을 맺는 두 명의 사람과 관련이 있다. 한 사람은 자신의 행동을 변화시킬 것이다. 다른 사람은 변화에 대해 그 사람에게 보상을 해줄 것이다. 이러한 계약은 단기간을 위한 것이다. 교수는 바람직한 행동에 대해 학생에게 작은 금별을 주기로 동의했다. 나쁜 행동에 대해서는 그것을 빼앗아갔다. 행동 계약 덕분에, 학생의 행동은 개선되었다.

Task 5 Showing a Cousin around Campus

Listening

> *Notes*
>
> **The Problem:** the woman's cousin is visiting campus, but she has to lead a film discussion
>
> **Solution 1:** have a friend show the cousin around campus
>
> **Solution 2:** cancel the film discussion

Script 2-44

M Student: Mary, are you ready for the film discussion today?

W Student: Oh my goodness. I totally forgot about the discussion.

M: That shouldn't be a problem. You've seen that film a lot of times. I know you can talk about it without preparing anything.

W: It's not that. It's just that my cousin is coming to campus today. She's going to be here for two hours to look around the school. She's coming at four and leaving at six.

M: Uh, but the discussion starts at four, too. Hmm . . . Why don't you have one of your friends show her around campus?

W: I'd like to do that. But she's extremely shy. She might not talk to my friend at all.

M: That's not good. In that case, I guess you'd better cancel the film discussion for today. That way, you can show your cousin around campus.

W: I guess so. But that doesn't seem fair to all the students who will attend today's discussion. They're expecting me to give them an analysis of the film.

M: That's true. You'd better decide on something. It's already twelve o'clock.

W: Let me think about it.

Translation

M Student: Mary, 오늘 영화 토론에 대한 준비를 했니?

W Student: 이런 세상에. 토론에 대해서 완전히 잊고 있었어.

M: 문제가 되지는 않을 거야. 너는 여러 차례 그 영화를 봤잖아. 아무런 준비를 하지 않아도 네가 그에 대한 이야기를 할 수 있을 것 같아.

W: 그런 것이 아니야. 오늘 내 사촌이 캠퍼스에 오기로 해서 그래. 학교를 구경하기 위해 2시간 동안 이곳에 있을 예정이지. 4시에 와서 6시에 떠날 거야.

M: 어, 하지만 토론도 4시에 시작하는군. 흠… 친구 중 한 명을 시켜서 그녀에게 캠퍼스를 소개하도록 하면 어떨까?

W: 그렇게 하고 싶어. 하지만 그녀는 매우 수줍음이 많아. 내 친구에게 전혀 말을 건네지 않을 수도 있어.

M: 좋지 않군. 그런 경우라면, 네가 오늘 영화 토론을 취소하는 것이 나을 것 같아. 그렇게 하면, 네가 사촌에게 캠퍼스를 구경시켜 줄 수 있어.

W: 그럴 수도 있겠지. 하지만 그러면 오늘 수업에 참석하는 모든 학생들에게 공정하지 않을 것 같아. 그들은 내가 자신들에게 영화에 대한 분석을 해주기를 기대하고 있거든.

M: 그건 사실이지. 무언가 결정을 내리는 것이 좋을 것 같군. 벌써 12시야.

W: 생각해 볼게.

Speaking

Guided & Sample Response 1: First Solution  2-45

The woman has a problem. She is supposed to lead <u>a film discussion</u>, but her cousin is coming to school at the same time. The man and woman suggest two solutions to her problem. The first is for her to <u>ask a friend</u> to show her cousin around campus. The second is for her to <u>cancel the film discussion</u>. In my opinion, the first choice is better. By having a friend <u>guide her cousin</u>, the woman can lead the film discussion. So she <u>won't let down</u> all of those students. Also, meeting a new person will be good for the woman's cousin. Maybe she can help <u>overcome her shyness</u> that way.

Translation

여자에게는 문제가 하나 있다. 그녀는 영화 토론을 주재하기로 예정이 되어 있는데, 그녀의 사촌이 같은 시간에 학교에 올 것이다. 남자와 여자는 여자의 문제에 대해 두 가지 해결 방안을 제시하고 있다. 첫 번째는 그녀가 친구에게 부탁을 해서 사촌에게 캠퍼스를 소개해 달라고 하는 것이다. 두 번째는 그녀가 영화 토론을 취소하는 것이다. 내 생각으로는, 첫 번째 방안이 더 낫다. 친구로 하여금 사촌에게 안내를 부탁함으로써, 여자는 영화 토론을 주재할 수 있다. 따라서 모든 학생들을 낙담시키지 않을 것이다. 또한, 새로운 사람을 만나는 것은 여자의 사촌에게 좋을 것이다. 그렇게 하면 아마도 그녀가 수줍음을 극복하는데 도움이 될 수 있을 것이다.

Guided & Sample Response 2: Second Solution 

The woman has a problem. She is supposed to lead <u>a film discussion</u>, but her cousin is coming to school at the same time. The man and woman suggest two solutions to her problem. The first is for her to <u>ask a friend</u> to show her cousin around campus. The second is for her to <u>cancel the film discussion</u>. In my opinion, the second choice is better. <u>Family is important</u>, so the woman should show her cousin around campus. In addition, since her cousin <u>is so shy</u>, it wouldn't be nice for the woman to ask a friend <u>to speak with her cousin</u>. That is something the woman should do herself.

Translation

여자에게는 문제가 하나 있다. 그녀는 영화 토론을 주재하기로 예정이 되어 있는데, 그녀의 사촌이 같은 시간에 학교에 올 것이다. 남자와 여자는 여자의 문제에 대해 두 가지 해결 방안을 제시하고 있다. 첫 번째는 그녀가 친구에게 부탁을 해서 사촌에게 캠퍼스를 소개해 달라고 하는 것이다. 두 번째는 그녀가 영화 토론을 취소하는 것이다. 내 생각으로는, 두 번째 방안이 더 낫다. 가족이 중요하기 때문에, 여자는 사촌에게 캠퍼스를 소개해 주어야 한다. 또한, 그녀의 사촌은 수줍음을 많이 타기 때문에, 사촌과 말을 나누도록 친구에게 부탁을 하는 것은 옳지 못하다. 그것은 여자 자신이 해야 하는 일이다.

Task 6   Zoology: Ant Foraging

📁 Listening

<table>
<tr><td colspan="1">Notes</td></tr>
</table>

Topic: zoology; ant foraging methods

Detail 1: movement

move in same direction; can't find food; move in another direction; no longer move in original direction

Detail 2: carrying food

find big piece of food; don't break it apart; carry it together; fewer ants needed to carry the food

Key Words: very efficient in the paths they take; fail to find food; head in a different direction; no more ants will move south; work together to carry large pieces of food; quite strong; could break fruit up; work together; by combining their strength, fewer ants are needed

Script 

W Professor: I find that ants are some of nature's most unique creatures. I've studied them for a couple of decades. And the more I study them, the more, uh, impressed with ants I become. When ants forage for food, they have some effective methods. Basically, uh, they are able to obtain the greatest amount of food for the smallest amount of effort.

If you watch ants for long enough, you'll notice something about them. They are very efficient in the paths they take when foraging. By that, I mean that some ants might start heading toward the south while looking for food. However, if they fail to find any food, all of the ants will head in a different direction. They might turn, uh, westward. And here's the interesting part: No more ants will move south. Somehow, they realize that there's no food in that direction. So they stop moving that way.

Here's something else they do . . . Ants often work together to carry large pieces of food. Ants, by the way, are quite strong for their size and body weight. Let's say that some ants find a piece of fruit. Now, uh, the ants could break the fruit up. But then it would take fifty ants to carry the pieces back to the anthill. However, if they work together, ten ants can carry the entire piece of fruit. By combining their strength, fewer ants are needed.

Translation

W Professor: 저는 개미들이 자연에서 가장 독특한 생물 중 하나라는 점을 알아냈습니다. 20년 동안 그들에 대한 연구를 하고 있죠. 그리고 그에 대해 더 많이 알수록, 더 많이, 어, 개미들에 대해 더 많은 감명을 받습니다. 개미들이 먹이를 구하러 돌아다닐 때, 이들은 몇 가지 효과적인 방법을 사용합니다. 기본적으로, 어, 이들은 최소한의 노력으로 최대한의 먹이를 얻을 수 있습니다.

충분히 오랫동안 개미들을 지켜보면, 그에 관한 무언가를 알아낼 수 있습니다. 먹이를 찾아 돌아다니는 경우, 이들이 택하는 경로는 매우 효과적입니다. 제 말의 의미는, 일부 개미들이 먹이를 찾는 동안 남쪽으로 향하기 시작할 수도 있습니다. 하지만, 이들이 먹이를 찾는데 실패하면, 모든 개미들은 다른 방향으로 가게 될 것입니다. 그들은, 어, 서쪽으로 방향을 돌릴 수도 있습니다. 그리고 흥미로운 점이 있습니다: 개미들은 더 이상 남쪽으로 이동하지 않습니다. 어느 정도, 이들은 그러한 방향에 먹이가 없다는 점을 깨닫고 있습니다. 따라서 그러한 방식으로 이동하는 것을 중단합니다.

그들이 하는 또 다른 것이 있습니다… 개미들은 종종 서로 협력해서 커다란 먹이를 다룹니다. 그건 그렇고, 개미들은 몸집 및 몸무게에 비해 상당히 힘이 셉니다. 일부 개미들이 과일 조각을 찾아냈다고 가정해 봅시다. 자, 어, 개미들은 과일을 분해시킬 수 있습니다. 하지만 그러면 그 조각들을 개미집으로 가지고 가는데 50마리의 개미들이 필요할 것입니다. 하지만, 협동을 한다면, 10마리의 개미가 과일 조각 전체를 옮길 수 있습니다. 힘을 합침으로써, 필요한 개미들이 적어지는 것입니다.

📁 Speaking

Guided & Sample Response

The professor lectures about the foraging habits of ants. She mentions that ants <u>have effective means</u> of foraging. She describes two of them. The first concerns the direction ants move when <u>looking for food</u>. Ants will walk in <u>a certain direction</u> to find food. But, if there is no food, they will all move in a different direction. And no ants will continue moving in <u>the original direction</u>. Also, ants <u>often work together</u> to carry back large pieces of food. Ants don't break up the food into small pieces. Instead, <u>a small number of</u> ants pick up a large piece of food and carry it back to their colony together.

Translation

교수는 먹이를 찾는 개미들의 습성에 대해 강의를 하고 있다. 그녀는 개미들이 먹이를 찾는데 효과적인 수단을 가지고 있다고 언급한다. 그녀는 그중 두 가지에 대해 설명한다. 첫 번째는 먹이를 찾아 다닐 때 개미들이 이동하는 방향과 관련이 있다. 개미들은 먹이를 찾기 위해 특정한 방향으로 나아갈 것이다. 하지만, 먹이가 없으면, 모두가 다른 방향으로 이동을 할 것이다. 그리고 어떤 개미도 원래의 방향으로 계속 이동하지는 않을 것이다. 또한, 개미들은 종종 협력을 해서 커다란 먹이를 가지고 간다. 개미들은 먹이를 작은 조각들로 분해하지 않는다. 대신, 적은 수의 개미들이 커다란 먹이를 들어 올려서 다함께 개미집으로 가지고 간다.

Task 1 A Facility You Want Your School to Construct

📁 Brainstorming

Idea Web

A Facility You Want Your School to Construct: Gym

Reason 1: *rains a lot in city*

Detail: *cancel P.E. when rains; can't go outside in rain*

Reason 2: *play indoor sports*

Detail: *no basketball and volleyball; could play them in gym*

📁 Organizing

A Facility You Want Your School to Construct: gym

First Reason: *rains a lot in city*

Details: *cancel P.E. when it rains; can't go outside; can play indoors if have gym*

Second Reason: *play indoor sports*

Details: *no basketball and volleyball; can't play at school; could play them in gym*

📁 Speaking

Guided & Sample Response  2-49

I would really like for my school <u>to construct a gym</u>. There are two reasons that I want a gym. The first is that <u>it rains a lot</u> in my city. When it rains, we have to <u>cancel P.E. class</u> since we can't go outside. But if we have a gym, we <u>can play indoors</u> on rainy days. The second reason is that having a gym will let us <u>play indoor sports</u> such as basketball and volleyball. We can't play either sport at my school now. However, we could play them if we had a gym.

Translation

나는 학교측이 체육관을 짓기를 정말로 바란다. 내가 체육관을 원하는 것에는 두 가지 이유가 있다. 첫 째는 우리 도시에 많은 비가 내린다는 점이다. 비가 내리면, 밖으로 나갈 수가 없기 때문에 우리는 체육 수업을 취소해야 한다. 하지만 체육관이 있다면, 비가 오는 날에도 실내에서 운동을 할 수가 있다. 두 번째 이유는 체육관이 있으면 농구와 배구와 같은 경기를 실내에서 할 수 있기 때문이다. 현재 우리 학교에서는 그중 어떤 경기도 할 수가 없다. 하지만, 체육관이 있다면, 그러한 경기를 할 수 있을 것이다.

Task 2 The Same Activities or Different Ones

📁 Brainstorming

Idea Web

Do the Same Activities // Do Different Activities

Reason 1: *can become very skilled // doing the same thing is boring*

Detail: *play basketball every day; am good basketball player // try to vary routine; do different activities*

Reason 2: *makes people feel comfortable // can learn new skills*

Detail: *friend watches movies every weekend; feels comfortable at theater // best friend does something different daily; is incredibly skilled*

📁 Organizing

My Choice: Do the Same Activities // Do Different Activities

First Reason: *can become very skilled // doing the same thing is boring*

Details: *play basketball every day; am good basketball player // try to vary routine; meet friends one day; exercise or stay home other days*

Second Reason: *make people feel comfortable // can learn new skills*

Details: *friend watches movies every weekend; feels comfortable at movie theater // best friend does different activity every day; studies English; learns computer programming; takes swimming lessons; is incredibly skilled*

📁 Speaking

Guided & Sample Response 1: Same Activities  2-50

In my opinion, it's better for people to do the same activities every day. The first reason is that this will let people become <u>very good at</u> these activities. For instance, I play basketball with my friends every day. Since I <u>play it so often</u>, I have become quite a good basketball player. The second reason is that familiar activities make people <u>feel comfortable</u>. One of my friends watches movies every weekend. I asked her why she does this. She responded that <u>she feels comfortable</u> at the movie theater. So she does an activity that <u>makes her feel good</u>.

Translation

내 의견으로, 매일 같은 활동을 하는 것이 더 좋다. 첫 번째 이유는, 그렇게 하면 그러한 활동들에 매우 능숙해지기 때문이다. 예를 들어, 나는 내 친구들과 매일 농구를 한다. 매우 자주 하기 때문에, 나는 농구를 매우 잘하게 되었다. 두 번째 이유는, 익숙한 활동을 하면 편안한 기분이 들기 때문이다. 내 친구 중 한 명은 매주 주말 마다 영화를 본다. 나는 그녀가 왜 그렇게 하는지를 물어 보았다. 그녀는 자신이 영화관에서 편안함을 느낀다고 대답했다. 따라서 그녀는 자신의 기분을 좋게 만들어 주는 활동을 하고 있는 것이다.

Guided & Sample Response 2: Different Activities 2-51

I strongly believe that people should do different activities every day. One reason I feel this way is that always doing <u>the same thing</u> is boring. I try to vary my routine. Some days, I meet my friends. Other days, I exercise or <u>stay home and read</u>. Another reason I feel this way is that doing different activities <u>can teach you</u> new skills. My best friend does <u>something different</u> each day of the week. For example, he studies English on Mondays. He learns computer programming on Tuesdays. And he takes swimming lessons on Wednesdays. He's an incredibly <u>skilled person</u>.

Translation

나는 매일 다양한 활동을 해야 한다고 굳게 믿는다. 내가 그렇게 생각하는 한 가지 이유는, 항상 같은 일만 하면 지루해지기 때문이다. 나는 내 일상에 변화를 주려고 노력한다. 어떤 날에는, 친구들을 만난다. 다른 날에는, 운동을 하거나 집에 머물면서 책을 읽는다. 내가 그렇게 생각하는 또 다른 이유는, 다양한 활동을 하면 새로운 기술을 배울 수가 있기 때문이다. 내 가장 친한 친구는 주중 매일마다 서로 다른 일을 한다. 예를 들어 월요일에는 영어를 공부한다. 화요일에는 컴퓨터 프로그래밍을 배운다. 그리고 수요일 마다 수영 수업을 듣는다. 그는 매우 재주가 많은 사람이다.

Task 3 Free E-Readers for Students

📁 Reading

Translation

모든 학생들이 무료 전자책 판독기를 받게 될 것입니다

전자책의 인기가 증가하고 있으므로, 학교측은 다음 학기를 시작으로 모든 학생들에게 무료 전자책 판독기를 제공해 줄 예정입니다. 이로써 학생들은 교과서 및 기타 참고 서적들의 전자책 버전을 구입할 수 있습니다. 또한 전자책 판독기로 인터넷 서핑 및 기타 다양한 기능들을 이용할 수 있습니다. 학생들은 3개의 서로 다른 전자책 판독기 중에서 하나를 선택하게 될 것입니다. 학교측은 세 개의 전자책 판독기 모두에 대한 정보들을 학생들에게 이메일로 보내 줄 것입니다. 그러면 학생들은 자신이 원하는 전자책 판독기를 학교측에 알려 줄 수 있을 것입니다.

📁 Listening

Notes

The woman (**agrees** / disagrees) with the decision.

Reason: *art history books expensive; e-book versions are cheaper; can save money; won't have to carry heavy books*

Key Words and Details: *going to save money with this e-reader; books are incredibly expensive; more than two hundred dollars; electronic versions of the books are much cheaper; going to save a ton of money; art books are heavy; hate having to carry around a backpack full of them; won't have to do that anymore*

Script 🎧 2-52

W Student: This is such great news. I've been happy all day long.

M Student: What? What happened?

W: The school is going to provide us with free e-readers. What a great decision.

M: I can't say I agree with you. It seems like a huge waste of money.

W: On the contrary, I'm going to save money with this e-reader. I'm an art history major you know. Most of our books are incredibly expensive. In fact, some cost, uh, more than two hundred dollars.

M: Really? You can't be serious.

W: I am. They have lots of color photographs. So that makes them expensive. But the electronic versions of the books are much cheaper. So I'm going to save a ton of money.

M: Oh, I see. I'm an English major, so this won't affect me too much.

W: There's another way I'm going to benefit. Many art books are heavy. I hate having to carry around a backpack full of them. I won't have to do that anymore.

M: That's cool. I suppose lots of art history students must be as happy as you are.

Translation

W Student: 정말 멋진 소식이야. 하루 종일 기분이 좋았어.

M Student: 뭐? 무슨 일이 있었는데?

W: 학교측에서 우리에게 무료 전자책 판독기를 제공할 예정이야. 정말로 멋진 결정이지.

M: 나는 네 말에 동의한다고 할 수 없을 것 같군. 막대한 돈 낭비가 될 것으로 보여.

W: 그 반대로, 나는 이번 전자책 판독기로 비용을 절약하게 될 거야. 알겠지만 나는 미술사를 전공하고 있어. 우리 책 대부분은 정말로 값이 비싸. 실제로, 몇몇 책은, 어, 200달러 이상의 비용이 들어.

M: 정말이니? 진담일 리가 없어.

W: 진담이야. 많은 컬러 사진들이 들어 있거든. 그래서 책이 비싸지지. 하지만 전자책 버전은 훨씬 값이 싸. 그래서 많은 돈을 절약하게 될 거야.

M: 오, 알겠어. 나는 영어가 전공이라, 그래서 이번 일이 나에게는 그렇게 큰 영향을 미치지는 않을 거야.

W: 내게 혜택이 되는 또 다른 측면이 있어. 많은 미술 서적들은 무거워. 나는 그런 책들이

가득 들어 있는 가방을 메고 다니는 것이 싫어. 이제 더 이상 그렇게 하지 않아도 될 거야.

M: 잘 되었구나. 많은 미술사 전공 학생들이 틀림없이 너만큼 기뻐할 것이라고 생각해.

📁 Speaking

Guided & Sample Response 🎧 2-53

The speakers are discussing the fact that the school will <u>give free e-readers</u> to students next semester. This will let them <u>purchase electronic books</u>. The woman supports this decision by the school. She tells the man two reasons that she is in favor of the school's decision. First, she states that the art books she must buy <u>are very expensive</u>. However, the e-book versions are much less expensive. So she <u>will save money</u>. She also notes that art books <u>weigh a lot</u>. Since she will have e-books in the future, she <u>won't have to carry</u> around any heavy books.

Translation

화자들은 다음 학기에 학교측이 학생들에게 무료 전자책 판독기를 제공해 줄 것이라는 사실에 대해 논의하고 있다. 이로써 학생들은 전자책을 구입할 수 있게 될 것이다. 여자는 학교측의 이러한 결정을 지지한다. 그녀는 남자에게 자신이 학교의 결정을 선호하는 두 가지 이유에 말한다. 첫째, 그녀는 자신이 구입해야 하는 미술 서적들이 매우 비싸다고 주장한다. 하지만, 전자책 버전은 훨씬 더 값이 싸다. 따라서 그녀는 돈을 절약하게 될 것이다. 그녀는 또한 미술 서적들이 무게가 많이 나간다고 언급한다. 앞으로 그녀는 전자책을 갖게 될 것이므로, 무거운 책들을 가지고 다닐 필요가 없을 것이다.

Task 4 ## Psychology: Short-Term Memory

📁 Reading

Translation

단기 기억

사람들은 장기 기억과 단기 기억 모두를 가지고 있다. 사람들에게 있어서 장기 기억은 수십 년 동안 지속될 수 있다. 단기 기억은 매우 빨리 사라진다. 단기 기억은 단지 몇 초나 몇 분간만 지속될 수도 있다. 혹은 몇 시간이나 며칠 동안 지속될 수도 있다. 대부분의 경우, 그러한 기억에 중요성이 없기 때문에 단기 기억은 사라진다. 더 이상 중요하지 않게 될 때까지만 기억을 유지한다. 그 후에는, 뇌가 그러한 기억을 잊게 된다.

📁 Listening

Notes

Topic: *short-term memory*

Detail 1: *decay*
memory fades when don't use; happens with phone numbers

Detail 2: *interruption*
interrupted in middle of conversation; forget what were talking about

Key Words: *decay; memory fading from your mind; phone numbers; remember it; don't call her for three days; can't recall her number; didn't use it, so it disappeared; interruption; talking to a friend; received a text message; restart the conversation; had forgotten what I was talking about*

Script 🎧 2-54

M Professor: You've probably had experiences where you forgot something someone told you almost immediately after hearing it. For instance, maybe someone told you a person's name. A few seconds later, you forgot it. Why did that happen . . . ? It happened because of how short-term memory operates.

One reason you forget things quickly has to do with decay. This refers to a memory fading from your mind. This often happens with phone numbers. Say that your friend tells you her phone number. You don't write it down. Instead, you remember it. You call her a couple of times. So it's easy to remember her number. But, um, you don't call her for three days. Suddenly, you can't recall her number. The reason is that this particular memory decayed. You didn't use it, so it disappeared.

Interruption also happens with short-term memory. This happens to me frequently. Yesterday, I was talking to a friend about a family matter. Suddenly, I received a text message on my cell phone. I stopped talking and read the text message. Then, I tried to restart the conversation. However, I had forgotten what I was talking about. Because of interruption, my short-term memory of that conversation had disappeared.

Translation

M Professor: 아마도 누군가가 여러분들께 이야기한 것을 여러분이 거의 듣자마자 잊어버린 기억이 있으실 것입니다. 예를 들어, 아마 누군가가 여러분에게 그 사람의 이름을 말해 주었을 수 있습니다. 몇 초 후, 여러분들은 그 이름을 잊어 버렸습니다. 왜 그런 일이 일어났을까요…? 단기 기억이 작동하는 원리 때문에 그런 일이 일어났던 것입니다.

무언가를 빨리 잊게 되는 한 가지 이유는 기억 쇠퇴와 관련이 있습니다. 이는 머릿속에서 기억이 서서히 사라지는 것을 의미합니다. 전화번호에 있어서 이러한 일이 종종 일어납니다. 가령 여러분 친구가 여러분에게 자신의 전화 번호를 말해 주었다고 가정해 봅시다. 여러분은 그것을 받아 적지 않습니다. 대신, 그것을 기억해 둡니다. 여러분들은 두어 차례 그녀에게 전화를 겁니다. 그러면 번호를 외우는 것이 쉽습니다. 하지만, 음, 여러분들이 3일 동안 그녀에게 전화를 걸지 않았습니다. 갑자기, 여러분들은 그녀의 번호를 생각해 낼 수가 없습니다. 그 이유는 이러한 특정 기억이 쇠퇴하기 때문입니다. 사용하지 않았기 때문에, 사라져 버린 것이었죠.

단기 기억에서는 방해 또한 일어납니다. 이러한 일은 제게 빈번히 일어납니다. 어제, 저는 친구와 가족 문제에 대해 이야기하고 있었습니다. 갑자기, 저는 휴대 전화로 문자 메시지를 받았습니다. 저는 이야기를 중단하고 문자 메시지를 읽어 보았습니다. 그리고 나서, 저는 대화를 재개하려고 했습니다. 하지만, 제가 무엇에 대해 이야기하고 있었는지를 잊어 버렸습니다. 방해 때문에, 대화에 관한 제 단기 기억이 사라졌던 것이었죠.

📁 Speaking

Guided & Sample Response 🎧 2-55
The professor tells the students about how short-term memory can disappear. Short-term memories <u>are different from</u> long-term memories. <u>They only last</u> for a few seconds, minutes, hours, or days. Then, they disappear. One reason they disappear is decay. When you <u>don't use a memory</u>, it decays. The professor says that memories of <u>phone numbers</u> may decay. If you don't call a person for a while, you might forget that person's phone number. Interruption makes short-term memories disappear, too. <u>During a conversation</u>, the professor received a text message. He read the message. However, because of the interruption, he forgot <u>what he'd been discussing</u>.

Translation

교수는 학생들에게 단기 기억이 사라지는 방식에 대해 이야기하고 있다. 단기 기억은 장기 기억과 다르다. 몇 초, 몇 분, 몇 시간, 혹은 며칠 동안만 지속될 뿐이다. 그리고 나면, 사라져 버린다. 단기 기억이 사라지는 한 가지 이유는 기억 쇠퇴 때문이다. 사용하지 않으면, 기억은 사라져 버린다. 교수는 전화번호에 대한 기억이 쇠퇴할 수 있다고 말한다. 한동안 누군가에게 전화를 걸지 않으면, 그 사람의 전화번호는 잊어 버리게 될 수 있다. 방해 역시 단기 기억을 사라지게 만든다. 대화를 하던 도중, 교수는 문자 메시지를 받았다. 그는 메시지를 읽어 보았다. 하지만, 방해 때문에, 자신이 논의하려고 했던 것을 잊어 버렸다.

Task 5 Making Plans for a Party

📁 Listening

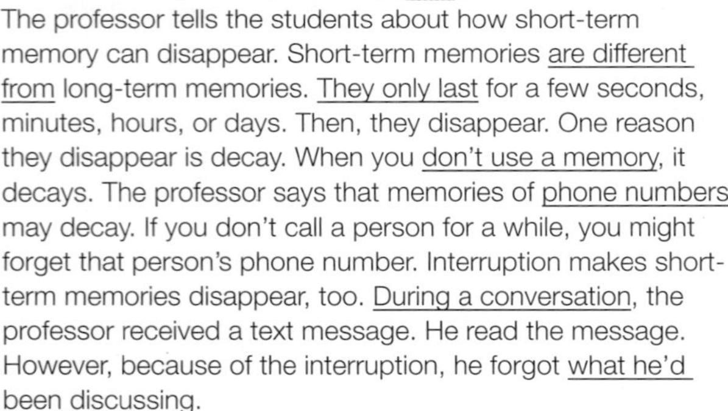

Script 🎧 2-56
M Student: Sarah, is everything ready for the big party at your place? I can't wait to go over to your house tonight.

W Student: Well, I'm having the party, but I don't know if it'll be fun.

M: How come?

W: The heater at my house just broke. And since it's winter, my house is going to be freezing cold. I'm trying to figure out what to do.

M: Hmm . . . Just have the party at a nearby restaurant. Aren't there lots of restaurants near your house?

W: There are, but I can't afford to take everyone out to dinner. There are nineteen people coming to the party. I don't have enough money in my budget to cover everyone's meal.

M: Oh, that could be a problem.

W: Do you have any suggestions?

M: Well . . . Have the party at your house, but contact your guests before they come. Tell them about the heater. So make sure that they wear some heavy clothes. You know, they can bring a sweater or two.

W: That might work. But it would be pretty inconvenient to have to wear so many heavy clothes indoors. Some of my guests might not enjoy that.

Translation

M Student: Sarah, 너희 집에서 열리는 성대한 파티에 대한 모든 준비가 끝났니? 오늘밤 너희 집에 정말로 가보고 싶어.

W Student: 음, 파티를 하기는 할 건데, 하지만 재미있을지 잘 모르겠어.

M: 어째서?

W: 집에 있는 난방기가 고장 났거든. 그리고 겨울이기 때문에, 집이 몹시 추울 거야. 어떻게 해야 할지 알아 보고 있어.

M: 흠… 근처의 식당에서 파티를 열어. 너희 집 근처에 식당들이 많지 않니?

W: 많이 있지만, 모든 사람들을 저녁 식사에 데리고 갈 여유는 없어. 파티에 올 사람은 19명이야. 내 예산 상 모든 사람들의 식비를 감당할 수 있는 충분한 돈은 없어.

M: 오, 문제가 될 수도 있겠군.

W: 제안할 것이 있니?

M: 음… 집에서 파티를 하되, 하지만 손님들이 오기 전에 먼저 연락을 해. 난방기에 대해 이야기해 줘. 그러면 확실히 두꺼운 옷을 입게 될 거야. 알겠지만, 스웨터 한두 벌을 가지고 올 수가 있지.

W: 그럴 수도 있을 거야. 하지만 실내에서 그처럼 많은 두꺼운 옷들을 입어야 한다는 점은 꽤 불편한 일이 될 거야. 손님 중 몇 명은 그러한 점을 좋아하지 않을 수도 있어.

📁 Speaking

Guided & Sample Response 1: First Solution 🎧 2-57
The woman's problem is that she's having a party at her house, but <u>her heater broke</u>. <u>Since it's winter</u>, her house is going to

be cold. The man and woman come up with two solutions to her problem. The first is for the woman to have the party <u>at a restaurant</u> near her house. The second is for the woman to tell her guests to <u>wear heavy clothes</u> to her house. I support the first solution because having the party at a restaurant will be <u>comfortable for the guests</u>. Secondly, the guests can help <u>pay for their dinners</u>. If they do that, then the woman won't have to spend too much money.

Translation

여자의 문제는 그녀가 집에서 파티를 할 것인데, 하지만 난방기가 고장이 났다는 점이다. 겨울이기 때문에, 그녀의 집은 추울 것이다. 그녀의 문제에 대해 남자와 여자는 두 가지 해결 방안을 생각해 내고 있다. 첫 번째는 여자가 집 근처의 식당에서 파티를 여는 것이다. 두 번째는 여자가 손님들에게 두꺼운 옷을 입고 집에 오라고 말을 해주는 것이다. 식당에서 파티를 하는 것이 손님들에게 편할 것이기 때문에, 나는 첫 번째 방안을 지지한다. 둘째로, 손님들은 식사 비용을 지불하는데 있어서 도움을 줄 수도 있다. 그들이 그렇게 해준다면, 여자는 너무 많은 돈을 지출하지 않아도 될 것이다.

Guided & Sample Response 2: Second Solution 🎧 2-58

The woman's problem is that she's having a party at her house, but <u>her heater broke</u>. <u>Since it's winter</u>, her house is going to be cold. The man and woman come up with two solutions to her problem. The first is for the woman to have the party <u>at a restaurant</u> near her house. The second is for the woman to tell her guests to <u>wear heavy clothes</u> to her house. I support the second solution because it <u>will help save</u> the woman money. She can't afford to go to a restaurant. Additionally, a party at a person's house is always fun. Even if it's cold, her guests will <u>have a great time</u>.

Translation

여자의 문제는 그녀가 집에서 파티를 할 것인데, 하지만 난방기가 고장이 났다는 점이다. 겨울이기 때문에, 그녀의 집은 추울 것이다. 그녀의 문제에 대해 남자와 여자는 두 가지 해결 방안을 생각해 내고 있다. 첫 번째는 여자가 집 근처의 식당에서 파티를 여는 것이다. 두 번째는 여자가 손님들에게 두꺼운 옷을 입고 집에 오라고 말을 해주는 것이다. 여자가 돈을 절약하는데 도움이 될 것이기 때문에, 나는 두 번째 방안을 지지한다. 여자는 식당에 갈 여력이 되지 않는다. 또한, 집에서 하는 파티는 언제나 재미있다. 비록 추울지라도, 그녀의 손님들은 재미있는 시간을 갖게 될 것이다.

Task 6　Psychology: Peer Reinforcement

📁 Listening

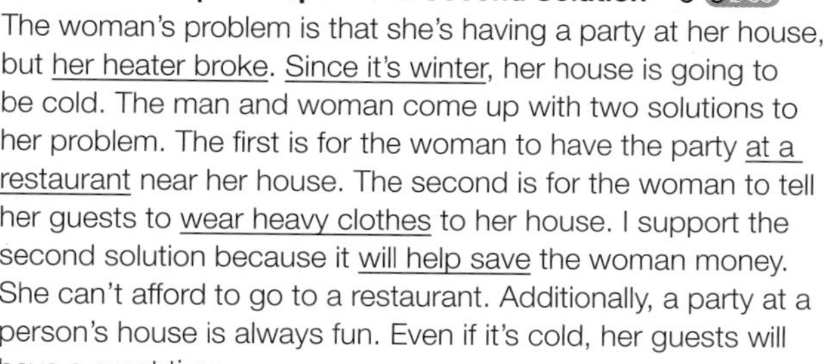

Notes

Topic: psychology; peer reinforcement

Detail 1: how to do it

don't punish bad students; ignore; praise good students; bad students want praise; will improve behavior

Detail 2: personal example

Danielle never picked up blocks; Greg did; praised Greg; Danielle started picking up blocks; praised her; no more bad behavior

Key Words: don't punish bad students; ignore them; praise the students who act properly; bad students notice; want to get praised; start to act like the students you're praising; Danielle; never cleaning up; Greg; always put his blocks away; praised him; Danielle started picking up her blocks; made sure to praise her; kept putting her blocks away

Script 🎧 2-59

W Professor: Many of you are planning to be teachers in the future. How are you going to control unruly students? You can't use corporal punishment on them . . .　Well, one way is to use peer reinforcement. I find that it's very effective, especially for elementary school students.

We often punish bad students. Or we at least chastise them for misbehaving. But this doesn't always get them to change their behavior. With peer reinforcement, you don't punish bad students. Instead, you ignore them no matter what they do. However . . . you make sure to praise the students who act properly. The bad students always notice this. And, most of the time, they want to get praised as well. So they, uh, they start to act like the students you're praising. If you do it properly, you can get the entire class acting well.

Here's an example . . .　I taught at an elementary school a few years ago. I had a student named Danielle. She had this bad habit of never cleaning up. For example, after playtime ended, she always left her wood blocks on the floor. Greg, on the other hand, was a great student. He always put his blocks away. So I praised him for doing that. After a few days, Danielle started picking up her blocks. Of course, I made sure to praise her. She liked that. So she kept putting her blocks away.

Translation

W Professor: 여러분 중 다수는 장차 교사가 될 계획을 세우고 계십니다. 다루기 힘든 학생들은 어떻게 통제하실 건가요? 그들에게 체벌을 가할 수는 없습니다… 음, 한 가지 방법은 또래 칭찬을 사용하는 것입니다. 저는, 특히 초등학교 학생들에게 있어서, 이것이 매우 효과적이라는 점을 알아냈습니다.

우리는 종종 행실이 나쁜 아이들에게 벌을 줍니다. 혹은 적어도 잘못된 행동에 대해서 꾸짖습니다. 하지만 이로써 항상 그들이 행동을 변화시키는 것은 아닙니다. 또래 칭찬에 있어서는, 행실이 나쁜 학생들에게 벌을 주지 않습니다. 대신, 이들이 무엇을 하던 무시를 합니다. 하지만… 적절한 행동을 한 학생들에게는 반드시 칭찬을 해줍니다. 행실이 나쁜 학생들은 항상 이를 주목합니다. 그리고, 대부분의 경우, 자신들도 칭찬받기를 원합니다. 따라서 그들은, 어, 여러분이 칭찬하는 학생들처럼 행동하기 시작합니다. 적절히 사용한다면, 여러분들은 학급 전체가 올바른 행동을 하도록 만들 수 있습니다.

예를 하나 들어 드리죠… 저는 몇 년 전에 초등학교에서 교편을 잡았습니다. Danielle이라는 이름의 학생이 있었습니다. 그녀는 결코 정리를 하지 않는 습관이 있었습니다. 예를 들어, 놀이 시간이 끝난 후에는, 언제나 나무 블록을 바닥에 놔두었습니다. 반면, Greg은 착한 학생이었습니다. 항상 자신의 블록을 치웠습니다. 그래서 저는 그러한 점에 대해 그에게 칭찬을 해주었습니다. 며칠 후, Danielle은 자신의 블록을 치우기 시작했습니다. 물론, 저도 잊지 않고 그녀를 칭찬해 주었고요. 그녀는 좋아했습니다. 그래서 계속 자신의 블록들을 치웠습니다.

📁 Speaking

Guided & Sample Response 🎧 2-60

In her lecture, the professor talks about peer reinforcement. She states that <u>it's a good way</u> to make some students behave. First, she explains how to do peer reinforcement. She tells the students <u>not to punish</u> or say anything negative to bad students. Instead, they <u>should praise students</u> who act properly. The bad students want <u>to get praised</u>. So they will begin behaving. The professor talks about her own personal experience. One girl never <u>put her blocks away</u>, but a boy did. She praised the boy and <u>ignored the girl</u>. Soon, the girl began to put her blocks away. So the professor praised her. The girl behaved well after that.

Translation

강의에서, 교수는 또래 칭찬에 대해 이야기하고 있다. 그녀는 그것이 일부 학생들 하여금 올바른 행동을 할 수 있도록 만드는 좋은 방법이라고 말한다. 우선, 그녀는 어떻게 또래 칭찬을 하는지에 대해 설명한다. 그녀는 학생들에게 행실이 나쁜 학생들을 벌하거나 부정적인 말을 해서는 안 된다고 말한다. 대신, 올바른 행동을 하는 학생들을 칭찬해 주어야 한다. 행실이 나쁜 학생들은 칭찬을 받고 싶어한다. 따라서 올바른 행동을 하기 시작할 것이다. 교수는 자신의 개인적인 경험에 대해 이야기한다. 한 여자 아이는 결코 블록을 치우지 않았지만, 한 남자 아이는 그렇게 했다. 그녀는 남자 아이를 칭찬해 주고 여자 아이는 무시했다. 곧, 여자 아이가 블록을 치우기 시작했다. 따라서 교수는 그녀에게 칭찬을 해주었다. 그 후 여자 아이는 올바른 행동을 했다.

Chapter 4
Writing

Unit 01

p.150

Task 1 Sociology: The Shortage of Primary Care Doctors

📁 Reading

Translation

미국은 1차 진료 의사의 부족 문제를 겪고 있다. 최근, 다수의 1차 진료 의사들이 은퇴를 하고 있다. 안타깝게도, 이들은 동일한 수의 의사들로 대체가 되지 못하고 있다.

이러한 부족 현상의 한 가지 이유는 의과대학의 막대한 비용과 관련이 있다. 최근, 의과대학의 등록금이 증가하고 있다. 미국의 일류 의과대학의 학비는 연간 50,000달러가 넘는다. 학생들은 또한 숙식비 및 기타 경비에 대한 지출을 해야 한다. 보통은 학생들이 일을 하지 않기 때문에, 대부분의 학생들은 대출을 받는다. 졸업 후, 이들은 갚아야 할 수 십만 달러의 대출금을 떠안게 된다. 1차 진료 의사들은 다른 의사들보다 적은 급여를 받는다. 따라서 의과대학 학생 중 1차 진료 의사가 되기로 선택한 학생들은 거의 없다. 그들에게 금전적으로 도움이 되지 않는다.

1차 진료 의사들이 갖고 있는 또 다른 문제는 그들이 해야 할 서류 작업이 매우 많다는 점이다. 이러한 의사들은 매일 많은 환자들을 진찰한다. 보험과 다른 문제들로 인해, 이들은 항상 서류 작업을 하고 있다. 이로써 많은 의사들이 장시간 동안 근무를 한다. 서류 업무를 하는 동안에는 수입을 얻지 못한다. 이로써 많은 사람들에게 1차 진료 의사가 되는 것은 매력이 없다. 상황이 바뀌기 전까지, 미국에서 이러한 의사들은 계속 부족할 것이다.

📁 Listening

Script 🎧 3-01

W Professor: Did you read the article I assigned? I'm talking about the one that mentioned the shortage of primary care doctors. Now, uh, it's true there are fewer primary care doctors these days. But I disagree with the writer's reasoning. Here's why . . .

First of all, there are ways to avoid paying the high costs of medical school. Yes, medical schools are expensive. However, most students never pay full price. For example, most medical schools offer scholarships. By receiving a scholarship, a student can reduce his or her debt load considerably. There are organizations that offer scholarships as well. Some groups and hospitals will pay for a person's schooling. In return, the doctor must work for them for a few years after graduating. By doing that, a person can have zero debt after graduating.

While it's true that hospitals and health clinics have more paperwork than ever, doctors don't do most of it. Instead, nurses and administrators do a lot of the paperwork. Doctors only have to do a small amount. And nurses are being trained better every year. So now they can complete many of the forms. In addition, administrative employees are responsible for doing insurance paperwork. So, uh, these aren't the reasons there are fewer primary care doctors.

Translation

W Professor: 제가 과제로 나누어 드린 기사를 읽어 보셨나요? 1차 진료 의사의 부족 현상을 언급하는 기사를 말씀드리는 것입니다. 자, 어, 오늘날 1차 진료 의사들이 적어졌다는 점은 사실입니다. 하지만 저는 글쓴이의 추론에 대해서는 동의하지 않습니다. 왜 그런지를 알려 드리죠…

우선, 의과대학의 높은 학비를 지불하지 않을 수 있는 방법이 있습니다. 네, 의과대학을 다니는 것에는 많은 비용이 듭니다. 하지만, 대부분의 학생들은 결코 전액을 지불하지 않습니다. 예를 들어, 대부분의 의과대학들은 종종 장학금을 지급합니다. 장학금을 받음으로써, 학생은 자신의 대출금을 상당히 감소시킬 수 있습니다. 또한 장학금을 제공해 주는 기관들도 있습니다. 몇몇 단체들과 병원들이 개인의 교육비를 지불해 줄 것입니다. 그에 대한 보답으로, 해당 의사는 졸업 후 몇 년 동안 그들을 위해 일을 해야 합니다. 그렇게 함으로써, 졸업 후에 빚이 없어질 수 있습니다.

병원 및 진료소에 어느 때보다 많은 서류 작업이 있는 것은 사실이지만, 의사들이 대부분의 일을 하는 것은 아닙니다. 대신, 간호사와 행정 직원들이 많은 서류 작업을 합니다. 의사들은 그중 적은 부분만을 하면 됩니다. 그리고 간호사들이 매년 양질의 교육을 받고 있습니다. 따라서 현재 많은 양식들을 처리할 수가 있습니다. 또한, 행정 직원들이 보험과 관련된 서류 작업을 책임지고 있습니다. 따라서, 어, 이는 1차 진료 의사들의 줄고 있는 이유가 되지 않습니다.

📁 Tandem Note-Taking

Reading	*Listening*
Main Idea: The United States is suffering from a shortage of primary care doctors.	**Main Idea:** It's true there are fewer primary care doctors these days. But I disagree with the writer's reasoning.
First Supporting Argument: One reason for this shortage concerns the great expense of medical school.	**First Supporting Argument:** There are ways to avoid paying the high costs of medical school.
Supporting Details: more than $50,000 a year; other charges as well; take out loans; huge debt to repay; make less money than other doctors	**Supporting Details:** most students never pay full price; get scholarships; get free schooling from organizations or hospitals
Second Supporting Argument: Another problem primary care doctors have is the large amount of paperwork they must do.	**Second Supporting Argument:** Nurses and administrators do a lot of the paperwork.
Supporting Details: work long hours because of paperwork; can't make money when doing paperwork	**Supporting Details:** doctors do little paperwork; nurses and other administrators do it

📁 Writing

Sample Response

The reading passage explains why there are not enough primary care doctors in the United States. The professor, however, casts doubt on the points made by the author of the reading passage.

To begin with, the professor points out that many students get scholarships to medical school. She says there are many ways for students to graduate with no debt to repay. This goes against the argument in the reading passage. The author states that medical school is very expensive. Plus, students have to spend money on other costs while in school. As a result, many of them finish school with huge amounts of debt.

The professor also mentions that doctors do not do very

much paperwork. This refutes the author of the reading passage, who believes that primary care doctors spend a lot of time doing paperwork. The professor claims that nurses and other employees actually fill out most of the forms.

Translation

읽기 지문은 미국에 1차 진료 의사들이 충분하지 않은 이유에 대해 설명하고 있다. 하지만, 교수는 읽기 지문을 쓴 사람이 제시한 요점에 대해 의문을 제기한다.

우선, 교수는 많은 학생들이 장학금을 받으면서 의과대학을 다닌다는 점을 지적한다. 그녀는 학생들이 갚아야 할 빚을 지지 않고서도 졸업을 할 수 있는 많은 방법들이 있다고 말한다. 이는 읽기 지문의 주장과 반대된다. 글쓴이는 의과대학의 비용이 매우 비싸다고 주장한다. 또한, 학생들은 학교에 다니는 동안 기타 비용을 지출해야 한다. 따라서, 다수의 학생들이 많은 빚을 지고서 학교를 마치게 된다.

교수는 또한 의사들이 그렇게 많은 서류 작업을 하는 것은 아니라고 말한다. 이는 읽기 지문의 글쓴이를 논박하는 것인데, 글쓴이는 1차 진료 의사들이 서류 작업을 하느라 많은 시간을 소비하고 있다고 믿는다. 교수는 실제로 간호사와 기타 직원들이 대부분의 양식을 작성하고 있다고 주장한다.

Task 2 Following Directions or Finding New Ways

📁 Planning

<table>
<tr><td>

Following Directions

Thesis Statement: I would prefer to have employees who are good at following directions.

First Supporting Idea: You always know what to expect from an employee who follows directions.

Supporting Examples: worker will follow boss's instructions; will not do anything different; follow boss's instructions at part-time job; boss likes me; coworker doesn't follow instructions; may get fired

Second Supporting Idea: Employees that follow directions rarely make mistakes.

Supporting Examples: cook at restaurant; follow cooking directions; no customer complaints; valuable employee

Conclusion: I think it is much better for employees to follow directions.

</td><td>

Finding New Ways

Thesis Statement: I believe that more employees should try to discover new and different methods of doing their jobs.

First Supporting Idea: Employees can use their creativity to come up with new and different ways to do their jobs.

Supporting Examples: inventors use creativity; find newer, better, and more efficient ways; advance because of creative spirit

Second Supporting Idea: Sometimes the methods people are using cause them to make many mistakes.

Supporting Examples: sister is computer programmer; found mistakes in programming method; fixed problem; no more mistakes

Conclusion: By finding new and different ways of doing their jobs, employees can make various improvements.

</td></tr>
</table>

📁 Writing

Sample Response 1: Following Directions

Some bosses like for their employees to be creative. But I disagree with them. I would prefer to have employees who are good at following directions.

First, you always know what to expect from an employee who follows directions. Thus a boss can tell a worker what to do, and the worker will do that. The worker will not do anything the boss did not tell him or her to do. I have a part-time job. I always follow my boss's instructions. My boss likes me a lot. However, one of my coworkers likes to do things his own way.

He insists that he knows how to do his job better than my boss does. My boss dislikes him very much because he does not follow directions. I think my coworker might get fired soon.

Second, employees that follow directions rarely make mistakes. Again, at my part-time job, I have never made any mistakes. I work at a fast-food restaurant. I am a cook there. I always follow the directions concerning how long to cook the food and at what temperature. The customers never complain about the food I make. They do not complain because I follow directions, so I do not make mistakes. That makes me a valuable employee at my restaurant.

Creativity can be a positive feature at some jobs. But I think it is much better for employees to follow directions.

Translation

어떤 상사들은 자신의 직원들이 창의적이기를 바란다. 하지만 나는 이에 동의하지 않는다. 나는 지시 사항을 잘 따르는 직원들이 있는 것이 더 낫다고 생각한다.

첫째, 지시 사항을 따르는 직원으로부터는 무엇을 기대할 수 있을지 항상 알 수가 있다. 따라서 상사가 직원에게 무엇을 하라고 말할 수 있으며, 그 직원은 그렇게 할 것이다. 그러한 직원은 상사가 자신에게 하라고 말하지 않은 것을 하려고 하지 않을 것이다. 나는 아르바이트를 하고 있다. 나는 항상 상사의 지시 사항을 따른다. 상사는 나를 매우 좋아한다. 하지만, 내 동료 중 한 명은 자신의 방법대로 일하는 것을 좋아한다. 그는 자신이 상사보다 일을 더 잘할 수 있는 방법을 알고 있다고 주장한다. 상사는 그가 지시 사항을 따르지 않기 때문에, 그를 매우 싫어한다. 나는 내 동료가 곧 해고될 것이라고 생각한다.

둘째, 지시 사항을 따르는 직원들은 실수를 하는 법이 거의 없다. 또 다시, 내 아르바이트 직장에서, 나는 결코 실수를 한 적이 없다. 나는 패스트푸드 식당에서 일을 한다. 그곳의 요리사이다. 나는 음식을 얼마나 오래 요리해야 하는지와 어떤 온도에서 요리해야 하는지에 관해 항상 지시 사항을 따르고 있다. 내가 만든 음식에 대해 고객들은 결코 불평을 하지 않는다. 내가 지시 사항을 따르기 때문에 불평을 하지 않는 것이며, 따라서 나는 실수를 하지 않는다. 그러한 점은 식당에서 나를 소중한 직원으로 만들고 있다.

몇몇 직장에서 창의성은 긍정적인 특성이 될 수 있다. 하지만 나는 직원들이 지시 사항을 따르는 것이 훨씬 더 좋다고 생각한다.

Sample Response 2: Finding New Ways

Many workers follow their boss's directions. However, I believe that more employees should try to discover new and different methods of doing their jobs.

The first reason I feel this way is that employees can use their creativity to come up with new and different ways to do their jobs. We progress because people get tired of doing activities in the same way. Inventors, for example, try to use their creativity to find newer, better, and more efficient ways to do work. Without this creative spirit, our technology would be much less advanced than it is today. We need people to act differently than others. That is how we progress.

The second reason I feel this way is that sometimes the methods people use cause them to make many mistakes. Therefore, people who look for new and different methods of doing something can keep from making these mistakes. For example, my sister works as a computer programmer. One time, her boss told her to use a certain programming method. But that method caused her to make many mistakes. She came up with a solution to that. Now, she does not make any mistakes at all. By being creative, she solved a problem.

By finding new and different ways of doing their jobs, employees can make various improvements. And that provides benefits for everyone. I wish more employees did that instead of just following directions.

많은 직원들이 상사의 지시 사항을 따르고 있다. 하지만, 나는 보다 많은 직원들이 일을 하는데 있어서 새롭고 특이한 방법들을 찾기 위해 노력해야 한다고 생각한다.

내가 그렇게 생각하는 첫 번째 이유는 직원들이 창의성을 이용하여 일을 처리할 수 있는 새롭고 특이한 방법들을 생각해 낼 수 있기 때문이다. 동일한 방법으로 행동을 하면 지치기 때문에 발전이 이루어지는 것이다. 예를 들어, 발명가들은 자신의 창의성을 이용하여 일을 하는데 보다 새롭고, 보다 뛰어나고, 그리고 보다 효율적인 방법들을 찾아내려고 노력한다. 창의력이 없다면, 우리의 기술은 현재 보다 훨씬 더 발전하지 못했을 것이다. 우리에게는 남들과 다르게 행동하는 사람들이 필요하다. 그것이 바로 우리가 발전을 이루어 낸 방법이다.

내가 그렇게 생각하는 두 번째 이유는 때때로 사람들이 사용하는 방식들이 많은 실수를 일으킨다는 점에 있다. 따라서, 무언가를 하는데 있어서 새롭고 다양한 방식을 찾는 사람들이 이러한 실수를 예방할 수 있다. 예를 들어, 내 누나는 컴퓨터 프로그래머로서 일하고 있다. 한 번은, 그녀의 상사가 그녀에게 특정 프로그래밍 방법을 사용하라고 말했다. 하지만 그러한 방법은 그녀로 하여금 많은 실수를 하도록 만들었다. 그녀는 그에 대한 해법을 찾아 냈다. 현재, 그녀는 전혀 실수를 하지 않는다. 창의적이었기 때문에, 그녀는 문제를 해결했다.

일을 하는데 있어서 새롭고 특이한 방법을 찾아냄으로써, 직원들은 다양한 발전을 이룰 수 있다. 그리고 그러한 점은 모두에게 혜택을 가져다 준다. 나는 보다 많은 직원들이, 단지 지시 사항만을 따르는 대신, 그렇게 하기를 바란다.

Unit 02

p.154

Task 1 Zoology: The American Burying Beetle

📂 Reading

Translation

북미산 송장벌레는 북아메리카의 토착 곤충 종이다. 이들은 사체 – 죽은 동물의 시체를 먹고 산다. 송장벌레는 한때 북아메리카 전역에서 서식했다. 미국의 35개 주에서 서식한다고 알려져 왔다. 하지만, 지난 세기 동안, 미국 내 송장벌레의 개체 수는 급감했다. 현재에는 단 5개 주에서만 발견되고 있다.

과학자들은 인간이 그들의 영역에 침입했기 때문에 미국산 송장벌레의 개체 수가 감소했다고 추측한다. 송장벌레는 사체만을 먹는다. 따라서 먹이를 먹기 위해서는 사체를 필요로 한다. 인간이 숲을 베어 내고 들을 개간함에 따라, 송장벌레의 서식지는 파괴되고 있다. 따라서 송장벌레가 살 수 있는 지역이 감소하고 있으며, 또한 이들이 먹이로 삼을 수 있는 동물들도 줄어들고 있다. 따라서, 개체 수가 감소하고 있는 것이다.

또한 송장벌레는 농부들이 사용하는 화학 물질에 의해서도 영향을 받고 있다. 송장벌레는 민감한 후각을 지니고 있다. 매우 먼 거리에서도 동물의 사체를 감지해 낼 수가 있다. 또한 죽은 지 얼마 되지 않은 동물들을 감지해 낼 수 있다. 하지만 농부들이 사용하는 특정 화학 물질들은 이들의 감각을 방해할 수 있다. 이러한 화학 물질들로 인해 송장벌레들은 먹이를 찾지 못하게 된다. 따라서 송장벌레들은 결국 굶어 죽는다.

📂 Listening

Script 🎧 3-02

W Professor: Look at the picture on page . . . page 104 in your textbooks. It's the American burying beetle. I doubt any of you have ever seen one in person. The reason is, um, that the beetle population has declined recently. The beetles used to live almost everywhere. Now, they're found only in a handful of states. Nobody knows why they're disappearing. Some people have made various suggestions. But each theory has holes in it.

The theory that humans are reducing the size of the beetle's habitat is appealing, but I can tell you that it simply is not true. First, as more people move to cities, lots of land is reverting to the wild. And remember that farmers are producing more food on less land these days. So the beetles should have more land to live on nowadays.

It's also impossible that chemicals used by farmers are interfering with the beetle's senses. You see, um, the beetle population started declining twenty years prior to the widespread use of these chemicals. In addition, remember that the beetles are not extinct. They're merely endangered. If the chemicals were harmful, the beetles would already be dead. After all, farmers have been using them for several decades. So I don't believe the chemicals are harming the beetles.

Translation

W Professor: 여러분 교재에 있는… 104쪽의 그림을 봐 주세요. 북미산 송장벌레입니다. 여러분 중에 직접 이를 본적이 있는 사람이 있는지 궁금하군요. 그 이유는, 음, 송장벌레의 개체 수가 최근 감소하고 있기 때문입니다. 송장벌레들은 한때 거의 모든 지역에서 살았습니다. 현재에는, 소수의 주에서만 발견될 뿐이죠. 이들이 왜 사라지고 있는지는 아무도 모릅니다. 몇몇 사람들이 다양한 추측을 하고 있습니다. 하지만 각각의 이론에는 맹점이 있습니다.

인간들이 송장벌레 서식지의 크기를 감소시키고 있다는 이론은 매력적이지만, 저는 여러분들께 그것이 사실과 다르다고 말씀드릴 수 있습니다. 우선, 보다 많은 사람들이 도시로 이주를 하고 있기 때문에, 많은 토지가 다시 야생 상태로 되돌아가고 있습니다. 그리고 오늘날 농부들은 적은 토지에서 많은 식량을 생산해 내고 있습니다. 따라서 현재 송장벌레들이 살 수 있는 지역은 더 넓어졌습니다.

또한 농부들이 사용하는 화학 물질이 송장벌레의 감각에 방해가 될 수도 있습니다. 아시겠지만, 음, 송장벌레의 개체 수는 이러한 화학 물질이 널리 사용되기 20년 전에 감소하기 시작했습니다. 또한, 송장벌레가 멸종한 것은 아니라는 점을 기억해 주세요. 단지 멸종 위기에 처해 있을 뿐입니다. 화학 물질이 해로운 것이라면, 송장벌레들은 이미 죽었을 것입니다. 어찌되었던, 농부들은 수십 년 동안 화학 물질을 사용해 왔으니까요. 따라서 저는 화학 물질이 송장벌레에게 피해를 입히고 있다고 생각하지 않습니다.

📂 Tandem Note-Taking

Reading	*Listening*
Main Idea: In the past century, the beetle population in the United States has declined dramatically.	**Main Idea:** Nobody knows why they're disappearing.
First Supporting Argument: Scientists suspect that the American burying beetle population has declined because humans have encroached on its territory.	**First Supporting Argument:** The theory that humans are reducing the size of the beetle's habitat is appealing, but I can tell you that it simply is not true.
Supporting Details: humans cut down forests and clear fields; less land to live on; fewer animals to feed on	**Supporting Details:** people move to cities; farmers use less land; is more land for beetles to live on
Second Supporting Argument: It is also possible that the beetles are being affected by chemicals used by farmers.	**Second Supporting Argument:** It's also impossible that chemicals used by farmers are interfering with the beetle's senses.
Supporting Details: acute sense of smell; use to find food; chemicals interfere with smell; can't find food; starve to death	**Supporting Details:** beetles began disappearing 20 years before chemical used; chemicals can't be harmful; if harmful, would have killed beetles already

📂 Writing

Sample Response

The professor discusses the decline of the American burying beetle. In her lecture, she refutes the two points made in the reading passage.

First, the professor talks about the decline in the beetle's habitat. According to the reading, humans have reduced the amount of land that the beetles can live on. But the professor stresses that there is more land available for beetles to live on today. She says that farmers are using less land and that more people are living in cities. So there is plenty of land for the beetles.

Second, the professor mentions the chemicals that farmers use. She does not believe that they are interfering with the beetle's senses. This is what the reading passage claims. But the professor says that the chemical are not harmful. She believes that, if they were harmful, the beetles would be extinct by now. Since they are still alive, then the chemicals are not harming them.

Translation

교수는 북미산 송장벌레의 감소에 관해 논의하고 있다. 강의에서, 그녀는 읽기 지문에서 제기된 두 가지 논지를 반박한다.

첫째, 교수는 송장벌레 서식지의 감소에 대해 이야기한다. 읽기 지문에 따르면, 인간들이 송장벌레가 살 수 있는 지역을 감소시키고 있다. 하지만 교수는 오늘날 송장벌레들이 살 수 있는 지역이 더 넓어졌다는 점을 강조한다. 그녀는 농부들이 토지를 더 적게 사용하고 있으며 보다 많은 사람들이 도시에서 살고 있다고 말한다. 따라서 송장벌레들에게는 많은 땅이 있다.

둘째, 교수는 농부들이 사용하는 화학 물질에 대해 언급한다. 그녀는 화학 물질이 송장벌레의 감각을 방해한다고 생각하지 않는다. 이는 읽기 지문이 주장하는 바이다. 하지만 교수는 화학 물질이 해롭지 않다고 말한다. 그녀는, 만약 해로운 것이라면, 송장벌레가 현재 멸종해 있을 것이라고 믿는다. 그들이 여전히 살고 있기 때문에, 화학 물질은 그들에게 해로운 것이 아니다.

Task 2 Helping Others

📁 Planning

<table>
<tr><td>Agree</td><td>Disagree</td></tr>
<tr><td>

Thesis Statement: I strongly believe that the younger generation today helps people more than previous generations did.

First Supporting Idea: So many young people volunteer nowadays.

Supporting Examples: volunteer at many places; young generation eager to help; volunteer at hospital; friends volunteer, too

Second Supporting Idea: Another way the young generation helps others is through the Internet.

Supporting Examples: friend runs website; helps people in Africa; donates money; visits Africa; is a teenager

Conclusion: Young people today help much more than people in past generations did.

</td><td>

Thesis Statement: The young generation does not provide that much help these days.

First Supporting Idea: The young generation today is extremely self-centered.

Supporting Examples: teens look out for selves; play video games; hang out; help less than parents and grandparents did

Second Supporting Idea: In the past, groups that helped others had many members, but that is not the case today.

Supporting Examples: Boy Scouts and Girl Scouts had many members in past; have few members today

Conclusion: Young people provide assistance for others much less than people in previous generations did.

</td></tr>
</table>

📁 Writing

Sample Response 1: Agree

I strongly believe that the younger generation today helps people more than previous generations did. I think this for a couple of reasons.

One is that so many young people volunteer nowadays. You can often see young people volunteering at hospitals, libraries, homeless shelters, and other places. These places are full of young people lending a hand. In the past, you rarely ever saw people doing that. But today's generation of young people truly wants to help people out. In fact, they are eager to provide assistance. I volunteer at a hospital twice a week. Most of my friends also volunteer their time. We do not want any money. We just want to improve people's lives.

Another way the young generation helps others is through the Internet. Thanks to the Internet, it is possible to help people all around the world. One of my friends runs a website to help starving children in Africa. He accepts donations and then sends the money to charity groups in Africa. He also organizes volunteers to visit Africa. He has been there twice himself. And he is still a teenager. There are many young people who use the Internet to help others. This was not possible for past generations to do.

It is easy to see how the young generation helps many people in need. Young people today do that much more than people in past generations did.

Translation

나는 오늘날 젊은 세대들이 기존 세대들보다 더 많이 사람들을 돕고 있다고 굳게 믿는다. 나는 두 가지 이유에서 그렇게 생각한다.

하나는 너무나 많은 젊은 사람들이 현재 자원 봉사를 하고 있기 때문이다. 병원, 도서관, 노숙자 쉼터, 그리고 기타 장소에서 젊은 사람들이 자원 봉사를 하는 것을 볼 수가 있다. 이러한 장소들은 도움을 주고 있는 젊은 사람들로 가득하다. 과거에는, 그렇게 하는 사람들을 거의 보지 못했다. 하지만 오늘날 젊은 세대의 사람들은 정말로 사람들을 돕고 싶어한다. 실제로, 이들은 도움을 주기를 갈망하고 있다. 나는 일주일에 두 번씩 병원에서 자원 봉사를 한다. 또한 내 친구들 대부분이 시간을 내서 자원 봉사를 하고 있다. 우리는 돈을 원하지 않는다. 단지 사람들의 삶을 향상시켜 주고 싶을 뿐이다.

젊은 세대들이 다른 사람들을 돕고 있는 또 다른 방법은 인터넷을 통해서이다. 인터넷 덕분에, 전 세계의 사람들을 돕는 것이 가능하다. 내 친구 중 한 명은 아프리카에서 굶고 아이들을 돕기 위한 웹사이트를 운영하고 있다. 그는 기부를 받아서 그 돈을 아프리카의 자선 단체에 보낸다. 또한 자원 봉사단을 조직하여 아프리카를 방문하고 있다. 그 자신이 그곳에 두 번 갔다 왔다. 그리고 그는 아직 십대이다. 인터넷을 이용하여 다른 사람들을 돕고 있는 많은 젊은 사람들이 있다. 기성 세대들이 그렇게 하는 것은 가능하지 않았다.

젊은 세대들이 도움이 필요한 많은 사람들을 어떻게 돕고 있는지는 쉽게 찾아볼 수 있다. 오늘날 젊은 사람들은 기성 세대들이 했던 것보다 훨씬 더 많이 그렇게 하고 있다.

Sample Response 2: Disagree

I have heard some people argue that the young generation helps others more than previous generations. I could not disagree more with this statement. The young generation does not provide that much help these days.

To begin with, the young generation today is extremely self-centered. They have no interest in helping other people. Today's young people only look out for themselves. I do not know of any teenagers who volunteer. Instead, they stay at home playing video games, or else they just hang out with their friends. Those actions do not help others. Those teenagers' parents' and grandparents' generations helped others much more than they do.

In the past, groups that helped others had many members, but that is not the case today. For example, the Boy Scouts and Girl Scouts were quite popular in the past. These groups do many activities. And one of them is volunteer work. In the past, the Boy Scouts and Girl Scouts had large memberships.

But they are shrinking in size today. In fact, many schools have no students in the Boy Scouts or Girl Scouts. One reason is that young people have no interest in helping others. So they do not want to join these groups or others like them.

I wish that the young generation wanted to help others, but that is not the case. Young people provide assistance for others much less than people in previous generations did.

Translation

나는 젊은 세대들이 기존 세대보다 더 많이 다른 사람들을 돕고 있다고 몇몇 사람들이 주장하는 것을 들어 본 적이 있다. 나는 이러한 진술에 결코 동의할 수 없다. 현재 젊은 세대들은 그처럼 많은 도움을 주고 있지 않다.

우선, 오늘날의 젊은 세대들은 극도로 자기 중심적이다. 다른 사람들을 돕는 일에는 전혀 관심이 없다. 오늘날 젊은 사람들은 자신의 이익만을 추구한다. 나는 자원 봉사를 하는 십대에 대해서 아는 바가 없다. 대신, 그들은 집에서 비디오 게임을 하거나, 혹은 친구들과 어울려 다닐 뿐이다. 그러한 행동은 다른 사람들을 돕지 못한다. 그러한 십대들의 부모 및 조부모 세대들이 그들보다 훨씬 더 많이 다른 사람들을 도왔다.

과거에는, 다른 사람들에게 도움을 주는 단체에 많은 회원들이 있었지만, 오늘날에는 더 이상 그렇지 않다. 예를 들면, Boy Scouts와 Girl Scouts는 과거에 꽤 인기가 좋았다. 이러한 단체는 많은 활동을 한다. 그리고 그중 하나가 자원 봉사이다. 과거, Boy Scouts와 Girl Scouts에는 많은 회원들이 있었다. 하지만 오늘날 그 규모는 작아지고 있다. 실제로, 많은 학교의 Boy Scouts와 Girl Scouts에 학생들이 없다. 한 가지 이유는 젊은 사람들이 다른 사람을 돕는 일에 관심이 없기 때문이다. 따라서 그들은 이러한 단체나 이와 같은 다른 단체에 가입하고 싶어하지 않는다.

나는 젊은 세대들이 다른 사람들을 돕기를 바라지만, 현실은 그렇지가 않다. 젊은 사람들은 다른 사람들을 돕는데 있어서 기존 세대의 사람들보다 훨씬 더 적은 도움을 주고 있다.

Unit 03
p.158

Task 1 Astronomy: The Ashen Light of Venus

📁 Reading

Translation

1643년 이래로, 금성을 관찰하던 사람들은 그 행성에서 이상한 점을 찾아냈다. 금성의 빛이 없는 부분에서 부드러운 빛이 방출되는 것처럼 보이는 것이다. 이는 금성의 애센광이라고 알려져 있다. 무엇으로 인해 이러한 일이 발생하는지는 아무도 모른다.

많은 사람들이 믿고 있는 한 가지 이론은 번개로 인해 금성에 빛이 생긴다는 것이다. 금성에는 매우 두꺼운 대기층이 있다. 따라서 그 표면에서는 종종 폭풍이 일어난다. 2007년, 인공위성인 *카시니*호가 토성으로 가는 도중 금성을 지나치게 되었다. 행성 가까이를 지나가면서, 여러 가지 관측을 했다. 때때로 번개에 의해 생성되는 몇 개의 저주파가 탐지되었다. 또한, 차후 NASA의 임무로, 금성에는 번개가 존재한다는 점이 확인되었다. 지구에서보다 더 많은 번개가 칠 수도 있다. 따라서 번개가 금성에서의 빛을 만들어낸다는 것은 가능한 일이다.

애센광은 금성으로 인해 만들어지는 것이 아니라, 그 대신 지구에 의해 만들어지는 것이라고 주장하는 사람들도 있다. 이러한 사람들은 지구의 대기가 금성에서 나오는 빛을 왜곡시킨다고 주장한다. 예를 들어, 공기 중에 습도가 높으면 대기 내에서 왜곡이 발생한다. 비와 눈과 같은 강수도 그렇게 할 수 있다. 이러한 날씨 상황에서 망원경을 통해 금성을 관찰하면, 잘못된 상을 보게 된다. 따라서 애센광은 환영에 불과할 수도 있다.

📁 Listening

Script  3-03

M Professor: Ever since Galileo first looked at the heavens with his telescope, people have scoured the night skies. During this process, they've learned a lot about the solar system. Yet there's one mystery we haven't solved. I'm referring to the Ashen Light of Venus. Some people believe they know what causes it, but I think they're wrong. Every theory has problems.

A few scientists claim that lightning causes it, but I happen to disagree with them. First of all, while there is lots of lightning on Venus, it's not that bright. There's no way that any telescope could see lightning on Venus from Earth. Remember that people have observed the Ashen Light since the 1600s. And their telescopes weren't any good. They couldn't possibly have seen weather conditions on another planet.

The suggestion that Earth's atmosphere creates the illusion of the Ashen Light is wrong as well. Think about it . . . People have observed the light from everywhere on the planet. They've seen it in all kinds of weather conditions. It's just not possible that all weather conditions on Earth create the illusion of Ashen Light on Venus. I don't believe it's possible. There has to be an explanation for the light. But neither of those two is correct.

Translation

M Professor: 갈릴레오가 망원경을 가지고 최초로 하늘을 관찰한 이래로, 사람들은 밤하늘을 면밀히 살펴보고 있습니다. 이러한 과정에서, 사람들은 태양계에 대해 많은 것을 알게 되었습니다. 하지만, 아직 해결되지 못한 한 가지 미스터리가 있습니다. 금성의 애센광을 말씀드리는 것입니다. 일부 사람들은 그것이 무엇으로 인해 생겨나는 것인지 알고 있다고 생각하지만, 저는 그들이 틀렸다고 생각합니다. 모든 이론에 문제가 있습니다.

몇몇 과학자들은 번개가 그 원인이라고 주장하지만, 저는 그들의 말에 동의하지 않습니다. 우선, 금성에서는 번개가 많이 치지만, 그렇게 밝지는 않습니다. 지구에서 금성의 번개를 볼 수 있는 망원경은 없습니다. 1600년대 이후로 사람들이 애센광을 관찰해 왔다는 점을 기억해 주세요. 그리고 그들의 망원경은 뛰어난 것이 아니었습니다. 다른 행성의 날씨 상황을 볼 수는 없었을 것입니다.

지구의 대기가 애센광이라는 환영을 만들어 낸다는 주장 또한 잘못된 것입니다. 생각해 보세요… 사람들은 지구 어디에서든 빛을 관찰해 왔습니다. 온갖 종류의 날씨 상황에서 보아 왔던 것이죠. 지구 상의 모든 날씨 상황에서 금성의 애센광이라는 환영이 만들어졌다는 것은 가능하지 않습니다. 저는 그것이 가능하지 않다고 믿습니다. 그러한 빛에 대한 설명이 있어야 합니다. 하지만 두 이론 중 어느 것도 맞지가 않습니다.

📁 Tandem Note-Taking

Reading	*Listening*
Main Idea: No one is sure what causes the Ashen Light of Venus to occur.	**Main Idea:** Every theory about the Ashen Light of Venus has problems.
First Supporting Argument: Lightning causes it.	**First Supporting Argument:** A few scientists claim that lightning causes it, but I happen to disagree with them.
Supporting Details: are storms on Venus; is known to be much lightning on Venus; maybe more than on Earth	**Supporting Details:** lightning isn't that bright; people saw Ashen Light with poor telescopes; couldn't have seen weather from Earth
Second Supporting Argument: The Ashen Light is not a product of Venus but comes from Earth instead.	**Second Supporting Argument:** The suggestion that Earth's atmosphere creates the illusion of the Ashen Light is wrong as well.
Supporting Details: Earth's atmosphere distorts images; certain weather conditions; creates illusion of light	**Supporting Details:** have observed light from everywhere on Earth; different weather conditions; can't all create illusion

Supporting Examples: doctors working on cure for disease; other team finds vital info; if share, doctors can find cure for disease; if don't share, can't find cure

Conclusion: People should announce all of their scientific discoveries to the world.

Conclusion: Scientists should not have to share their discoveries with others if they do not want to.

📁 Writing

Sample Response

The lecturer challenges two arguments that the reading passage makes about the Ashen Light of Venus. In doing this, the lecturer argues that no one knows what causes the light to occur.

The lecturer first talks about lightning causing the Ashen Light. The lecturer states that lightning cannot be so bright that people on Earth can see it. He notes that people observed it centuries ago. But their telescopes were of poor quality. They could not have identified weather conditions on Venus. So the lecturer challenges the claim made in the reading that lightning causes the Ashen Light.

The lecturer further refutes the notion that Earth's atmosphere causes an illusion that creates the Ashen Light. The writer claims that humidity, rain, and snow can cause the illusion of Ashen Light. But the professor says that people have observed the Ashen Light in all kinds of weather conditions. They have also seen the light from many different places on the planet.

Translation

교수는 읽기 지문에 제시되어 있는 금성의 애센광에 대한 두 가지 주장을 반박하고 있다. 그렇게 하면서, 교수는 무엇이 그러한 빛을 만들어 내는지에 대해 아무도 모르고 있다고 주장한다.

교수는 먼저 애센광을 일으키는 번개에 대해 이야기한다. 교수는 그러한 번개가 지구에 있는 사람들이 볼 수 있을 만큼 밝은 빛을 낼 수 없다고 주장한다. 그는 사람들이 수 세기 전에 그것을 관찰했다는 점에 주목한다. 하지만 그들의 망원경은 성능이 떨어졌다. 금성의 날씨 상황을 확인할 수 없었을 것이다. 따라서 교수는 읽기 지문에서 제시된 번개가 애센광을 일으킨다는 주장을 논박하고 있다.

교수는 더 나아가 지구의 대기가 애센광을 만들어 내는, 환영의 원인이라는 주장을 반박한다. 글쓴이는 습도, 비, 그리고 눈이 애센광이라는 환영을 만들어낼 수 있다고 주장한다. 하지만 교수는 사람들이 모든 종류의 날씨 상황 속에서 애센광을 관찰해 왔다고 말한다. 또한 그러한 빛을 지구의 여러 다양한 지역에서 지켜봐 왔다.

Task 2 Sharing Scientific Discoveries

📁 Planning

Agree	Disagree
Thesis Statement: I prefer that scientists share the news of their discoveries with others.	**Thesis Statement:** I disagree with the statement that scientists should share news about their discoveries with other people.
First Supporting Idea: They ought to let others, such as scientists, know about the discovery because they can help advance human knowledge.	**First Supporting Idea:** Scientists have no obligation to share their knowledge with others.
Supporting Examples: can benefit millions; if one person knows, others don't benefit; should share knowledge; can advance society	**Supporting Examples:** fund own research; don't have to share; no obligation to others
Second Supporting Idea: This knowledge can sometimes help other people make even more advances.	**Second Supporting Idea:** Some knowledge is too dangerous to share.
	Supporting Examples: found genetic makeup of deadly flu; others could use for bioterrorism; could kill millions; keep chemical and nuclear weapon info secret, too

📁 Writing

Sample Response 1: Agree

When scientists make a new discovery, they have a choice: They can announce the discovery. Or they can keep it secret. I prefer that scientists share the news of their discoveries with others.

They ought to let others, such as scientists, know about the discovery because they can help advance human knowledge. There are many scientific discoveries that can benefit millions of people around the world. However, if only one person knows about it, then no one gains from that knowledge. And if something happens to that person, the knowledge could be lost forever. Knowledge should be shared with others. This will improve the overall amount of knowledge humans have. And that will let us advance society further.

In addition, this knowledge can sometimes help other people make even more advances. For example, perhaps a team of doctors is working on a cure for a disease such as cancer. The team might lack some important information. If another group discovers that information and announces it to the world, then the other team of doctors can use it. They might be able to cure the disease they are studying. But, if the group keeps its discovery a secret, then the doctors might not find a cure for the disease.

Obviously, people should announce all of their scientific discoveries to the world. It will help people out considerably. And it could save a lot of lives.

Translation

과학자들이 새로운 발견을 하는 경우, 그들은 선택을 할 수 있다: 그러한 발견을 발표할 수도 있다. 혹은 그것을 비밀로 유지할 수도 있다. 나는 과학자들이 발견에 대한 소식을 다른 사람들과 공유하는 것이 더 낫다고 생각한다.

발견은 인류의 지식을 증대시키는데 도움이 될 수 있기 때문에, 그들은 과학자와 같은 다른 사람들이 그러한 발견에 대해 알 수 있도록 해야 한다. 전 세계 수백만 명의 사람들에게 혜택이 될 수 있는 많은 과학적 발견들이 존재한다. 하지만, 단 한 사람만이 그에 대해 알고 있다면, 누구도 그러한 지식으로부터 이익을 얻을 수 없다. 그리고 그러한 사람에게 무슨 일이 발생한다면, 그 지식은 영원히 손실될 것이다. 지식은 다른 사람들과 공유되어야 한다. 이로써 인류가 가지고 있는 지식의 전체적인 양이 증대될 것이다. 그리고 우리는 사회를 보다 더 발전시키게 될 것이다.

또한, 이러한 지식은 때때로 다른 사람들이 더 많은 발전을 이루는데 도움이 될 수 있다. 예를 들어, 한 팀의 의사들이 암과 같은 질병의 치료에 관한 연구를 하고 있을 수 있다. 이러한 팀에는 몇 가지 중요한 정보가 결여되어 있을 수 있다. 또 다른 그룹이 그러한 정보를 발견해서 이를 세상에 알린다면, 다른 팀의 의사들이 그것을 이용할 수 있다. 자신들이 연구하던 질병을 치료할 수 있게 될 것이다. 하지만, 그러한 그룹이 자신의 발견을 비밀로 유지한다면, 의사들은 질병에 대한 치료법을 찾지 못하게 될 것이다.

분명, 모든 과학적 발견들은 세상에 알려져야 한다. 그럼으로써 사람들은 막대한 도움을 받게 될 것이다. 그리고 이로써 많은 생명을 구하게 될 것이다.

Sample Response 2: Disagree

I disagree with the statement that scientists should share news about their discoveries with other people. I do not believe that scientists have to do that at all.

Many scientists do research to satisfy their own personal curiosity. So they have no obligation to share their knowledge with others. After all, these scientists use their own money to fund their research. No one else is paying for it. So they can do whatever they want with their research. If they want to share it, that is fine. If they do not want to share it, that is fine, too. We might wish that they would share important discoveries. But they do not have to.

Furthermore, some knowledge is too dangerous to share. I recently read about some scientists that had determined the genetic makeup for a deadly strain of the flu. If they released that information, other people could use that to create a very harmful virus. Those people could use the virus for bioterrorism. That could kill millions of people. Additionally, I think that discoveries about chemical or nuclear weapons should remain secret as well. In my opinion, it is sometimes better not to reveal certain knowledge to others.

Scientists should not have to share their discoveries with others if they do not want to. In some cases, it is actually desirable that they not share their knowledge. The results could be disastrous.

Translation

나는 과학자들이 자신의 발견에 관한 소식을 다른 사람들과 공유해야 한다는 주장에 동의하지 않는다. 나는 과학자들이 전혀 그럴 필요가 없다고 생각한다.

많은 과학자들은 개인적인 호기심을 충족시키기 위해 연구를 한다. 따라서 자신의 지식을 다른 사람들과 공유할 의무는 없다. 어찌되었든, 이러한 과학자들은 자신의 돈을 사용하여 연구비를 마련한다. 다른 어떤 사람들도 그 비용을 지불해 주지 않는다. 따라서 그들은 연구에 있어서 그것이 무엇이든 원하는 것을 할 수 있다. 그것을 공유하고자 한다면, 그럴 수 있다. 그것을 공유하고자 하지 않는다면, 그 또한 그렇게 할 수 있다. 우리는 그들이 중요한 발견들을 공유하기를 바랄 수 있다. 하지만 그들이 꼭 그렇게 해야 하는 것은 아니다.

게다가, 일부 지식들은 공유하기에 너무나 위험하다. 나는 최근에 치명적인 독감 바이러스에 대한 유전적 성분을 밝혀낸 몇몇 과학자들에 대한 글을 읽었다. 그들이 그러한 정보를 발표한다면, 다른 사람들이 이를 이용하며 매우 해로운 바이러스를 만들어 낼 수도 있다. 그러한 사람들은 바이러스를 이용하여 생물학 무기를 이용한 테러를 저지를 수도 있을 것이다. 그러면 수백만 명의 사람들이 목숨을 잃게 될 것이다. 또한, 나는 화학무기 혹은 핵무기에 관한 발견도 비밀로 유지되어야 한다고 생각한다. 내 의견으로, 때로는 다른 사람들에게 특정 정보를 공개하지 않는 것이 더 낫다.

자신이 원하지 않는 경우에, 과학자들이 자신의 발견을 다른 사람들과 공유해야 할 필요는 없다. 일부 경우에는, 실제로 자신들의 지식을 공유하지 않는 것이 바람직하다. 그 결과가 끔찍한 것이 될 수도 있다.

Unit 04

p.162

Task 1 Zoology: The Ivory-Billed Woodpecker

Reading

Translation

큰 흑백색 딱따구리는 한때 미국의 동남부에 서식했던 딱따구리의 한 종이다. 인간의 영역이 확대됨에 따라, 이 딱따구리의 개체 수는 1800년대에 감소하기 시작했다. 오늘날에는, 멸종된 종으로 여겨진다.

하지만, 일부 사람들은 그러한 딱따구리가 여전히 살아있다고 주장한다. 최근, 한 사람이 큰 흑백색 딱따구리라고 주장하는 새의 사진을 찍어 왔다. 사진 속의 새는 분명 큰

흑백색 딱따구리이다. 하지만 사진의 화질이 좋지 않다. 따라서 사진으로부터 세부적인 사항을 알아내는 것이 어렵다. 큰 흑백색 딱따구리는 쉽게 알아볼 수 있는, 눈에 잘 띄는 하얗고 빨간 무늬를 가지고 있다. 하지만, 사진 속 딱따구리는 그러한 색을 가지고 있는 것처럼 보이지 않는다. 따라서 큰 흑백색 딱따구리가 아닐 가능성이 높다.

지난 몇 년 간, 몇몇 학자들이 큰 흑백색 딱따구리의 둥지를 찾기 시작했지만, 아무것도 찾아 내지 못했다. 이 새들은 죽은 나무의 몸통 안에 둥지를 튼다. 학자들은 넓은 습지대 지역을 탐사했다. 딱따구리들이 둥지를 트는데 선호하는 지역이다. 광범위한 조사에도 불구하고, 단 하나의 큰 흑백색 딱따구리의 둥지도 발견되지 않았다. 큰 흑백색 딱따구리가 여전히 살고 있다는 증거는 없다. 몇 년 동안 한 마리도 보이지 않았다. 아마도 멸종했을 것이다.

Listening

Script 🎧 3-04

M Professor: For many years, people believed that the ivory-billed woodpecker had gone extinct. However, in 2004, a team of scientists from a university went to a swamp in Arkansas. They claimed they found evidence the woodpecker was still alive. Some people don't believe them though.

Then, a little later, a person produced a picture. According to him, the bird in the picture was an ivory-billed woodpecker. The quality of the picture was low. So some people doubt that it's actually an ivory-billed woodpecker. I, however, disagree. First, the person saw the bird. He knows a lot about birds. And he claimed it was an ivory-billed woodpecker. So, uh, even though the picture isn't good . . . we have an eyewitness. He got an up-close look at the bird. And I believe him.

Sometime later, some scientists started actively looking for ivory-billed woodpecker nests. They didn't find any. That, they said, proved that the birds were extinct. Well, um, let me tell you about their nesting habits. These birds don't build nests close to one another. In fact, you might only find a single nest in an area covering several square kilometers. In other words, I wouldn't expect the scientists to find any nests. They're just too hard to find in general.

Translation

M Professor: 수년 동안, 사람들은 큰 흑백색 딱따구리가 멸종했다고 믿고 있었습니다. 하지만, 2004년, 한 대학의 과학자 팀이 아칸소 주의 습지대를 찾아갔습니다. 이들은 자신들이 그 딱따구리가 여전히 살고 있다는 증거를 발견해 냈다고 주장했습니다. 하지만 일부 사람들은 그들의 말을 믿지 않습니다.

이후, 얼마 후에, 한 사람이 사진을 찍었습니다. 그에 의하면, 사진 속의 새는 큰 흑백색 딱따구리였습니다. 사진의 화질은 좋지 않았습니다. 그래서 몇몇 사람들은 그것이 실제 큰 흑백색 딱따구리인지에 대해 의심을 하고 있습니다. 하지만, 저는 그들의 말에 동의하지 않습니다. 먼저, 그 사람은 새를 보았습니다. 그는 새에 대해 많이 알고 있습니다. 그리고 그것이 큰 흑백색 딱따구리라고 주장했습니다. 따라서, 어, 화질이 좋지 않더라고… 우리에게는 증인이 있는 것입니다. 그는 그 새를 가까이에서 보았습니다. 그리고 저는 그의 말을 믿습니다.

얼마 후, 몇몇 과학자들이 적극적으로 큰 흑백색 딱따구리의 둥지를 찾기 시작했습니다. 그들은 아무것도 찾아내지 못했습니다. 그러한 점은, 그들이 말하길, 그 새가 멸종했다는 점을 입증해 주는 것이었습니다. 글쎄요, 음, 그들이 둥지를 트는 습성에 대해 제가 말씀을 드리죠. 이 새들은 서로 가까운 곳에 둥지를 짓지 않습니다. 실제로, 몇 평방 킬로미터에 걸쳐 있는 지역에서 단 하나의 둥지만을 찾게 될 수도 있습니다. 즉, 저는 과학자들이 둥지를 찾아낼 것이라고 예상하지 않았습니다. 일반적으로 찾기가 너무나 어렵습니다.

📁 Tandem Note-Taking

<table>
<tr><td colspan="2" align="center">●   ●</td></tr>
<tr><td align="center">Reading</td><td align="center">Listening</td></tr>
<tr><td>

Main Idea: The ivory-billed woodpecker is considered extinct today.

First Supporting Argument: The picture does not really show an ivory-billed woodpecker.

Supporting Details: picture is low quality; can't get details; no distinct markings in picture

Second Supporting Argument: In the past few years, some researchers began looking for ivory-billed woodpecker nests yet found nothing.

Supporting Details: explored swampland; didn't find woodpecker nests; no evidence are still alive

</td><td>

Main Idea: It is possible that the birds are still alive today.

First Supporting Argument: The person who took the picture believes the bird is an ivory-billed woodpecker.

Supporting Details: person saw the bird; knows a lot about birds; professor believes him

Second Supporting Argument: Finding ivory-billed woodpecker nests is very difficult.

Supporting Details: don't build nests close to one another; only one in several square kilometers; too hard to find nests

</td></tr>
</table>

📁 Writing

Sample Response

The professor believes that there is evidence showing that the ivory-billed woodpecker is still alive. The professor's arguments challenge those made by the writer of the reading passage.

The professor states that there is a recent picture showing an ivory-billed woodpecker. While the picture is not clear, the professor says that the person who took the picture knows about birds. The photographer believes the picture shows an ivory-billed woodpecker. So the professor believes him. This counters the argument made in the reading passage. The writer claims that the picture does not show the distinctive colors of the ivory-billed woodpecker.

The professor further claims that he expected the researchers looking for ivory-billed woodpecker nests to fail. He mentions that the birds build their nests very far apart. As a result, finding their nests in swampland would be impossible. This refutes the writer of the reading passage. The writer believes that the scientists should have found some nests in the swamp.

Translation

교수는 큰 흑백색 딱따구리가 여전히 살고 있다는 증거가 존재한다고 믿는다. 교수의 주장은 읽기 지문을 쓴 사람의 주장과 반대되는 것이다.

교수는 큰 흑백색 딱따구리를 보여 주는 최근의 사진이 있다고 말한다. 사진이 선명하지는 않지만, 교수는 사진을 찍은 사람이 새에 대해 아는 사람이라고 말한다. 사진을 찍은 사람은 그 사진이 큰 흑백색 딱따구리를 나타낸다고 믿고 있다. 따라서 교수는 그의 말을 믿는다. 이는 읽기 지문에서 제기된 주장과 반대된다. 글쓴이는 그러한 사진 속에 큰 흑백색 딱따구리의 눈에 잘 띄는 색깔이 나타나 있지 않다고 주장한다.

더 나아가 교수는 큰 흑백색 딱따구리 둥지를 찾던 학자들이 실패할 것으로 예상했다고 주장한다. 그는 그 새들이 매우 멀리 떨어져서 둥지를 짓는다고 언급한다. 그 결과, 습지대에서 그들의 둥지를 찾아내는 것은 불가능한 일이 될 것이다. 이는 읽기 지문을 쓴 사람을 논박하는 것이다. 글쓴이는 과학자들이 습지대에서 몇몇 둥지들을 찾아낼 수도 있었을 것이라고 믿었다.

Task 2 Setting Aside Land to Protect Animals and Plants

📁 Planning

<table>
<tr><td colspan="2" align="center">●   ●</td></tr>
<tr><td align="center">Agree</td><td align="center">Disagree</td></tr>
<tr><td>

Thesis Statement: I consider it important for the government to set aside land to protect wild animals and plants for future generations.

First Supporting Idea: We must have a diversity of species on the planet.

Supporting Examples: many species extinct or endangered; dying because of humans; cut down rainforests; pollution; should protect

Second Supporting Idea: Plants and animals provide many benefits to humans.

Supporting Examples: medicines come from plants and plant products; undiscovered species; could cure illnesses or diseases

Conclusion: Humans are rapidly destroying the habitats of animals and plants, so the government should set aside land to preserve them.

</td><td>

Thesis Statement: I do not like the idea of the government setting aside land to protect wild animals and plants.

First Supporting Idea: I do not believe that there are many animals or plants in danger of going extinct.

Supporting Examples: most people live in cities; cover small area; other areas unpopulated; lots of room for plants and animals

Second Supporting Idea: The government should not be involved in something like this.

Supporting Examples: government is inefficient; let private groups preserve land; will do better job than government

Conclusion: The government has no business getting involved in creating preserves for animals and plants.

</td></tr>
</table>

📁 Writing

Sample Response 1: Agree

I agree with the statement. I consider it important for the government to set aside land to protect wild animals and plants for future generations.

To start, we must have a diversity of species on the planet. Nowadays, many animal and plant species have gone extinct or are endangered. Human actions are often the reasons that these animals and plants are dying. For instance, when humans cut down rainforests, they destroy the habitats of many animals and plants. In addition, pollution created by humans kills many other species. It is therefore important to set aside land for animals and plants to make sure we have a wide variety of species on the planet. We ought to protect all of these species.

Also, plants and animals provide many benefits to humans. For instance, there are a lot of medicines that come from plants and plant products. There are also many species of plants that humans have not discovered yet. Many of these plants are in the Earth's rainforests. It is possible that some of these plants could be the key to curing illnesses or diseases such as cancer. Because of that, we should make sure to preserve the lands that these plants grow on. Saving these plants could help humanity in the future.

Humans are rapidly destroying the habitats of animals and plants, so the government should set aside land to preserve them. Doing that will greatly help future generations.

나는 그러한 주장에 동의한다. 나는 정부가 미리 세대를 위하여 야생 동식물을 보호하기 위한 지역을 따로 설정해 두는 것이 중요하다고 생각한다.

우선, 지구 상에는 다양한 종이 있어야 한다. 오늘날, 많은 동식물의 종이 멸종했거나 멸종 위기에 처해 있다. 종종 인간의 활동이 이러한 동식물들이 소멸하고 있는 이유가 된다. 예를 들어, 인간이 산림을 벌목하면, 많은 동식물들의 서식처가 파괴된다. 또한, 인간이 만든 오염으로 인해 기타 많은 종들이 목숨을 잃고 있다. 따라서 지구 상에 다양한 종이 있도록 하기 위해서 동식물을 위한 지역을 따로 설정해 두는 것이 중요하다. 우리는 이러한 모든 종들을 보호해야만 한다.

또한, 식물과 동물들은 인간에게 많은 혜택을 가져다 준다. 예를 들어, 식물과 식물 제품으로부터 비롯되는 많은 의약품들이 있다. 또한 인간이 아직까지 발견해 내지 못한 많은 종의 식물들도 있다. 이러한 식물 중 다수는 지구의 우림 지대에 있다. 이러한 몇몇 식물들은 암과 같은 질병이나 질환을 치료하는데 실마리가 될 수도 있다. 그러한 점 때문에, 우리는 이러한 식물들이 자라고 있는 지역을 반드시 보존해야 한다. 이러한 식물들을 보호한다면 차후 인간에게 도움을 줄 수 있을 것이다.

인간들이 빠르게 동식물들의 서식지를 파괴시키고 있기 때문에, 정부는 그들을 보호하기 위한 지역을 따로 설정해 두어야 한다. 그렇게 함으로써 미래의 세대에게 도움을 줄 수 있을 것이다.

Sample Response 2: Disagree

I do not like the idea of the government setting aside land to protect wild animals and plants. There are two reasons that I feel this way.

First of all, I do not believe that there are many animals or plants in danger of going extinct. There are huge areas around my country that have no people in them. In fact, almost the entire population of my country lives in large cities. These cities take up very little space in the country. The rest of the country is mostly unpopulated. So there is plenty of space for animals to live and plants to grow. Therefore they already have enough room. We do not need to set aside more land for them.

Another reason is that the government should not be involved in something like this. Governments do not do anything efficiently. If the government sets aside land, then there will likely be many problems. On the other hand, if private groups want to purchase land to preserve it, then I support their decision. People who genuinely care for nature are members of these private groups. If they create nature preserves, then they will probably be very effective. As a result, plants and animals will be preserved without any government involvement.

The government has no business getting involved in creating preserves for animals and plants. So I disagree with the statement.

Translation

나는 정부가 야생 동식물 보호를 위해 지역을 따로 설정해 두어야 한다는 생각에 찬성하지 않는다. 내가 그렇게 생각하는 것에는 두 가지 이유가 있다.

우선, 나는 멸종 위기를 겪고 있는 동식물이 많다고 생각하지 않는다. 우리 나라에는 사람이 살지 않은 거대한 지역이 있다. 실제, 우리 나라 전체 인구의 거의 대부분이 대도시에서 살고 있다. 이러한 도시들은 우리 나라에서 매우 적은 면적만을 차지한다. 우리 나라의 나머지 지역에서는 통상 사람들이 살지 않는다. 따라서 동물들이 살고 식물들이 자랄 수 있는 장소는 많다. 그러므로, 그들에게는 이미 충분한 공간이 있다. 우리가 그들을 위해 더 많은 지역을 따로 설정해 둘 필요는 없다.

또 다른 이유는 정부가 이와 같은 일에 개입해서는 안 되기 때문이다. 정부는 효율적으로 일을 하지 않는다. 정부가 토지를 따로 설정해 둔다면, 아마도 많은 문제들이 생기게 될 것이다. 반면, 민간 단체가 보호를 목적으로 토지를 구입하고자 한다면, 나는 그들의 결정을 지지한다. 성실하게 자연을 돌보는 사람들은 이러한 민간 단체의 회원들이다. 그들이 자연 보호 구역을 만든다면, 매우 효과적일 가능성이 높다. 따라서, 정부의 개입 없이도 식물 및 동물들은 보존이 될 것이다.

정부에게는 동식물들을 위한 보호 지역을 설정할 권리가 없다. 따라서 나는 그러한 주장에 동의하지 않는다.

Unit 05

p.166

Task 1 Marine Biology: Turtle Exclusion Devices

Reading

Translation

새우잡이들은 – 새우를 잡는 어부들은 – 종종 해저까지 닿는 그물을 친다. 이러한 그물에는 새우 이외의 바다거북과 같은 동물들도 잡힌다. 따라서, 새우잡이들은 바다거북 어획 방지 장비(TED)가 있는 그물을 사용한다. TED는 거북들이 그물에서 빠져나갈 수 있도록 해준다. 따라서 목숨을 잃는 거북들이 줄고 있다. 하지만 많은 TED들이 제대로 작동하지 않고 있다. 따라서 새우잡이들의 그물로 인해 여전히 많은 거북들이 죽고 있다.

이러한 문제를 해결하기 위해 몇몇 사람들이 다양한 방법들을 제안하고 있다. 하나의 아이디어는 모든 새우잡이들이 매분 마다 그물을 표면으로 걷어 올리는 것이다. 거북들은 수중에서 호흡을 할 수 없다. 따라서 공기 중의 산소를 호흡하기 위해 표면으로 올라와야 한다. 많은 거북들이 그물에 걸려 있을 때 물에 빠져 죽는다. 하지만, 새우잡이들이 그물을 던진 후 곧바로 표면으로 걷어 올리면, 익사하는 거북의 수는 줄어들 것이다.

또 다른 제안은 TED를 더 크게 만드는 것이다. 많은 바다거북들은 상당히 큰 크기로 자란다. 예를 들어, 몇몇 붉은바다거북들은 길이가 2.5미터 이상이 될 수도 있다. 무게는 130킬로그램 이상으로 나갈 수 있다. 이처럼 커다란 거북들은 TED에서 빠져나올 수 없다. 그러한 장비를 보다 크게 만듦으로써, 거북들은 빠져나갈 수 있게 될 것이다. 그리고 새우잡이들도 계속해서 충분한 양의 새우를 포획할 수 있을 것이다.

Listening

Script 🔊 3-05

W Professor: TEDs are a great idea. They've saved the lives of many turtles. Yet sea turtles are endangered. We should do everything possible to save them. Some people have made a few suggestions. Yet I don't think they're satisfactory.

One suggestion is to instruct shrimpers to bring their nets to the surface every few minutes. That's a great idea, but it's impractical. Firstly, shrimpers insist that their nets need to be underwater for a long period of time. Otherwise, they won't catch enough shrimp. Also, even if this suggestion becomes a law, it would be impossible to enforce. After all, you can't put government agents on every boat. I just don't see how this suggestion would work.

Some also claim that TEDs should be made larger, but I don't think that's practical either. There are two reasons why . . . One, the shrimpers say that, uh, increasing the size of TEDs might cause them to catch fewer shrimp. Two, the shrimpers already paid a large amount of money to purchase TEDs for their nets. If we make them buy larger ones, they'll have to spend even more money. Shrimpers don't make that much money to begin with. Adding extra costs might cause some to go bankrupt.

Translation

W Professor: TED는 멋진 아이디어입니다. 많은 거북들의 목숨을 보호해 주죠. 하지만 바다거북은 멸종 위기에 처해 있습니다. 우리는 그들을 구하기 위해 할 수 있는 모든 일들을 해야 합니다. 몇몇 사람들이 몇 가지의 제안을 하고 있습니다. 하지만 저는 그것들이 만족스러운 것이라고 생각하지 않습니다.

하나의 제안은 새우잡이들에게 매분 마다 그물을 걷어 올리라고 지시하는 것입니다. 멋진 아이디어지만, 현실적이지 않습니다. 먼저, 새우잡이들은 자신의 그물이 장시간

수중에 있어야 한다고 주장합니다. 그렇지 않으면, 충분한 새우를 잡지 못하게 될 것입니다. 또한, 이러한 제안이 법으로 제정된다면, 법을 집행하는 것도 불가능할 것입니다. 어찌되었든, 정부 요원들을 모든 배에 태울 수는 없으니까요. 이러한 제안이 얼마나 효과가 있을지는 저는 잘 모르겠습니다.

또한 일부 사람들은 TED가 더 크게 만들어져야 한다고 주장하지만, 저는 그것 역시 현실적이지 않다고 생각합니다. 왜 그런지에 대한 두 가지 이유가 있는데… 하나는, 새우잡이들이, 어, TED의 크기를 증대시키면 그들이 잡게 되는 새우의 양이 더 적어질 것이라고 말하기 때문입니다. 둘째, 새우잡이들은 그물용 TED를 구입하기 위해 이미 막대한 양의 돈을 지불했습니다. 그들로 하여금 더 큰 것을 구입하도록 한다면, 그들은 훨씬 더 많은 돈을 소비해야 할 것입니다. 새우잡이들은 그렇게 할 수 있을 정도로 많은 돈을 벌지 못합니다. 추가 비용을 부담하게 되면 일부는 파산할 수도 있습니다.

📁 Tandem Note-Taking

<table>
<tr><td>

Reading

Main Idea: TEDs should save sea turtles, but they do not always work properly.

First Supporting Argument: One idea is to make sure that all shrimpers bring their nets to the surface every few minutes.

Supporting Details: turtles can't breathe underwater; need air; bring nets up to surface quickly; turtles don't drown

Second Supporting Argument: People should make TEDs larger.

Supporting Details: some turtles very large; if TEDs larger, then big turtles can escape

</td><td>

Listening

Main Idea: The suggestions made to save sea turtles are not effective.

First Supporting Argument: Having shrimpers bring their nets to the surface every few minutes is impractical.

Supporting Details: shrimpers say nets should be underwater long time; impossible to enforce

Second Supporting Argument: Some also claim that TEDs should be made larger, but I don't think that's practical either.

Supporting Details: larger TEDs means will catch fewer shrimp; TEDS are expensive; might make shrimpers go bankrupt

</td></tr>
</table>

📁 Writing

Sample Response

The lecturer claims that two of the solutions to the killing of sea turtles by shrimpers would not be effective. She challenges the claims made in the reading passage. The writer of the reading passage believes both solutions will work.

The first point the lecturer challenges concerns making shrimpers raise their nets every few minutes. According to the reading, this will let sea turtles caught in the nets breathe. Thus the turtles will not drown. The lecturer thinks this will not work for two reasons. First, the shrimpers will not agree to it. Second, no one can make sure the shrimpers will obey the law.

The second point the lecturer challenges concerns the size of turtle exclusion devices (TED). The lecturer says that shrimpers will not want to buy more TEDs. Also, larger TEDs will make shrimpers catch fewer shrimp. The writer of the reading passage thinks that increasing the size of TEDs will let large turtles escape. The lecturer disagrees though.

Translation

교수는 새우잡이에 의해 바다거북이 죽고 있는 문제에 관한 두 가지 해결 방안이 효과적이지 않을 것이라고 주장한다. 그녀는 읽기 지문에서 제기된 주장들을 반박하고 있다. 읽기 지문을 쓴 사람은 두 가지 해결 방안 모두 효과가 있을 것이라고 생각한다.

교수가 반박하는 첫 번째 논지는 새우잡이로 하여금 매분 마다 그물을 건져 올리도록 하는 것과 관련된 것이다. 읽기 지문에 따르면, 이로써 그물에 잡힌 바다거북이들이 호흡

할 수 있게 될 것이다. 따라서 거북들은 익사하지 않을 것이다. 교수는 두 가지 이유로 이것이 효과가 없을 것이라고 생각한다. 첫째, 새우잡이들이 동의하지 않을 것이다. 둘째, 새우잡이들이 법을 준수할 것인지는 아무도 확신할 수 없다.

교수가 반박하는 두 번째 논지는 바다거북 어획 방지 장비(TED)의 크기와 관련된 것이다. 교수는 새우잡이들이 더 이상의 TED를 구입하는 것을 원치 않을 것이라고 말한다. 또한, 보다 큰 TED는 새우잡이들로 하여금 보다 적은 양의 새우를 잡도록 만들 것이다. 읽기 지문을 쓴 사람은 TED의 크기를 증가시킴으로써 크기가 큰 거북들이 빠져나가게 될 것이라고 생각한다. 하지만 교수는 이에 동의하지 않는다.

Task 2 A Good Location or a Good Friend

📁 Planning

<table>
<tr><td>

A Good Location

Thesis Statement: When I travel, I think that the location is more important.

First Supporting Idea: When I travel, I love to visit new places.

Supporting Examples: took trip to Europe; visited several cities; saw many sights; had greatest trip of life

Second Supporting Idea: The location can turn a good trip into a great one.

Supporting Examples: cousin took trip to Hawaii; argued a lot; should have had bad trip; but were in Hawaii, so enjoyed their vacation

Conclusion: It is clear to me that the location is the most important thing when going on a trip.

</td><td>

A Good Friend

Thesis Statement: A good friend is much more important when traveling than going to a good location.

First Supporting Idea: There are very few people who enjoy traveling alone or with people they dislike.

Supporting Examples: friend provides companionship; enjoy experiences more when with friend

Second Supporting Idea: A good friend can also help make a bad trip a good one.

Supporting Examples: went to U.S. with friend; car broke down; expensive to fix; lost time; friend was positive; both had fun

Conclusion: I always make sure to travel with a good friend. That way, I know that I will enjoy my trip.

</td></tr>
</table>

📁 Writing

Sample Response 1: A Good Location

Some people prefer to go on trips with a good friend. However, when I travel, I think that the location is more important.

When I travel, I love to visit new places. As a result, the location is of great importance to me. Last year, I went to several cities in Europe. I visited Rome, Venice, Athens, and Prague. I saw all kinds of amazing sights in those cities. I got to visit several museums and art galleries, too. It was the greatest trip of my life. For me, the location of my trip was crucial. I could not have had the same experience by traveling to a place near my home.

Additionally, the location can turn a good trip into a great one. For example, my cousin and his family traveled to Hawaii last year. On the trip, everyone in his family argued all the time. They got into several fights. Normally, that would make a vacation be terrible. However, they were on vacation in a tropical paradise for two weeks. So, even though they fought a lot, all of them still had a great trip. And the reason for this was the location of their trip.

It is clear to me that the location is the most important thing when going on a trip. I recommend that everyone think carefully about where they are going on their next vacation.

Translation

어떤 사람들은 친한 친구와 함께 여행하는 것을 선호한다. 하지만, 내가 여행을 하는 경우라면, 장소가 더 중요하다고 생각한다.

여행을 할 때, 나는 새로운 장소들을 찾아가 보는 것을 좋아한다. 그 결과, 내게는 장소가 매우 중요하다. 작년, 나는 유럽의 몇몇 도시에 가보았다. 로마, 베니스, 아테네, 그리고 프라하를 방문했다. 나는 그러한 도시에서 온갖 종류의 멋진 광경들을 보았다. 또한 몇 군데의 박물관과 미술관에도 가보았다. 내 인생에서 가장 멋진 여행이었다. 나로서는, 여행 장소가 매우 중요하다. 집에서 멀지 않은 장소로 여행을 떠났다면 그와 똑같은 경험을 하지는 못했을 것이다.

또한, 장소는 즐거운 여행을 굉장한 여행으로 바꾸어 놓을 수 있다. 예를 들어, 내 사촌과 그의 가족들은 작년에 하와이로 여행을 갔다. 여행에서, 가족 모두는 항상 말다툼을 벌였다. 몇 차례 싸움을 벌이기도 했다. 보통, 그런 일이 있으면 휴가를 망치게 된다. 하지만, 그들은 2주 동안 열대 지방의 낙원과 같은 곳에서 휴가를 보냈다. 따라서, 많이 싸웠을지라도, 그들 모두는 멋진 여행을 보냈다. 그리고 그러한 이유는 바로 여행 장소 때문이었다.

여행을 하는 경우에 장소가 가장 중요한 점이라는 점은 내게 분명하다. 나는 모든 사람들이 다음 휴가로 어디에 갈 것인지에 관하여 주의 깊게 생각해 볼 것을 추천한다.

Sample Response 2: A Good Friend

A good friend is much more important when traveling than going to a good location. Let me explain why I feel that way.

There are very few people who enjoy traveling alone or with people they dislike. Traveling alone can be a very lonely experience. And traveling with people you dislike is never fun either. That is why you need a good friend to go on a trip with. A good friend will provide you with companionship. You will not only have great experiences on your trip, but you will also enjoy them more because of the person you are with. You should always take a good friend with you when you travel.

A good friend can also help make a bad trip a good one. Two years ago, my friend and I went on a trip to the United States. We rented a car on that trip. But our car developed an engine problem while we were driving across the country. Because of the engine problem, we had to pay several hundred dollars for repairs. And we lost a couple of days on our trip as well. We could have been miserable. But my friend stayed positive. She made sure that we both had fun. Thanks to her, our trip was not ruined.

I always make sure to travel with a good friend. That way, I know that I will enjoy my trip.

Translation

여행을 할 때는 멋진 장소에 가는 것보다 친한 친구가 훨씬 더 중요하다. 그렇게 생각하는 이유에 대해 설명해 보도록 하겠다.

혼자서 혹은 자신이 싫어하는 사람과 여행을 떠나는 것을 좋아하는 사람은 거의 없다. 혼자서 하는 여행은 매우 외로운 경험이 될 수 있을 것이다. 그리고 본인이 싫어하는 사람과 떠나는 여행 역시 결코 재미있지 않을 것이다. 그것이 바로 여행을 할 때 친한 친구가 필요한 이유이다. 친한 친구는 우정을 선사해 줄 것이다. 여행에서 멋진 경험을 하게 될 뿐만 아니라, 또한 함께 있는 사람으로 인하여 그러한 경험을 보다 더 즐기게 될 것이다. 여행을 떠나는 경우에는 항상 친한 친구와 함께 가야 한다.

또한 친한 친구는 불쾌한 여행을 즐거운 여행으로 만드는데 도움이 될 수 있다. 2년 전, 내 친구와 나는 미국으로 여행을 갔다. 그 여행에서 우리는 자동차를 빌렸다. 하지만 차를 타고 미국을 돌아다니는 동안, 차에 엔진 문제가 발생했다. 엔진 문제로 인해, 우리는 수리 비용으로 수백 달러를 지불해야 했다. 그리고 또한 여행에서 이틀을 허비하게 되었다. 끔찍한 상황이 될 수도 있었을 것이다. 하지만 내 친구는 긍정적이었다. 그녀는 우리 둘 모두가 재미있게 지내도록 만들었다. 그녀 덕분에, 우리 여행은 엉망이 되지 않았다.

나는 항상 친한 친구와 여행을 하려고 한다. 그렇게 함으로써, 여행을 즐기게 될 것이라는 점을 나는 알 수 있다.

Actual Test 1

Answers

1. Ⓐ (Vocabulary Question)

2. Ⓒ (Sentence Simplification Question)

3. Ⓑ (Negative Factual Question)

4. Ⓒ (Rhetorical Purpose Question)

5. Ⓑ (Factual Question)

Translation

빙산의 형성

북극 및 북대서양의 차가운 수역에서는, 선장들이 주의를 기울여야 한다. 바다에 다수의 커다란 얼음 조각들이 떠다니고 있다. 이러한 빙산들은 자신과 충돌하는 선박들에게 피해를 주고 이들을 침몰시킬 수 있다.

빙산은 바다에 있는 작은 산과 같다. 보통은 꼭대기 부분이 하얗고 바닥 부분은 푸른색을 띄는 것처럼 보인다. 이는 빙산의 다양한 표면에 빛이 반사되는 방식 때문에 그렇다. 빙산은 크기와 형태에 있어서 다양할 수 있다. 일부는 그 크기가 단 수 미터에 불과한 반면, 일부는 수십 킬로미터에 이를 수도 있다. 몇몇 빙산들은 물 밖으로 높이 솟아 있을 수도 있지만, 얼음 덩어리의 대부분은 수중에서 발견된다.

빙산은 항상 바다에서 발견된다; 하지만, 염수로 이루어져 있지는 않다. 대신, 담수로 구성되어 있다. 북반구에서, 거대한 양의 빙산들은 그린란드, 알래스카, 캐나다 북부, 그리고 스칸디나비아의 일부 지역에 있는 빙하 혹은 빙붕의 가장 자리로부터 나온다. 빙하 및 빙붕 모두는 바다 쪽으로 이동하거나 확대되는 경향을 보인다. 이중 하나가 바다에 닿으면, 그 가장자리가 물에 떠오르기 시작한다. 그러면, 조수와 파도 모두가 이 얼음에 영향을 미치기 시작한다. 이로써 분리 빙하라고 알려진 과정이 일어난다. 얼음에 피로 골절이 나타난다. 이것이 확대되어, 결국에는, 얼음 덩어리가 바다에 떨어져 나가게 된다. 이러한 방식으로, 빙산이 형성된다.

전문가들은 매년 10,000개와 15,000개 사이의 빙산이 만들어진다고 믿고 있다. 빙산이 바다에서 자유롭게 떠다니게 되면, 조류, 해풍, 그리고 해류를 따라 이동하게 된다. 많은 빙산들이 북쪽의 차가운 수역에 남아 있다. 하지만, 보다 따뜻한 수역으로 가는 것들도 있다. 이러한 일이 발생하면, 이들은 녹아서 작아지기 시작한다. 때때로 보다 작은 빙산들로 분해되기도 한다. 안타깝게도, 많은 빙산들이 대양 항로로 들어간다. *타이타닉*호가 빙산으로 인해 침몰한 가장 유명한 선박이지만, 이들로 인하여 다른 수많은 선박들도 난파되었다. 반면, 일부 빙산들은 육지에 닿기도 한다. 이들은 항구에 방해가 되며 해변을 지저분하게 만든다. 그러면, 완전히 녹을 때까지 문제로 남게 된다.

Answers

6. Ⓒ (Reference Question)

7. Ⓐ (Factual Question)

8. Ⓓ (Vocabulary Question)

9. Ⓑ (Rhetorical Purpose Question)

10. **1, 3, 6** (Prose Summary Question)

Translation

라디오와 미국 사회

이탈리아의 발명가인 굴리엘모 마르코니는 1800년대 후반에 전파에 관한 연구를 했다. 그는 주로 통신용으로 이를 사용하는 것에 관심을 가졌다. 그는 그러한 분야에서의 선구자였다. 마르코니 이후, 기타 많은 사람들 또한 전파에 대한 연구를 시작했다.
그러한 노력의 한 가지 결과로 1920년대에 공영 라디오 방송이 시작되었다. 이는 큰
인기를 얻었다. 1930년대경에는, 전 세계 수백 만 명의 사람들이 라디오를 듣고 있었다.
청취자들이 매우 많았기 때문에, 라디오는 이러한 20년 동안 사회에 많은 영향을 끼치게
되었다.

　　1920년대, 미국에서 정규 라디오 방송이 시작되었다. 라디오는 즉각적인 성공을
이루었다. 미국 전역에서 라디오 방송국들이 빠르게 생겨났다. 이들은 다양한
프로그램들을 방송했다. 여기에는 뉴스, 스포츠 경기, 코미디 쇼, 그리고 드라마가
포함되어 있었다. 라디오는 미국에서 가장 인기 있는 형태의 오락 거리 중 하나가 되었다.
1930년대 무렵, 미국인들이 라디오 주변에 앉아 라디오를 청취하는 것은 일상적인
일이었다. 이들은 미국을 하나로 묶는데 도움을 준 경험을 공유하게 되었다. 예를 들어,
수백 만 명의 사람들이 야구 경기와 권투 시합과 같은 스포츠 경기를 생중계로 들을
수 있었다. 신문에서 그 결과를 알기 위해 더 이상 그 다음 날까지 기다려야 할 필요가
없었다.

　　1930년대, 미국은 경제 대공황의 중심에 있었다. 이는 국가 경제에 심각한 문제를
일으켰다. 1940년대 초, 미국은 세계 2차 대전에 참전하고 있었다. 이때는 미국 역사상
절망적인 시기였다. 프랭클린 D. 루즈벨트 대통령은 라디오를 효과적으로 이용하는
법을 알게 되었다. 1933년에서 1944년까지, 그는 일련의 라디오 방송을 했다. 이는 노변
환담이라고 불려졌다. 그의 연설은 미국이 직면하고 있는 문제에 대해 설명해 주는
것이었다. 그는 그처럼 힘든 시기에 미국인들을 위로하고 격려해 주었다.

　　사람들은 사실상 사회의 모든 측면에서 라디오의 용도를 찾아냈다. 군대는 라디오를
사용하여 메시지를 주고 받았다. 선박과 비행기들 또한 이를 이용했다. 이들은 날씨에
대한 보고를 받을 수 있었다. 그리고 문제가 생기는 경우에 라디오를 이용하여 메시지를
보낼 수 있었다.

Answers

11. Ⓑ (Inference Question)

12. Ⓐ (Negative Factual Question)

13. Ⓑ (Factual Question)

14. Ⓓ (Vocabulary Question)

15. 3rd (Insert Text Question)

Translation

오랑우탄

　　고릴라, 원숭이, 침팬지, 그리고 인간을 포함하여 많은 영장류들이 있다. 가장 특이한
영장류 중 하나는 인도네시아와 말레이시아의 지역에서 서식한다. 바로 오랑우탄이다. 이
동물은 지능이 매우 높다. 고릴라 다음으로, 인간과 가장 밀접한 관련이 있는 동물이다.
안타깝게도, 이는 가까운 미래에 멸종될 위기에 직면해 있는 멸종 위기의 종이다.

　　오랑우탄은 그 신체적 특성으로 인해 알아보기 쉽다. 두꺼운 목, 길고 튼튼한
팔, 그리고 구부러진 모양의 다리를 가지고 있다. 다른 영장류들과 달리, 꼬리는 없다.
가장 손쉽게 알아볼 수 있는 특징은 털이다. 얼굴을 제외한 몸 전체를 덮고 있는 길고
붉은 빛이 나는 털을 지지고 있다. 오랑우탄에는 두 가지 종류가 있다. 첫 번째는 둥그런
얼굴과 진한 색의 털을 가지고 있는 것이다. 두 번째는 길쭉한 얼굴과 밝은 색의 털을
가지고 있는 것이다. 하지만, 이 둘 모두는, 마주보는 엄지손가락이 달린 손을 가지고
있다. (이로써 오랑우탄은 사냥용과 같은 간단한 도구를 이용할 수 있다.) 그리고
30년에서 50년까지의 수명을 갖는다.

　　오랑우탄은 열대 우림에 집을 짓는다. 지면에서 시간을 보내는 것보다 나무의 높은
곳에 머무르는 것을 더 좋아한다. 그 결과, 오랑우탄은 기다란 팔을 갖도록 진화되었다.
이로써 나무를 오르는 일이 쉬워진다. 오랑우탄은 야행성이라기 보다는 주행성 동물이다.
나무에 지어 놓은 단상이나 둥지에서 밤에 잠을 잔다. 이들은 나뭇잎과 나뭇가지로
만들어진다. 잡식성인 오랑우탄은 주로 식물을 먹는데, 과일류를 선호한다. 하지만
나뭇잎, 씨앗, 나무껍질, 꽃, 그리고 식물의 구근도 먹는다. 때때로 고기도 – 주로 작은
동물들의 고기도 먹는다.

　　많은 영장류들과 달리, 오랑우탄은 사회적 동물이 아니다. 수컷은 혼자서 지내는
경향을 보인다. 1년에 며칠 동안만 암컷과 교제를 할 뿐이다. 짝짓기를 목적으로 그렇게
한다. 그런 다음에는 암컷들이 혼자서 새끼를 기른다. 새끼 오랑우탄은 성숙해 지기
전까지 약 7년 동안 어미 곁에 머무른다.

　　오랑우탄의 서식지는 현재 줄어들고 있다. 한 가지 이유는 오랑우탄이 살고 있는
우림을 인간들이 베어내고 있기 때문이다. 또 다른 이유는 많은 새끼 오랑우탄들이
동물원에 갇혀 길러지기 위해 포획되고 있기 때문이다. 안타깝게도, 오랑우탄은 현재
멸종 위기에 처해 있다. 그리고 그 숫자는 매년 감소하고 있다.

Actual Test 2

Answers

1. Ⓑ (Reference Question)

2. Ⓐ (Rhetorical Purpose Question)

3. Ⓒ (Vocabulary Question)

4. 4th (Insert Text Question)

5. 2, 3, 4 (Prose Summary Question)

Translation

지진 측정

　　지구의 지각은 많은 판으로 구성되어 있다. 일부는 막대한 지역에 걸쳐져 있다. 보다
작은 것들도 있다. 이러한 판들은 고정되어 있는 것이 아니라, 서로를 향해 이동하거나
혹은 서로로부터 멀어지고 있으며 때로는 충돌하기도 한다. 이들이 움직이면, 지면이
흔들린다. 이는 지진, 혹은 지동이라고 알려져 있다. 지진은 그 강도에 있어서 다양하다.
대부분은 약하기 때문에, 인식을 할 수가 없다. 사람들에 의해 느껴지는 것들도 있는데,
이들은 미약한 피해를 입힐 수 있다. 너무나 강력해서 도시 전체를 파괴시키는 것들도
있다. 지진의 다양한 특성으로 인해, 과학자들은 지진을 측정할 수 있는 방법들을 고안해
냈다. 주로 활용되고 있는 몇 가지 방법이 있다.

　　가장 잘 알려진 지진 측정 시스템은 리히터 척도이다. 미국인 과학자 찰스 리히터가
1935년에 이를 개발했다. 리히터 척도는 0에서 시작하는 숫자들로 지진의 등급을
매김으로써 진동의 정도를 측정한다. 지진계를 사용하여 그렇게 한다. 이 장비에는
지진이 발생하는 동안 움직이는 바늘이 달려 있다. 전 세계에 지진계가 설치되어 있다.
여러 지진계로부터 나오는 측정값을 취합함으로써, 과학자들은 어떤 지진이 얼마나
강력한 것인지를 알아낼 수 있다. 가장 약한 지진은 리히터 척도에서 가장 낮은 쪽에
있다. 2 혹은 그보다 낮게 측정되는 진동은 사람에 의해 느껴질 수 없다. 상당한 손해를
입히고 사망 피해를 줄 수 있는 지진은 6 혹은 그보다 높은 수치로 측정된다. (예를 들어,
1906년의 샌프란시스코 지진은, 3,000명 이상의 사람들의 목숨을 앗아갔는데, 약 7.8의
값으로 측정되었다.) 역사상 가장 강력했던 지진은 리히터 척도로 9.5의 값을 기록했다.

　　일부 과학자들은 리히터 척도를 사용하지 않고, 대신 다른 방법으로 지진을 측정한다.
이들은 지진이 일으키는 피해가 어느 정도인지에 따라 진동을 평가한다. 지진이 일어난 후,
이들 과학자들은 해당 지역의 건물 및 토지에 발생한 피해를 조사한다. 그런 다음, 지진의
등급을 매긴다. 이 방법은 두 가지 이유로 리히터 척도보다 신뢰도가 낮다. 첫째, 사람이
거주하지 않는 지역에서도 강력한 지진이 발생할 수 있지만, 손상되는 건물이 없기
때문에 이는 낮은 등급을 받게 된다. 둘째, 일본과 같이 지진에 취약한 국가에서는 내진
설계로 건물들이 지어진다. 따라서 일본에서는 강력한 지진이 거의 피해를 주지 않을
수도 있는 반면, 다른 곳에서의 보다 약한 지진은 막대한 피해를 가져다 줄 수도 있다.

Answers

6. Ⓐ (Sentence Simplification Question)

7. Ⓒ (Vocabulary Question)

8. Ⓓ (Factual Question)

9. Ⓑ (Reference Question)

10. Ⓐ (Negative Factual Question)

동물에게 소화 불량을 일으킬 수 있는 화학적 방어 수단을 가지고 있다.

식물의 방어 수단 중 세 번째 유형은 상리 공생이다. 이는 공생의 한 형태이다. 상리 공생에서, 식물과 또 다른 생물은 – 통상 동물이 되는데 – 밀접한 관계를 갖는다. 식물은 먹이 혹은 휴식처와 같은 것을 동물에게 제공해 준다. 그에 대한 보답으로, 동물은 보호를 해준다. 아카시아 나무는 개미의 한 종과 이러한 종류의 관계를 맺고 있다. 개미가 나무에서 살며 그 과즙을 먹는다. 그에 대한 보답으로, 개미는 나무의 잎을 먹으려고 하는 다른 생물들을 공격해서 쫓아낸다.

Listening

p.184

Actual Test 1

Answers

1. (A) (Gist-Purpose Question)

2. (B) (Understanding Attitude Question)

3. (B) (Making Inferences Question)

4. (D) (Understanding Attitude Question)

Script 🎧 4-01

W1 Professor: Jenny, welcome back from Spain. It's great to see you again.

W2 Student: Thanks, Professor Dillard. It's good to be back home as well.

W1: So, tell me . . . How was your semester abroad in Spain? Did you enjoy your time there?

W2: [4]It was the most amazing three months of my life. I had such an incredible semester in Spain. I got to do so many things . . . see so many places . . . learn so many things. **It's quite a shame that I had to come back when I did.** But I have to get a job for the summer, so here I am.

W1: Well, it sounds like you had a great experience. I know it would be nice to get to spend more time there. Um, but at least you got to go in the first place.

W2: That's true.

W1: So, uh, what brings you to my office?

W2: Next year's classes.

W1: Oh, that's right. You haven't registered yet, have you?

W2: That's correct. I have the list of classes I want to take right here. Take a look . . . I shouldn't have any problems getting into any of them.

W1: Hmm . . . Yes, I don't imagine any of these classes will be full. That's a good thing since most students have already registered. Oh, I need to ask . . . Which requirements do these classes fill?

W2: Two of them are for my major . . . One is my last science requirement. And the other two are electives. In the spring semester next year, I'll only have to take two more requirements in order to graduate.

W1: Excellent. You're really on the ball. Okay, let me sign this form, and then you can take it to the Registrar's Office.

W2: Thanks so much, Professor Dillard.

Translation

폰세 데 레온

1492년에 콜럼버스가 신대륙을 발견한 후, 스페인 사람들은 대서양을 횡단하는 많은 원정대를 보내기 시작했다. 하층 계급 및 귀족들 모두가 새롭게 발견된 대륙으로 길을 떠났다. 그곳을 여행했던 한 명의 귀족이 후안 폰세 데 레온이었다. 1474년에 태어난 폰세 데 레온은 신대륙을 향한 콜럼버스의 두 번째 여행에서 그와 함께 항해를 했다. 해외에서의 긴 여정의 시작이었다.

콜럼버스와의 항해에서, 폰세 데 레온은 히스파니올라 섬을 탐험했다. 그의 인생에서 그 다음 몇 년 동안은 모호하다. 평생 신대륙에서 머물렀을 수도 있고, 혹은 스페인으로 돌아왔을 수도 있다. 하지만, 1504년경, 그는 확실히 히스파니올라에 있었다. 당시, 그는 섬 원주민들과 전투를 벌이고 있었다. 그의 지도력에 대한 보상으로, 그는 그 지역의 총독이 되었다.

총독의 역할을 담당하는 동안, 폰세 데 레온은 종종 원주민 부족의 구성원들과 만났다. 그는 비옥한 토지 및 상당량의 금이 있는 장소에 관한 여러 이야기들을 듣게 되었다. 1508년, 폰세 데 레온은 이러한 장소를 찾기 위해 푸에르토리코로의 탐험대를 이끌었다. 그는 그곳에서 약간의 금을 발견했고 이후 그 섬의 총독으로 임명되었다. 푸에르토리코에서, 그는 원주민들로부터 계속 이야기를 들었다. 몇몇 이야기들은 북서쪽에 위치한 지역에 관한 것이었다. 바하마 제도에 있는 섬인 비미니와 관련된 것들도 있었다.

전설에 의하면, 비미니에는 '청춘의 샘'이 있었다. 이 샘에는 그곳에서 목욕을 하는 모든 사람에게 영원한 젊음을 가져다 준다는 물이 있다고 생각되었다. 호기심에 찬 폰세 데 레온은 이 샘을 찾기 위해 원정대를 조직했다. 1513년에 항해를 떠나서, 폰세 데 레온과 그의 동료들은 오늘날의 플로리다 세인트오거스틴 시 근처에 상륙했다. 그와 그의 동료들은 자신들이 섬에 있다고 생각했지만, 실제로는 북아메리카 대륙에 도착한 것이었다. 이들은 8개월 동안 플로리다를, 그가 그렇게 불렀는데, 탐험했다. 몇 년 후인 1521년에, 폰세 데 레온은 플로리다로 돌아왔다. 그곳에서, 그는 원주민들과의 전투로 부상을 입었고 그 후 곧 목숨을 잃었다.

Answers

11. (B) (Negative Factual Question)

12. (D) (Factual Question)

13. (B) (Inference Question)

14. (D) (Factual Question)

15. **Physical: 4, 7   Chemical: 1, 2, 5** (Fill in a Table Question)

Translation

초식 동물에 대한 식물들의 방어 수단

많은 동물들이 초식 동물이다. 따라서 이들은 식물로부터 영양분을 얻는다. 일부는 과일 및 과즙을 섭취하는 반면, 잎이나 식물 자체를 먹는 동물들도 있다. 이러한 동물들에 대응하여, 식물은 오랜 시간에 걸쳐 여러 가지 방어 시스템을 진화시켜 왔다. 식물들이 사용하는 방어 수단에는 세 가지 주요한 유형이 있다. 물리적 방어 수단, 화학적 방어 수단, 그리고 다른 생물들과의 상호 관계가 그것이다.

물리적 방어 수단은 – 또한 기계적 방어 수단이라고도 알려져 있는데 – 식물의 표면에서 발견된다. 예를 들어, 가시는 흔한 물리적 방어 수단 중의 하나이다. 블랙베리 및 산딸기와 같은 식물들은 가시를 지니고 있다. 이로써 동물들은 그들의 과일을 먹지 못하게 된다. 많은 동물들은 가시에 의해 상처를 입는 것을 원하지 않는다. 따라서 식물들을 가만히 나두게 된다. 다른 식물들은, 특히 나무는, 지면 근처가 아니라 지면으로부터 높은 곳에 나뭇가지들을 둔다. 이로써 사슴과 같은 동물들은 그들의 잎을 먹을 수가 없다. 단단한 껍질을 지닌 과일이나 견과를 가지고 있는 식물들도 있다. 이에 대한 두 가지 예로 호두와 코코넛이 있다.

식물들의 화학적 방어 수단은 화합물과 관련된 것이다. 사용되는 화학 물질들은 식물의 성장이나 번식과는 관련이 없다. 그 대신 이들은 2차적인 화학 물질이다. 일반적인 화학적 방어 수단 중 하나는 식물로 하여금 초식 동물에게 좋지 않은 맛을 내도록 하는 것이다. 예를 들어, 식물의 잎에 많은 양의 알칼로이드가 들어 있는 경우, 이는 동물들에게 쓴 맛이 나도록 할 수 있다. 따라서 동물들은 이러한 잎을 먹으면 안 된다는 점을 알게 된다. 덩굴 옻나무와 같은 다른 식물들은 동물들의 피부에 통증을 일으킬 수 있다. 이로써 동물들은 차후에 이러한 식물들을 먹지 않게 된다. 심지어 일부 식물들은

Translation

W1 Professor: Jenny, 스페인에서 돌아온 것을 환영해요. 다시 만나게 되어 기쁘군요.

W2 Student: 고맙습니다, Dillard 교수님. 저 또한 집으로 오게 되어 기뻐요.

W1: 그러면, 말씀해 보세요… 스페인에서의 학기는 어땠나요? 그곳에서 즐거운 시간을 보냈나요?

W2: 제 인생에서 가장 멋진 3개월이었어요. 스페인에서 믿을 수 없을 정도로 멋진 학기를 보냈어요. 많은 것들을 하게 되었고… 많은 장소에도 가보았으며… 너무나 많은 것들을 배우게 되었죠. 다시 돌아와야 한다는 점이 상당히 아쉬웠어요. 하지만 여름 동안에는 일을 해야 하기 때문에, 여기에 온 것이죠.

W1: 음, 학생이 멋진 경험을 한 것처럼 들리는군요. 그곳에서 더 많은 시간을 보냈으면 좋았을 것이라고 생각해요. 음, 하지만 어쨌거나 학생은 그곳에 가보았죠.

W2: 맞는 말씀이세요.

W1: 그러면, 어, 왜 제 사무실에 왔나요?

W2: 내년의 수업 때문이에요.

W1: 오, 그래요. 아직 등록을 하지 않았죠, 그렇죠?

W2: 맞아요. 여기에 제가 수강하고자 하는 수업의 리스트를 가지고 왔어요. 보세요… 그중 어떤 수업이라도 수강하는데 문제가 없어야 해서요.

W1: 흠… 네, 이 중 어떤 수업에서도 인원이 다 차게 될 것 같지는 않군요. 대부분의 학생들이 이미 수강 신청을 해두었기 때문에, 다행스러운 일이에요. 오, 물어볼 것이 있는데… 이들 수업이 어떤 요건을 충족시키게 되나요?

W2: 그중 두 개는 제 전공을 위한 것이에요… 하나는 마지막으로 남은 과학 필수 과목이죠. 그리고 다른 두 개는 선택 과목이고요. 졸업을 하기 위해서는 내년 봄 학기에 두 개의 필수 과목만 더 들으면 되죠.

W1: 훌륭하네요. 정말로 잘 알고 있군요. 좋아요, 제가 이 양식에 서명을 해드리면, 이것을 학적과로 가지고 갈 수 있을 거에요.

W2: 정말 고맙습니다, Dillard 교수님.

Answers

5. Ⓑ (Gist-Content Question)

6. Ⓓ (Understanding Organization Question)

7. **Fact:** 1, 4 **Not a Fact:** 2, 3 (Detail Question)

8. Ⓒ (Detail Question)

Script 🎧 4-02

W Professor: Another animal that lives around the Galapagos Islands is the giant tortoise. Please note that the giant tortoise is not exclusive to that area. It lives around the Seychelles Islands and the Mascarene Islands in the Indian Ocean, too. Many years ago, it lived along the coasts of both South America and Madagascar. It became extinct in those places though.

Compared to other tortoise species, the giant tortoise is, uh, as its name suggests, very large. It can grow to be nearly two meters in length. And it can weigh as much as 300 kilograms. Direct your attention to the screen, please. Here is a picture of a zookeeper feeding a giant tortoise . . . Look at how big it is in comparison to the man. Here's another shot for you . . .

The giant tortoise is among the longest-lived creatures on Earth. It can live for more than a century. One tortoise that was kept in captivity in an Australian zoo was 170 years old when it died. Incredible, isn't it . . . ? As you might expect, because the giant tortoise lives so long, it develops slowly. It doesn't reach its mating age until it is between twenty and twenty-five years old. The males are bigger than the females. Additionally, it's the males that initiate mating. Sometimes males act aggressively toward other males when they're competing for mates. They stretch their necks very high and bite each other. Here's a picture of that for you to see . . .

After mating, a female lays her eggs in sandy soil and then buries them. Most tortoises lay between six and sixteen eggs. The number mainly depends on the subspecies of tortoise. The eggs themselves are round and about the size of, oh, a tennis ball or a billiard ball. When the eggs hatch, the baby tortoises are quite small. They're about eight centimeters long. Since they hatch underground, the first thing the babies must do is dig their way out of the sand.

M Student: Don't the parents watch over their eggs until they hatch?

W: No, they don't. That's behavior more common in birds than in reptiles. The parents actually play no role after laying the eggs. As a result, the life of a baby giant tortoise is filled with danger. Many fall victim to predators. Birds in particular feed upon them. Dogs, cats, and rats have been known to attack and eat them as well. So, uh, many babies fail to survive to adulthood. However, those that survive long enough for their shells to become fully grown are extremely hard to kill. While their necks and tails are vulnerable, the tortoises can quickly pull them into their protective shells.

Interestingly, the giant tortoise lacks teeth. Instead, it has sharp, bony ridges on its mouth that help it crush food. It mainly eats plants. It drinks water but can survive for a long amount of time without it. The reason is that the tortoise gets a lot of the moisture it requires from the food it eats.

Translation

W Professor: 갈라파고스 제도 주변에서 살고 있는 또 다른 동물은 코끼리거북입니다. 코끼리거북이 그 지역에만 있는 것은 아니라는 점에 주목해 주세요. 인도양의 세이셸 및 마스카렌 제도 주변에서도 서식을 합니다. 수년 전에는, 남아메리카와 마다가스카르의 해안을 따라 살기도 했죠. 하지만 이러한 지역에서는 멸종을 했습니다.

다른 거북 종들과 비교해 볼 때, 코끼리거북은, 어, 그 이름이 암시하듯이, 매우 커다랗습니다. 길이가 거의 2미터까지 되도록 자랄 수 있습니다. 그리고 300킬로그램 정도의 무게가 나갈 수 있습니다. 화면에 주목해 주세요. 코끼리거북에게 먹이를 주고 있는 사육사의 사진이 있습니다… 사람과 비교했을 때 이것이 얼마나 큰지를 보십시오. 여러분께 보여 드릴 사진이 하나 더 있습니다…

코끼리거북은 지구상에서 가장 오래 사는 생물 중 하나입니다. 100년 이상을 살 수가 있습니다. 호주의 동물원에서 사육되었던 한 거북이는 죽었을 당시 170살이었습니다. 믿기지가 않죠, 그렇지 않나요…? 예상하실 수도 있겠는데, 코끼리거북은 매우 오래 살기 때문에, 천천히 발달합니다. 20살에서 25살 사이가 되어서야 짝짓기를 할 수 있는 연령에 도달합니다. 수컷들이 암컷들보다 더 큽니다. 또한, 짝짓기를 주도하는 것도 수컷이고요. 때때로 수컷들은 짝짓기 상대를 두고 경쟁을 할 때, 다른 수컷들에게 공격적인 행동을 합니다. 목을 매우 높이 치켜들고 서로 뭅니다. 여러분들이 볼 수 있는 그러한 사진이 여기에 있습니다…

짝짓기를 한 후, 암컷은 모래흙에 알을 낳고 이를 묻습니다. 대부분의 거북들은 6개에서 16개 사이의 알을 낳습니다. 그러한 숫자는 주로 거북의 아종에 따라 달라집니다. 알 자체는 둥글고, 대략, 오, 테니스 공이나 당구공 정도의 크기입니다. 알이 부화를 하면, 새끼 거북들은 꽤 작습니다. 길이가 약 8센티미터 정도이죠. 땅 속에서 부화를 하기 때문에, 새끼들이 해야 할 첫 번째 일은 구멍을 파서 모래 밖으로 나오는 것입니다.

M Student: 부화할 때까지 부모 거북들이 알을 보살피지 않나요?

W: 아니오, 그렇지 않습니다. 그것은 파충류보다 조류에 있어서 보다 흔한 행동입니다. 알을 낳은 후 실제로 부모 거북들은 어떠한 역할도 담당하지 않습니다. 그 결과, 새끼 코끼리거북의 삶은 위험으로 가득차 있습니다. 많은 새끼들이 포식자의 희생물이 됩니다. 특히 새들이 이들을 잡아먹습니다. 개, 고양이, 그리고 쥐들도 이들을 공격해서 잡아먹는다고 알려져 있고요. 따라서, 어, 많은 새끼들이 성인까지 살아남지를 못합니다. 하지만, 껍질이 충분히 성장할 정도로 오래 살아남은 거북은 죽이기가 극도로 어렵습니다. 목과 꼬리가 취약한 부분이지만, 거북들은 보호용 등딱지 속으로

빠르게 그러한 부분을 집어 넣을 수 있습니다.

흥미롭게도, 코끼리거북은 이빨을 가지고 있지 않습니다. 대신, 입 안에 먹이를 씹는데 도움이 되는 날카롭고 딱딱한 부분이 돌출되어 있습니다. 주로 식물을 먹습니다. 물을 마시지만 물을 마시지 않고서도 오랜 시간 동안 살아갈 수 있습니다. 그 이유는 이 거북들이 섭취하는 먹이로부터 필요한 많은 수분을 얻기 때문입니다.

Answers

9. Ⓐ (Gist-Content Question)

10. Ⓒ (Understanding Function Question)

11. Ⓓ (Detail Question)

12. Ⓑ (Understanding Organization Question)

Script 🎧 4-03

M Professor: Economists often mention the term complementary goods. This refers to two or more products that go well with one another. Here are some examples . . . Uh, hotdogs and hotdog buns are complementary goods. So are shoes and shoelaces. And, uh, cars, of course, require gasoline to run. That makes cars and gasoline complementary goods as well.

Why do we use this particular term? Well, let me tell you . . . In many cases, when customers buy one of these goods, they tend to purchase the other as well. These complementary goods may be absolute necessities . . . Uh, a car won't run without gas, for instance . . . Or they may simply be good options to buy. For example, you don't need hotdog buns when you buy hotdogs. But hotdogs taste better when you eat them on buns, don't they?

People typically associate complementary goods with one another. As a result, businesses group them together to make shopping more convenient for their customers. That's why I know I can always find a pair of shoelaces at a shoe store. Likewise, I will always be able to buy hotdogs, hotdog buns, and, um, condiments such as ketchup and mustard at a supermarket. This is the reason there are so many specialty stores. Think of that party shop near campus. You can get everything you need for a party at that store. It specializes in complementary goods.

Some complementary goods go together most of the time. Again, let me mention shoes and shoelaces. Most shoes require shoelaces. Without them, the shoes are pretty much worthless. They won't fit properly as they will slide off your feet. Other complementary goods go well with one another but don't need to be together all the time. Let's talk about hotdogs and hotdog buns again. Many people eat hotdogs on buns. But not all of them do. Some people eat hotdogs plain or put them in soups or pasta dishes. So it's not always necessary to have hotdog buns to eat hotdogs. The same is true of condiments. Ketchup and mustard are complementary goods for hotdogs, but they're not always necessary. For instance, I never eat mustard. So mustard and hotdogs aren't complementary goods for me. But they are for other people.

Finally, there are products that won't work without a complementary good. Motor vehicles and gasoline are the best example. A motor vehicle . . . uh, a car . . . needs fuel to move. Without it, it's useless. A long time ago, oil companies realized the profits to be made by selling gas. They set up their own distribution centers: gas stations. These gas stations became centers for other complementary goods besides fuel. Think

about what many gas stations sell . . . They sell oil, tires, and other spare parts for cars. These are all complementary goods that cars must have in order to run.

Translation

M Professor: 경제학자들은 종종 보완재라는 용어를 사용합니다. 이는 서로 잘 어울리는 두 개 혹은 그 이상의 상품들을 지칭하는 것입니다. 몇 가지 예를 알려 드리죠… 어, 핫도그 소시지와 핫도그 빵은 보완재입니다. 신발과 신발 끈도 그렇고요. 그리고, 어, 자동차는. 물론, 달리기 위해서 가솔린을 필요로 합니다. 따라서 자동차와 가솔린 역시 보완재가 됩니다.

왜 이와 같은 특정한 용어를 사용하는 것일까요? 음, 말씀해 드리죠… 많은 경우, 소비자들이 이러한 상품 중 하나를 구입하면, 이들은 다른 하나도 구입하는 경향이 있습니다. 이러한 보완재는 반드시 필요한 것일 수 있습니다… 어, 예를 들면, 자동차는 가솔린이 없으면 움직이지 않습니다… 아니면 단지 구입을 하는 것이 좋은 선택이 될 수도 있습니다. 예를 들어, 핫도그 소시지를 살 때 핫도그 빵이 필요하지 않을 수도 있습니다. 하지만 핫도그 소시지를 핫도그 빵에 넣어 먹을 때 맛이 더 좋습니다. 그렇지 않나요?

일반적으로 사람들은 보완재를 서로 연관시킵니다. 그 결과, 기업들은 이들을 묶음으로써 소비자들이 쇼핑을 보다 편리하게 할 수 있도록 합니다. 신발 가게에서는 신발 끈 한 짝을 항상 발견할 수 있다는 점을 제가 알고 있는 이유입니다. 마찬가지로, 슈퍼마켓에서는 항상 핫도그 소시지와 핫도그 빵, 그리고 음, 케첩과 머스터드와 같은 소스를 구입할 수 있습니다. 이는 그렇게 많은 전문점들이 존재하는 이유가 됩니다. 캠퍼스 주변의 파티 숍을 생각해 보세요. 그러한 매장에서는 파티에 필요한 모든 것들을 구입할 수가 있습니다. 보완재를 전문으로 하고 있는 것이죠.

몇몇 보완재들은 대부분의 경우 함께 어울리는 것들입니다. 또 다시, 신발과 신발 끈을 언급하도록 하겠습니다. 대부분의 신발들은 신발 끈을 필요로 합니다. 신발 끈이 없다면, 신발의 가치는 상당히 떨어지게 됩니다. 발에서 미끄러져 나갈 것이기 때문에 발에 제대로 맞지 않을 것입니다. 서로 잘 어울리지만, 항상 같이 있을 필요는 없는 보완재들도 있습니다. 다시 핫도그 소시지와 핫도그 빵에 대해 이야기해 봅시다. 많은 사람들이 빵에 핫도그 소시지를 넣어 먹습니다. 하지만 모든 사람들이 그와 같이 먹는 것은 아닙니다. 어떤 사람들은 핫도그 소시지를 그냥 먹거나 이를 수프나 파스타 요리에 넣기도 합니다. 따라서 핫도그 소시지를 먹기 위해 항상 핫도그 빵이 있어야 할 필요는 없습니다. 소스에 있어서도 마찬가지입니다. 케첩과 머스터드는 핫도그 소시지에 대한 보완재가 되지만, 항상 필요한 것은 아닙니다. 예를 들어, 저는 머스터드를 먹지 않습니다. 따라서 머스터드와 핫도그 소시지는 제게 보완재가 아닙니다. 하지만 다른 사람들에게는 보완재입니다.

마지막으로, 보완재가 없으면 효과가 없는 상품들이 있습니다. 차량과 가솔린이 가장 좋은 예입니다. 차량은… 어, 자동차는… 움직이기 위해 연료를 필요로 합니다. 연료가 없으면 쓸모가 없습니다. 오래 전, 석유 회사들은 가솔린을 판매함으로써 생기게 될 이익을 깨달았습니다. 그들은 자신들의 유통 센터를 세웠습니다: 바로 주유소입니다. 이러한 주유소들은 연료 이외의 기타 보완재들에 대한 판매처가 되었습니다. 많은 주유소에서 판매하고 있는 것들을 생각해 보십시오… 오일, 타이어, 그리고 자동차를 위한 기타 예비 부품들을 판매합니다. 이들 모두는 자동차가 달리기 위해서 반드시 있어야 하는 보완재들입니다.

Answers

13. Ⓐ (Gist-Purpose Question)

14. Ⓒ (Making Inferences Question)

15. **Fact:** ① , ④ **Not a Fact:** ② , ③ (Detail Question)

16. Ⓒ (Understanding Attitude Question)

Script 🎧 4-04

W Student: Jeremy, do you mind if I come in for a moment? I need to speak with you about something important.

M Resident Assistant: Sure, Sarah. Come on in and have a seat in that chair. Uh, you don't look very happy. What's the matter?

W: My next-door neighbors are driving me crazy. I don't think I can stand listening to their music any longer.

M: Uh, are you referring to Lewis and Walt?

W: Yes, those two. They play their music way too loudly. And they do that day and night. I can never concentrate on my studies when they're playing their music.

M: Have you tried asking them to turn their music down?

W: Of course I have. I've asked them a bunch of times. So has my roommate. And so have Jason and Todd. Uh, you know . . . They're in the room directly across the hall from Lewis and Walt.

M: And what was their reaction when you asked them to be quiet?

W: They said no. Then, they slammed the door in my face and turned their music up even louder. They do that to everyone. They're so rude. Surely you must have heard their music. I mean, uh, you live here in the dorm, too.

M: Yeah, but I'm not around that much, so I wasn't aware of the problem until now. I guess they're bothering lots of people . . . Okay, uh, I'm going to have a chat with them.

W: Thanks. I appreciate it.

M: Those two need to learn to be good neighbors. I'll make sure they turn their music down. And, if they behave improperly again in the future, let me know immediately. I'll put a halt to that. I don't want there to be any problems like that in this dorm.

Translation

W Student: Jeremy 선생님, 잠시 들어가도 될까요? 중요한 일에 대해 선생님과 이야기를 해야 해서요.

M Resident Assistant: 물론이에요. Sarah. 들어와서 저쪽 의자에 앉으세요. 어, 기분이 그다지 좋아 보이지 않는군요. 무슨 일인가요?

W: 제 옆에 사는 이웃들 때문에 미치겠어요. 더 이상 그들의 음악을 듣는 것을 견딜 수가 없을 것 같아요.

M: 어, Lewis와 Walt를 말하는 건가요?

W: 네, 그 둘이요. 음악을 너무 크게 틀어 놓아요. 그리고 밤낮을 가리지 않고 그렇게 하죠. 그들이 음악을 틀어 놓을 때면 저는 공부에 전혀 집중을 할 수가 없어요.

M: 그들에게 음악 소리를 줄여달라고 요청해 본 적이 있나요?

W: 물론 그랬어요. 수 차례 요청을 해보았죠. 제 룸메이트도 그랬고요. 그리고 Jason과 Todd도 그렇게 했어요. 어, 아시겠지만… 그들은 복도를 사이에 두고 Lewis와 Walt와 바로 맞은 편에 있는 방에 묵고 있죠.

M: 조용히 해달라고 요청했을 때 반응이 어땠나요?

W: 그렇게 할 수 없다고 말하더군요. 그런 다음, 제 면전에서 문을 세게 닫고 음악 소리를 더 크게 올렸어요. 모든 사람들에게 그렇게 해요. 정말로 예의가 없죠. 분명 선생님도 그들의 음악 소리를 들어보셨을 거에요. 제 말은, 어, 선생님도 기숙사에서 생활하잖아요.

M: 그래요, 하지만 그렇게 자주 있는 편은 아니라서, 지금까지 그러한 문제를 몰랐네요. 그들이 많은 사람들에게 폐를 끼치고 있는 것 같군요… 좋아요, 어, 제가 그들과 이야기를 해볼게요.

W: 고마워요. 감사합니다.

M: 그 두 사람은 좋은 이웃이 되는 법을 배워야 할 것 같군요. 확실히 그들이 음악 소리를 줄이도록 만들게요. 그리고, 차후에 그들이 또 다시 부적절한 행동을 한다면, 즉시 제게 알려 주세요. 제가 중단시킬게요. 이곳 기숙사에서 그와 같은 문제가 생기는 것을 원치 않거든요.

Answers

17. Ⓒ (Gist-Content Question)

18. Ⓓ (Detail Question)

19. **Diamond:** 1, 3, 4 **Ruby:** 2
(Connecting Content Question)

20. Ⓑ (Understanding Attitude Question)

Script 🎧 4-05

M Professor: There are dozens of gemstones. They include diamonds, rubies, sapphires, and emeralds. Most gemstones are forms of various minerals. However, each has undergone some type of change from its original mineral. As you surely know, people have considered gemstones valuable ever since ancient times. There are two reasons for that. First, they are both beautiful and lustrous. Second, most gemstones are rare. So their scarcity makes them increase in value.

One thing you ought to know about gemstones is that they look much different when people dig them out of the ground. Uh, I mean, they aren't shiny at all. In fact, their appearance is quite rough. They're often embedded in rocks and dirt. The gemstones therefore need to be cleaned first. Then, they are polished to make them shine more brightly. Sometimes, jewelers cut them down to certain sizes so that they can be used to make jewelry such as necklaces, pendants, and rings. Additionally, some gemstones have facets. These are small, flat sections. Jewelers cut them in symmetrical patterns on gems. Gemstones with facets reflect light much better than ones without facets. Diamonds are almost always cut with facets.

Now, uh, what about the uses of gemstones? Okay, obviously, we use them for jewelry. But there are a number of other uses for some gemstones. Most of them are industrial in nature. Think about diamonds for instance. They are the hardest substance known to man, so they make excellent cutting tools. Many types of industrial saws have diamond-edged blades. Oh, but most of the diamonds used by industries are artificial, not natural. Real diamonds are almost always used to make jewelry. But here's another example. Rubies were used in some of the first lasers that were made decades ago. And many advanced lasers utilize artificial rubies these days.

There are also some who believe that gemstones have special healing properties. This is a belief that dates back thousands of years. For instance, the ancient Egyptians thought that lapis lazuli . . . uh, that's a kind of gemstone . . . they thought that lapis lazuli could cure a headache if it was placed on a person's head. It's also supposed to help ease high blood pressure in people. Some people claim that moonstones, quartz, and agates can balance people's emotions if they are worn as jewelry. In addition, jade, opal, amethyst, and turquoise are said to be able to heal people.

Now, um, many people are skeptical about what I just said. This is actually a somewhat controversial topic. But large numbers of people swear that they feel better when they have certain gems on their bodies. How does this work? Well, one theory is that the sun's light waves enter the body differently when they pass through a gemstone. This causes the light waves to have a different effect on the body. I have no idea if that's true or not. However, there is some evidence that supports this claim.

M Professor: 수십 가지의 보석들이 있습니다. 여기에는 다이아몬드, 루비, 사파이어, 그리고 에메랄드가 포함됩니다. 대부분의 보석들은 다양한 광물의 형태를 띠고 있습니다. 하지만, 각각은 원래의 암석으로부터 일정한 종류의 변화를 겪은 것들입니다. 틀림없이 여러분들도 알고 있을 텐데, 고대로부터 사람들은 보석을 귀중하게 생각했습니다. 그에 대해서는 두 가지 이유가 있습니다. 첫째, 이들은 아름다운 동시에 반짝거립니다. 둘째, 대부분의 보석들은 희귀합니다. 따라서 희소성으로 인하여 가치가 증대됩니다.

보석에 관해 여러분들이 알아야 할 한 가지는 땅에서 파낼 때 이들이 상당히 다르게 보인다는 점입니다. 어, 제 말은, 전혀 빛이 나지가 않습니다. 실제, 이들의 표면은 상당히 거칩니다. 종종 암석이나 흙 속에 들어가 있습니다. 따라서 먼저 보석들은 세척이 되어야 합니다. 그런 다음, 보다 밝게 빛이 날 수 있도록 광택을 내야 합니다. 때때로, 목걸이, 펜던트, 그리고 반지와 같은 보석 제품을 만들기 위해 보석 세공인들은 일정한 크기로 보석을 자릅니다. 또한, 일부 보석들은 단면을 지니고 있습니다. 이는 작고 평평한 부분입니다. 보석 세공인들은 대칭적인 형태로 보석을 깎습니다. 단면을 지닌 보석들은 단면이 없는 보석보다 빛을 더욱 잘 반사시킵니다. 다이아몬드는 거의 항상 단면을 갖도록 깎입니다.

자, 어, 보석의 용도는 어떨까요? 그래요, 분명, 우리는 이들을 보석 제품으로 사용합니다. 하지만 일부 보석에 있어서는 그와 다른 많은 용도들이 있습니다. 그중 대부분은 본질적으로 공업용입니다. 예를 들어 다이아몬드를 생각해 보세요. 인간에게 알려져 있는 가장 단단한 물질이기 때문에, 다이아몬드는 뛰어난 절삭 도구가 됩니다. 많은 유형의 산업용 톱에는 다이아몬드 날이 있습니다. 오, 하지만 산업체에서 사용되는 대부분의 다이아몬드는 천연 다이아몬드가 아니라 인조 다이아몬드입니다. 진짜 다이아몬드는 거의 항상 보석 제품을 만드는데 사용됩니다. 하지만 또 다른 예가 있습니다. 수십 년 전에 만들어졌던 최초의 레이저에서는 루비가 사용되었습니다. 그리고 오늘날 많은 첨단 레이저들이 인조 루비를 활용하고 있습니다.

또한 보석들이 특별한 치유 능력을 가지고 있다고 믿는 사람들도 있습니다. 그 기원이 수천 년 전으로 거슬러 올라가는 믿음입니다. 예를 들어, 고대 이집트 사람들은 청금석… 어, 일종의 보석인데… 그들은 청금석을 사람의 머리에 올려놓으면 이것이 두통을 치료해 줄 수 있다고 생각했습니다. 또한 사람들 사이에서는 이것이 고혈압을 경감시키는데 도움이 된다는 믿음이 존재합니다. 몇몇 사람들은 월장석, 석영, 그리고 마노를 보석 제품으로 착용하면 이들이 평정심을 가져다 준다고 주장합니다. 또한, 비취, 오팔, 자수정, 그리고 터키석도 사람의 병을 치료해 줄 수 있다고 말해집니다.

자, 음, 제가 방금 말씀드린 것에 대해 많은 사람들이 회의적입니다. 실제로 다소 논란이 있는 주제입니다. 하지만 많은 사람들은 자신의 몸에 특정 보석을 착용했을 때 기분이 더 좋아진다고 단언합니다. 어떻게 그럴 수가 있을까요? 음, 하나의 이론에 따르면, 태양의 광파는 보석을 통과하는 경우 신체에 다른 방식으로 들어온다고 합니다. 이로써 광파가 신체에 다양한 효과를 미치게 되는 것이고요. 그것이 사실인지 아닌지는 저도 잘 모르겠습니다. 하지만, 그러한 주장을 뒷받침하는 몇 가지 증거들이 있습니다.

Answers

21. Ⓑ (Gist-Content Question)

22. Ⓒ (Detail Question)

23. Ⓐ (Understanding Attitude Question)

24. Ⓑ (Making Inferences Question)

Script 🎧 4-06

W Professor: Australia has been inhabited for more than 40,000 years. The people who first settled it were the Aborigines. The descendants of these people still live there today. While Australia was settled long ago, it was unknown to the rest of the world for centuries. It wasn't until the Age of Exploration that it was rediscovered. And it wasn't settled by any Europeans until the 1700s.

Australia was one of the last places the, um, the Europeans discovered. There were, however, rumors about its existence for a long time. Some sailors may have seen it, but they never landed there. The first actual landing on Australia by Europeans happened in 1606. It was a ship from the Netherlands . . . uh,

a Dutch ship, that is, that first visited the continent. Later, both Dutch and Spanish ships sighted Australia and sometimes made landfall during the 1600s. But nobody founded a permanent settlement. The Dutch managed to chart most of Australia's coasts though. And Dutch explorers also discovered New Zealand, Tasmania, and Fiji during that time.

M Student: Why didn't the Dutch settle there?

W: The Dutch basically saw the land as having no value. You see, um, Australia has a harsh climate in many places. In addition, the Aborigines led a very primitive lifestyle. They didn't trade in gold, silk, or spices. So the Dutch realized there were no immediate profits to make. Oh, and Australia is rather far from Europe, so any colony would have needed to be mostly self-sufficient. A few people proposed colonizing the land, but nothing ever came of their ideas.

In 1770, though, Captain James Cook, the famous British explorer and navigator, charted the east coast of Australia. He noticed that Botany Bay, a natural harbor, might be a good place for a settlement. Cook subsequently claimed the land for Britain. The British were initially slow to colonize the land. Then, the American Revolution ended in 1783, and the British lost the American colonies. Why is that important . . . ? Well, for decades, the British had transported criminals to the American colonies. These convicts worked as indentured servants until their sentences ended. But, when the American Revolution began in 1775, new convicts couldn't be sent to America anymore. Instead, many were kept in prisons and onboard ships in British harbors. The conditions in these places were, uh, simply atrocious.

Joseph Banks and James Marta then came up with a plan. Both men had visited Australia with Cook, so they were familiar with the land. They proposed that a colony be established at Botany Bay. Marta suggested that convicts could settle the land there. The proposal was accepted. So eleven ships departed England and arrived at Botany Bay in January 1788. There were more than 1,000 settlers aboard the ships. Most of them were convicts. The leaders soon decided to leave Botany Bay. They moved to Port Jackson, which they considered a better site. This became the first European settlement in Australia. Today, Port Jackson is where Sydney is located. Now, as for that colony, here's what happened . . .

Translation

W Professor: 사람들은 40,000년이 넘는 기간 동안 호주에 거주해 왔습니다. 그곳에 처음으로 정착했던 사람들은 호주 원주민이었습니다. 그러한 사람들의 후손들은 오늘날까지도 그곳에서 살고 있습니다. 사람들이 호주에 정착을 한 것은 오래 전 일이었지만, 호주는 수 세기 동안 다른 곳에 알려져 있지 않았습니다. 탐험의 시대가 되어서야 호주는 재발견되었습니다. 그리고 1700년대가 되어서야 유럽인들이 정착을 하기 시작했고요.

호주는, 음, 유럽인들이 발견해 낸, 가장 마지막 지역 중의 하나였습니다. 하지만, 오래 동안 그에 관한 소문들이 존재했습니다. 몇몇 선원들이 그곳을 보았을 수도 있지만, 결코 그곳에 상륙하지는 않았습니다. 실제로 유럽인들이 처음으로 호주에 상륙한 것은 1606년이었습니다. 화란, 어, 즉 네덜란드 선박이 호주 대륙을 최초로 방문했습니다. 이후, 네덜란드 선박과 스페인 선박 모두가 호주를 발견했고 1600년대에는 때때로 상륙을 하기도 했습니다. 하지만 누구도 영구적인 정착촌을 세우지는 않았습니다. 하지만 네덜란드인들은 호주 해안가의 대부분의 지역에 대한 지도를 만들었습니다. 그리고 네덜란드 탐험가들은 이 시기 동안에 뉴질랜드, 태즈메이니아, 그리고 피지도 발견해 냈죠.

M Student: 네덜란드인들은 왜 그곳에 정착하지 않았나요?

W: 네덜란드인들은 기본적으로 그곳을 가치가 없는 지역으로 여겼습니다. 아시겠지만, 음, 호주의 여러 지역에서는 기후가 혹독합니다. 게다가, 원주민들은 매우 원시적인

생활을 하고 있었습니다. 금, 비단, 혹은 향료에 대한 거래를 하지 않았습니다. 따라서 네덜란드인들은 즉각적으로 얻을 수 있는 이익이 존재하지 않는다는 점을 깨달았습니다. 오, 그리고 호주는 유럽에서 다소 멀리 떨어져 있기 때문에, 식민지가 있었다면 주로 자급자족을 해야 할 것이었습니다. 소수의 사람들이 호주 지역을 식민화 할 것을 제안했지만, 그러한 생각으로부터 돌아오는 것은 아무것도 없었습니다.

하지만, 1770년, 유명한 영국인 탐험가이자 항해사인 제임스 쿡 선장이 호주의 동쪽 해안에 대한 지도를 만들었습니다. 그는 천연 항구인 보터니 만이 정착을 하기 위한 좋은 장소가 될 것이라는 점에 주목을 했습니다. 이후 쿡은 호주가 영국의 땅이라고 주장했습니다. 영국인들에 의한 호주의 식민지화는 초기에 더디게 이루어졌습니다. 그 후, 미국 혁명이 1792년에 끝났고, 영국인들은 아메리카 대륙의 식민지들을 잃게 되었습니다. 왜 그러한 점이 중요할까요…? 음, 수십 년 동안, 영국인들은 범죄자들을 아메리카 식민지로 이송시켰습니다. 이러한 죄수들은 형이 끝날 때까지 연한 계약 노동자로서 노동을 했습니다. 하지만, 미국 혁명이 1775년에 시작되자, 새로운 죄수들을 더 이상 아메리카 대륙으로 보낼 수가 없었습니다. 대신, 많은 이들이 수감되어 영국 항구의 선박에 승선해 있었습니다. 이러한 곳에서의 상황은, 어, 끔찍했습니다.

그 후 조지프 뱅크스와 제임스 마트라가 하나의 계획을 세웠습니다. 두 사람은 쿡과 함께 호주를 방문한 적이 있었기 때문에, 그 지역에 익숙했습니다. 그들은 보터니 만에 식민지를 건설할 것을 제안했습니다. 마르타는 죄수들이 그곳 땅에 정착할 수 있을 것이라고 주장했습니다. 그러한 제안은 받아들여졌습니다. 그래서 11척의 선박이 영국을 떠나 1788년 1월에 보터니 만에 도착했습니다. 배에는 1,000명 이상의 정착민들이 승선해 있었습니다. 그들 대부분은 죄수들이었습니다. 얼마 후 지도자들은 보터니 만을 떠나기로 결정했습니다. 이들은 잭슨 항으로 이동했는데, 그들은 그곳이 더 좋은 장소라고 생각했습니다. 이곳은 호주에서 최초의 유럽 정착촌이 되었습니다. 오늘날, 잭슨 항은 시드니가 위치해 있는 곳입니다. 자, 그러한 식민지에 있어서, 어떤 일이 있었는지를 알려 드리면…

Actual Test 2

Answers

1. Ⓑ (Gist-Content Question)

2. Ⓓ (Making Inferences Question)

3. Ⓑ (Detail Question)

4. Ⓒ (Understanding Attitude Question)

Script 🎧 4-07

W Student: Professor Roberts, I'm so glad you're in your office. Do you mind if I come in for a moment?

M Professor: Not at all, Cathy. Please be my guest.

W: Thanks so much. Um, I have a problem, and I think you can help me. At least, uh, I hope you can help me.

M: How so?

W: You're teaching a seminar next semester, right? Uh, the seminar on the history of colonialism in the Americas I mean.

M: Yes, that is correct. It should be a fun class. I taught it three years ago, and the students seemed to enjoy it a lot then.

W: I'm sure they did. Well, uh, anyway, I tried to register for the class, but I wasn't allowed to. Apparently, only seniors are allowed to sign up for a seminar. As you know, I'm only a junior, but, uh, is there any way I can get into your class?

M: Hmm . . . That's a good question.

W: What do you mean?

M: Well, all history majors have to take a seminar before they graduate. So, uh, senior students are always allowed to register for the class first. In addition, the class is limited to fifteen students. That way, everyone can participate in the

discussions.

W: [4]I see . . . So you're saying I won't be able to get into the class? That's too bad. I was really looking forward to taking it.

M: Slow down a minute. There is actually a small chance that you can take it. If fewer than fifteen seniors sign up, then juniors in the History Department can enroll in the class. I'll put you on the waitlist. You'll be the first junior who gets to join if there is enough room. How does that sound?

W: Some chance is better than no chance at all. It's not a perfect result, but it's better than nothing. Thanks, sir.

Translation

W Student: Roberts 교수님, 사무실에 계셔서 정말 다행이에요. 잠시 들어가도 될까요?

M Professor: 물론이죠, Cathy. 어서 들어오세요.

W: 정말 고맙습니다. 음, 제게 문제가 하나 있는데, 교수님께서 저를 도와 주실 수 있을 것 같아서요. 적어도, 어, 교수님께서 도와 주실 수 있기를 바라요.

M: 어떻게요?

W: 다음 학기에 교수님께서 세미나 수업을 하실 거죠, 그렇죠? 어, 아메리카 대륙의 식민주의 역사에 관한 세미나 수업을 말씀드리는 거에요.

M: 네, 맞아요. 재미있는 수업이 될 거에요. 3년 전에 가르쳤는데, 당시 학생들이 많이 좋아했던 것 같아요.

W: 분명 그랬을 거에요. 음, 어, 어쨌든, 저는 그 수업에 등록을 하려고 했지만, 승인을 받지 못했어요. 듣자 하니, 4학년들만 수업에 등록을 할 수가 있더군요. 아시겠지만, 저는 3학년일 뿐인데, 하지만, 어, 제가 교수님의 수업을 들을 수 있는 방법이 있을까요?

M: 흠… 좋은 질문이군요.

W: 무슨 말씀이시죠?

M: 음, 모든 역사 전공 학생들은 졸업을 하기 전에 세미나 수업을 들어야 해요. 그래서, 어, 4학년 학생들이 항상 제일 먼저 수업에 등록을 할 수가 있죠. 또한, 그 수업은 인원이 15명으로 제한되어 있어요. 그렇게 함으로써, 모든 학생들이 수업 토론에 참여할 수가 있죠.

W: 그렇군요… 그러면 제가 그 수업을 들을 수 없을 것이라는 말씀이신가요? 안 되었네요. 정말로 그 수업을 듣고 싶었거든요.

M: 잠시 진정하세요. 실은 학생이 수강을 할 수 있는 기회가 약간 있어요. 15명 미만의 4학년 학생들이 수강 신청을 하면, 역사학과의 3학년 학생들도 수업에 등록을 할 수가 있죠. 대기자 명단에 학생의 이름을 올려 놓을 게요. 자리가 충분히 비는 경우, 학생은 수업을 듣게 될 첫 번째 3학년생이 될 거에요. 어떻게 들리나요?

W: 기회가 약간 있는 것이 전혀 없는 것보다는 낫죠. 완벽한 결과는 아니지만, 없는 것보다는 나아요. 고맙습니다, 교수님.

Answers

5. 1 , 4 (Detail Question)

6. Ⓒ (Understanding Organization Question)

7. Ⓒ (Gist-Purpose Question)

8. Ⓑ (Understanding Attitude Question)

Script 🎧 4-08

M1 Professor: People rarely think of birds as predators. However, there are many species of birds that hunt. Some are the condor, hawk, eagle, falcon, buzzard, vulture, and owl. They are collectively referred to as birds of prey. For the most part, they eat small mammals and other birds. Most birds of prey attack by swooping down suddenly from above. They surprise their victims and kill them with their sharp claws and beaks.

All birds of prey have several characteristics in common

that make them good hunters. For one thing, they have keen eyesight. This allows them to see potential prey from far away or from high above. They have sharp claws that let them kill animals. They also have very sharp beaks. These enable the birds to tear the flesh of animals. Their beaks are usually curved and pointy. Look at the screen here . . . You can see an eagle's beak . . . Note the sharp tip here . . . and the downward turn of the end of the beak . . . In this picture . . . look at the claws, or talons, as we call them . . . They can grasp and tear at the same time.

Many birds of prey share those physical characteristics. But don't misunderstand. There are also many differences between them. The shapes of their wings often differ. Some, such as the eagle . . . and the condor . . . have broad wings. These let the birds soar high above the ground while they search for prey down below. Others, such as the falcon here . . . and the hawk here . . . have short, compact wings. These are ideal for swiftly diving on prey. Another difference is that most birds of prey hunt during the day. Owls, on the other hand, are night hunters. Over the years, their eyes have evolved so that they have excellent night vision. This makes them extremely fearsome nocturnal hunters. Do you have a question, Tina?

W Student: Yes, sir, I do. You mentioned that buzzards and vultures are birds of prey. Is that correct? I have never thought of them as being hunters.

M1: Ah, yes. Thank you for bringing that up. That's rather observant of you. Let me explain, class . . . While most birds of prey are hunters, some are scavengers. They occasionally hunt, but they prefer carrion . . . Yes?

M2 Student: Carrion? I'm not familiar with that term.

M1: It means the body of a dead animal. You know, uh, a carcass. That is what buzzards and vultures usually eat. Nevertheless, we consider them birds of prey since they have all of their physical features. Everybody got that . . . ? Good.

In total, there are somewhere around 500 species of birds of prey. They are found in virtually every climate and terrain. [8]Among birds of prey, the condor, eagle, and vulture are the largest. The Andean condor has a wingspan of more than three meters. Conversely, falcons, hawks, and owls are among the smallest birds of prey. **One species of owl—the elf owl— is only around twelve centimeters long and weighs next to nothing.**

Translation

M1 Professor: 조류를 포식자로 생각하는 경우는 거의 없습니다. 하지만, 사냥을 하는 많은 종의 조류들이 존재합니다. 그중 일부는 콘도르, 매, 독수리, 팔콘, 대머리수리, 벌쳐, 그리고 올빼미입니다. 이들은 통칭해서 맹금류라고 불립니다. 주로, 작은 포유류나 다른 새들을 잡아먹죠. 대부분의 맹금류들은 위쪽에서 갑자기 급강하함으로써 공격을 합니다. 희생물을 놀라게 하여 날카로운 발톱과 부리를 가지고 목숨을 빼앗습니다.

모든 맹금류들은 자신들을 훌륭한 사냥꾼으로 만들어 주는 몇 가지 공통적인 특성을 지니고 있습니다. 우선, 뛰어난 시력을 가지고 있습니다. 이로써 먼 곳으로부터 혹은 높은 곳으로부터 먹이가 될 수 있는 대상을 볼 수가 있습니다. 이들은 동물의 목숨을 빼앗도록 해주는 날카로운 발톱을 지니고 있습니다. 또한 매우 날카로운 부리도 가지고 있습니다. 이는 맹금류로 하여금 동물의 살점을 찢어낼 수 있도록 합니다. 이들의 부리는 보통 구부러져 있으며 끝이 뾰족합니다. 여기 스크린을 보시면… 독수리의 부리를 보실 수 있습니다… 여기 날카로운 끝을 주목해 주시고… 그리고 부리 끝 쪽이 아래로 향해 있는 것도 주목해 주십시오… 이 사진에서… 발톱과 혹은 소위 탤런이라고 불리는 것을 봐 주세요… 이들은 먹이를 잡아채는 동시에 살점을 찢을 수가 있습니다.

많은 맹금류들이 그와 같은 신체적인 특징들을 공유하고 있습니다. 하지만 오해하지는 마세요. 또한 그들 간에는 여러 가지 차이점들도 존재합니다. 종종 날개의 형태가 다릅니다. 일부는, 예컨대 독수리와… 그리고 콘도르는… 폭이 넓은 날개를

가지고 있습니다. 이러한 점은 아래에 있는 먹이를 찾을 때 지면 높은 곳에서 이들이 비행할 수 있도록 해줍니다. 또 다른 새들, 예컨대 여기 팔콘과… 여기에 있는 매는… 짧고 작은 날개를 가지고 있습니다. 이는 먹이를 향해 빠르게 하강하는데 이상적입니다. 또 다른 차이점은 대부분의 맹금류들이 낮 동안에 사냥을 한다는 점입니다. 반면, 올빼미는 야간에 사냥을 합니다. 수 년에 걸쳐, 눈이 진화되어 이들은 뛰어난 밤눈을 가지고 있습니다. 이로써 이들은 매우 무시무시한 야간 사냥꾼이 됩니다. 질문이 있나요, Tina?

W Student: 네, 교수님, 있습니다. 대머리수리와 벌쳐가 맹금류라고 말씀하셨는데요. 그것이 사실인가요? 그들을 맹수라고 생각해 본 적이 없어서요.

M1: 아, 네. 그 점을 생각나게 해줘서 고맙네요. 관찰력이 상당히 좋군요. 설명해 드리죠, 여러분… 대부분의 맹금류들은 맹수지만, 일부는 청소 동물입니다. 때때로 사냥을 하지만, 썩은 고기를 더 좋아합니다… 네?

M2 Student: 썩은 고기요? 그러한 용어는 익숙하지가 않은데요.

M1: 죽은 동물의 시체를 의미합니다. 아시겠지만, 어, 사체죠. 대머리수리와 벌쳐가 보통 먹는 것입니다. 그럼에도 불구하고, 이들은 맹금류의 신체적 특징을 모두 가지고 있기 때문에, 우리는 이들을 맹금류로 간주합니다. 모두들 알겠나요…? 좋습니다.

모두 합해서, 약 500여종의 맹금류가 존재합니다. 사실상 모든 기후 및 모든 지형에서 발견됩니다. 맹금류 중에서, 콘도르, 독수리, 그리고 벌쳐가 가장 큽니다. 안데스 콘도르의 날개 길이는 3미터가 넘습니다. 반면, 팔콘, 매, 그리고 올빼미는 가장 작은 맹금류에 속합니다. 올빼미 중 한 종은 – 엘프 올빼미는 – 길이가 12센티미터 정도일 뿐이며 몸무게가 가장 적게 나갑니다.

Answers

9.   Ⓓ (Gist-Content Question)

10.   Ⓑ (Understanding Attitude Question)

11.   Ⓐ (Detail Question)

12.   Ⓑ (Making Inferences Question)

Script 🎧 4-09

W Professor: For the next two weeks, we're going to focus on *The Canterbury Tales*. I'd like to give you a brief introduction at this moment. And then I'll dismiss you for the day. Oh, uh, be sure to read the general prologue by the next class. That's the very beginning of the poem in case you don't know.

Okay, um, *The Canterbury Tales* . . . It was written by Geoffrey Chaucer. He started working on it in 1387. When he died in 1400, his masterpiece was incomplete. Hmm . . . Actually, I think "incomplete" might be an improper word. Let me explain why. You see, Chaucer wrote his poem by using a method common during his time. He wrote many relatively short poems and combined them by using a framework. So *The Canterbury Tales* can be taken as one very long poem. Or it can be considered a compilation of many smaller poems.

M Student: What was the framework for the story, Professor Madison?

W: Basically, the poem is about a group of people going on a pilgrimage from London to Canterbury. They're going to Canterbury to visit the shrine of Saint Thomas Becket. There are thirty people in the group. They have various backgrounds . . . The group includes a knight, a priest, a nun, some craftsmen, and a lawyer, among others. They meet in a tavern near London before starting their journey. The tavern owner suggests that they have a storytelling contest. He says that each person should tell two stories on the way to Canterbury and two more on the way back.

So, uh, if all thirty characters tell four tales each, there would be 120 tales, right? However, Chaucer only wrote twenty-four. How come . . . ? Some people believe Chaucer stopped writing in order to revise his first twenty-four stories. Then, he died before he could write any more. Others have different theories. Whatever the case, *The Canterbury Tales* isn't anywhere close to, um, to being as long as Chaucer had planned. In fact, in the story, the pilgrims never even make it to Canterbury. The poem ends before they get there.

But we're not going to focus on the pilgrimage itself. Of more importance are the stories. These stories are told by people with various backgrounds. As you can imagine, this results in the stories being quite different from one another. The knight's tale, for instance, is a poem about chivalry. But other tales, such as that told by the wife of Bath, are cruder. Some of the tales are funny. Others are not. The themes of many of the stories focus on religion and the differences between the various social classes of the day. We'll examine these various themes as we read the poems. Oh, and we're going to read *The Canterbury Tales* in the original language, which was Middle English. It's quite different from modern English, so you'll have to get used to it quickly. I hope that all of you can manage to do that.

Translation

W Professor: 다음 2주 동안에는, *캔터베리 이야기*에 대해 초점을 맞추어 보도록 하겠습니다. 지금은 여러분께 간단히 소개를 해드리고자 합니다. 그리고 나서는 수업을 마치도록 하겠습니다. 오, 어, 다음 수업 때까지 잊지 말고 서문을 읽어 오세요. 모르시는 분을 위해 말씀을 드리면, 시의 첫 부분입니다.

좋아요, 음, *캔터베리 이야기*는 제프리 초서에 의해 쓰여졌습니다. 그는 1387년에 그것에 대한 작업을 시작했습니다. 그가 1400년에 사망할 당시, 그의 걸작은 미완성 상태였습니다. 흠… 사실, 저는 "미완성"이란 말이 부적절한 단어가 될 수 있다고 생각합니다. 그 이유를 설명해 드리죠. 아시겠지만, 초서는 당시에 일반적이던 방법을 사용하여 자신의 시를 썼습니다. 비교적 짧은 시를 많이 쓰고, 하나의 틀을 사용해서 그들을 연결시켰습니다. 따라서 *캔터베리 이야기*는 하나의 매우 긴 시로서 간주될 수 있습니다. 혹은 많은 짧은 시들로 이루어진 편집본으로서 간주될 수도 있죠.

M Student: 이야기에 대한 틀이 무엇이었나요, Madison 교수님?

W: 기본적으로, 그 시는 런던에서 캔터베리로 순례 여행을 떠났던 한 무리의 사람들에 관한 것입니다. 이들은 성인 토마스 베켓의 성지를 방문하기 위해 캔터베리로 가고 있습니다. 무리에는 30명의 사람이 있었고요, 그들은 다양한 배경을 가지고 있습니다… 무리에는 기사, 성직자, 수녀, 몇 명의 장인들, 그리고 한 명의 법관이 다른 사람들과 함께 포함되어 있었습니다. 이들은 여정을 시작하기 전에 런던 근처의 한 여관에서 모이게 됩니다. 여관 주인은 이들이 이야기 지어내기 시합을 할 것을 제안합니다. 각자가 캔터베리로 가는 도중에 두 개의 이야기를 말하고 돌아오는 길에 두 개의 이야기를 더 말해야 한다고 말을 합니다.

그래서, 어, 30명의 인물들이 각각 4개의 이야기를 한다면, 120개의 이야기가 나오게 될 것입니다, 그렇죠? 하지만, 초서는 24개만을 썼습니다. 왜 그랬을까요…? 몇몇 사람들은 초서가 첫 24개의 이야기를 수정하기 위해 글 쓰는 것을 잠시 중단했다고 믿고 있습니다. 그런 다음, 이야기를 더 쓰기 전에 사망을 한 것이죠. 다른 이론을 가지고 있는 사람들도 있습니다. 어떤 경우이던, *캔터베리 이야기*는 음, 초서가 계획했던 것과 전혀 다른 것이 되었습니다. 사실, 이야기에서, 순례자들은 결코 캔터베리에 가지 않습니다. 그들이 그곳에 도착하기 전에 시가 끝나버립니다.

하지만 우리가 순례 그 자체에 초점을 맞추지는 않을 것입니다. 보다 중요한 것 중의 하나는 이야기입니다. 이 이야기들은 다양한 배경을 가진 사람들에 의해 말해집니다. 상상할 수 있듯이, 이는 그 결과로서 서로 매우 다른 이야기들을 만들어 냅니다. 예를 들어, 기사의 이야기는 기사도에 관한 시입니다. 하지만 바스 부인이 말한 것과 같은 다른 이야기들은 보다 저속합니다. 몇몇 이야기들은 재미있습니다. 그렇지 않은 것들도 있고요. 많은 이야기들의 주제는 종교 및 당시 다양한 사회 계층 간의 차이에 초점을 맞추고 있습니다. 시를 읽으면서 우리는 이러한 다양한 주제들에 관해 검토해 볼 것입니다. 오, 그리고 원어로, 즉 중세 시대의 영어로 캔터베리 이야기를 읽게 될 것입니다. 현대 영어와는 다소 차이가 나기 때문에, 여러분들은 빠르게 적응을 하셔야 할 것입니다. 여러분 모두가 그렇게 하실 수 있기를 바랍니다.

Answers

13. Ⓒ (Gist-Content Question)

14. Ⓐ (Gist-Purpose Question)

15. ② , ④ (Detail Question)

16. Ⓐ (Understanding Attitude Question)

Script 🎧 4-10

W Librarian: Good afternoon. Is there anything I can do for you?

M Student: Yes, there is. I am trying to find a book, but it seems to be checked out. Is there some way I can, uh, I don't know, reserve the book? I mean, when the person returns it, can I be the next one to check it out? Is that possible?

W: Yes, you can do that. I can put a hold on the book for you.

M: Uh, what exactly does that mean?

W: When you put a hold on a book, the person has to return it within ten days. So, first, we'll send a notice to the person who has the book. Then, when the book is returned, we'll call you. After that, you can come and check it out.

M: Awesome. What do I have to do?

W: Just fill out this form. Oh, I need to see your student ID, too.

M: Sure thing . . . Here you are.

W: Looks good to me. Thank you.

M: Ah, there's one more thing. I need to renew my library books. I think a few of them are due tomorrow. You can do that for me, right?

W: Yes, I can do that now. Let me check your account . . . Hmm . . . You have eleven books checked out . . . You're right. Four are due tomorrow. I'll just go ahead and renew all eleven.

M: Thanks so much for doing that. What's the new due date?

W: It's November seventeenth. That's two weeks from today. You can renew those books two more times before you have to return them. Now, finish filling out that form, and I will put the hold on the book you want.

Translation

W Librarian: 안녕하세요. 학생을 위해 제가 해드릴 일이 있나요?

M Student: 네, 있어요. 책을 한 권 찾고 있는 중인데, 대출이 된 것 같아요. 제가, 어, 뭐라고 해야 할지 잘 모르겠는데, 책을 예약해 둘 수 있는 방법이 있을까요? 제 말은, 그 사람이 책을 반납을 할 때, 제가 그 책을 대출할 수 있는 바로 다음 차례가 될 수 있을까요? 그것이 가능한가요?

W: 네, 그렇게 할 수 있죠. 학생을 위해 제가 도서 예약을 해드릴게요.

M: 어, 그것이 정확히 어떤 의미인가요?

W: 도서 예약을 하면, 대출자가 10일 이내에 책을 반납해야 해요. 그래서, 우선은, 책을 가지고 있는 사람에게 저희가 통지를 해줄 거에요. 그런 다음, 책이 반납되면, 학생에게 전화를 할 것이고요. 그 후에는, 학생이 이리로 와서 그 책을 대출할 수가 있죠.

M: 멋지군요. 제가 어떻게 하면 되나요?

W: 이 양식에 내용만 기입해 주세요. 오, 학생의 학생증도 확인해야 해요.

M: 물론이에요… 여기 있어요.

W: 괜찮아 보이네요. 고마워요.

M: 아, 한 가지가 더 있어요. 도서관 책들의 대출 기간을 연장해야 해서요. 그중 몇 권은 내일까지 반납해야 하는 것으로 알고 있어요. 그렇게 해주실 수 있죠, 그렇죠?

W: 네, 지금 해드릴게요. 학생의 대출 내역을 확인해 볼게요… 흠… 11권의 책을 대출하셨군요… 학생 말이 맞아요. 4권의 반납일이 내일까지네요. 11권 모두에 대해 제가 대출 기간을 연장해 드릴게요.

M: 그렇게 해주신다니 정말로 고맙습니다. 새로운 반납 기한은 어떻게 되나요?

W: 11월 17일이에요. 오늘부터 2주 후죠. 책들을 반납을 하기 전에 두 차례 더 대출 기간을 연장하실 수 있어요. 자, 양식에 내용을 다 기입해 주시면, 제가 학생이 원하는 책에 대해서 도서 예약을 해드릴게요.

Answers

17. Ⓑ (Detail Question)

18. **Wind:** 2 , 4 **Fetch:** 1 , 3
    (Connecting Content Question)

19. Ⓑ (Making Inferences Question)

20. Ⓐ (Understanding Function Question)

Script 🎧 4-11

M Professor: Waves are mainly caused by the action of the wind on the surface of the water. How so . . . ? Well, the wind produces friction on the water's surface. This causes the water to start to ripple. Gradually, these ripples become larger. Soon, a wave forms. Each wave has a crest—its highest point—and a trough, which is its lowest point.

When a wave forms, it appears as though the water is moving forward. Yet that's an illusion. Very little water actually moves forward. It's the wave's energy that causes the water to appear to move. The reason is that water is a fluid medium. I'll explain that in a bit. Okay . . . ?

Now, uh, sometimes you might have seen some wavelike motion on the ocean when there's no wind. These waves are called swells. Have you ever wondered what swells are . . . ? Uh, maybe not . . . Anyway, swells are the remains of waves that formed in other locations where it was windy. [20]The wave energy is still present in the water, so that's why they occur. Swells produce a gentler, more rolling motion than waves.

Okay, I got sidetracked a little there. I'm sorry. Let me get back to the main topic: wave formation. There are five main factors that affect wave formation and the sizes of waves. Let me tell you a little about each. The first factor is wind speed. When the wind is weak, it produces small waves. When the wind blows harder, it produces more friction. This results in higher waves. The second factor is fetch. This refers to how far across the water the wind has blown. You see, uh, on the ocean, the wind can move greater distances than it can on a river or lake. Thus ocean waves are bigger than river and lake waves.

Now, uh, the third factor is the width of the area the wind blows on. When it blows on a wide area, the waves are larger than when it blows on a narrow area. Fourth concerns the amount of time the wind blows. If it blows a long time, the waves are higher. The final factor is the depth of the water. Some waves in shallow water can build up to great heights before crashing onto shore. Yes, Amanda?

W Student: So, uh, the waves near shore are the biggest ones?

M: No, they aren't. Some monster waves, or, uh, rogue waves, can reach shore. But the biggest recorded waves are formed far out on the ocean. Many monster waves have been recorded at heights of thirty meters. That's as high as a cruise ship or oil tanker. These waves were once thought to be extremely rare. Yet they happen more often than we had thought, which is unfortunate since they can be deadly.

But don't worry too much. Most waves are just a few meters in height. Now, since Amanda brought up the topic . . . let's examine what happens to a wave as it reaches shallow water.

Translation

M Professor: 파도는 수면에 부는 바람의 작용에 의해 주로 생성됩니다. 어떻게요…? 음, 바람이 수면에 마찰을 일으킵니다. 이로써 물에 물결을 생기기 시작합니다. 점차적으로, 이러한 물결은 보다 커지게 됩니다. 곧, 파도가 생성됩니다. 각각의 파도는 물마루와 – 가장 높은 지점과 – 가장 낮은 지점인 골을 갖습니다.

파도가 형성되면, 물이 앞으로 이동하는 것처럼 보입니다. 하지만 이것은 착각입니다. 실제로 물이 앞으로 이동하는 경우는 거의 없습니다. 물이 이동하는 것처럼 보이게 만드는 것은 바로 파도의 에너지입니다. 그 이유는 물이 액체로 된 매체이기 때문입니다. 잠시 그에 대해 설명해 드리도록 하겠습니다. 괜찮겠죠…?

자, 어, 때때로 바람이 없을 때 바다에서 파도와 같은 움직임을 보신 적이 있으실 것입니다. 이러한 파도는 너울이라고 불립니다. 너울이 무엇인지 궁금해 하신 적이 있나요…? 어, 아마도 그렇지 않으셨을 것 같군요… 어쨌든, 너울은 바람이 부는 또 다른 위치에서 형성된 파도의 잔여물입니다. 파랑 에너지는 물속에 계속 존재하는데, 따라서 이것이 너울이 생성되는 이유가 됩니다. 너울은 파도보다 더욱 부드럽고 완만한 운동을 합니다.

좋아요, 잠시 옆길로 빠졌군요. 죄송합니다. 다시 주제로 돌아가도록 하겠습니다: 파도의 형성입니다. 파도의 형성과 파도의 크기에 영향을 미치는 5개의 주요 요인들이 있습니다. 각각에 대해 짧게 말씀해 드리도록 하겠습니다. 첫 번째 요인은 풍속입니다. 바람이 약하면, 작은 파도가 생성됩니다. 바람이 보다 세차게 불면, 더 많은 마찰이 일어납니다. 그 결과 보다 높은 파도가 생성됩니다. 두 번째 요인은 대안거리입니다. 이는 수면에서 바람이 불 수 있는 거리를 지칭합니다. 아시다시피, 어, 바다에서는, 강이나 호수에서보다 바람이 더 먼 거리를 이동할 수 있습니다. 따라서 바다에서의 파도는 강과 호수에서의 파도보다 더 큽니다.

자, 어, 세 번째 요인은 바람이 부는 지역의 넓이입니다. 넓은 지역에서 바람이 불면, 좁은 지역에서 불 때보다 파도가 더 큽니다. 네 번째는 바람이 부는 시간의 양과 관련이 있습니다. 오래 동안 바람이 불 때, 파도가 보다 높아집니다. 마지막 요인은 수심입니다. 수심이 얕은 수역에서의 일부 파도들은 해안가에 부딪히기 전에 막대한 높이로 점점 커질 수 있습니다. 네, Amanda?

W Student: 그러면, 어, 해안가 근처의 파도가 가장 큰 파도인가요?

M: 아니오, 그렇지 않습니다. 일부 괴물 파도들, 즉, 어, 거대한 파도들이 해안가에 닿을 수도 있습니다. 하지만 기록상 가장 큰 파도는 바다에서 멀리 떨어진 곳에서 형성되었습니다. 많은 괴물 파도들이 30미터의 높이를 가지고 있었다고 기록된 바 있습니다. 유람선이나 유조선 정도의 높이입니다. 이러한 파도들은 한때 극히 드문 것으로 생각되었습니다. 하지만 생각했던 것보다 자주 발생하고 있는데, 파도가 치명적일 수 있기 때문에 이는 안타까운 일입니다. 하지만 너무 걱정하지는 마세요. 대부분의 파도들은 높이가 수 미터에 지나지 않습니다. 자, Amanda가 주제를 제시해 주었으므로… 얕은 수역에 도달하는 경우, 파도에 어떤 일이 일어나는지 검토해 보도록 합시다.

Answers

21. Ⓒ (Gist-Content Question)

22. Ⓒ (Detail Question)

23. Ⓓ (Understanding Organization Question)

24. Ⓑ (Making Inferences Question)

Script 🎧 4-12

M Professor: What exactly was the Cold War? I think we can best define it as a period of tension that was mostly between the United States and the Soviet Union. The Cold War lasted from 1946 to 1991. It ended when the Soviet Union collapsed and broke apart into several nations. But, before we begin today's lesson on the Cold War, I'd like to look briefly at what led it to happen.

Two of the main causes of the Cold War were communism and World War II. In 1917, World War I was still going on. We covered that already, right . . . ? Well, the Russian Revolution took place in that year. It enabled the communists to come to power. Thus Russia soon became the Soviet Union. Almost immediately, there was a great deal of tension between the Soviet Union and democratic nations such as Great Britain, France, and the United States. Counterrevolutionary forces tried to overthrow the communists. This resulted in the Russian Civil War being fought right after the Russian Revolution. Many Western democracies provided aid and even sent soldiers to help the counterrevolutionaries. But the communists emerged victorious.

For the next two decades . . . uh, the 1920s and 1930s . . . there was a great deal of unease between the Soviet Union and the West. They weren't exactly enemies, but, um, they weren't friends either. Many in the West feared the spread of communism. Yet this didn't happen to a great extent. Then, in 1939, World War II began. At that time, Josef Stalin was the leader of the Soviet Union. He and Adolf Hitler of Germany signed a nonaggression pact. They even conquered and divided Poland between their countries. This angered many in the West. But Hitler soon turned on Stalin and invaded the Soviet Union on June 22, 1941. By default, the West and the Soviet Union became allies. Ultimately, of course, Germany was defeated. But, in doing so, the Soviet Union's armies came to occupy much of Eastern Europe. This set the stage for the Cold War.

The Soviets began setting up and backing communist governments throughout Eastern Europe. The West was unhappy yet did nothing but protest. In 1946, British politician Winston Churchill gave a famous speech. He stated that an "iron curtain" had descended across Europe. It was dividing the democratic West from the communist East. The iron curtain would become a symbol of the Cold War.

Now, uh, what you need to remember about the Cold War was that there was no direct fighting between the Soviets and the West. Yes, there were proxy wars, such as the Korean War and the Vietnam War. But Western troops and Soviet troops never battled one another openly. One of the hotspots of the Cold War, however, was Berlin, Germany. After Germany lost the war in 1945, it was divided into four zones. They were the Soviet, American, British, and French zones. Berlin, Germany's capital, was divided the same way. Naturally, this led to a lot of tension. Here's what happened . . .

Translation

M Professor: 냉전이란 정확히 무엇이었을까요? 주로 미국과 소련 사이에 있었던 일정 기간 동안의 긴장 상태라고 가장 잘 정의를 내릴 수 있을 것 같습니다. 냉전은 1946년부터 1991년까지 지속되었습니다. 소련이 붕괴되어 여러 개의 나라들로 분리되었을 때 끝이 났고요. 하지만, 냉전에 대한 오늘 수업을 시작하기에 앞서서, 무엇이 냉전을 이끌어 냈는지에 대해 간략히 살펴보고자 합니다.

냉전의 두 가지 주요 요인은 공산주의와 세계 2차 대전이었습니다. 1917년, 세계 1차 대전은 여전히 진행 중이었습니다. 그에 대해서는 우리가 이미 다루어 보았습니다. 그렇죠…? 음, 러시아 혁명이 그 해에 일어났습니다. 공산주의들로 하여금 권력을 잡도록 했죠. 따라서 러시아는 곧 소련이 되었습니다. 거의 즉각적으로, 소련과 민주주의 국가들, 예컨대 영국, 프랑스, 그리고 미국과 같은 나라들 사이에는 막대한 긴장감이 생겨났습니다. 반혁명 세력들은 공산주의를 전복시키려고 했습니다. 그 결과로서 러시아 혁명 직후에 러시아 내전이 발생하였습니다. 많은 서구 민주주의 국가들은 반혁명 세력을 돕기 위해 원조를 제공해 주었고 심지어는 군대도 보내 주었습니다. 하지만 공산주의자들이 승리한 것으로 판명되었습니다.

다음 20년 동안… 어, 1920년대와 1930년대에… 소련과 서방 사이에는 커다란 불안감이 존재했습니다. 정확히 적국은 아니었지만, 음, 또한 우방도 아니었죠. 서구의 많은 사람들은 공산주의가 확대되는 것을 두려워했습니다. 하지만 상당한 범위로 이루어지지는 않았습니다. 그 후, 1939년, 세계 2차 대전이 시작되었습니다. 당시, 요셉 스탈린이 소련의 지도자였습니다. 그와 독일의 아돌프 히틀러는 불가침 조약에 서명했습니다. 심지어 그 사이에 있는 폴란드를 점령하여 이를 분할하기도 했습니다. 이는 서구의 많은 사람들을 분노하게 만들었습니다. 하지만 히틀러는 곧 스탈린을 공격하여 1941년 6월 22일에 소련을 침공했습니다. 자연스럽게, 서구와 소련은 동맹국이 되었습니다. 결국, 물론, 독일이 패배했습니다. 하지만, 그러는 동안, 소련의 군대가 동유럽의 많은 지역을 점령하게 되었습니다. 이로써 냉전의 무대가 마련되었습니다.

소련 사람들은 동유럽 전역에 공산주의 정부를 세우고 이를 지원하기 시작했습니다. 서방은 달가워하지 않았지만 항의하는 것 이외에는 아무것도 하지 못했습니다. 1946년, 영국의 정치인인 윈스턴 처칠이 유명한 연설을 했습니다. 그는 "철의 장막"이 유럽에 드리워지고 있다고 주장했습니다. 그것은 서구와 공산주의 동구권을 구분 짓는 것이었습니다. 철의 장막은 냉전의 상징이 되었습니다.

자, 어, 냉전에 대해 여러분들이 기억해야 할 것은 소련과 서구 간에 직접적인 전투가 없었다는 점입니다. 네, 한국 전쟁과 베트남 전쟁과 같은 대리 전쟁은 있었습니다. 하지만 서구의 군대와 소련의 군대는 공식적으로 서로 전투를 벌인 적이 결코 없었습니다. 하지만, 냉전의 위험 지대는 독일의 베를린이었습니다. 1945년에 패전을 한 후, 독일은 4개의 점령 지역으로 나뉘었습니다. 소련 점령 지역, 미국 점령 지역, 영국 점령 지역, 그리고 프랑스 점령 지역이 그것이었습니다. 독일의 수도인 베를린도 같은 방식으로 나뉘었습니다. 당연하게도, 이로써 많은 긴장감이 생기에 되었습니다. 어떤 일이 있었는지 말씀을 드리면…

Speaking

p.196

Task 1

Sample Response  4-13

Many people like shopping on the Internet, but I don't. In fact, I dislike it very much. Most of the time, products sold online don't look like the pictures on the websites. Once, I bought a shirt from an online store. But the shirt I received looked totally different from the picture. It's also difficult to return items that you purchase if you aren't satisfied with them. Many online stores have a no-return policy. You have to be careful when you buy from them. If you aren't happy with your purchase, you won't get your money back.

Translation

많은 사람들이 인터넷으로 쇼핑하는 것을 좋아하지만, 나는 그렇지 않다. 사실, 나는 인터넷 쇼핑을 매우 싫어한다. 대부분의 경우, 온라인에서 판매되는 제품들은 웹사이트에 있는 사진과 같이 보이지 않는다. 한번은, 온라인 매장에서 셔츠를 구입한 적이 있었다. 하지만 내가 받은 셔츠는 사진과 완전히 다르게 보였다. 또한 제품에 만족을 하지 못하는 경우, 구입한 제품을 반품하는 것도 어렵다. 많은 온라인 매장들이 규정상 반품을 받지 않는다. 그러한 곳에서 구입을 할 때는 주의해야 한다. 구입에 만족을 하지 않는 경우라도, 환불을 받지 못할 것이다.

Task 2

Sample Response 1: Agree 4-14

I strongly agree with the statement. Student evaluations of their teachers are definitely valuable. First of all, teachers always read their evaluations. So they can learn what they are doing wrong. Last year, several students in my class criticized a teacher for giving too much homework. The next semester, he gave less homework. Those student evaluations were effective. Secondly, teachers can also learn what they are doing right. Students often compliment teachers for certain actions. Thus teachers will know which actions of theirs the students like. For those two reasons, student evaluations of teachers are clearly important.

Translation

나는 그러한 진술에 강력히 찬성한다. 교사에 대한 학생들의 평가는 매우 가치가 있다. 우선, 교사들은 항상 자신에 대한 평가 내용을 읽는다. 따라서 자신들이 무엇을 잘못하고 있는지를 알 수 있다. 작년, 우리 반 학생들은 과제를 너무 많이 내준다고 담당 교사를 비판했다. 다음 학기에, 그는 과제를 덜 내주었다. 그러한 학생들의 평가는 효과적이었다. 둘째, 교사들은 또한 자신이 무엇을 잘 하고 있는지를 알 수 있다. 학생들은 종종 특정한 행동에 대해 교사들을 좋게 평가한다. 따라서 교사들은 자신의 어떤 행동들을 학생들이 좋아하는지 알게 될 것이다. 이러한 두 가지 이유로, 교사에 대한 학생들의 평가는 분명 중요하다.

Sample Response 2: Disagree 🎧 4-15

I disagree with the statement. I think that student evaluations of teachers are worthless. The first reason I feel this way is that most students make useless comments. For example, students with bad grades usually write that the teacher was horrible. And students with good grades usually write that the teacher was great. Those comments don't help anyone. Second of all, many students don't even write any comments. They just fill out their evaluations as quickly as they can. If the students don't provide any input, then the teachers won't know how to improve.

Translation

나는 그러한 진술에 반대한다. 나는 교사에 대한 학생들의 평가가 가치가 없다고 생각한다. 내가 그렇게 생각하는 첫 번째 이유는 대부분의 학생들이 쓸모 없는 평가를 하기 때문이다. 예를 들어, 성적이 나쁜 학생들은 통상 교사가 형편없다고 적는다. 그리고 성적이 좋은 학생들은 보통 교사가 뛰어나다고 적는다. 그러한 평가는 누구에게도 도움이 되지 않는다. 둘째, 많은 학생들이 평가 내용을 적지도 않는다. 가능한 빨리 평가 양식에 내용을 채울 뿐이다. 학생들이 내용을 기입을 하지 않으면, 교사들은 어떻게 개선시킬 것인지를 모르게 될 것이다.

Task 3

📁 Reading

Translation

기숙사에서 공중 전화가 철거될 예정입니다

대학 기숙사 내 모든 공중 전화가 이번 주 토요일인 10월 3일에 철거될 예정입니다. 대부분의 학생들이 휴대 전화를 가지고 있기 때문에, 현재 공중 전화는 거의 사용되지 않고 있습니다. 또한, 대학측은 공중 전화로 인해 손실을 보고 있습니다. 공중 전화를 설치하고 관리하는데 비용을 부담해야 합니다. 그리고 매달 요금을 지불해야 합니다. 따라서 대학 행정 당국은 공중 전화를 철거함으로써 비용을 절약하기로 결정을 내렸습니다. 하지만, 학과 건물 내의 공중 전화는 철거되지 않을 것입니다.

📁 Listening

Script 🎧 4-16

M Student: Hey, the school is finally removing the payphones from the dorms. It's about time.

W Student: Hmm . . . I have to disagree with you. I think it's a bad decision.

M: Why do you say that? I mean, uh, I've never used a
payphone in three years here.

W: Maybe you haven't. But I have. I sometimes forget to recharge my cell phone's batteries. So I need to use one of the payphones downstairs to make important calls. Now, I'm not going to be able to do that anymore.

M: But what about the fact that the school is losing money because of the payphones? Times are tough economically. I am glad that the school is trying to save money.

W: Come on. I don't believe that. The school doesn't have to pay any phone bills. After all, people pay every time they use the phone. That's why they're called payphones.

M: Oh . . . yeah. You may be right about that.

W: I'm going to talk to someone in the administration. Maybe I can convince the school to leave some of the payphones.

Translation

M Student: 이봐. 학교 측이 마침내 기숙사에서 공중 전화를 철거할 예정이군. 그럴 때가 되었지.

W Student: 흠… 나는 네 말에 동의할 수 없어. 그것은 좋지 못한 결정이라고 생각해.

M: 왜 그렇게 말하는 거지? 내 말은, 어, 나는 여기서 3년 동안 공중 전화를 사용해 본 적이 없어.

W: 아마 그랬을 수도 있겠지. 하지만 난 사용해 봤어. 가끔 전화기 배터리를 충전해야 한다는 점을 잊어. 그래서 중요한 전화를 하기 위해서는 아래층의 공중 전화 중 하나를 사용해야 해. 이제, 더 이상 그렇게 하지 못할 거야.

M: 하지만 공중 전화로 인해 대학측이 손실을 보고 있다는 사실은 어떻게 하지? 경제적으로 힘든 시기야. 학교측이 비용을 절약하려고 한다는 점은 반가운 일이야.

W: 봐봐. 나는 그렇게 생각하지 않아. 학교측은 공중 전화 요금을 지불할 필요가 없어. 어찌되었든, 사람들이 전화를 이용할 때 마다 요금을 지불하는 것이거든. 공중 전화라고 불리는 이유가 그것이지.

M: 오… 그래. 그 점에 대해서는 네 말이 맞을 수도 있겠군.

W: 학교 행정 당국의 누군가에게 이야기를 해야겠어. 아마 학교측을 설득해서 공중 전화 몇 대는 남겨 둘 수 있을 거야.

Sample Response 🎧 4-17

The man and woman are discussing an announcement by the school's management office. The school has decided to remove the payphones from the dormitories. The woman disagrees with this decision. She gives two reasons for disagreeing with it. The first is that she sometimes uses the payphones. Her cell phone often runs out of batteries. When that happens, she uses a payphone. Also, she claims that the school isn't losing money on the phones. She states that people pay the phone bills when they use the phones. For those reasons, she wants the school to keep some of the payphones.

Translation

남자와 여자는 학교 관리처의 공지 사항에 대해 논의를 하고 있다. 대학측은 기숙사에서 공중 전화를 철거하기로 결정했다. 여자는 이러한 결정에 반대한다. 그녀는 자신이 반대하는 것에 대한 두 가지 이유를 제시한다. 첫 번째는 그녀가 때때로 공중 전화를 이용한다는 점이다. 그녀의 휴대폰은 종종 방전이 된다. 그런 일이 발생하면, 그녀는 공중 전화를 이용한다. 또한, 그녀는 학교측이 공중 전화로 손실을 보고 있는 것은 아니라고 주장한다. 그녀는 사람들이 공중 전화를 사용할 때 전화 요금을 지불한다고 언급한다. 이러한 이유로, 그녀는 학교측이 공중 전화 몇 대는 계속 유지시킬 것을 원한다.

Task 4

📁 Reading

Translation

동물들의 협동

종종 같은 종의 동물들은 서로 협력을 한다. 여러 가지 방식으로 함께 행동을 한다. 때때로 함께 먹이를 찾아 다니거나 사냥을 한다. 다 자란 동물들은 종종 포식자로부터 새끼나 어린 동물들을 보호하기도 한다. 몇몇 동물들이 먹이를 먹을 때, 다른 동물들은 포식자 혹은 다른 형태의 위험 요인들을 경계해 주기도 한다. 서로 협력을 함으로써, 동물들은 충분한 음식을 얻고 스스로를 안전하게 지킬 수 있다. 이로써 보다 더 오래 살 수 있다.

📁 Listening

Script 🎧 4-18

M Professor: People love to watch monkeys at the zoo. But I prefer to watch them in the wild. In the wild, monkeys often act together. They truly cooperate with one another. Here are a couple of examples.

Monkeys share their food with one another. For instance, some monkeys may be too old or sick to find their own food. So, um, other monkeys bring food to them. In addition, baby monkeys can't find food of their own. So the babies' mothers and other adults provide food for them. This lets baby monkeys get enough to eat. Therefore, they can grow to become healthy adults.

Monkeys protect one another, too. I'm going to show you a video in a moment. This is what you're going to see. A leopard approaches a colony of monkeys. Some monkeys are feeding. But others are watching for danger. When the monkeys spot the leopard, they start making noise. This alerts the other monkeys of the danger. As a result, the monkeys scatter, and the leopard can't kill any of them. By cooperating in this way, the monkeys all stay alive. Now, um, let's take a look at that video. I want you to see this for yourselves.

Translation

M Professor: 사람들은 동물원에서 원숭이를 구경하는 것을 좋아합니다. 하지만 저는 야생에 있는 원숭이를 보는 것을 더 좋아합니다. 야생에서, 원숭이들은 종종 함께 행동합니다. 정말로 서로 협동을 하고 있는 것이죠. 두 개의 예를 들어 드리도록 하겠습니다.

원숭이들은 서로 먹이를 공유합니다. 예를 들어, 몇몇 원숭이들은 너무 늙거나 병들어서 스스로 먹이를 찾지 못할 수도 있습니다. 그러면, 음, 다른 원숭이들이 이들에게 먹이를 가져다 줍니다. 또한, 새끼 원숭이는 자신의 먹이를 찾을 수가 없습니다. 따라서 새끼 원숭이들의 어미와 다른 다 자란 원숭이들이 이들에게 먹이를 제공해 줍니다. 이로써 새끼 원숭이들은 먹을 수 있는 충분한 먹이를 얻게 됩니다. 따라서, 성장해서 건강한 성체가 될 수 있습니다.

원숭이들은 또한 서로를 보호해 줍니다. 잠시 후에 비디오를 보여 드리도록 하겠습니다. 여러분들께서 보시게 될 내용을 알려 드리죠. 표범 한 마리가 원숭이 서식지에 다가갑니다. 몇몇 원숭이들은 먹이를 먹고 있습니다. 하지만 다른 원숭이들이 위험 요인을 경계해 줍니다. 원숭이들이 표범을 발견하자, 소리를 지르기 시작합니다. 이는 다른 원숭이들에게 위험을 경고해 줍니다. 그 결과, 원숭이들은 흩어지고, 표범은 그 중 누구도 죽일 수가 없게 됩니다. 이러한 방식으로 협동을 함으로써, 원숭이들은 모두 살게 됩니다. 자, 음, 그 비디오를 봅시다. 여러분들 스스로가 이러한 점을 찾게 되기를 바랍니다.

Sample Response 🎧 4-19

The professor tells the students that monkeys usually cooperate with one another. He gives them two examples. First, monkeys share their food with other monkeys. Healthy monkeys find food for old and sick monkeys. They also provide food for baby monkeys. In addition, monkeys protect each other from danger. When a leopard approaches, some monkeys spot the leopard. They make noises to warn the other monkeys. As a result, all of the monkeys survive. Both of these actions are related to animal cooperation. By working together, the monkeys can help each other stay alive. So they can live much longer.

Translation

교수는 학생들에게 원숭이들이 통상적으로 서로 협동을 한다고 말한다. 그는 학생들에게 두 가지 이유를 제시한다. 첫째, 원숭이들은 다른 원숭이와 먹이를 공유한다. 건강한 원숭이들이 늙고 병든 원숭이들을 위해 먹이를 찾는다. 또한 새끼 원숭이들에게 먹이를 공급해 준다. 게다가, 원숭이들은 위험으로부터 서로를 보호해 준다. 표범이 접근하면, 몇몇 원숭이들이 표범을 발견해 낸다. 이들은 소리를 질러 다른 원숭이들에게 경고를 해준다. 그 결과, 모든 원숭이들이 생존한다. 이러한 두 가지 행동 모두는 동물들의 협동과 관련이 있다. 협력을 함으로써, 원숭이들은 서로가 생존하는데 도움을 주고 받을 수 있다. 따라서 훨씬 더 오래 살 수 있다.

Task 5

📁 Listening

Script 🎧 4-20

W Student: Daniel, you don't look like you're doing all right. Is something wrong with you?

M Student: Yeah, I have a big problem. I've got a horrible toothache right now. My tooth is killing me.

W: You'd better go to see the dentist right away.

M: I agree, but that's not possible. I called the dentist, but he can't see me until tomorrow.

W: Tomorrow? Can you wait that long?

M: Well, there's another dentist that I can see. He takes emergency patients. It'll take me an hour to get to his office though. And, if I go there, I'll miss a review lesson in my chemistry class. I'm not that good at chemistry. So, um, I'm not sure I can afford to miss the lecture.

W: You've got to take care of your health. But I see your point. What else can you do?

M: I can just endure the pain. I made an appointment with my regular dentist for tomorrow at one o'clock. I can probably make it until then.

W: I guess you'll get to go to the review lesson. But what if you're in too much pain to focus on the lesson?

M: Oh, right. I hadn't thought of that.

Translation

W Student: Daniel, 괜찮아 보이지가 않네. 무슨 문제라도 있어?

M Student: 응, 큰 문제가 하나 있어. 지금 심한 치통을 앓고 있는 중이야. 이빨 때문에 정말로 아파.

W: 지금 당장 치과에 가보는 것이 좋을 것 같군.

M: 나도 그렇게 생각하지만 그럴 수가 없어. 치과에 전화를 했는데, 내일까지는 진찰을 받을 수가 없다는군.

W: 내일이라고? 그렇게 오래 기다릴 수 있겠어?

M: 음, 진찰을 받을 수 있는 또 다른 치과가 있어. 응급 환자를 받지. 하지만 그 치과에 가는데 한 시간이 걸릴 거야. 그리고, 그곳에 간다면, 화학 수업의 복습 수업을 놓치게 될 거고. 나는 화학을 잘 하지 못해. 그래서, 음, 강의를 놓쳐도 될 여유가 있는지 잘 모르겠어.

W: 건강을 신경써야 해. 하지만 네 요지는 알겠어. 그 밖에 어떤 일을 할 수 있을까?

M: 고통을 참으면 되지. 내일 1시에 단골 치과에 예약을 해두었거든. 아마도 그때까지는 참을 수 있을 거야.

W: 네가 복습 수업을 들을 수도 있을 것이라고 생각해. 하지만 너무 고통스러워서 수업에 집중을 못하면 어떻게 하지?

M: 오, 맞아. 그 점은 내가 생각하지 못했군.

Sample Response 1: First Solution 

The man's problem is that he has a toothache but his dentist cannot see him until tomorrow. The speakers discuss two solutions to the man's problem. The first solution is for the man to visit a dentist who takes emergency patients. The second solution is for him to see the dentist tomorrow. I support the first solution. To begin with, the man says he's in a lot of pain. It's an emergency, so he should see a dentist immediately. Secondly, his tooth is hurting him very much. So he won't be able to concentrate on the review lesson. Thus going to it would be a waste of time.

Translation

남자의 문제는 그가 치통을 앓고 있지만 내일까지는 치과의 진찰을 받을 수 없다는 점이다. 화자들은 남자의 문제에 대한 두 가지 해결 방안을 논의하고 있다. 첫 번째 방안은 남자가 응급 환자를 받는 치과에 가는 것이다. 두 번째 방안은 남자가 내일 치과에 가는 것이다. 나는 첫 번째 방안을 지지한다. 우선, 남자는 자신이 매우 고통스럽다고 말한다. 긴급 상황이기 때문에, 그는 즉시 치과에 가야 한다. 둘째, 그의 이빨 때문에 그가 매우 고통스러워 하고 있다. 따라서 그는 복습 수업에서 집중을 하지 못하게 될 것이다. 따라서 수업에 가는 것은 시간 낭비가 될 것이다.

Sample Response 2: Second Solution 

The man's problem is that he has a toothache but his dentist cannot see him until tomorrow. The speakers discuss two solutions to the man's problem. The first solution is for the man to visit a dentist who takes emergency patients. The second solution is for him to see the dentist tomorrow. I support the second solution. One reason is that the man needs to attend the review lesson. Otherwise, he might do poorly in his chemistry class. Another reason is that the other dentist is too far away. Going there would be a two-hour round trip. It might be a waste of time to go that far.

Translation

남자의 문제는 그가 치통을 앓고 있지만 내일까지는 치과의 진찰을 받을 수 없다는 점이다. 화자들은 남자의 문제에 대한 두 가지 해결 방안을 논의하고 있다. 첫 번째 방안은 남자가 응급 환자를 받는 치과에 가는 것이다. 두 번째 방안은 남자가 내일 치과에 가는 것이다. 나는 두 번째 방안을 지지한다. 한 가지 이유는 남자가 복습 수업에 참석해야 하기 때문이다. 그렇게 하지 않는다면, 그는 화학 수업에서 좋지 못한 성적을 받게 될 것이다. 또 하나의 이유는 다른 치과가 너무 멀리 떨어져 있기 때문이다. 그곳에 다녀오면 총 2시간이 걸릴 것이다. 그렇게 멀리까지 가는 것은 시간 낭비가 될 것이다.

Task 6

📁 Listening

Script (4-23)

M Professor: Take a look at these pictures of birds. Here's an eagle . . . Here's one of an owl . . . This is a robin . . . And this is a duck . . . Do you notice anything different about these birds . . . ? Okay, let me tell you then. It's the placement of their eyes. Some birds have eyes on the front of their heads. Other birds have eyes on the sides of their heads. This is why . . .

Birds such as eagles, owls, and hawks have their eyes on the front of their heads. These birds are all predators. They need their eyes positioned that way so that they can judge depth. Uh, you know, this gives them depth perception. So, when an eagle is diving to attack its prey, it can judge the distance accurately. It can do that because of its eyes. That's the easiest way to identify if a bird is a predator. Just look for eyes in the front of its head.

Birds that are prey animals have eyes on the sides of their heads. There's a reason for this, too. The reason is that these birds have eyes that can see just about 360 degrees. This enables them to keep a watch out for predators. Notice how many of these birds often move their heads around. They're doing that to look for danger. Thanks to the positioning of their eyes, they can do this much more easily.

Translation

M Professor: 새에 관한 이 그림들을 봐 주세요. 독수리가 있습니다… 올빼미가 있고 이것은 개똥지빠귀입니다… 그리고 이것은 오리고요… 이 새들에 있어서 서로 다른 무언가를 알아 차리셨나요…? 좋아요, 그러면 제가 말씀을 드리겠습니다. 바로 눈의 위치입니다. 몇몇 새들은 머리 앞쪽에 눈이 달려 있습니다. 다른 새들은 머리의 측면에 눈이 있죠. 왜 그런 지를 알려 드리겠습니다…

독수리, 올빼미, 그리고 매와 같은 새들은 머리의 앞쪽에 눈이 달려 있습니다. 이러한 새들은 모두 포식자입니다. 깊이감을 판단할 수 있도록 그런 식으로 눈이 위치해야 있어야 합니다. 어, 아시겠지만, 이로써 그들은 깊이감을 인식할 수 있습니다. 따라서, 먹이를 공격하기 위해 하강을 할 때, 독수리는 그러한 거리를 정확하게 판단할 수 있습니다. 눈 때문에 그렇게 할 수 있는 것이죠. 어떠한 새가 포식자인지를 확인해 볼 수 있는 가장 손쉬운 방법입니다. 머리 앞쪽에 눈이 있는지를 보면 됩니다.

피식자인 새들은 머리의 측면에 눈이 있습니다. 이에 대해서도 이유가 있습니다. 그 이유는 이러한 새들이 360도를 볼 수 있는 눈을 가지고 있다는 점에 있습니다. 이로써 포식자를 경계할 수 있습니다. 이러한 새 중 얼마나 많은 수가 종종 머리를 이리저리 움직이는지에 주목해 보십시오. 위험 요인을 찾기 위해 그렇게 하고 있는 것입니다. 눈의 위치 때문에, 보다 쉽게 그럴 수가 있습니다.

Sample Response (4-24)

The professor lectures about the positions of birds' eyes. He says that some birds have eyes in the front of their heads. But the eyes of other birds are on the sides of their heads. The professor mentions that birds with eyes in the front of their heads are predators. These are birds like owls, hawks, and eagles. Their eye position gives them depth perception. So they can hunt other animals much better. Birds that are prey animals have eyes on the sides of their heads. This gives them a wider range of vision. So they can look out for danger from many directions at the same time.

Translation

교수는 새의 눈 위치에 대해 강의를 한다. 그는 몇몇 새들은 머리의 앞쪽에 눈이 달려 있다고 말한다. 하지만 눈이 머리의 측면에 달려 있는 새들도 있다. 교수는 머리 앞쪽에 눈이 있는 새들은 포식자들이라고 언급한다. 올빼미, 매, 그리고 독수리와 같은 새들이 그러하다. 눈의 위치로 인해 이들은 깊이감을 인식할 수 있다. 따라서 다른 동물들을 보다 잘 사냥할 수 있다. 피식 동물인 새들은 머리의 측면에 눈이 있다. 이로써 시야가 넓어진다. 따라서 한 번에 여러 군데의 방향에서 나올 수 있는 위험 요인들을 주의할 수 있다.

Task 1

📁 Reading

Translation

북아메리카에는 몇몇 종의 소나무 딱정벌레들이 있다. 이 딱정벌레들은 매년 막대한 수의 소나무를 죽이고 있다. 실제로, 이들은 그 어떤 것보다 많은 소나무들을 죽이는 원인이 되고 있다. 소나무 딱정벌레들이 만연한 숲에서는 수천 그루의 나무들이 죽을 수 있다. 다행히도, 소나무 딱정벌레를 막을 수 있는 몇 가지 방법들이 존재한다.

소나무를 지킬 수 있는 한 가지 방어 수단은 자연 자체로부터 나온다: 바로 추운 날씨이다. 소나무는 종종 날씨가 추운 북아메리카 지역에서 자란다. 산이나 추운 겨울이 찾아 오는 지역에서 높이 자랄 수 있다. 소나무 딱정벌레는 추운 날씨에 잘 적응하지 못한다. 장기간 동안 기온이 낮은 경우에 특히 그러하다. 곤충이기 때문에, 소나무 딱정벌레는 추운 날씨에 활동을 하지 못한다. 온도가 매우 낮은 경우, 딱정벌레들은 종종 죽는다. 따라서 자연은 다수의 딱정벌레를 죽이는 원인이 된다.

소나무 딱정벌레는 나이가 많고 병든 나무들을 공격하는 경향이 있다. 이러한 나무들이 가장 취약하다. 젊고 성숙한 나무들은 소나무 딱정벌레로부터 종종 스스로를 보호할 수 있다. 그 결과, 일부 숲에서는 나이가 많고 병든 나무들을 벌목하기 위한 노력이 진행되고 있다. 이로써 소나무 딱정벌레들이 공격하기에 이상적인 나무들이 없어진다. 취약한 나무들을 베어냄으로써, 소나무 딱정벌레들을 제거할 수 있다. 소나무 딱정벌레들이 없다면, 숲 전체가 이들로부터 안전하게 될 것이다.

📁 Listening

Script 🎧 ④4-25

W Professor: Take a look at this insect . . . It's the western pine beetle. It's one of the numerous species of pine beetles in North America. These beetles kill millions of pine trees during some infestations. It's simply horrible what a pine beetle outbreak can do to a forest. And there's not much we can do about them either.

Now, uh, it's true that cold weather deters beetles. However, many pine trees grow in areas that never see freezing temperatures. So beetles living in the southern United States are never threatened by cold weather. In addition, some parts of the United States have been getting warm winters recently. These mild winters haven't killed as many pine beetles as they normally do. Unfortunately, that means there are more pine beetles than ever before.

You know that pine beetles often attack old and diseased trees, right? It would be great if we could cut those trees down. And people are doing it in some places. But, in other places, there are problems. You see, uh, the problems are caused by environmentalists. They're suing to prevent logging in some forests. They don't want any trees, uh, even old and sick ones, to be cut down. The environmentalists are doing more harm than good. We need to cut these trees down to keep the stronger trees safe. But we're not allowed to do that.

Translation

W Professor: 이 곤충을 봐 주세요⋯ 서양 소나무 딱정벌레입니다. 북아메리카 내 수많은 소나무 딱정벌레의 종 중 하나입니다. 이 딱정벌레들이 만연하는 몇몇 경우에는 수백만 그루의 소나무들이 죽습니다. 소나무 딱정벌레의 급증이 숲에 끼칠 수 있는 영향은 끔찍합니다. 그리고 그에 대해 우리가 할 수 있는 일도 많지가 않습니다.

자, 어, 추운 날씨가 딱정벌레들을 억지한다는 점은 사실입니다. 하지만, 많은 소나무들은 결코 기온이 낮아지지 않은 지역에서 자라고 있습니다. 따라서 미국의 남부에 서식하는 딱정벌레들은 결코 추운 날씨에 의한 위협을 받지 않습니다. 게다가, 최근 미국의 일부 지역들은 따뜻한 겨울을 맞이하고 있습니다. 이러한 온화한 겨울은 평상시

정도의 수만큼 소나무 딱정벌레들을 죽이지 못하고 있습니다. 안타깝게도, 이러한 점은 그 어느 때 보다 소나무 딱정벌레가 많아졌다는 점을 의미합니다.

소나무 딱정벌레가 종종 나이 많고 병든 나무들을 공격한다는 점을 여러분들께서는 알고 계실 것입니다, 그렇죠? 그러한 나무들을 베어 버릴 수 있다면 좋을 것입니다. 그리고 일부 지역에서는 사람들이 그렇게 하고 있습니다. 하지만, 다른 지역에서는, 문제가 있습니다. 아시겠지만, 어, 문제는 환경보호론자들로부터 나오고 있습니다. 이들은 일부 숲에서 벌목 행위를 저지하기 위해 소송을 제기하고 있습니다. 그들은 어떤 나무라도, 어, 심지어 나이가 많고 병든 나무일지라도 벌목되는 것을 원치 않습니다. 환경보호론자들은 백해무익한 일을 하고 있습니다. 우리는 그러한 나무를 베어 내어 보다 튼튼한 나무들이 계속 안전할 수 있도록 해야 합니다. 하지만, 그렇게 할 수가 없습니다.

Sample Response

The professor provides two reasons that defenses against pine beetles are not successful. These two reasons challenge the claims made in the reading passage. The author of the reading passage believes that there are effective defenses against pine beetles.

The first defense the author of the reading passage mentions is cold weather. Many pine trees grow in regions that have cold weather. The cold weather often kills beetles. This prevents them from damaging any pine trees. However, the professor refutes this point. She claims that the weather in many places is not cold enough to kill the beetles. In addition, some places that are usually cold are having mild winters these days. As a result, fewer beetles are dying.

The reading passage also notes that people are cutting down old, sick trees. Pine beetles usually attack these trees. The professor admits there is logging in some forests. So people are cutting down the old, sick trees. But she states that environmentalists are preventing logging in many other forests. She believes they are causing harm to these forests.

Translation

교수는 소나무 딱정벌레를 막기 위한 방법이 성공적이지 못하고 있는데 대한 두 가지 이유를 제시하고 있다. 이러한 두 가지 이유는 읽기 지문에서 제기된 주장을 반박한다. 읽기 지문을 쓴 사람은 소나무 딱정벌레를 막을 수 있는 효과적인 방법이 존재한다고 믿는다.

읽기 지문을 쓴 사람이 언급하는 첫 번째 방어 수단은 추운 날씨이다. 많은 소나무들이 추운 날씨를 보이는 지역에서 자란다. 추운 날씨는 종종 딱정벌레들을 죽인다. 이는 소나무들이 피해를 입는 것을 방지해 준다. 하지만, 교수는 이러한 점을 반박한다. 그녀는 여러 지역의 날씨가 딱정벌레를 죽이기에 충분히 춥지는 않다고 주장한다. 또한, 통상 추웠던 일부 지역에서 현재 온화한 겨울이 나타나고 있다. 그 결과, 딱정벌레들이 죽는 경우가 줄어들었다.

또한 읽기 지문은 사람들이 나이 들고 병든 나무들을 베어 내고 있다는 점에 주목한다. 소나무 딱정벌레는 통상 이러한 나무들을 공격한다. 교수는 일부 숲에서 벌목이 이루어지고 있다는 점을 인정한다. 따라서 오래되고 병든 나무들이 베어지고 있다. 하지만 기타 많은 숲에서는 환경보호론자들이 벌목 행위를 방해하고 있다고 주장한다. 그녀는 이들이 숲에 해를 끼치고 있다고 믿는다.

Task 2

Sample Response 1: By Email

I sometimes have to discuss upsetting problems with other people. Doing that by email is better than talking about it over the phone.

For one, you can explain the problem much easier in an email. This way, people know exactly what you are trying to say. Last week, one of my friends got fired from her job. I wanted to give her some encouragement. So I wrote a long email to her. However, before I sent her the email, I read it over.

I made a few small changes to it. That made the letter better. Because I was able to proofread the letter, I did not offend my friend. She appreciated my email and felt much better after she read it.

In addition, the recipient of an email can read the letter again and again. This can let the person understand the news much better. For instance, my sister received some bad news by email recently. She got extremely upset because of the letter. But, later, she went back and read the letter again. She found some lines in it that improved her mood. Because she reread the letter, she gained a better understanding of the situation. As a result, she calmed down a lot.

No one is ever happy to get bad news. I would definitely prefer to get bad news by email than over the telephone though.

Translation

때때로 나는 다른 사람들과 말하기 어려운 문제를 논의해야 한다. 이메일로 그렇게 하는 것이 전화로 그에 대해 이야기하는 것보다 더 낫다.

우선, 이메일로 문제를 보다 더 쉽게 설명할 수 있다. 그렇게 하면, 사람들은 무엇을 말하고자 하는지를 정확하게 알게 된다. 지난 주, 내 친구 중 한 명이 직장에서 해고되었다. 나는 그녀에게 용기를 주고 싶었다. 그래서 장문의 이메일을 그녀에게 보냈다. 하지만, 그녀에게 이메일을 보내기 전에, 나는 그것을 검토해 보았다. 몇 가지 부분을 고쳤다. 그럼으로써 편지가 더 좋게 되었다. 편지의 교정을 볼 수 있었기 때문에, 나는 내 친구의 기분을 나쁘게 만들지 않았다. 그녀는 내 이메일에 고마워했고 이메일을 읽은 후 훨씬 더 기분이 좋아졌다.

또한, 이메일의 수취인은 편지를 계속해서 읽어 볼 수 있다. 이로써 그 사람은 소식을 훨씬 잘 이해할 수 있다. 예를 들어, 내 여동생은 최근에 이메일로 나쁜 소식을 접했다. 그녀는 편지 때문에 몹시 기분이 상했다. 하지만, 이후, 그녀는 다시 편지를 읽어 보았다. 그녀는 편지에서 자신의 기분을 좋게 만든 몇 가지 문구를 찾아냈다. 편지를 다시 읽었기 때문에, 그녀는 상황을 보다 잘 이해하게 되었다. 그 결과, 그녀는 많이 진정되었다.

나쁜 소식을 듣고서 행복해 하는 사람은 없다. 하지만 나는 전화를 통해서가 아니라 이메일로 나쁜 소식을 접하는 것을 확실히 선호한다.

Sample Response 2: Over the Telephone

I know that some people like to give bad news to others by email. However, in my opinion, telling someone about upsetting news is better to do on the telephone.

To begin with, when you receive bad news, you always want to hear another person's voice. The sound of that person's voice can be very comforting. When my grandmother died, my mother called to tell me. I was upset about it. My grandmother and I had been close to each other. But my mother was able to comfort me. Her words on the phone made me calm down and feel better. So, even though I was upset about my grandmother's death, I was still in control.

There is another reason that giving upsetting news over the phone is better. The reason is that the person giving the news can answer the other person's questions instantly. For example, my best friend's father was hospitalized last month. He had been in a car accident. My friend's mother called to tell him the bad news. My friend asked his mother a lot of questions over the telephone. He got instant answers. He might not have gotten immediate answers by email. Since his mother called him, however, he knew everything that she did.

Clearly, it is better to hear upsetting news on the telephone than to read about it in an email. The telephone provides a personal touch that email lacks.

Translation

나는 몇몇 사람들이 이메일로 다른 사람에게 나쁜 소식을 전하는 것을 선호한다고 알고 있다. 하지만, 내 의견으로, 말하기 어려운 소식에 관해 누군가에게 말을 할 때는 전화로 하는 것이 더 좋다고 생각한다.

우선, 나쁜 소식을 접하는 경우에는, 항상 다른 사람의 목소리가 듣고 싶다. 그 사람의 목소리는 큰 위로가 될 수 있다. 내 할머니께서 돌아가셨을 때, 어머니께서는 전화를 걸어 내게 말씀을 해주셨다. 나는 그에 대해 매우 속상했다. 할머니와 나는 서로 친한 사이였다. 하지만 어머니께서 나를 위로해 주실 수 있었다. 전화로 들리는 어머니의 말씀은 나를 진정시켰고 내 기분이 나아지게 만들었다. 그래서, 할머니의 죽음으로 기분이 좋지 않았음에도 불구하고, 나는 진정이 되었다.

말하기 어려운 소식을 전화로 전하는 것이 더 나은 또 다른 이유가 있다. 그 이유는 소식을 전하는 사람이 다른 사람의 질문에 즉각적으로 대답을 해줄 수 있기 때문이다. 예를 들어, 나의 가장 친한 친구의 아버님께서 지난 달에 입원하셨다. 그분께서는 자동차 사고를 당하셨다. 친구의 어머님이 그에게 나쁜 소식을 전했다. 내 친구는 전화로 어머님께 많은 질문을 드렸다. 그는 즉각적인 대답을 들었다. 이메일로는 즉각적인 답변을 듣지 못했을 것이다. 하지만, 그의 어머니께서 그에게 전화를 해주셨기 때문에, 그는 그녀가 한 모든 일에 대해 알게 되었다.

분명, 전화로 말하기 어려운 소식을 듣는 것이 이메일로 그에 관한 글을 읽는 것보다 더 낫다. 전화는 이메일에 들어 있지 않은 인간적인 교감을 제공해 준다.

Smart TOEFL® iBT Pre-Intermediate

Smart TOEFL® iBT Pre-Intermediate is intended for
students with a low-intermediate knowledge of English.
Therefore the passages are shorter, and the questions are
easier than those found on the TOEFL® iBT. Nevertheless,
the passages and questions are written in the TOEFL®
iBT style, so students will be able to prepare themselves
for the test when they actually take it. *Smart TOEFL® iBT
Pre-Intermediate* will also provide students with a basic
introduction to many different academic topics. Thus
students will learn important information and specialized
vocabulary in a number of topics.

<Smart TOEFL® iBT Pre-Intermediate> Components

- Main Book
- Answers, Listening Scripts, and Translations
- Free MP3 Downloads
  For More Student and Teacher Support Materials,
  Free Downloads at **http://www.darakwon.co.kr**